BASIC
DATA
PROCESSING

BASIC
DATA
PROCESSING

JANET K. BUDZIK
Morton West High School
Berwyn, Illinois

CLARENCE A. SIMS
Northern Illinois University

GEORGE E. MAYCOCK

**ADDISON-WESLEY
PUBLISHING COMPANY**
Reading, Massachusetts
Menlo Park, California
London • Don Mills, Ontario

To my husband Dick,
for without his encouragement
this book would never have been started
or completed

Janet K. Budzik

To my wife Dorothy,
for her encouragement

Clarence A. Sims

ACKNOWLEDGMENTS

We wish to thank the following associations or companies for their cooperation and for supplying us with photographs: The British Crown Copyright, Science Museum, London, Fig. 12.1. EAI (Electronic Associates, Inc.), Figs. 15.6; 15.7(a), (b), (c); 15.8; 15.9; 24.1. Graphic Services, Inc., Fig. 1.4(a). Honeywell (Information Systems), Figs. 12.2; 12.6; 12.8; 13.13; 13.18; 24.6; 25.1. I.B.M. (International Business Machines), Figs. 1(a), (b), (c), (d), (e), (g), (h); 1.5; 1.6(a), (b), (d), (e), (f); 5.2; 6.12; 6.13; 6.22; 7.1; 7.2; 7.3; 7.5; 7.7; 7.8; 7.11; 7.17; 7.18; 7.20; 7.21; 8.1; 8.3; 8.7; 9.1; 9.2; 9.4; 9.5; 9.7; 9.8; 10.1; 10.10; 10.17; 11.1; 11.2; 12.5; 12.7; 13.2; 13.7; 13.12; 13.14; 13.17; 13.19; 13.20; 13.21; 13.22; 14.4; 14.11; 14.13; 14.17; 14.18; 15.2; 15.5; 24.3; 24.4; 25.2; 26.1. John Hancock Mutual Life Insurance Company, Fig. 24.5. Monroe (International, Inc.), Fig. 5.1, (Calculator Company), 5.3. NASA (National Aeronautics and Space Administration), Fig. 1.6(c). NCR (National Cash Register Company), Figs. 10.8; 10.9; 12.3; 12.4; 13.6; 13.16; 13.23; 14.10; 14.15; 14.16; 14.19; 15.1. Royal Typewriter (Litton Business Systems, Inc.), Figs. 1.3(a); 1.4(b); 7.6. Singer Company (Friden Division), Fig. 1.4(c). Standard Register Company, Figs. 1.3(b), (c), (d); 1.4(d). Teletype Corporation, Figs. 13.5; 24.2. Univac (Division of Sperry Rand Corporation), Figs. 1.1(f); 1.6(g), 10.2; 10.3; 10.4; 10.6; 10.7; 13.1; 15.4. Wright Line Division, Figs. 6.14; 8.2.

PREFACE

It has been said many times that we are living in the "age of the computer," and, in a sense, this observation is certainly appropriate. The greatest growth in our economy and the greatest advances in our standard of living have occurred during the past twenty-five years. High-speed information processing has played a significant part in this growth, and will become even more important in the continued development of our economy. As a result, increasing attention is being given to this phase of our culture, one that has revolutionized so many of our business and scientific procedures, one that is giving employment to increasingly large numbers of skilled and professional workers.

Because of the wide range of interests in modern data processing and the reasons for these interests, this book was planned with three major objectives in mind: *to provide*

1. A broad insight into the nature of data processing—with its concepts, objectives, techniques, applications, and results—for those readers desiring a general knowledge of modern data processing;

2. A comprehensive foundation for readers who intend to pursue some aspect of data processing, to select some area for further study; and

3. Increased and up-dated information for readers whose occupational effectiveness requires a knowledge of the techniques and terminology of modern data processing methods, even though they themselves may not be directly involved in the data processing operations.

To attain these three very distinct objectives, we avoided oversimplification. We also avoided step-by-step "how to" instructions for operating the equipment and in-depth, minute details concerning specific aspects of various points in the discussion. However, sufficient detail is provided to explain the purposes and operating sequences of the equipment. At the end of each chapter, appropriate questions will be found to reinforce the important facts and concepts of the chapter.

The use of this book with complete understanding requires no prior knowledge or exposure to the computer or other equipment, no background in mathematics, and no equipment. However, supplemental films and/or field trips are always helpful to show the various aspects of modern data processing systems in operation.

Although we put major emphasis on the computer and punched cards, we feel that the well-informed reader should have a knowledge of related topics, including all commonly used data processing techniques and the correlation of the data processing function with the overall business needs.

Although it is primarily designed for use in introductory college-level courses, the book can also be used successfully for juniors and seniors in high schools, especially if it is supplemented by the workbook/project set.

Special features of this textbook are

1. Introductory data (five chapters) to give the person with little or no prior business knowledge a basic understanding of the data processing needs of business firms and the role of the data processing function.

2. Separate chapters for three currently and widely used programming languages: COBOL, FORTRAN, AND PL/I, in sufficient detail so that a person will understand how to write or interpret a basic program in each language.

3. A thorough but brief explanation of the punched card methods, which can be scanned if necessary because of time limitations.

4. Explanation of both the standard 80-column card and the newer 96-column card.

5. Introduction to the new IBM System/3 computer and other new computers.

Chapters devoted to related topics discuss the role and place of modern data processing, and they include such subjects as the objectives and organization of the data processing function; how the computer is affecting people and organizations; the strengths and weaknesses of the computer; management's need for information and for effective planning, control, delegation of authority, and communication; the role of systems analysis and design; the scientific and manufacturing uses of the computer; and a look into the future of the computer. An entire chapter is devoted to the opportunities in the field of data processing.

Because of the accelerated rate of change in the electronic data processing field, we have not only included the most recent new developments, but we have included general concepts that cross the wide areas of change so that we could eliminate or at least reduce the "generation gap." Our distinct and separate backgrounds in the technical aspects and office management aspects of data processing have, we hope, enabled us to offer a comprehensive blend of these interrelated topics.

October, 1971   J.K.B.
                                                                  C.A.S.

CONTENTS

Chapter 5   The Data Processing Function

PART II   PUNCHED CARD DATA PROCESSING

Chapter 6   Recording Media

Chapter 7   Recording Methods

Chapter 8   Operations with Punched Cards: Part 1

Chapter 9   Operations with Punched Cards: Part 2

Chapter 14   Central Processing Unit of the Computer

Chapter 15   Samples of Typical Computer Systems in Use Today

PART IV   COMPUTER PROGRAMMING AND SYSTEMS DESIGN

Chapter 16   Flowcharting and Programming

PART I

INTRODUCTION
TO
AND
HISTORY
OF
DATA
PROCESSING
CONCEPTS

BASIC
DATA
PROCESSING
CONCEPTS

CHAPTER 1

THE PURPOSE OF DATA PROCESSING

Data processing is not a new concept or activity. Clay tablets found by archaeologists among the ruins of ancient Babylonian cities show wedge-shaped symbols that represent numbers. The Egyptians used highly stylized pictures of fish, lotus blossoms, etc. Documents dating back to the ancient Greek and Roman civilizations bear witness to extensive commerce, banking activities, and taxation which even though not as complex as those we know, required many detailed records.

The trend in data processing has always been to reduce—or even replace—mental and manual efforts by the use of techniques and equipment that can take over more and more of the routine data processing function. Today the demand for data processing is so great in business that there is a shortage of data processing personnel with business knowledge.

We all know that we live in the Age of the Computer. Our lives have been influenced by the computer in countless ways and will be affected even more in the years to come as we get more sophisticated in our uses of the computer. We have learned to take for granted live television programs broadcast by satellite, astronauts walking on the moon, credit cards, direct dialing of long-distance telephone calls, and many other conveniences all made possible by the use of computers.

With the rapid advancement of data processing by electronic means, you may find that your business career will involve you with computers more than you expect. Your job will have been designed so that its routine aspects can be done better by machines. Even if your work does not tie in with machines directly, it will have to be processed more accurately or in a more even flow because many related details of the business will be channeled into one data processing system. Thus, even though you may be majoring in business administration, you need firsthand knowledge of computer technology and data processing operations.

Computer technology, then, is in the driver's seat. The computer is revolutionizing the business world—and just about every other aspect of our society. The only thing that can slow its progress is a shortage of EDP (Electronic Data Processing) personnel. This shortage exists even though EDP is one of the few professions which does not require a college degree. The traits stressed most in this profession are aptitude and a logical mind.

It is therefore important that you be aware not only of the possibilities of data processing systems, but that you be able to make constructive use of them. Business needs a work force that is highly skilled and capable of performing the tasks of data processing; it needs competent computer operators.

JOBS AVAILABLE

The new data processing machines, including computers, create many new jobs and change an even greater number of traditional job duties. Some of the jobs that directly relate to data processing machines are pictured in Fig. 1.1 (a), (b), (c), (d), (e), (f), (g), and (h). These jobs will be discussed more fully after we have gained an understanding of the data processing machines and their uses.

DATA PROCESSING DEFINED

Data processing, then, is not a new concept or word to us even if we have never worked in an office or taken a business course. However, though we have heard the term "data processing" frequently, few of us would agree on exactly what it means in a business sense. Due to abuse in definition it means different things to different people. Perhaps you would define it by saying, "It is a procedure for processing data." Substituting just a few explanatory phrases for the terms "procedure" and "processing" gives us a more workable definition:

Data processing is performing a predetermined related series of operations on facts (data) to obtain useful end results.

(a) Librarian—
tape files

(b) Sales
representative
of computer
manufacturer

(c) Computer
programmer

(d) Machine
operator

FIG. 1.1 Jobs related to data processing

FIG. 1.1   cont.

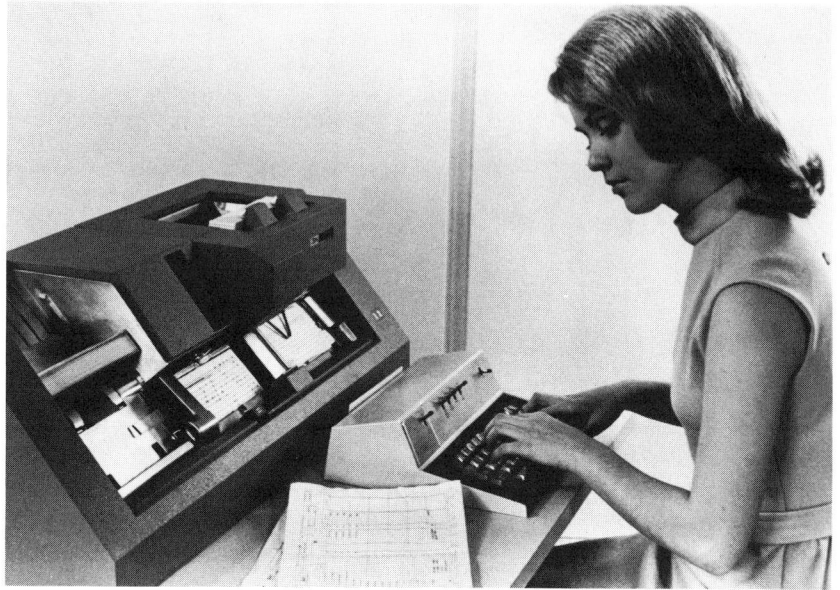

(e)   Keypunch operator

(f) Computer engineers

(g)   Computer maintenance technician

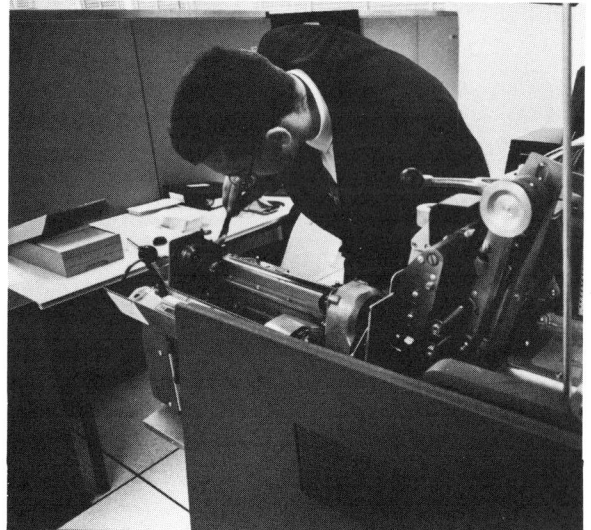

FIG. 1.1   cont.

(h) **Computer operators**

DATA AND BUSINESS DATA

The term *data* refers to facts. The rules for playing volley ball can be referred to as data; so can a list of the capitals of the states. However, *business data* refers only to those facts that are useful or meaningful to a given company. The rules for playing volley ball are probably not useful to any business; therefore they are not business data, but are merely data. A list of capitals of the states might be useful to some companies but not to all companies; therefore, this list would be considered as business data by some companies and not by others. The Federal Income Tax Withholding Tables, however, are business data to all companies because all companies must deduct the stated amount from each employee's salary and send it to the federal government (see Fig. 1.2).

A list of all the names and addresses of people who have recently received driver's licenses in a town is considered as data. To what types of businesses could this list be useful? It would be useful to automobile dealers and insurance agencies; so it would be business data to them. It would probably not be useful to a driver's training school, and hence this list would not be business data to them. Another term used to mean business data is *information*.

THE RULES OF GOLF

Golf consists in playing a ball from successive tees into a series of cups or holes in accordance with certain rules:

1. No part of the club may be movable or separable or capable of being adjusted during a round of play.

2. The grip shall be a continuation of the shaft to which material may be added for the purpose of obtaining a firm hold. The grip shall be substantially straight and plain in form, may have flat sides. It may not have a channel or furrow or molded part in the handle.

3. The weight of the ball shall not be greater than 1.620 ounces avoirdupois, and the size not less than 1.680 inches in diameter.

4. Before starting a stipulated round, a player shall select his clubs, which must not exceed fourteen in number. He is limited to the clubs so selected for that round except that, without unduly delaying play he may. . . . .

MARRIED Persons — WEEKLY Payroll Period

And the wages are—		And the number of withholding exemptions claimed is—										
At least	But less than	0	1	2	3	4	5	6	7	8	9	10 or more
		The amount of income tax to be withheld shall be—										
$100	$105	$13.10	$11.10	$9.10	$7.00	$4.80	$2.80	$1.00	$0	$0	$0	$0
105	110	13.90	11.90	9.90	7.80	5.70	3.60	1.70	0	0	0	0
110	115	14.70	12.70	10.70	8.70	6.50	4.40	2.40	.70	0	0	0
115	120	15.50	13.50	11.50	9.50	7.40	5.30	3.10	1.40	0	0	0
120	125	16.30	14.30	12.30	10.30	8.20	6.10	4.00	2.10	.30	0	0
125	130	17.10	15.10	13.10	11.10	9.10	7.00	4.80	2.80	1.00	0	0
130	135	17.90	15.90	13.90	11.90	9.90	7.80	5.70	3.60	1.70	0	0
135	140	18.70	16.70	14.70	12.70	10.70	8.70	6.50	4.40	2.40	.70	0
140	145	19.50	17.50	15.50	13.50	11.50	9.50	7.40	5.30	3.10	1.40	0
145	150	20.30	18.30	16.30	14.30	12.30	10.30	8.20	6.10	4.00	2.10	.30
150	160	21.50	19.50	17.50	15.50	13.50	11.50	9.50	7.40	5.30	3.10	1.40
160	170	23.10	21.10	19.10	17.10	15.10	13.10	11.10	9.10	7.00	4.80	2.80
170	180	25.00	22.70	20.70	18.70	16.70	14.70	12.70	10.70	8.70	6.50	4.40
180	190	26.90	24.50	22.30	20.30	18.30	16.30	14.30	12.30	10.30	8.20	6.10
190	200	28.80	26.40	24.10	21.90	19.90	17.90	15.90	13.90	11.90	9.90	7.80
200	210	30.70	28.30	26.00	23.60	21.50	19.50	17.50	15.50	13.50	11.50	9.50
210	220	32.60	30.20	27.90	25.50	23.10	21.10	19.10	17.10	15.10	13.10	11.10
220	230	34.50	32.10	29.80	27.40	25.00	22.70	20.70	18.70	16.70	14.70	12.70
230	240	36.40	34.00	31.70	29.30	26.90	24.50	22.30	20.30	18.30	16.30	14.30
240	250	38.30	35.90	33.60	31.20	28.80	26.40	24.10	21.90	19.90	17.90	15.90
250	260	40.20	37.80	35.50	33.10	30.70	28.30	26.00	23.60	21.50	19.50	17.50
260	270	42.10	39.70	37.40	35.00	32.60	30.20	27.90	25.50	23.10	21.10	19.10
270	280	44.10	41.60	39.30	36.90	34.50	32.10	29.80	27.40	25.00	22.70	20.70
280	290	46.20	43.60	41.20	38.80	36.40	34.00	31.70	29.30	26.90	24.50	22.30
290	300	48.30	45.70	43.10	40.70	38.30	35.90	33.60	31.20	28.80	26.40	24.10

FIG. 1.2 Business data

WHY PROCESS DATA?

A company will process only data that are useful in conducting its business. A list of data is of little, if any, use unless you do something with it. For example, the list of names and addresses of people who have recently obtained driver's licenses could be used to send out ads to potential car buyers. A list containing the names and number of hours worked by each employee during a week would be used to calculate his earnings, make out pay checks, and establish permanent records. From these examples, we can understand that each business, regardless of its size, needs to process data.

THE ROLE OF THE DATA PROCESSING FUNCTION IN BUSINESS

Information processing—keeping books, accounting, and developing reports and statistics—is an integral part of every business organization. Most office procedures are concerned with gathering, processing, recording, and communicating information. Responsibility for these functions has traditionally been in the hands of what we referred to as "office management." A newer concept, however, is gaining acceptance, and the new term is *information management*. Today we do not call the management of a factory "factory management" but "manufacturing management" or "industrial management," because the term factory refers to the place while the terms *manufacturing* and *industrial* refer to the function. The two are separate elements in our thinking about a factory. The same holds true in our thinking about the office: The office is the place, but information processing is the function. The quality of information is strongly influenced by the systems that create it. The basic function of an information system is to provide data to decision-makers in a form most suitable for their work in making intelligent policy decisions. The need for and uses of data will be discussed more fully in Chapter 2. Management and information concerning the decisions that management faces today will be discussed in Chapter 3.

The manager of the information system has to think of three separate but interrelated functions: systems, records management, and data processing.

A *system* is a network of related procedures developed according to the specific needs of a given business. Thus there are several systems used in an office: accounting systems, filing systems, communication systems, and others.

Records management is important, but records cannot be accumulated indefinitely. With management's increasing dependence on written records and the ease of obtaining duplicate copies, the problem of records management is growing in size and importance.

Our basic concern here, however, is not with the total information system nor with records management. Instead, we are concerned with *data processing* and how it aids these other two functions of information management. We must learn to decide what data are to be processed and how we will go about it. Data processing, as the functional part of the information system, provides the tools and techniques for the task.

Data processing is a *part* of the information system. It is not the *entire* system (although many professional data processors would like to think so), and has no proper decision-making or policy-making function outside the information system. As a part of the information system, the data processing function encompasses eight operations, each of which is discussed in the next section.

DATA PROCESSING OPERATIONS

Data processing is the heart of the office or information function of business. We must understand the data processing operations in order to understand today's office procedures. The prime purpose of the data processing function is to turn facts into meaningful information on which management can base policy decisions. To achieve this purpose, we perform eight basic operations on business data. These are:

1. Recording	5 Calculating
2. Duplicating	6. Summarizing
3. Classifying	7. Communicating
4. Sorting	8. Storing and retrieving

When processing a specific type of business data, we do not always perform these eight operations in the order listed above, because

1. not all these operations may be needed, or
2. some of these operations might have to be performed more than once.

The eight operations are discussed below.

Recording. Data are written and transcribed in a form that can be handled by the system. Data are recorded so that they can be processed and saved.

Duplicating. Data that have already been recorded are reproduced because usually more than one copy of a document is needed and as insurance against loss. Duplicating may be done simultaneously by using carbons, or it can be done later with ditto duplicators or photo-copying machines.

Classifying. In this operation data are separated and developed by some characteristic selected to distinguish them from other data. Classifying usually involves using code numbers or letters to group data for easier and faster processing.

Sorting. The data are arranged in a sequence or order by means of the numbers and/or letters which were used in the classifying operation. Sorting is done so that the data is processed, accumulated, and reported in a desired order.

Calculating (computing). The mathematical operations of adding, subtracting, multiplying, and dividing may be performed on the data according to the way the material is to be used. This is an important operation because most business data consist primarily of numbers which are either quantities of items or dollar values.

Summarizing. This operation provides the results obtained from the data. Not all the details used in arriving at the answer are included; the data are condensed to show just the desired main results of the computations. A more comprehensive summary is frequently called a report, and the summarizing operation is sometimes called reporting. A simple example might be that at the end of each day the total value of sales is important to the store manager or owner, but the individual amount of each sale is less important.

Communicating. Data may be transferred from one point to another, for example, from one machine to another, so that the next operation can be performed. Data are also transferred to the person or people who will use the results. In order to be of value, data that have been processed must be available to a person who needs it *when* he needs it.

Storing and retrieving. The data are filed so that they can be found and used when needed in the future. One can store data whether they have been only partially processed or completely processed. A part of the storing operation is the retrieval, that is, getting the data from storage when they are needed.

METHODS OF PROCESSING DATA

The four common classifications of data processing methods used today are:

1. Manual data processing
2. Mechanical data processing
3. Punched card data processing, or unit record data processing
4. Electronic data processing

These four classifications, considered in this order, actually represent the stages of mechanization in the development of data processing. In each subsequent stage, machines are used more and humans less. This will be discussed in greater detail in Chapter 4.

(a) Manual typewriter

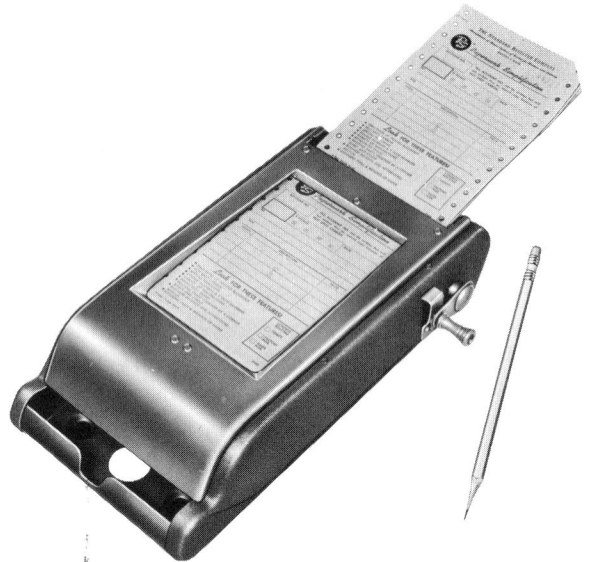

(b) Forms register

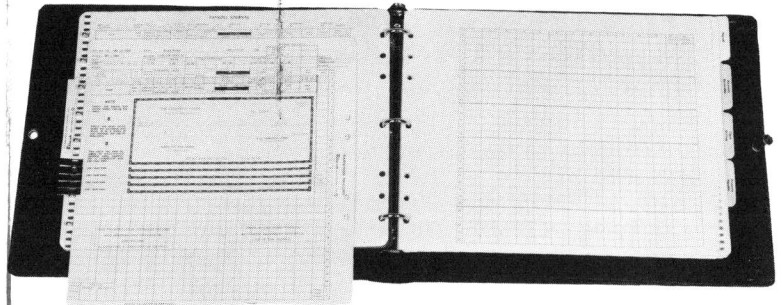

(c) Posting register

(d) Continuous forms

FIG. 1.3 Devices to aid manual data processing

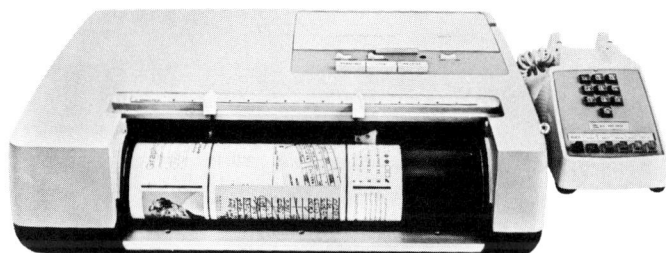

(a) Machine for receiving photos transmitted over telephone lines

(b) Electric typewriter

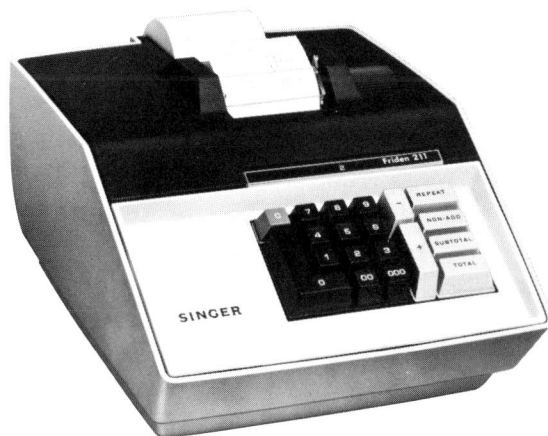

(c) Electric adding machine

FIG. 1.4 Machines used for mechanical data processing

(d) Electric forms register

Manual data processing. Data are sometimes processed by hand (manually) by people using paper, pen, or pencil or some of the numerous devices that have been developed such as forms registers, posing boards, filing cases, and typewriters (Fig. 1–3 (a), (b), (c), and (d)). Today, however, not all these devices are operated by hand. If the device has any moving parts that are not operated directly by hand

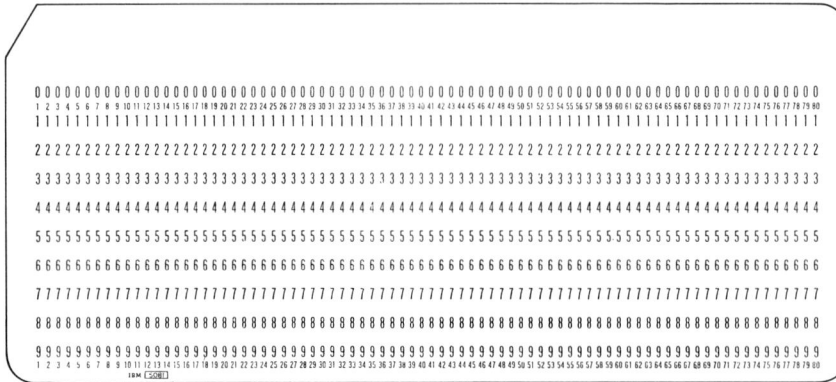

FIG. 1.5 A punched
card used for
punch card
data processing

(usually by electricity), then it is a mechanical data processing device;
the operation is no longer considered a manual data process.

Mechanical data processing. The data are processed with mechanical
equipment which is usually electrically operated. This development
increased the speed and accuracy of the processing. The more common mechanical data processing machines are electric cash registers,
electric adding and calculating machines, and electric typewriters (Fig.
1.4 (a), (b), (c), and (d)).

Punched card data processing. This involves the data which have been
recorded on cards. The special machines used operate electrically.
Punched card data processing is actually a part of mechanical data
processing, but is considered separately because it is so distinct from
all other mechanical data processing methods. Speed and accuracy
are improved because this operation requires less human effort than
manual or other mechanical types of data processing. The more common punched card machines are the keypunch, collator, and sorter.
Each card contains specific data about one person or transaction,
called a unit. Hence this type of data processing is also called *unit
record data processing.* The machines that use punched cards can be
called punched card machines or unit record machines. A punch
card is shown in Fig. 1.5.

Electronic data processing. The data are processed by computer. The
important difference between a computer and the mechanical and
punched card machine is its greater speed and higher degree of

accuracy. The enormous increase in speed is due to the fact that the computer processes the data by electronic impulses while the other types of machines process data by the movement of mechanical machine parts. Computers also work with data recorded on magnetic tapes and disks which are faster than punched cards.

TYPES OF COMPUTERS

Two basic types of work are performed by computers, and special computer systems have been developed for each type of work. One type operates with numbers, that is, it adds, subtracts, multiplies, and divides with them; this is a *digital computer*. The other type measures and manipulates physical processes such as voltage or temperature; it is called an *analog computer*. Therefore, the digital computer works with digits, and the analog computer works with analogous physical situations. Since the analog computer works with physical quantities rather than actual numbers, it is not used for business data processing, but is used for some engineering, scientific, and manufacturing problems. The digital computer works with actual numerical values (such as dollars and cents, number of hours worked, quantities of items), and is the one that is used in business data processing. Digital computers are also used for some scientific and engineering problems, though. Since it is the digital computer that is used for business data processing, this is the type we will discuss in this book.

MODERN DATA PROCESSING AND THE COMPUTER

Most people hearing the term data processing think of punched cards and computers. Actually, this term applies to all four methods of processing data because manual and mechanical methods also process data. A more precise term that should be used when we refer specifically to punched card equipment and computers is *modern data processing*. Only a minimum amount of human effort is required for data processing that is increasingly more efficient.

The computer is a machine designed to aid man by doing work for him. At the present time, it represents the most advanced stage of mechanization in the office. Mechanization refers to the use of machines. Some speak of automation in the office or automated data processing when referring to the use of computers. But, technically, the word "automation" means that work is performed with *no* human

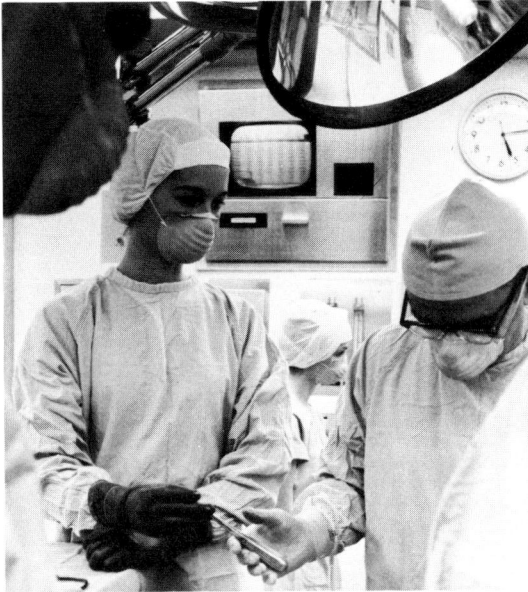

(a) **Medical work:**
Display terminal
in operating room

(b) **Flight navigation**

(c) **Apollo spacecraft center**

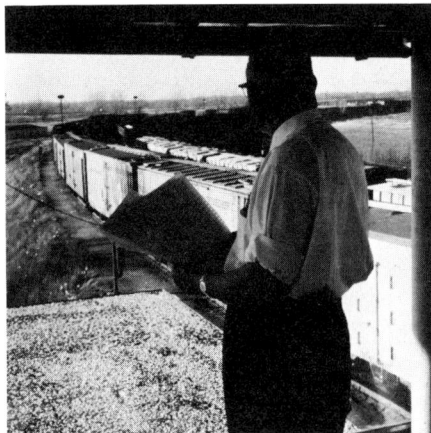

(d) **Planning and scheduling railroad operations**

FIG. 1.6 Computer applications

effort other than that of directing the machine. Computers cannot
be used to this extent in office work. Therefore, when a person uses
the term automated or automation, he really means that there is only
limited human effort; he does not mean that there is no human effort.
Some of the applications of computers are shown in Fig. 1.6 (a), (b),
(c), (d), (e), (f), and (g).

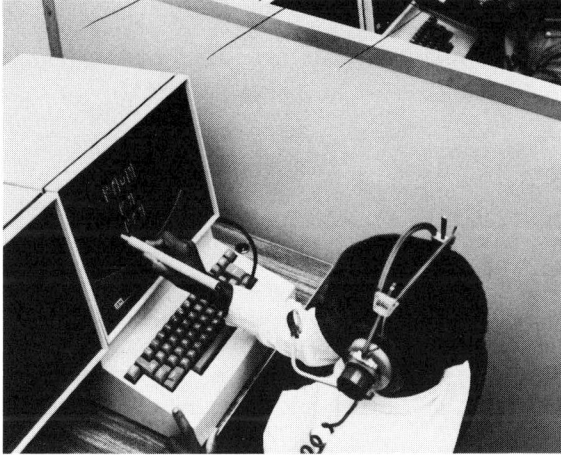

(e) Education:
terminal in the
classroom

(f) Scientific research

(g) Executive
decision-making

QUESTIONS AND PROBLEMS

1. Explain why we are in the Age of the Computer.
2. What is the main barrier to the computer revolution?
3. Define "data processing."
4. Explain the difference between "data" and "business data."
5. Define "information."
6. Why is the present trend toward "information management" rather than "office management"?
7. List and define the three major functions of information management.
8. List and define the eight data processing operations.
9. List, in order, and briefly describe the four classifications of data processing methods.
10. Briefly describe the primary difference between the two basic types of computers.
11. Discuss why data processing is not new.

THE DEVELOPMENT OF DATA PROCESSING

In this chapter we digress a little to give some background against which data processing must be seen in order to appreciate its role within the total economy. The population of the United States has increased a little more than two and a half times since 1900. The American labor force has increased about three times. The clerical work force, however, has increased eleven and a half times. Table 2.1 shows that from 1870 to 1968 the proportion of clerical workers in the total labor force has steadily risen, increasing from 2.4 percent in 1870 to 16.7 percent in 1968. Stated differently, in 1870 about one worker in 40 was an office worker; in 1968 about one in six was an office worker. Except for operators of various kinds of machines, in the years 1960 to 1968 the clerical group was larger than any other occupational group.

The next question then is, "What industry or industries employ the clerical workers?" Clerical workers are, to some degree, employed in every industrial group. However, the proportion of clerical workers to total labor varies with different industries. As we can see from Table 2.2, the largest *percentage* was employed in finance, followed by public service and transportation. Manufacturing holds first place in employing a greater *number* of clerical workers than any other group, followed by trade, public service, and finance. It is interesting that three groups—manufacturing, trade, and public service—employed around 55 percent of all the clerical workers in 1960; finance and professional service are very close to the third-place industry, public service.

A significant change has also occurred in the male versus female ratio of clerical workers. Table 2.3 shows that in 1968, of 12,731,000   19

TABLE 2.1   Total labor force of the United States, and clerical occupations: 1870–1968

Period	Total labor force	Clerical occupations	Percent of clerical occupations to total labor force
1968[a]	76,364,000	12,731,000	16.7
1960[b]	64,646,563	9,303,231	14.4
1950[c]	55,803,520	6,865,960	12.3
1940[d]	45,166,083	4,612,356	10.2
1930[e]	48,829,920	4,025,324	8.2
1920[e]	41,614,248	3,111,836	7.5
1910[e]	38,167,336	1,718,458	4.5
1900[f]	29,073,233	1,068,993	3.7
1890[f]	22,735,661	801,505	3.5
1880[f]	17,392,099	518,439	3.0
1870[f]	12,505,923	305,502	2.4

[a] United States Department of Labor, *Employment and Earnings and Monthly Report on the Labor Force*, Vol. 15, No. 5, Nov. 1968, p. 11.

[b] United States Bureau of the Census, *U. S. Census of Population, 1960, Subject Reports, Occupation by Industry*, Final Report PC(2)–7C, U. S. Government Printing Office, Washington, D. C., 1963, Table 2, p. 7.

[c] United States Bureau of the Census, *U. S. Census of Population: 1950. Vol. IV, Special Reports*, Part 1, Chapter C, *Occupation by Industry*, p. 13.

[d] United States Bureau of the Census, *Sixteenth Census of the United States: 1940, Population, Vol. III, The Labor Force, Part 1: U. S. Summary*, pp. 75–76.

[e] United States Bureau of the Census, *Fifteenth Census of the United States: 1930, Population, Vol. V, General Report on Occupations*, pp. 10 and 22.

[f] United States Bureau of the Census, *Twelfth Census of the United States: 1900, Special Reports: Occupations*, pp. 1 and 1i.

clerical workers, there were approximately three women doing clerical work for every man. From 1870 to 1968 the number of both male and female clerical workers has increased substantially. But, in proportion to the total clerical work force, males have lost ground: they made up 97.3 percent of the clerical force in 1870 but only 25.6 percent in 1968. The proportion of women clerical workers to men clerical workers has

TABLE 2.2   Percentage of clerical workers by industry, 1960

Industry	Labor force 1960	Clerical[a] workers 1960	Percent clerical workers per industry	Percent of total clerical workers
Agricultural pursuits	4,252,849	26,540	.62	.29
Forestry and fishing	91,460	5,003	5.50	.05
Mining	653,979	48,446	7.41	.52
Manufacturing	17,529,762	2,096,927	11.96	22.54
Transportation	4,458,549	1,064,680	23.88	11.45
Trade	11,797,899	1,621,486	13.74	17.43
Public service	3,194,250	1,350,262	42.27	14.51
Professional service	7,574,472	1,112,721	14.69	11.96
Domestic and personal service	5,967,906	529,824	8.88	5.69
Construction	3,817,678	168,842	4.42	1.82
Finance	2,695,498	1,249,811	46.37	13.43
Industry not reported	2,612,261	28,669	1.10	.31
Totals	64,646,563	9,303,231	14.39	100.00

[a] United States Bureau of the Census, *U. S. Census of Population 1960, Subject Reports, Occupation by Industry*, Table 2, summary of figures, pp. 7–146.

changed from one out of 37 to three out of four. Another interesting point is that of the employed women, the largest group in 1968 was made up of clerical workers. Approximately one-third of employed women were clerical workers in 1968.* Men tend to work in the professional groups and/or managerial groups. A breakdown by types of clerical occupations is shown in Table 2.4.

Thus the clerical occupation group is a very large one, increasing not only in absolute numbers but also in proportion of the total labor work force. This occupation covers a great many different jobs. The more important of these are: accountants, auditors, bookkeepers, stenographers, typists, machine operators, general office clerks, messengers, office boys and girls, and agents. These workers are divided

* United States Department of Labor, Wage and Labor Standards Administration, *Background Facts on Women Workers in the United States*, Sept. 1968, p. 11.

TABLE 2.3   Sex of clerical workers, 1870–1968

Period	Clerical workers	Male	Female	Percent male	Percent female
1968[a]	12,731,000	3,256,000	9,475,000	25.6	74.4
1960[b]	9,303,231	3,027,732	6,275,499	32.5	67.5
1950[c]	6,865,960	2,593,030	4,272,930	37.8	62.2
1940[d]	4,612,356	2,336,853	2,375,503	48.5	51.5
1930[e]	4,025,324	2,038,494	1,986,830	50.6	49.4
1920[e]	3,111,836	1,689,911	1,421,935	54.3	45.7
1910[e]	1,718,458	1,129,849	588,609	65.7	34.3
1900[f]	1,068,993	816,813	252,180	76.4	23.6
1890[f]	801,505	685,335	116,170	85.5	14.5
1880[f]	518,439	487,195	30,744	94.0	6.0
1870[f]	305,502	297,399	8,103	97.3	2.7

[a] United States Department of Labor, Bureau of Labor Statistics, *Employment and Earnings and Monthly Report on the Labor Force*, Vol. 15, #5, November, 1968, p. 24.

[b] United States Bureau of the Census, *U. S. Census of Population, 1960, Subject Reports, Occupational Characteristics*, Final Report PC(2)–7A, Table 6, pp. 73 and 83.

[c] United States Bureau of the Census, *U. S. Census of Population; 1950. Vol. IV, Special Reports*, Part 1, Chapter C, *Occupation by Industry*, p. 13.

[d] United States Bureau of the Census, *Sixteenth Census of the United States: 1940, Population, Vol. III, The Labor Force, Part I: U. S. Summary*, pp. 75–76.

[e] United States Bureau of the Census, *Fifteenth Census of the United States: 1930, Population, Vol. V, General Report on Occupations*, pp. 10 and 22.

[f] United States Bureau of the Census, *Twelfth Census of the United States: 1900, Special Reports: Occupations*, pp. 1 and 1i.

into four categories for 1870 to 1900 and into six groups from 1910 on. The totals for each of these classifications are shown in Table 2.4.

This table brings out two interesting facts. Before 1900 typists were called "typewriters," as we can see from the 60th anniversary issue of Today's Secretary:

One of the greatest obstacles to the typewriter popularity and success was a lack of qualified operators . . . in 1881 . . . Remington started their own classes for "typewriters" as typists were then called. . . . Typewriters, neuter and feminine species, had their feet in the door.*

---

* Marua Mara, "Once Upon a Typewriter," *Today's Secretary*, Gregg Publishing Division of McGraw-Hill Book, Dayton, Ohio, 61:30, April, 1959.

TABLE 2.4   Clerical workers classified by clerical occupations, 1870–1960

	1870[a]	1880[a]	1890[a]	1900[a]
Bookkeepers and accountants			159,374	254,880
Clerks and copyists	296,785	504,454	557,358	630,127
Stenographers and Typewriters			33,418	112,364
Messengers, etc.	8,717	13,985	51,355	71,622
Totals	305,502	518,439	801,505	1,068,993

	1910[b]	1920[b]	1930[b]
Bookkeepers and accountants	486,700	734,688	930,648
General office clerks	720,498	1,487,905	1,958,902
Stenographers and typists	316,693	615,154	811,190
Messengers, etc.	108,035	113,022	90,379
Office machine operators			38,098
Agents, etc.	86,532	161,067	196,107
Totals	1,718,458	3,111,836	4,025,324

	1940[c]	1950[d]	1960[e]
Bookkeepers and accountants	856,448	946,170	1,515,608
General office clerks	2,387,200	3,939,690	4,073,154
Stenographers and typists	1,056,886	1,579,770	2,389,606
Messengers, etc.	54,360	55,200	266,209
Office machine operators	59,738	142,530	679,210
Agents, etc.	197,724	202,580	379,444
Totals	4,612,356	6,865,960	9,303,231

[a] United States Bureau of the Census, *Twelfth Census of the United States: 1900, Special Reports: Occupations,* pp. 1 and 1i.

[b] United States Bureau of the Census, *Fifteenth Census of the United States: 1930, Population, Vol. V,* p. 22.

[c] United States Bureau of the Census, *Sixteenth Census of the United States: 1940, Population,* Vol. III, p. 76.

[d] United States Bureau of the Census, *1950 Census of Population, Special Report P-E #1–B,* p. 17.

[e] United States Bureau of the Census, United States Census of Population, 1960, *Subject Reports, Occupation by Industry,* Table 2, p. 8.

The other fact is that until 1930 office machine operators were included in other clerical groups. Since 1930, however, they have been classified as a separate group. From 1930 to 1960 the number of workers in this group increased by 641,112 or approximately 1700 percent.

This brief overview of the situation regarding the amount of clerical work which has had to be done in our increasingly industrial society indicates clearly the importance of devices to carry out the work with the greatest accuracy and the least expenditure of time. Data processing has become an extremely important part of the American economy. The ever increasing magnitude and complexity of business has created a need by management for more information for the purpose of planning and control. There are other reasons for an increased dependency on the data processing function: (1) a changing economy and (2) developments that have caused new and increased demands for information.

A CHANGING ECONOMY

Managers are primarily interested in problems of production and income of the company they work for and are less concerned with the total production and income of the United States. At the same time, many realize that they play an important part in the total economy, which in turn affects the production and income of their firms. Production and income are higher when the economy of the country is prosperous because the demand for goods and services is higher than it is when the economy is in a slump.

The individual firm finds that it is operating in a growing national economy. One commonly accepted measure of growth is the gross national product, or GNP. This is the sum of the value of all the goods and services produced by the residents of a nation in a given period of time, including the services provided by the government. In 1930, the gross national product of the United States, valued in constant dollars of 1958 purchasing power, was 183.5 billion. In 1940, it was 227.2 billion—a 24 percent increase from 1930 to 1940. In 1950, it was 355.3 billion—reflecting a 56 percent increase from 1940. In 1960, the GNP was 487.8 billion and in 1968, 719.1 billion. From 1950 to 1960, the GNP increased by 37 percent and from 1960 to 1968, by 47 percent. The increase from 1930 to 1968 was 270 percent.

However, real gross national product is merely a quantitative concept of economic growth. By itself, it does not explain the tremendous absolute increase in the employment of clerical workers either in absolute numbers or in relation to other categories of workers.

The sustained change in total output of the United States economy is characterized in industrialization, that is to say, a shift upward in

TABLE 2.5   Relative position of the major occupations groups of the American labor force: 1900–1968

Occupation	1900[a]	1910[a]	1920[a]	1930[a]	1940[a]	1950[a]	1960[b]	1968[c]
Farm workers	37.6	30.8	27.0	21.1	17.4	11.7	8.1	4.4
Manual workers	35.9	38.1	40.3	39.6	39.9	41.2	36.2	36.3
Service workers	9.1	9.7	7.8	9.9	11.7	10.5	12.6	12.3
White-collar workers	17.4	21.4	24.9	29.4	31.0	36.6	43.1	47.0
Total	100.0	100.0	100.0	100.0	100.0	100.0	100.0	100.0

[a] U. S. Bureau of the Census, *Historical Statistics of the United States, Colonial Times to 1957*, Washington, D. C., 1960, p. 74.

[b] U. S. Bureau of the Census, *Statistical Abstract of the United States: 1968*, Washington, D. C., 1968, p. 225.

[c] U. S. Department of Labor: Bureau of Labor Statistics, *Employment and Earnings*, Vol. 15, #5, p. 25.

the relative importance of the industrial system within the American economy and a shift downward in the relative importance of the agrarian component.

To illustrate what has happened, we present Table 2.5 which shows the percentage changes in the distribution of the labor force by major occupations from 1900 to 1968. In 1900, the farm worker group was the largest. However, since 1900 the farm worker group has been steadily losing ground until in 1968 it was the smallest group (see Table 2.5). Until the turn of the century, the United States had primarily an agricultural economy. The proportion of nonfarm workers grew from approximately 62 percent of the labor force in 1900 to approximately 95 percent in 1968. The proportion of white-collar workers grew from approximately 17 percent of the labor force in 1900 to approximately 47 percent in 1968, becoming the largest group since the 1950's.

By 1968, the structure of employment had changed radically, and principally because mechanization has decreased the need for people in the farming occupations. This indicates that the United States has become primarily an industrialized, commercialized, and professional nation instead of a nation that is primarily engaged in agriculture. The growth of American industry and commerce has been astonishing.

With the increase in a nation's population, it becomes increasingly difficult to continue to increase per capita income through agriculture. Economic development follows a typical pattern. First an economy is relatively self-sufficient—agriculture absorbs a major part of the energies of the population. Second, industries develop—the economy becomes industrialized. Third, manufacturing increases to such a degree that auxiliary commercial services are required. Clark, an English economist at Oxford University, shows that this pattern has three stages:

Stage 1: development of primary industries, such as agriculture, forestry, fishing, and hunting;

Stage 2: development of secondary industries, such as manufacturing, mining, construction, and the hand trades;

Stage 3: development of tertiary industries, such as marketing, finance, communication, transportation, warehousing, professional and governmental services.[1]

A growing and changing economy is not, in itself, the reason for the growth of the clerical work force. Instead, the reason is the shift from an agricultural economy with little demand for clerical services to our industrial, commercial, and professional economy which has an enormous demand for clerical workers. The reason for the enormous growth of the data processing function, then, is not a larger economy but a different economy which has shifted activities utilizing little information to those requiring a high degree of information.

In addition to the overall change in the business economy, there are internal changes that have taken place within the individual business firms, which in turn have increased the need for the data processing function.

First, let's examine the question of size. Perhaps it should be pointed out why the emphasis is on "large" business. A small business has direct, oral lines of communication. The manager of the small business does most of his managing in a face-to-face situation. He knows what is happening in his firm through personal observation and through talking with his subordinates. The information he needs can be carried either in his head or maintained by a very simple office sys-

EXHIBIT 2.1   Distribution of firms and paid employment by size of firm, 1966

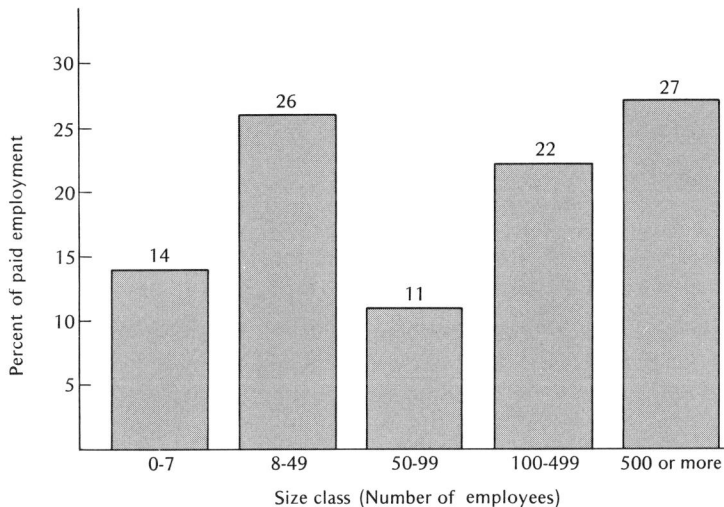

Source: Compiled from the U.S. Bureau of the Census, Statistical
Abstract of the United States: 1968, Washington, D.C., 1968, p. 476.

tem of files, records, reports, and the like. As a business firm grows,
lines of communication get larger, and more information is required
to enable the manager to know what is happening in his firm.

To evaluate the importance of the size of business firms in its effect
on the need for information, we must compare the operations of small
and large firms. One of the best ways to show the impact of size is
to show the distribution of employees among businesses of various
sizes. According to Exhibit 2.1, firms with more than 50 employees
account for approximately 60 percent of all paid employment, firms
with more than 100 employees account for approximately 50 percent
of all paid employment, and those with more than 500 employees
account for 27 percent.

THE NEW AND INCREASED DEMANDS FOR INFORMATION

The growth of the American economy is closely intertwined with the
emergence of the corporation as the dominant form of business organization. The corporate form of legal organization permitted the
raising of needed capital and increased centralization of managerial

control. This form of organization enables investors to combine their capital and participate in the profits of business firms with a risk limited to the capital contributed and without peril to their own other personal resources. It is doubtful that the amount of capital needed for modern business could have been assembled in any other way.

One important continuing development is the increasing significance of market opportunities in terms of their international dimensions. United States business has responded to this international opportunity on a large scale, especially since World War II, as is shown by the rapid increase in the sale and production of goods abroad by United States companies. The best available indicator of this trend is the value of direct investments in foreign countries which rose approximately 57 percent from 1929 to 1950, a little over 132 percent from 1950 to 1958, and approximately 343 percent from 1958 to 1967.

The data processing function becomes important to the firm engaged in international business as Professor Fayerweather of Columbia University points out:

A regular flow of information from the field into the home office is essential both for control and counseling purposes. The headquarters must keep informed about the course of operations abroad to make plans, to be able to devise the field units intelligently, and to keep the foreign managements from making minor decisions which cumulatively result in major deviations from company policies.[2]

The more a business grows, the more complicated becomes its flow of information, its organization, its product line, its internal relationships, its external relationships, and its facilities for operating. A great deal of coordination is required to achieve consistency in the quality and extent of the various activities. The more extensive a business becomes on an international basis, then, the more difficult it is to manage. More extensive information and analyses are needed for management control. Management needs more and more information, and in order to survive must find more effective and efficient means of processing data.

Perhaps in the development of larger and more complex business entities, it was inevitable that the function of planning be separated from the function of doing. Essentially the function of management is to determine what needs to be done and to allocate these tasks to competent specialists who can best handle them. Presidents of large companies have found that it is advantageous to delegate certain functions to staff specialists. The trend in the corporate organization is to have new and bigger staff groups, including a group whose function is to perform a series of operations on data—the data processing group. Supplying management with information from staff specialists goes back to the separation of planning from performance that F. W. Taylor advocated at the beginning of the 20th century.

The greater productivity of the manufacturing firms in the United States has been largely due to mechanization and improved methods of production resulting from improved technology. However, there is another reason, which is seldom recognized, why the American factory worker is one of the most productive in the world: he has more supervision and more staff work to support him.

Staff services provide pertinent data dealing directly with operations as well as with all areas in which policy decisions must be made. This need for information stems from management in that staff functions typically are of a consultive nature, providing special and technical information. Information usually involves summaries based on research, recommendations, record and statistical maintenance, and other specialized data.

This puts data processing as an organizational activity clearly in a staff capacity. (Line, staff, and line-and-staff will be explained in the section on organization in Chapter 20.) The advantage of having the data processing as a separate, distinct function was pointed out as early as 1886 by Henry C. Metcalfe in a paper he presented before the American Society of Mechanical Engineers on "The Shop Order System of Accounts."[3] In this paper, Metcalfe suggested a plan of organization on the fundamental division of work between the "work-shop" and the "office" which appears as an equivalent to F. W. Taylor's idea of the fundamental division of planning and performance.* In fact, Taylor, who was present at the meeting and participated in the discussion that followed the presentation of Metcalfe's paper, made the following remark:

We at the Midvale Steel Company have had the experience during the past ten years of organizing a system very similar to that of Mr. Metcalfe. The chief idea in our system, as in his, is that the authority for doing all kind of work

---

* Henry Metcalfe was the superintendent of several army arsenals from 1868–1893. He was a pioneer in devising a system for cost and material control which many feel makes sense even today. His system was concerned primarily with a continuous flow of information. F. W. Taylor is considered to be the father of Scientific Management which became the first systematic study of management in the United States.

should proceed from one central office to the various departments, and that the proper records should be kept of the work and reports made daily to the central office, so that the superintending department should be kept thoroughly informed as to what is taking place throughout the works, and at the same time no work could be done in the works without proper authority.[4]

Specialization has become an outstanding characteristic of the modern business office. The enormous increase in specialization has resulted in the need for an increasing volume of data. When the work load becomes too great for one individual, it is often split between two persons, each of whom does half the steps on all the tasks, rather than all the steps on half the tasks. The problem for the manager of the data processing function has become not whether to specialize but how far to carry the division of work. He has to weigh very carefully the advantages and disadvantages of various kinds of specialization. He has to consider whether specialization will result in easier, simpler, less complicated operations or whether specialization will make the work more difficult to manage.

To take advantage of automation, the manager of the data processing function is forced to streamline, coordinate, and integrate the system that he has designed through the use of the specialization concept. Automation does require specialists. Special skill, even though not complicated, is required to run a machine efficiently. Only a well-trained operator is able to run a machine efficiently. The manager of the data processing function has to attempt to find a "happy medium" between overspecialization and specialization.

Since the Hawthorne studies,* management has been interested in human relations, hoping to improve its ability to cope with people. Actually, the study of business has become in part a behavioral science, studying a sample of behavior in a particular context. Consequently, more records and reports are necessary. Maintenance of accurate and comprehensive records concerning the human element is becoming

---

* Elton Mayo, who with Fritz Roethlisberger, William J. Dickson, and others conducted a series of studies in the 1920's at the Hawthorne plant of Western Electric Company. They concluded that employees would be happy and productive only if they could belong to a cohesive and stable work group, that the "sense of belonging" was more important to them than anything else. For the complete account of the Hawthorne experiments, see F. J. Roethlisberger and William J. Dickson, *Management and the Worker*, Harvard University Press, Cambridge, Mass., 1939.

EXHIBIT 2.2   Corner Grocery Store
Income Statement (for year ended December, 1971)

Income:		
Sale of groceries		$51,360
Cost of groceries sold:		
Inventory January 1, 1971	$ 3,560	
Purchases	33,450	
Total available for sale	$37,010	
Less: Inventory December 31,1971	3,330	
Total		33,680
Gross profit on sales		$17,680
Expenses:		
Delivery	$ 300	
Rent	1,800	
Salary	5,200	
Supplies	633	
Utilities	530	
Insurance	342	
Miscellaneous	315	
Total expenses		9,120
Net income		$8,560

a major activity of business. Records concerning accidents, lay-offs, hours of work, or shift work may be required by law or union contract. Other records concerning labor turnover, absenteeism, grievances, ratings, transfer and promotions, suggestions, training and the like are essential for a successful human relations approach. Adequate performance records help management to make decisions concerning the employees.

Even employee benefit programs have increased the clerical activities of the business firm. Group insurance, group hospitalization plans, credit unions, wage incentive plans, labor negotiations, retirement programs and many other employee benefit programs have become an accepted and vital part of the business world today. Such programs require records, and such records mean an increase in the clerical activities of the firm.

The owner of a small store who hires no employees must still keep a record of his purchases and his sales in order to complete his tax forms for the Government, as shown in Exhibit 2.2. He does not have to keep a record on paper of how many of each particular item he has in his store—he can just walk over to the shelf, count the number of cans he has of chocolate syrup, and decide how many he should order because he can recall approximately how many he sold during the same part of the year last year. A large corporation must keep many more records and more accurate records, as shown in Exhibit 2.3. For example, the corporation that makes ice-cream bars cannot send a person to the stockroom to count the sticks or paper bags every week or to count the number of ice-cream bars in the freezers each month. It might take a day, or even longer, to do the counting. Therefore, the company must keep an up-to-date record of how many boxes are made, add this number to the amount on hand, and subtract the number sold from the amount they have. This example shows just one way in which larger companies must keep more accurate records and more detailed records than a small businessman. There is also a need for keeping payroll data and all income and expenses in order to prepare all the tax reports the state and the federal government require. The larger a business is, the more information or data it needs to keep. The methods used by each business to process its data depend on the following factors:

1. How quickly the data must be processed.
2. How many data are to be processed.
3. How much money it can spend initially to set up a data-processing system.

Data, as we have noted, is information that has been processed in some way directly by a person or indirectly by him through a computer. The manager needs to have up-to-date, pertinent information in order to plan, control, delegate, and communicate intelligently. These needs for information will be discussed in Chapter 3.

QUESTIONS AND PROBLEMS

1. What has been the rate of growth in the number of clerical workers?
2. What industry or industries employ clerical workers?
3. Explain the change that has occurred in the type of individuals doing office work.
4. Which clerical occupation showed the largest growth in number of employees from 1930 to 1960? Compare this increase with that in the other clerical occupations.

The Jones Company
17 West Lake Street
Chicago, Illinois

November, 1971

EXHIBIT 2.3   Operating statement

Index		AMOUNTS		PERCENTAGES	
		Current Month	Year to Date	Month	To Date
300	SALES				
301	Sales—Type A	13,261.79	105,479.86	32.0	35.7
302	Sales—Type B	27,440.86	181,080.40	66.3	61.4
303	Sales—Type C	712.49	8,557.33	1.7	2.9
399	Total Sales	41,415.14	295,117.59	100.0	100.0
400	COST OF SALES				
401	Cost of Sales—Type A	11,683.64	92,927.77	88.1	88.2
402	Cost of Sales—Type B	20,251.35	133,637.33	73.8	73.8
403	Cost of Sales—Type C	525.82	3,240.13	73.7	37.7
498	Total Cost of Sales	32,460.81	229,805.23	78.4	77.9
499	GROSS PROFIT	8,954.33	65,312.36	21.6	22.1
500	OPERATING EXPENSES				
508	Shipping Supplies	29.36	1,590.82	.1	.5
509	Export Crating		73.08		
510	Operating Supplies	23.04	278.81	.1	.1
511	Freight In	403.26	3,058.68	1.0	1.0
515	Gross Wages-Shop	2,146.62	23,237.33	5.2	7.9
516	Officers Salaries	1,000.00	5,000.00	2.4	1.7
520	Rent	1,500.00	8,000.00	3.6	2.7
526	Utilities		487.94		.2
530	Repairs & Maintenance	90.87	428.84	.2	.1
531	Tooling		194.30		.1
535	Insurance	44.74	223.70	.1	.1
536	Hospital Insurance	100.72	104.56	.2	
538	Uniforms		63.42		
540	State Unemployment		271.81		.1
542	Payroll Tax	149.89	772.58	.4	.3
564	Legal & Audit	45.00	395.00	.1	.1
566	Office Expense		37.59		
575	Depreciation	119.88	592.86	.3	.2
581	Laundry & Linen	10.61	20.74		
582	Freight-In Equipment		3.72		
596	Experimental & Engineering	336.00	336.00	.8	.1
597	Office Service Billed	1,750.00	8,750.00	4.2	3.0
598	Total Operating Expenses	7,749.99	53,921.78	18.7	18.2
599	PROFIT	1,204.34	11,390.58	2.9	3.9

5. Briefly indicate what the facts presented in this chapter indicate.

6. a) Discuss the changing economy in the United States.
   b) How does this place more importance upon the data processing function?

7. What is G.N.P.? Explain briefly.

8. Describe the changes in the distribution of the labor force by major occupations since 1900.

9. Briefly trace the typical pattern of economic developments in a nation.

10. Why does the problem of data processing emphasize the larger businesses?

11. Discuss the developments that have caused new and increased demands for information.

12. When the work load becomes too great for one individual, why is it advantageous to split it between two persons, each doing half the steps on all the tasks rather than each doing all the steps on half the tasks?

13. Why is it so necessary for organizations to process data?

14. What factors help determine the methods each business uses to process data?

REFERENCES

1. Colin Clark, *Conditions of Economic Progress,* (London: Macmillan, 1940), p. 182.

2. John Fayerweather, *Management of International Operations,* (New York: McGraw-Hill, 1960), p. 369.

3. Henry C. Metcalfe, "The Shop-Order System of Accounts," *Transactions of the American Society of Mechanical Engineers,* **7**:443, 1886.

4. *Ibid.,* p. 474.

THE ORGANIZATION OF DATA

Data are facts which can be used as a basis for reasoning; processing involves a series of operations performed on data to assemble it in a way which will be most useful to those who need it for decision-making. Thus facts are the raw material for the function of data processing. In today's business organization the number of relevant facts for decision-making at various levels within the organization is quite staggering, so that only the most pertinent facts can be reported in the normal course of operations. The prime purposes of the data-processing function are recording, duplicating, classifying, sorting, calculating, summarizing, communicating, and storing and retrieving the various facts that are collected in day-to-day operations. Data, then, are unorganized facts; information results from the collection and organization of data.

EFFECTIVE PLANNING

In research, engineering, manufacturing, finance, and sales, the key to progress is planning. A company grows by long-term planning and continuous re-evaluation of its operation in the light of new knowledge. The data processing function contributes to such planning by providing management with complete, accurate, and timely information which it can use to make such plans.

For management to be effective it must concern itself with policies and assign the details of day-to-day operation to its staff and/or line personnel. The staff or line executive is primarily interested in accomplishing the objectives of his own department. He has had professional training in his particular field, and concentrates his efforts on solving the problems of his particular professional field.

Like top management, the staff or line executive probably takes data processing for granted and is glad that the data processing function has been delegated to some other person. Nonetheless, he depends on the data processing function for the performance of many of his activities.

The quality of information is basic to the quality of management. American business is now in an era in which managerial skill is its greatest asset. Management is dynamic and not only adjusts to business changes but also initiates such changes. The office is the center of planning for innovation, and it is the data processing function that sets the pace by providing the information required in planning, such as data for the designing of control procedures, the planning of organization structures, the planning of organizational relationships, and for determining standards. Some of the important results of planning are to provide:

1. technical advice on organization and procedure,
2. assistance in installing improved procedures,
3. conditions that are conducive to maximum economy and effectiveness in the performance of staff or line functions,
4. efficient communication,
5. effective work force,
6. well-coordinated fast flow of information between offices, and
7. standards that will contribute to the accomplishment of the above objectives.

The above objectives apply to administrative planning as well as to operating planning, and both rely on the data processing function. All executives, whether staff, line, or administrative, carry out planning. The staff executives help some line executive plan and/or supervise the activities of others. The line executive controls the operative execution of plans. Administrators make plans of action for the organization as a whole or for its principal functions—finance, marketing, production, information, etc. For an administrator to plan efficiently he must have information on

1. general objectives that will keep the firm competitive, as well as profitable,
2. sales objectives,
3. profit and loss objectives,

4. product lines, and

5. personnel practice and policies.

It can be seen that the above objectives are related to one another. The data processing function will be of help to the administration in these objectives only if it has broad interests and is coordinated to cut across organization lines.

EFFECTIVE CONTROL

Control is only as good as the planning that precedes it and the action that follows it. Planning mechanisms and control mechanisms are very closely allied. Although control activities make extensive use of accounting data, they are by no means limited to accounting. Business and industry rely on staff operations at many key operational points— manufacturing, sales, finance, etc. An effective data processing system will provide the basis for planning and for management control.

PROPER DELEGATION OF RESPONSIBILITY

It is impossible for any one person to keep track of all the day-to-day details that must be watched to ensure efficient management of a company's affairs. The executive can delegate authority for various activities to others, but he must retain the responsibility for the work. The person to whom responsibility is delegated is accountable to his superior for his own acts and for those of the unit under his supervision. The executive who can no longer personally oversee various activities must rely on information in the form of records to tell him what is happening. On this data he must rely in his planning, organizing, and directing of the current and future activities for which he is responsible.

EFFECTIVE COMMUNICATION

Good controls over the delegation of authority will detect mistakes or failures in the performance of the staff. Adequate communication will prevent mistakes and failures resulting from misunderstandings. For this reason, adequate communication is a prerequisite to effective planning, effective control, and effective delegation and assignment of responsibility. Effective communication is basic to these functions for without it coordination is difficult.

Some information handling activities are concerned primarily with the origination phase of communications. Some examples are: correspondence supervision, central stenographic service, and printing and duplicating units. The organization phase of communications is concerned with the personnel, equipment, records, and supplies that are necessary to produce a message.

There are also data processing activities that deal with the transmission phase of communications, with conveying the written or spoken word from one location to another. Transmission must be accurate, quick, and low in cost. The mail unit, the communications center, input/output units, machine data-processing operations, and the central files are concerned with the problem of information transmission. These units are often beset by problems, and management expects the manager of the data processing function to help find solutions to these problems.

MANAGEMENT'S CHANGED ATTITUDE TOWARD THE USE OF INFORMATION

The rapid growth of corporations, separation of ownership from management, competition on both a national and international scale, and rapid technological advances have been the forces motivating management to plan, control, delegate, and communicate. Business decisions must be based on reliable and readily accessible facts.

Management is the directing, planning, and organizing group effort of an enterprise to reach effective decisions about the proper integration of both human and nonhuman resources to achieve the objectives and carry out the policies of the enterprise. To perform these activities effectively, managers on all levels need adequate information.

The frequency with which information is received varies from daily, to weekly, monthly, quarterly, or annually. Information may be transmitted in discussions, memoranda, reports, meetings, telephone calls, and visual exhibits. All these media involve the data processing function in varying degrees.

DECISION-MAKING AND THE DATA PROCESSING FUNCTION

Management is not a purely mechanistic activity. The effective application of the managerial functions of planning, organizing, and directing (commanding, communication, coordination, and control) is fraught with great difficulties. These stem from the dynamic aspects of these functions as they are carried out. No fixed formula can be followed in all cases.

Management must be capable of decision-making. Appraising a situation or condition and knowing what to do about it is the manager's job. The ability to make decisions is, by far, the most important aspect of management at all levels. As clearly stated by Peter F. Drucker: "Whatever a manager does he does through making decisions."[1]

Herbert Simon, Professor of Administration at Carnegie Institute of Technology, points out that the decision-making process does not consist solely of choosing between two or more alternatives. The decision-making process is not "the alert gray-haired businessman, sitting at the board of directors' table with his associates, caught at the moment of saying 'aye' or 'nay'."[2] Decision-making involves something more than the final choice which is the culmination of the decision-making process.

Decision-making is not a new concept. Philosophers, economists, educators, psychologists, and social psychologists have been interested in decision-making from the problem-solving viewpoint. One of the best descriptions of problem solving comes from the philosopher, educator, and psychologist John Dewey, who viewed decision-making, problem-solving, or managing as a three-stage process aimed at answering the following questions:

What is the problem?

What are the alternatives?

Which alternative is best?[3]

The connection between the data processing function and the decision-making process described by Simon and Dewey is basically one of information. Information of one kind or another is required at each stage of the problem-solving or decision-making process.

The management of business is carried on by a group who make many day-to-day decisions. These decisions involve the flow of information concerning money, methods, materials, men, and machines through a firm. These activities involve planning, organizing, and directing of information about financing, production, sales, engineering, research and development, public relations personnel, and legal activities. The quality and timing of these decisions are dependent upon the efficiency and effectiveness of the data processing function.

Felix Kaufman, Electronic Data Processing specialist of Lybrand, Ross Bros. and Montgomery, points out:

Two identifying and interrelated problems confront American management today. One is the growing mountain of paperwork, a product of prosperity, i.e. increased sales, as well as the increasing demand for reports by State and Federal agencies. The other problem is the need for some reliable data to make managerial decisions more quickly.

One result of all this is the rapid growth in the number of clerical workers compared to all workers . . . Another result is the momentous developments in the techniques of data processing. The entire field of information handling is now being viewed in a new light.[4]

The development in the techniques of data processing will be discussed in Chapters 4 and 5. The field of information handling is being viewed in a new light: information, the product of the data processing function, is seen (a) as binding all phases of executive work together, and (b) as linking all executive work with the environment in which it operates (see Chapter 2). If the information content answers management's needs, information integrates all facets into a true system.

It is not enough to update older data processing systems by introducing new techniques; in addition, the information generated by these techniques must be integrated and correlated creatively. The objective is to simplify and improve control and consequently simplify managing and controlling functions at all management levels. In many companies, this undoubtedly involves adjustments in existing organizational responsibilities and structures to provide for functional reassignments. This places the manager of the data processing function in a position in which he has new responsibilities and a new place in the corporate organization chart.

Logically, it would appear that we should discuss systems and organization. However, we prefer to review first information technology and the history of data processing, for these have had an effect on systems and organization of the data processing function as well as on the American business firm.

QUESTIONS AND PROBLEMS

1. Distinguish between facts and information useful to management.
2. Comment on the following statement: "Records are a necessity in the operation of every business entity."
3. Why does management need both internal and external information for effective planning?
4. Explain why management needs information for setting goals and maintaining effective control.
5. Why does the increasing need to delegate authority necessitate more elaborate methods of control?
6. Discuss how communication affects control.
7. "If a manager learns the techniques of planning, organizing, and directing, his job is purely mechanistic." Discuss.
8. How does the availability of information bind together all phases of executive work?
9. "The information a manager needs for planning, controlling, delegating, and communicating is interrelated." Discuss.

REFERENCES

1. Peter F. Drucker, *The Practice of Management,* (New York: Harper, 1954), p. 351; see *ibid.,* Chapter 28 for his effective and thorough analysis of the problem of making decisions. Professor Drucker is author, consultant, and lecturer in the field of general management. He is presently Professor of Management at the Graduate School of Business Administration of New York University.
2. Herbert F. Simon, *The New Science of Management Decision,* (New York, N.Y.: Harper, 1960), p. 1.
3. John Dewey, *How We Think,* (2nd Edition, Boston, Mass.: D. C. Heath, 1933), p. 120.
4. Felix Kaufman, "Data Processing, Present and Future," *American Business,* **29**:15, October 1959.

INFORMATION TECHNOLOGY

CHAPTER 4

THE NEW TREND IN MECHANIZATION

Mechanical devices should be used in the office whenever they save time, promote accuracy, or eliminate monotonous routine work. Mechanization transfers time and effort from the man to the machine, thus freeing the man for more creative work. In many companies the volume of data processing activities is great enough to warrant mechanization, but often the work is performed in separate units, of diverse kinds, and distributed throughout the organization. In the latter case, mechanization is too expensive. There are three reasons for excessive costs in electronic data processing: 1) lack of planning and preparation; 2) lack of management understanding; and 3) use of low-wage labor.[1]

For the last two decades, the manufacturers of electronic data processing equipment have come up with one new invention after another, steadily making the office a different kind of place in which to work. Into the computers, inventors have built increasing operating speeds and monumental degrees of accuracy. In order to appreciate the progress of EDP as it has evolved to its present stage, we next present a chronological review of data processing, the role of the computer in decision-making, and the history of data processing. The first two topics will be discussed in this chapter; the third in Chapter 5.

W. H. Leffingwell, the first writer on scientific office management, gave the following chronological breakdown of data processing:

to 1900   Copy press era

1900–1910   Systems era

1910–1920   Machine era

1920–   Management era[2]

Leffingwell died in 1934. Data processing function remained in the management era until 1949.[3] Recent developments in data processing are reflected by the following breakdown:

1920–1950   Management era

1950–1965   Administrative services era

1965–   Information management era

We mentioned earlier that the phrase "information management" is beginning to replace the traditional "office management." The emphasis is on "total systems" and thinking of the organization as an integrated process, or viewing it as "integrated systems." Either approach gives us the "information systems approach" of today.

Until 1900 relatively little was done to improve the efficiency of data processing. The business correspondence of the 1890's was written by hand. Good penmanship and ability in arithmetic appear to have been the prime prerequisites of an office worker. Other than copying by hand, the only method of duplicating a record or letter was by the copying press. Even though the typewriter was invented before 1900, people were reluctant to replace hand-copying by machines other than the copying press. It was felt that the typewritten page was too impersonal. Thus, the copy press was generally used for the duplication of records and letters.

During the first decade of the twentieth century, the data processing function was beginning to gain status. As business was becoming larger and more complex, the owner or manager of a firm could no longer retain all ideas, plans, facts, and other data either in his head or on papers "pigeon-holed" in his roll-top desk.

The work of providing and retaining data was delegated to a responsible person who was called chief clerk or office manager. (In today's help-wanted ads, the qualifications listed for an office manager are those of chief accounting clerk rather than a manager.) The chief clerk at the beginning of the century soon realized that he had to have a system. Issues of the magazine *System*, published in the early years of the twentieth century, reveal that a "system" was advocated for every activity performed in the office. The titles of some of the articles in the first few volumes are "System in Buying," "System in Collections," and "System in Selling." The "system" referred to was a card index system which gave office workers an orderly, systematic way of doing things. Hence, the name "systems era."

By 1910, machines were beginning to invade the office on a large scale. Office managers were convinced that systems plus machines would give the office the perfect formula for efficiency. Hence they were in favor of using machines wherever these could aid the system.

In 1913, J. W. Schulze, one of the pioneers in the office management field, described the telephone, telautograph, intercommunication equipment, stenotype machines, dictating machines, calculating machines, cash registers, and addressing machines,[4] as well as billing machines, duplication machines, check protectors and signers, folding and numbering machines, sealing, stamping, and mail-opening machines, the automatic typewriter, and even Hollerith punched-card equipment. Thus the basic office machines we know today were already in existence during the first quarter of the twentieth century. The period during 1925 to 1945 was characterized primarily by improvements of the machines existing in 1913. It is no wonder Leffingwell chose to call this period the "machine era."

The scientific management movement started by F. W. Taylor and his associates did not penetrate into the office until about 1920. The office manager was confronted with a large labor force, a maze of records, many systems, and a mass of machines—and therefore large-sized management problems. Taylor advocated separation of planning from performance and use of the scientific method in setting and maintaining standards of materials, equipment, methods, and performance in factories. Leffingwell applied Taylor's principles to data processing. A review of textbooks written on the management of data processing since 1920 reveals that these principles are considered as the "fundamentals" of data processing management. Hence, the designation of the "management era." The fifties have been called many things, among them the "automated decade," "electronic data processing era," "scientific computing era," "the computer age," etc. So many different titles arose because there were so many interpretations of the rapid spread of electronic data processing during that period.

Thus we see that the development of electronic devices and their application to office machines are bringing about revolutionary changes in the performance of data processing. Although these techniques do aid management in making effective decisions, they do not, of course, replace the decision-making process. Let's explore this subject further.

THE ROLE OF THE COMPUTER IN DECISION-MAKING

The development of efficient and trustworthy computers (along with many other technological improvements) has provided not only the means of collecting, manipulating, and presenting huge masses of facts, but it has necessitated study and development of proper techniques. It has been necessary to select and organize pertinent facts into useful answers to specific questions.

The value of the computer in decision-making is pointed out by Robert Caleo:

Computers do not make management decisions, but they do make managers better decision-makers. Processed data in meaningful form—the end product of the computer—reduces the need for assumption, thus minimizing the possibility of important decisions backfiring on management . . .

This is the big payoff of computers, not the ten to twenty-five percent clerical savings they effect in the office.[5]

At first, then, the work of the computer was confined to "simple" tasks such as bookkeeping and doing the payroll. Today, it is a key element in management decision-making. It comprises by vast communications networks, advanced hardware, and utilizes numerous scientific formulas and techniques. To provide the best possible data for the decision-maker, control and analysis formulas are fed into the computer.

A good example of one of the newer control and planning techniques is the Program Evaluation Review Technique (PERT). PERT enables management to anticipate trouble spots, and avoid unexpected delays. It is geared to schedule and control activities to ensure that all elements of a project move forward in a proper time relationship. It points out the cause of delays and brings these to the attention of the people who are able to correct the situation.

PERT is just one of a number of significant developments in management methods that have occurred during the past twenty years. Progressive managers have been quick to appreciate and utilize the better decision-making and managerial control made possible by a computer programmed with advanced management systems. The heart of the PERT system is the computer, which processes the PERT data, and then provides management with a series of reports that not only pinpoint present progress but also forecast the future of the program being analyzed. The rewards of PERT are in direct proportion to the use management makes of the reports and the importance management attaches to them.

The "Total Systems" approach to clerical work is considered one of the most important events in the past twenty years. People have been very optimistic about how "total systems" and computer technology would affect traditional concepts of office management:

At the three-day International Systems meeting of the Systems Procedures Association last month . . .

The dominant theme of them all was *Total Systems,* that concept of integrated administration tying together, for maximum efficiency, the many "fragmented" systems which had once been deemed good enough for any well-run company. A big order this, but a necessary one if management is economically to receive the "total" information it needs for its operating decisions. A big order, probably an impossible order heretofore, but a realistic goal now, thanks to computer technology.[6]

Thus, the systems approach, including computers, has a positive contribution to make to the art of management. It suggests a means of organizing elements into an integrated network designed to achieve predetermined results. Donald Caruth of North Texas State University examined the many definitions of "total systems" and offered the following definition:

An approach which conceives the business organization as a single entity which is composed of various interrelated and interdependent subsystems which attempt to provide timely and accurate information for management decision-making which leads to the optimization of overall enterprise goals.[7]

The systems approach became very popular several years ago when Secretary of Defense Robert S. McNamara applied systems principles used successfully at Ford Motor Company to the armed services, saving millions of dollars by standardizing purchasing and other operations that previously had been duplicated at high cost by various branches. In this case, "system" would be defined as a network of related procedures developed according to an integrated scheme for performing a major activity (purchasing) of the organization.

There is one factor or guideline that needs emphasis:

Those concerned with implementing the total systems concept should participate in its development.

When one takes part in the formulation of a plan, he feels responsible for making it work. On the other hand, resistance to change is a fundamental attitude present in all of us in different degrees. The reader probably doesn't have to think back very far to remember a situation in which a plan didn't have a chance to succeed because those principally engaged in carrying it out were not consulted in its development, and, as a result, made up their minds that the plan would not work. The problem of acceptance or of nonacceptance of any plan involves the philosophy of a person—that is, whether he is cautious, conservative, or progressive vis-à-vis change.

We have found, then, that computer technology is contributing to improved information (useful data) handling in three ways:

1. New methods are being developed for gathering and introducing information. Key-depression machines, such as typewriters, cash registers, and bookkeeping equipment prepare data for subsequent handling.

2. New machines and systems are being developed for information processing. The long established punched-card system, optical scanning, and the newer electronic data processing systems perform office work many times faster and better than office workers un-aided by machines.

3. The methodology of science and scientific knowledge is being adapted for use in executive decision-making of primary importance in the PERT system and the "Total Systems" concept.

QUESTIONS AND PROBLEMS

1. Discuss the interrelationship of the three reasons for excessive costs in EDP.

2. Explain why the period from 1920 to 1950 has been called the "management era."

3. Explain the changes that brought about the evolution to the "administrative services" era.

4. Discuss how the "information management" era encompasses the main thesis of the preceding eras.

5. What is the true role of the computer in decision-making?

6. Explain how the computer is the heart of the PERT system.

7. What is the role of the computer in the application of the "total systems approach"?

8. Discuss why we are concerned with the evolution of data processing.

REFERENCES

1. "Rising Costs Challenge Office Manager," *Administrative Management,* **22**:31, June 1961.

2. Cheney Archer, "The American Office—1949," *Office Management and Equipment,* **10**:19–23, January 1949.

3. *Ibid.,* p. 23.

4. J. W. Schulze, *The American Office,* (New York, N.Y.: Key Publishing, 1913).

5. Robert L. Caleo, "What's Happening in the Office," *Administrative Management,* **24**:24–25, January 1964.

6. "Toward Total Systems," Administrative Management, **22**:90, November 1961.

7. Donald L. Caruth, "The Total Systems Concept," *Business Studies,* School of Business Administration, North Texas State University, Denton, Texas, p. 69.

THE
DATA
PROCESSING
FUNCTION

CHAPTER 5

Part 1
The Background of
Data Processing

As we review the various stages in the development of data processing, we readily understand the motivation of inventors and scientists who worked in this field—each tried to invent a machine or process that would make his job easier. As processing methods developed, procedures became more complex, following the steps from manual to mechanical, to punched cards, and now to electronic data processing. To many of us, the computer seemed suddenly to be here one day, and immediately began to change our ways. However, its appearance on the scene was preceded by step-by-step progress toward our modern machines.

MANUAL DATA PROCESSING—THE ABACUS

Early man used his fingers for counting, and later stones or sticks. In this way he could add and subtract. Much much later, the abacus, the first calculating device, was developed. It was used in many countries, and is still being used in some parts of the world (Fig. 5.1).

The abacus is made of beads strung on wooden rods or wires. Each column of beads represents a digit. Each bead in the lower portion represents one unit, and each bead in the top portion represents

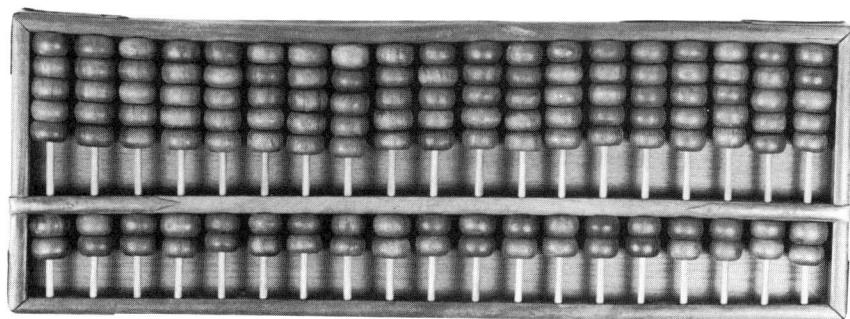

FIG. 5.1 Abacus, one of the first devices for figuring and counting

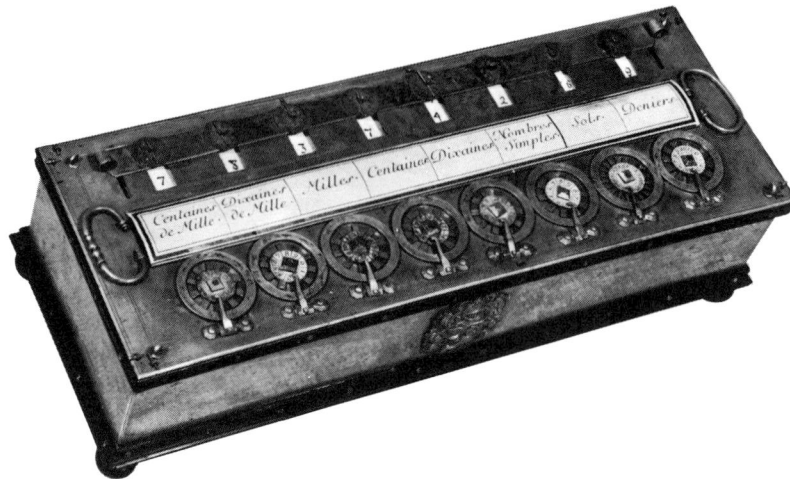

FIG. 5.2 Pascal's mechanical adding machine

five units. The beads to be counted are the ones pushed toward the center bar. When two 5-unit beads to be counted are the ones pushed toward the center, they can both be pushed back and one bead (1 unit) in the next column to the left pushed toward the center.

The abacus certainly seems primitive now, but originally it was such a successful invention that it was used for more than 5000 years.

MECHANICAL DATA PROCESSING—ADDING MACHINES

In 1642 a young Frenchman, Blaise Pascal, got tired of pushing beads up and down the abacus to add up figures in his tax collector father's office. He invented a machine whose gears and wheels were housed in a box (Fig. 5.2). The wheels on the top of the box corresponded to ones, tens, hundreds, and so on; each wheel could register the digits 0 to 9. A "one" was automatically carried to the next wheel when one wheel advanced from 9 to 0. Pascal thus built the world's first adding machine. Many adaptations were made in the years following to improve on the device.

In the United States Frank Baldwin introduced in 1872 a machine which operated on a different principle (Fig. 5.3). He and J. R. Monroe formed the Monroe Calculating Company and thereby laid the foundation for the calculating machine industry in this country.

FIG. 5.3 Baldwin calculator

PUNCHED CARDS—THE AUTOMATIC WEAVING LOOM

In 1801 another Frenchman, Jacquard, introduced his automatic weaving loom. Holes punched in heavy paper controlled the machine according to the pattern punched on the paper. For a repeat pattern, the same instructions were used over and over again. A variable pattern required many different instructions on thousands of these papers or cards. The same set of instructions could be reused to produce identical pieces. Jacquard was the first to store data by means of punched holes and control a machine in this manner. His loom was patented in 1801, but its use did not become widespread until many years later. Eventually it was realized that the loom's products could be sold at much lower prices than handwoven goods, and that the products woven by machines contained fewer flaws than those woven by people.

Punched cards, however, were not adapted to other uses for nearly another 100 years—not until 1887!

In 1830 a young Englishman named Babbage designed a "difference engine" to perform complex calculations accurate to twenty decimal places and to print the answer. He persuaded the British government to finance his building the machine. However, the best craftsmen could not make the necessary parts for this machine so that it would function properly, because many of Babbage's ideas were far ahead of their time. Lack of high-precision tools made it impossible to produce the parts with the accuracy required. His computer was designed to store information in the form of numbers on mechanical wheels. Mechanical devices were to be used to perform the arithmetic operations.

Babbage met a lady mathematician, Lady Lovelace, who devised the binary arithmetic that is still used in computers, but Babbage's machine still did not work. Babbage was convinced that a machine would make far fewer errors in calculations than humans, that it could be "programmed" or instructed for many consecutive steps, and that it could automatically print the answers. All these ideas are used in today's computers.

PUNCHED CARD DATA PROCESSING—THE UNITED STATES CENSUS

The United States entered the data processing series of events—by necessity. The U. S. Constitution requires that a census of the popula-

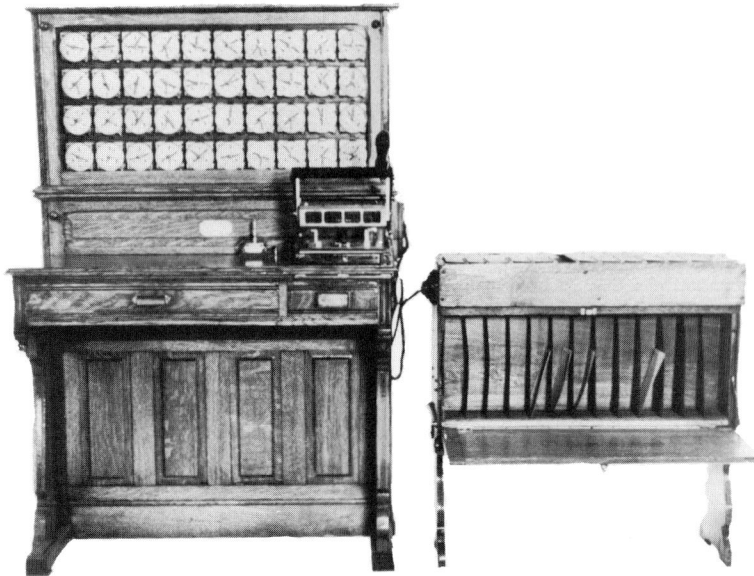

FIG. 5.4 Hollerith
punched card equipment

tion be taken every ten years. Because of the population increase during the period of 1870–1880, it took more than seven years to tabulate the results. Hollerith, a young man working in the U. S. Census office wanted to solve this problem. He developed the "Census Machine" which used punched cards to perform tabulations. Then he developed the "Electric Tabulating System" which was used in the 1890 census, and performed the calculations in one-third the time that was required in doing the 1880 census by hand methods. His method combined the ideas of Babbage and Jacquard—using punched holes and tabulating data by machine. (See Fig. 5.4.)

In Hollerith's original system, the census data were recorded on long strips of paper by punching holes on the strips in a specific pattern; each hole in a particular location meant a specific piece of data. Since the paper strips tore easily, they were soon replaced by heavier paper called *cards*.

Many improvements have been made in the use of punched cards. They were put to immediate use to keep pace with the technological changes of the early 1900's. In fact, punched card processing methods are still being used, studied, and improved.

Hollerith knew that his machine and idea had potential that exceeded mere census computations. He formed the Tabulating Machine Company in 1896. All his machines worked on the same principle, using a standard card with specific coding. Each machine could process groups of cards containing the same type of information much faster than the results could be obtained by hand methods. Each machine could perform a specific task. Each unit of information was contained on one record or punched card. The equipment came to be called unit record equipment, and the processing of data with these machines came to be called *unit record data processing*. Since these machines all use punched cards, they are sometimes called *punched card machines* rather than unit record machines.

Hollerith's machines were not used in the 1910 census. A competitor named Powers had taken over. Powers's success with his machine in the 1910 census prompted him to form the Powers Accounting Machine Company in 1911.

GROWTH OF PUNCHED CARD MACHINE COMPANIES

Both Powers's company and Hollerith's company got started at the right time. In the early 1900's the population of the United States grew rapidly and the country became industrialized. Both developments generated large volumes of data that had to be processed. Both companies were successful. Powers's company merged with several office supply companies in 1927 to form Remington-Rand Company; in 1955 it merged with Sperry Gyroscope and became the Sperry-Rand Corporation. Its punched card equipment and computers are known by their trade name of Univac.

Hollerith's company also underwent several mergers. In 1911, it merged to form the International Time Recording Company. In 1924, its name was changed to International Business Machines Corporation (IBM).

By 1940, both IBM and Remington-Rand had introduced most of the punched card machines that are still in use today, although changes continued to be made to increase the processing speed.

After Henry Ford introduced assembly-line mass production techniques, industry was able to produce goods—automobiles, refrigerators, radios, and later television sets—at lower prices and for ever-increasing markets. In the period from 1900 to 1940, factory methods improved at a much faster rate than did data processing methods.

Punched card equipment was being used, but it was not fast enough and could perform only relatively simple operations, one at a time. At this point both IBM and Remington-Rand turned their attention to the development of computers. World War II broke out, and with it came demands for improvements in office methods for handling data and making mathematical calculations. The reasons for these demands were

1. a shortage of manpower,

2. increased industrial output,

3. emergency government regulations requiring extensive record keeping, and

4. mathematical calculations required for automatic weapons and other technological advances.

After the war, the needs for processing data did not decrease, but became even greater. We experienced

1. a great demand for consumer products that had been produced only in limited quantities during the war,

2. a new demand for consumer goods by those returning to civilian life and setting up new homes,

3. an extraordinary increase in population which required more records, and

4. the emergence of many new businesses and the fast growth of others, with the result that more detailed and careful records had to be kept.

THE NEED FOR SOMETHING BETTER

Most machines that use punched cards can perform only one major function at a time, such as performing calculations, or putting cards in order, or punching cards, or combining stacks of cards. This limitation requires the use of several machines to obtain the desired results. To avoid multimachine use, those in charge of information management now shifted their interest from punched card machines to computers. However, the manufacturers of punched card equipment continued to improve their machines.

ELECTRONIC DATA PROCESSING—COMPUTERS

More than 100 years passed between the time when Babbage attempted to build his difference engine and when a similar machine was actually made and put into operation. In 1937 Howard Aiken, a Harvard professor, began to develop a computer which consisted of more than 70 adding machines and desk calculators hooked together and controlled by a set of instructions punched on paper tape. His machine was completed in 1944 and used by the U. S. Navy in World War II. It was called the Automatic Sequence Controlled Calculator, or Mark I, and could perform one addition or subtraction in three-tenths of a second.

In 1946, Mauchly and Eckert completed the first all-electric computer. The speed of calculation was significantly higher than that of previous equipment: it could perform 5000 additions in one second. Called the Eniac (Electronic Numerical Integrator and Calculator), it contained more than 500,000 soldered connections and more than 18,000 vacuum tubes. It weighed over 30 tons, and occupied more than 15,000 square feet of space.

Since 1946 there have been so many developments that we shall defer their description until we reach the chapters dealing in detail with computers.

Even before 1812, some people called machines that could add by the name computers, because they could technically perform computations.

COMPUTERS VERSUS PUNCHED CARD MACHINES

Although punched card equipment has many disadvantages compared to computers, punched card equipment continues to be used in business for the same reason that manual typewriters are still being used alongside electric ones.

1. Manual typewriters are less expensive.

   Punched card equipment is less expensive than a computer in some instances.

2. The typewriter is not used a sufficient number of hours each day to justify the expense of an electric typewriter.

   The computer would not be used enough hours of each day to justify its expense.

3. Some people who have always used a manual typewriter do not want to change to an electric typewriter.

The employees are used to punched card equipment and would rather not change.

Of course, there are as many arguments in favor of computers. Each company must determine its own needs and then decide what types of data processing methods are best: manual, mechanical, punched card, or electronic. In fact, in general a combination of methods is used. Companies that have computers still need punched card equipment and even mechanical and manual methods of processing data in their complete operation.

The arguments in favor of punched card equipment are quickly becoming outdated. The year 1969 saw the advent of small computers about the size of an office desk. Since these can be rented for $900 to $1000 a month, punched card equipment is no longer less expensive in many instances. The concept of time-sharing or renting time permits many companies with limited computer needs to take advantage of computers at a reasonable cost.

Some methods and devices cannot be classified as purely manual, mechanical, punched card, or electronic. One example is electromechanical equipment, such as a machine that uses punched cards but performs calculations electronically.

COMPUTER COMPANIES TODAY

IBM and Sperry-Rand's Univac Division are the largest manufacturers of punched card machines, with IBM far outnumbering Univac machines. In computer manufacturing, IBM has many more competitors. Well-known ones are Sperry-Rand, Honeywell Information Systems, Burroughs Corporation, National Cash Register Company, Philco Corporation, Radio Corporation of America (RCA), and Control Data Corporation. There are also smaller companies that manufacture special computers for specific uses and other equipment and supplies needed in conjunction with computers.

QUESTIONS AND PROBLEMS

1. Why is each inventor interested in developing a new device or process?
2. What did Pascal invent?
3. What did Jacquard invent?

4. How was the automatic weaving loom of 1801 controlled?

5. What is the significance to data processing of the weaving loom?

6. What did Babbage design?

7. Why wasn't Babbage able to have his machine made?

8. What did Lady Lovelace contribute to data processing?

9. What ideas did Babbage have that are true of computers today?

10. What situation urged Hollerith to invent his first punched card machine?

11. Why did Hollerith form the Tabulating Machine Company?

12. Whose machines were used for the 1910 census?

13. What events near the beginning of the twentieth century caused larger volumes of data to be processed?

14. Trace the mergers of Powers's Accounting Machine Company.

15. Trace the mergers of Hollerith's company.

16. Since the early 1940's, what progress have punched card machines had?

17. What factors caused the need for improved data processing methods in the early 1940's?

18. What factors caused the need for even greater improvements in data processing methods after World War II?

19. What limitations of punched card machines caused interest to grow in computer design and development?

20. Describe what Aiken invented in 1937.

21. Describe what Mauchly and Eckert invented in 1946.

22. Why do punched card machines continue to be used in spite of the advantages of the computer?

23. What is changing the lower cost advantage of punched card machines over computers?

24. List the major computer manufacturers in the United States.

The changes that have occurred thus far in the twentieth century are greater than those of any other century. The unprecedented advance of science and technology has profoundly affected the whole structure of society as well as the individual business firm that operates in this changing environment. The full import of the adjustments we will have to make cannot be comprehended. One of the chief roles of the data processing function has always been to help administrative management keep pace with the changes in its environment; hence arose the "administrative services" movement of the sixties. In this

Part 2
The Evolving
Role of the Data
Processing Function

period of rapid transition, vast modifications of the data processing function have been required. The business world and its managers have dictated the change from "office management" to "administrative management" to "information management."

The production and distribution of products and services are increasingly dependent on information. Specialists in market analysis, product research, accounting, systems and procedures, personnel administration, management research and development, and statistical analyses of all kinds have pyramided the need for records and reports.

To an ever-increasing degree, the executive is being pushed further and further away from the actual job of operating the business firm. Those executives who must make the crucial decisions concerning policy are becoming increasingly reliant on organized reports of all aspects of the business, particularly of all operations within their own companies. Since they have become insulated from first-hand information, their need for accurate and integrated information is a vital one. We can see the value of processing, integrating, and supplying information from "grass roots," and the necessity of data processing for any major organization. We can depend on an even wider use of computers because of the continuing increase in the size of business firms, the geographical decentralization of operations, the combination of businesses through mergers and acquisitions, the conglomerate movement, the development of multiple product lines with varying managerial requirements, the increase in management research and development, the development of multi-markets, and an increasing specialization sired by competition and the push for effectiveness and efficiency.

The data processing function, then, is in a unique position. The techniques, methods, procedures, and systems developed to perform the data processing function are the media through which information of all kinds travels through an organization. In the past, attention was concentrated more on other functions of business—production, marketing, finance, etc.—and the importance of the data processing function was not consciously recognized. The rapid growth of businesses since the forties has been forcing management to appreciate the actual and potential contributions of the data processing function in meeting specific demands on management for better planning, organizing, and directing. As business has grown, the data processing function has increased, using a greater number of employees and occupying a more significant place in the thinking of management.

Thus one comes to the problem of what and how much information is needed, the qualities necessary in a manager of the data processing division, and how to get the clerical force required to cope with it. Management's concern is in getting the information it needs, in the form in which it is most useful, and fast enough so that intelligent action can be taken promptly.

THE NEED FOR CONSOLIDATION OF INFORMATION

More functional specialists are needed today. No manager can possibly know all there is to know about any one single business function, much less all the functions of a business. Production personnel require certain sales and marketing statistics for establishing production requirements. Accounting personnel use these same figures under other headings. Engineering personnel need sales reports for product research, control, and the like. Since organization functions are often separated by geography, groups in a given area have a tendency to want to maintain and update the information on the basis of convenience.

No functional executive, however, can allow this sort of clannishness to develop. If he is to make sound decisions, he cannot do so without a reasonable grasp of the activities within related or parallel functions.

Each member of management must be given the information he needs to perform his particular role in the company. But somewhere in the organization there must be a clearing house for all information —a central point where all the facts and figures pertaining to the company are edited, classified, and routed on to various levels of management.

The need for accuracy. Intelligent decision-making depends upon having accurate information on which to make judgments. This is most important when major policy decisions are being made, of course. But statements or actions based on inaccurate data can antagonize customers and damage the goodwill of the company. A lack of proper understanding within the company also can have a deleterious effect on employee morale.

The need for faster delivery of goods. Emphasis is now on streamlining service cycles and furnishing faster delivery of goods to the customer. One way to provide faster and better service is to reduce the time to process data. Plans with regard to the data processing function are not self-executing. Management must take steps to see that they are carried out. The data processing function plays the leading role in the coordination of the activities of the different departments, units, and employees through the product it passes on to management—information.

THE CHALLENGE FOR IMPROVEMENT

Management is learning that information is the lifeblood of its business enterprise, and to be useful, the information must be available when it is needed and in the proper form. This job of gathering, processing, and distributing information is usually assigned to the data processing function with authority to carry out this responsibility. For this reason, Rathe says, "the office is destined to be the fountainhead of business information."[1]

THE DATA PROCESSING MANAGER

The man responsible for the data processing function must

1. analyze the present data processing function,
2. continue to develop an improved data processing system,
3. make recommendations concerning the data processing function, and
4. install whatever is economically sound to carry out the function.

The data processing manager must pay particular attention to his personal characteristics—his job responsibilities and authority cross departmental, divisional, and functional lines. He must not only have a high degree of specialization; he must be well informed in all the related functional areas of the business. More important, he must integrate and assimilate this related functional knowledge and present it in a meaningful way to the people who must make decisions. He must be trained to plan, organize, and direct the data processing function. He must also be able to communicate effectively with other functional managers and top management.

What type of education does the present-day data processing manager need? Requirements vary depending on the type of industry he may work in, but the following list is suggested as a minimum for the knowledge that is required of a data processing manager. He needs basic courses in

Management	Personnel	Office Management (or Information Management)
Accounting	Economics	Statistics
Mathematics	Production	Marketing
Finance	Data Processing	Social Psychology.

A college education in business administration would seem to be necessary for data processing managers. This is not necessarily true. These courses, however, do describe the type of knowledge the data processing manager of today must have to be effective in today's complex business world. The astute manager realizes that education directed toward these subjects will be valuable. The necessary knowledge can be obtained informally, but currently the emphasis is on formal education.

Software programmers or scientific programmers require a knowledge of science and mathematics. Commercial programmers need basic courses in

Management	Accounting	Finance
Marketing	EDP	

as well as knowledge of

Systems (methods and procedures)	Operations Research or Management Science
Management Analysis	
Organizational Structure.	Communication Analysis

The basic knowledge that a programmer must have, then, includes fundamentals of computer design, organization of data processing systems, basic concepts of computer programming, in addition to an understanding of the functions of business and management science (as operations research is commonly called today).

The challenge for improvement, in part, lies in education and training for the data processing manager, the EDP specialists, and the general clerical workers. The data processing function is constantly changing. Schools and industry have an obligation to keep up with these developments.

THE NEW ROLE OF THE DATA PROCESSING FUNCTION

The data processing function has to be a separate and independent activity with the proper authority given to the manager of the data processing function to plan, organize, and direct his function as a centralized unit on a companywide scale. Mr. Steven L. Shea, Vice President of Data Processing of the American Insurance Company, points out that "information alone is not enough."[2] He goes on to say that what is needed is business intelligence which is the result of selection, screening, and judgment applied to the mass of raw information. With this thought in mind, we can define the new role of the data processing function as a centralized, integrated processing and communication system, one capable of coordinating the activities of all functional departments by supplying them not only with accurate and up-to-date information when it is needed, but also a function directed by a manager who has a sound knowledge about the business and the devices which are most appropriate for his company. The data processing function is now operating on a company-wide scale. In fact, the activities of the data processing function now extend beyond the physical place called the office. The new role encompasses and directs all the business intelligence and communications activities of the company as an integrated whole.

Data processing has become an activity of a larger function—that of information, sometimes called *management services*. Management services are described as "staff services in the traditional functional areas of manufacturing, marketing, engineering, finance, and the like."[3] As such, management services concentrate on coordination of the functional subdivisions in accordance with the master direction and objectives of the company.[4] Research and development as well as current operating statistics become part of the material processed.

Evolutionary influences have been at work, and the *evolutionary cycle* of the data processing function may be observed in the development of the data processing in a firm that has grown from a small firm to one of medium size or large size. This cycle may be considered in terms of a number of phases.

Phase 1. Management realizes that records of transactions and the duplication of legal papers are necessary in running a business. In the initial phase one department usually "houses" all data processing activities—sales, finance, accounting, and office services. Office machinery is limited to typewriters, and some simple adding, addressing, and tabulating machines. Most of the data processing is still being done by hand.

Phase 2. Management realizes merely recording transactions and duplicating legal papers are not sufficient for effective planning. It recognizes that facts, ideas, and plans have to be put in writing. This demands an organized way of doing things. Thus systems are devised to increase efficiency.

Phase 3. Expansion brings about the need for more advanced machines to become a part of the system.

Phase 4. The natural growth of business brought forth a maze of records, many and varied systems, the extensive use of machines, and consequently a large office force. A data processing manager is needed to spend full time planning, organizing, and directing the data processing function. Using the scientific approach to solve the problems of the office becomes a necessity.

Phase 5. Management realizes that the communications function must be integrated with the data processing function and paperwork routines in order to reduce the cost of office work, increase accuracy, and reduce the time required to obtain the information for managerial reports.

The fifth phase, then, is the evolution back to complete integration of information reflecting the entire business effort. When the business is very small, this integration is possible because all facts, ideas, and plans are in the mind of a single owner or manager. But as the business expands, the firm becomes departmentalized, and many managers take the place of the original man. Then the problems start. One department does not always know what the other departments are doing. The larger the firm becomes, the more it is necessary to make a conscious effort to achieve the original advantage of complete integration. Present day processing techniques make possible automatic reporting and transmission of information between the plants, offices, and branches of a firm. Thus the cycle starts and ends with complete integration of information and the data processing function is able to produce the information that management needs for decision-making and control purposes.

QUESTIONS AND PROBLEMS

1. What responsibility of management has changed the "administrative services approach" to the "information management approach" in data processing?
2. How is the manager being pushed away from the task of operating the firm?
3. What is the unique position of the data processing function today?
4. What is the need for consolidation of information?
5. Why is accuracy so important?
6. How does data processing effect the delivery of goods?
7. What are the functions of the data processing manager?
8. What is the new role of the data processing function?
9. How does the new role of the data processing function aid the managers of other business functions perform their tasks more efficiently?
10. Apply the evolutionary cycle of the data processing in a typical growing firm.

REFERENCES

1. Alex W. Rathe, "The Role of the Office Manager in the Modern Business Enterprise," *The Changing Dimensions of Office Management,* AMA Management Report Number 41, American Management Association, Inc., New York, 1960, p. 13.
2. "Introduction: The Origins of and Need for a New Concept of Administrative Management," *Shaping a New Concept of Administrative Management,* AMA Management Report No. 56, American Management Association, Inc., New York, 1961, p. 7.
3. Marshall K. Evans, "Management Services at Westinghouse Electric Corporation," *Concept of Administrative Management,* p. 69.
4. *Idem.*

PART II

PUNCHED
CARD
DATA
PROCESSING

RECORDING MEDIA

CHAPTER 6

Before data can be processed with the numerous machines, the information must be recorded in a way that all these machines can use and can use quickly. The method that has been developed is by means of the punched card. All cards are a standard size and are made of a standard thickness of paper or card paper; they are uniform so that they can be used by all machines designed for them.

PUNCHED CARDS AS INPUT/OUTPUT

The data that enters a machine to be processed is called input; and the results or answers that the machine produces are called output. Punched card or unit record equipment uses punched cards both as input and output; sometimes during processing the same cards are both input and output, such as when they are being put in correct order by the sorter; and sometimes one card is input and another card is output, such as when the reproducer punches a duplicate card. Also some machines classified as unit record machines have punched cards as input but another type of output, such as in the printer where the output is printed paper.

Computers can also use punched cards both as input and as output, but they also use other faster methods such as magnetic tape and printed paper. When referring to both input and output, we usually write the words "input/output" or merely "I/O."

CARD SIZES

The standard card is $7\frac{3}{8}$" by $3\frac{1}{4}$" in size and is 0.007" thick (see Fig. 6.1). The cards need to be this thickness in order to pass through the machines at a fast speed and yet not wear out or tear with numerous uses. Special cards with plastic coating can be purchased; these last much longer.

A new size of IBM card, shown in Fig. 6.2, was introduced in 1969 but not used until 1970. It is $3\frac{1}{4}$" by $2\frac{5}{8}$" and was designed for use with IBM's new small desk-size computer, the System/3. The older,

67

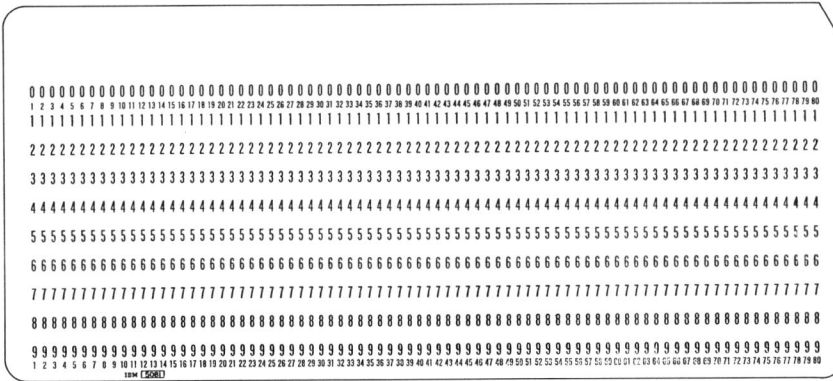

FIG. 6.1 Standard size IBM punched card

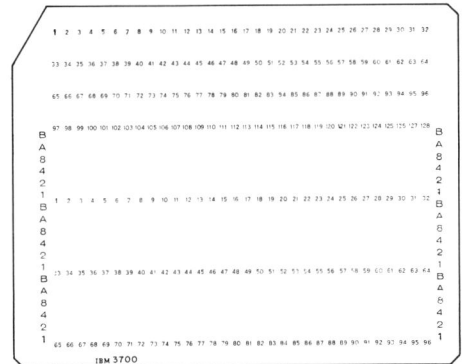

FIG. 6.2 Small size IBM punched card

larger punched card will be explained first, then the new, smaller punched card.

Data that are to be processed must be in a form that these machines can interpret. Coded holes are punched on the cards, as shown in Fig. 6.3.

CODING SYSTEMS—STANDARD SIZE CARD

At the present time, two coding systems are being used: the IBM Hollerith code and the Univac code. Although both coding systems are still in use, the Hollerith system is becoming the standard one, and the newer Univac machines are being made to use this coding system. Other equipment manufacturers, including most in foreign countries, are also accepting the Hollerith coding system as standard and are designing their machines to use it. In this way, each company or office is not limited to using just one manufacturer's equipment but can use specific advantageous equipment of a number of manufacturers.

This standardization does not cause great concern in the United States because most basic machines that use punched cards (called unit record equipment) are made by IBM Corporation. Other manufacturers that have designed machines for highly specific operations find that they have to use the same system so that they can sell their machines to companies that already use the more basic IBM punched card equipment.

Zone punches

Numeric punches

80-column scale

HOLLERITH CODE=   +-0123456789   ABCDEFGHI   JKLMNOPQR   /STUVWXYZ   .$,=)*(.

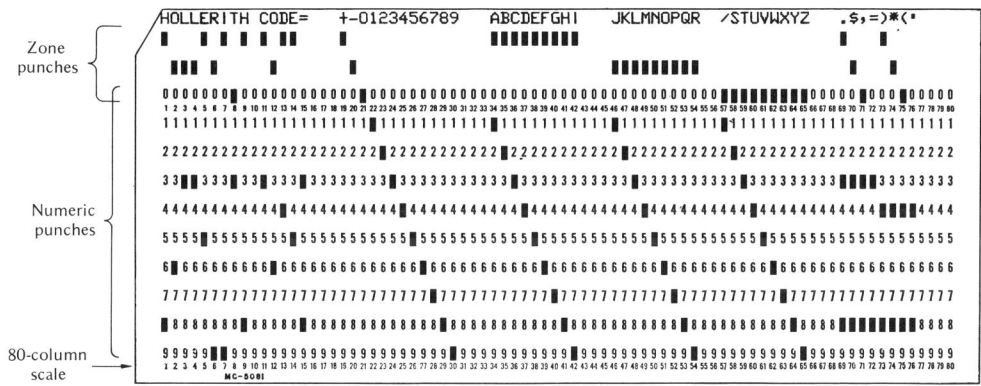

FIG. 6.3 Standard size IBM card-sections labeled—Hollerith Coding System

IBM CARD FORMAT

Figure 6.3 shows an IBM card. It contains 80 columns, and each column is numbered at two places—below the 0-row and below the 9-row. It contains 12 rows, 10 of which are numbered on the card from 0 through 9; the other two rows are the 11-row and the 12-row which are above the 0-row and are labeled on the card in Fig. 6.3. Each punching position can be referred to by its row and by its column.

The cards are usually purchased with the upper-left corner cut diagonally, as in Fig. 6.3. This makes it easy to see whether a card is backward or upside down in a stack of cards before they are inserted into a machine for processing. Cards can be purchased with no corner cut or with a corner cut in any of the three other corners. Also they are available in a variety of colors. These special features of the cards aid the people who handle and use the cards. For example, a company might have a card with the name, home address, phone number, and social security number of each employee. The cards for the full-time employees could be green and the cards for the part-time employees could be blue or another color, to distinguish them visually.

NUMBER CODES—HOLLERITH SYSTEM

Each column can represent only one number, letter, or symbol; therefore the highest number that can be in one column is the number 9. The number 89 takes 2 columns, and the number 1,879 takes 4 columns because punctuation is not usually used. The coding system for the numbers is very easy—each number is represented by a punch in its number row, in the correct column. See Fig. 6.4. To represent the number 3 in column 3, a hole is punched in the 3-row in column 3. To represent the number 50 in columns 15 and 16, a hole is punched in the 5-row in column 15 and in the 0-row in column 16. Columns with no punch are blank so we must always punch a 0 where necessary to distinguish it from no punch.

Keypunch machines automatically punch the correct hole when you depress the key. This will be explained in detail in the next chapter. Some keypunch machines print each character above the column in which it is punched and others do not. See Fig. 6.5. Sometimes when it is necessary to "read" the punches on a card that does not have the characters printed, it is helpful if we are familiar with this coding system.

LETTER CODE—HOLLERITH SYSTEM

Each letter of the alphabet is represented by 2 holes punched in the same column. When using the letter code, the 0-row, 11-row, and 12-row are considered as "zone" punches, and the 1 through 9 rows are considered as digit punches (or number punches), as in Fig. 6.6. Each letter has a zone punched and a digit punched.

The letter A begins with the top zone or 12-zone and the first digit is 1, since 0 is considered a zone in the alphabetic code. The next letters also use a 12-zone punch and each digit punch in order until the letter I has used the digit-9 punch, as shown in Fig. 6.6. Then we go on to use the next zone below, the 11-zone, with the digit 1 punch to represent the letter j. We continue with the 11-zone and each digit punch in order until the letter R has used the digit-9 punch. Then we go on to use the next zone below, the 0-zone with the digit 2 (we skip the digit 1) to represent the letter S. Continue with the 0-zone and each digit punch in order until the letter Z has been used with the digit-9 punch.

Why did we omit the number 1 punch with the 0-zone? When making up this system, Mr. Hollerith knew that using each of the three zones with each of the nine numbers could represent 27 characters and the alphabet contains only 26 characters. Since one code could be omitted, he knew it would be best to omit the 0-zone number 1 punch because this would require two punches, one next to the other.

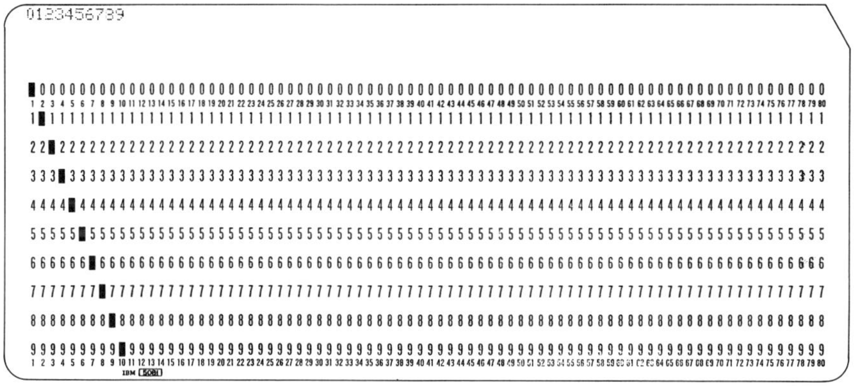

FIG. 6.4   Number codes (Hollerith)

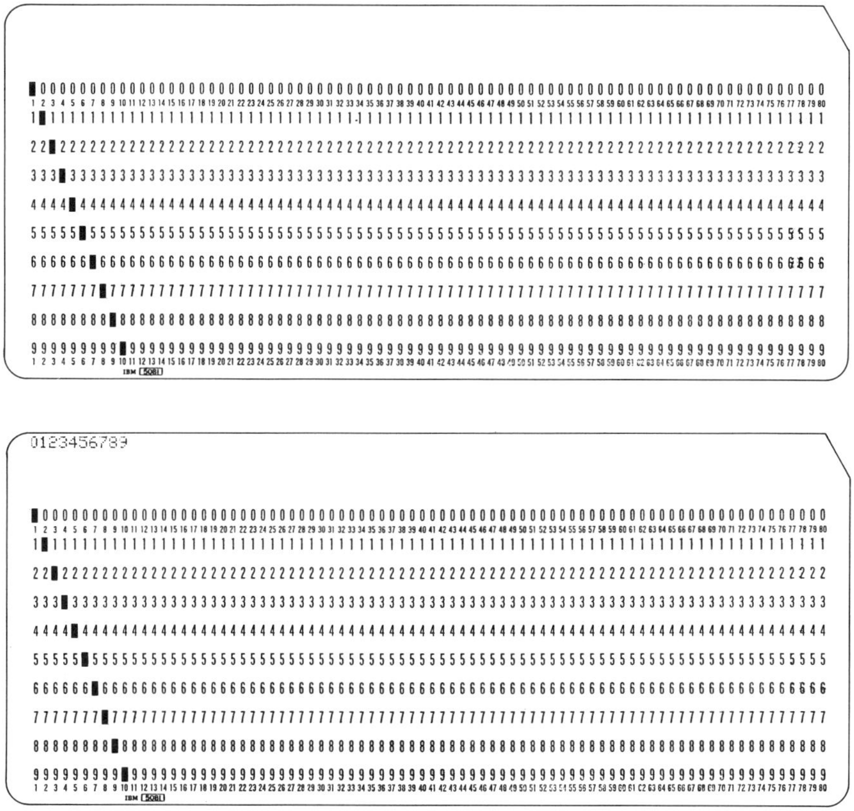

FIG. 6.5   Numbers punched with and without printing

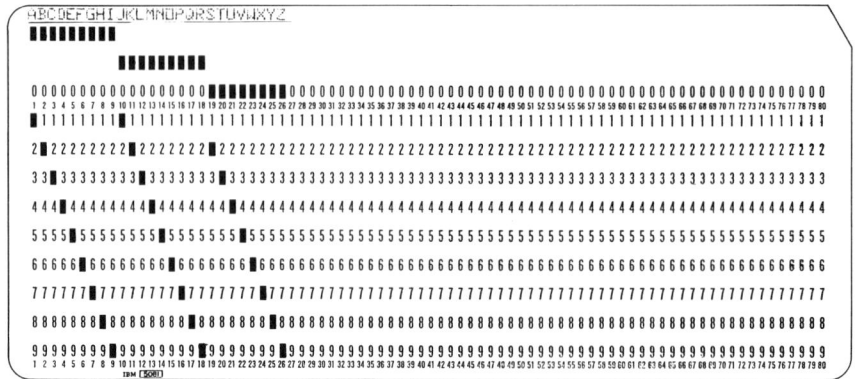

FIG. 6.6 Alphabetic codes (Hollerith)

The card would wear out or tear much more easily if there were such a small amount of card between two holes. In this way, no code requires two holes in rows next to each other.

To make it easier to remember this coding system for the alphabet, notice that the first and last letters in the 11-zone make "JR" the abbreviation for the word "Junior." On punched cards, there is no need to distinguish between capital and small letters; the keypunch machines print the characters at the top of the card in all capitals. When using the keypunch machine, the operator does not have to use these codes. He merely depresses the correct letters on the keyboard and the machine automatically makes the correct punches.

SPECIAL CHARACTER CODES—HOLLERITH SYSTEM

In the Hollerith coding system, there is no special system for easily remembering the codes for special symbols. However, these symbols are not used nearly so frequently as numbers and letters. The more common symbols are shown in Fig. 6.7; notice that some, such as the &-sign, require one punch in the column; some, such as the #-sign, require two punches in the column; and some, such as the $-sign, require three punches in the column.

There is a code for the period but it is seldom used. If we need to use an abbreviation, when punching addresses, for example, it saves time to omit the periods and just leave the one space between words. It is obvious that this is an abbreviation without the period. When

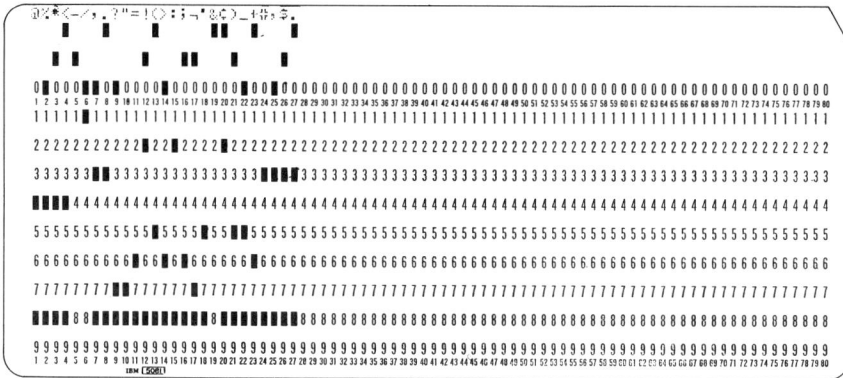

FIG. 6.7 Symbols and special characters (Hollerith)

FIG. 6.8 Bills with symbols printed and symbols omitted

punching numbers to represent amounts of money, the operators omit both the $-sign and the period that represents the decimal point. For consistency, we always use the two zeros to show the cents when the amount is an even dollar amount. Omitting these symbols is another efficient way to save time. The machines that process the cards do not need the symbols. After the cards are processed through several machines, a report is usually printed, such as a person's pay check or an invoice. The machine that does this printing can be instructed to insert these symbols, or they can already be printed on the forms, as the $-sign is on checks.

For example, an electric bill and a telephone bill omit some symbols and print others. In Fig. 6.8, the Northern Illinois Gas bill printed the decimal in the BTU number and did not print it in the amount due where it was already indicated on the form. In Fig. 6.9, the long-distance report of a telephone bill omits the $-signs and decimals in the amount column. Because these machines have so many bills to process each day, omitting these symbols saves an appreciable amount of time.

In summary, numbers are represented by one punch in the column; letters of the alphabet by two punches in the column; and special symbols by one, two, or three punches in the column.

LONG DISTANCE SERVICE

YOUR NUMBER	PAGE	DATE	CITY AND STATE	AREA OR TYPE	TELEPHONE NO.	AMOUNT
484 4538	1*	611	HOOPESTON ILL	217	283 5677	80
		612	BLOOMINGTN ILL	3RD	CHCAGO ILL	90
		616	INDIANAPLS IND	3RD	CHCAGO ILL	390

EXPLANATION OF
"AREA OR TYPE" COLUMN

AREA: The area code of the
    called telephone.
TYPE: The following abbrevia-
    tions may appear in place
    of the area code.
COLL - "Collect" call
CRCD - Credit Card Call
3RD - "Third Number Call" a
    call charged to your num-
    ber, but made between
    two others.
*Toll tickets and/or other
records supporting these
charges may be inspected by
arrangement with your
telephone business office for
six months from the bill's date.*

| *DIALED CALL | Includes | 1.70 | for calls within Illinois | | TOTAL CARRIED TO BILL | 560 |

subject to additional charge due to State tax and, where applicable, to City tax

FIG. 6.9 Telephone bill

PLANNING THE FIELDS OF A CARD

Cards with data punched on them are used by other machines to put the cards in a special order, to make calculations, and to print results. So that the cards can be used by these other machines, each type of data must be in specific columns of the card because these machines must be told where they can find the data needed on every card. The sorter cannot put a stack of cards in correct alphabetic order if the person's last name begins in column 1 of one card, in column 21 of the next card, and in column 7 of the next card. It does not matter in which column the data begins, but all the cards in the group *must* record the same kind of information in the same part of the card. Therefore, the columns of the cards to be used for each item of information must be planned very carefully. A card with the fields marked is shown in Fig. 6.10.

Each item of information is represented by a field of the card. A *field* is the column or columns of space that are reserved to punch a specific type of information on a card. If 5-digit identification numbers are to be recorded, a 5-column field is needed. A field can be one column such as a 1-digit code number, or it can be as large as 80 columns, the entire card. It can record only a person's last name, first name, middle initial with the remainder of the card left blank. When a limited length field must be used for the person's name, and a few

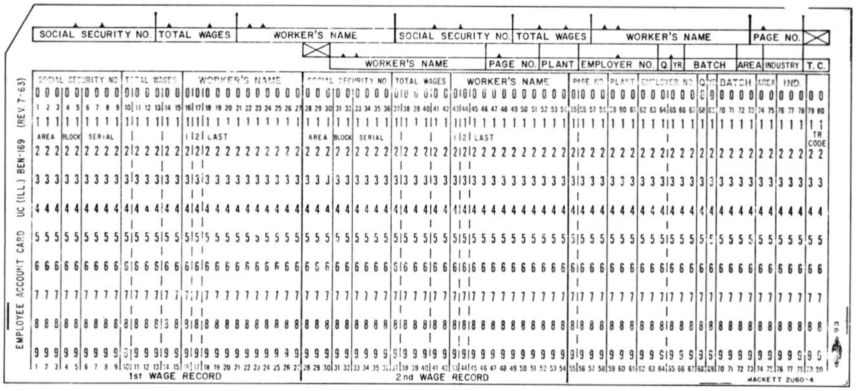

FIG. 6.10 Punched card with fields marked

names are longer than the space allowed, those names must be represented by using only initials for the first and/or middle names, or only part of the surname. In such a case, there is usually sufficient space to give enough of the name so that it can be easily distinguished from all other names. When planning fields for alphabetic data such as names, it is good practice to allow five extra spaces in addition to the space required for the longest name currently needed. This will probably allow sufficient space for any new names that may be added in the future. When planning fields for numbers, such as amounts of money, be sure to determine what could reasonably be the largest amount and allow for it.

These steps should be followed to plan the fields of a card:

1. List the types of information to be placed on the card.

2. Place these items in the most convenient order, depending on the raw data and the use to be made of the cards.

3. Specify the number of columns needed for each item.

4. Assign specific columns for each field of information.

5. Mark a sample card with the fields indicated, or use a card layout form.

To determine the best order for punching the items and the fields of data, you must consider the order in which the original data is located on the source documents from which the keypunch operator will be working. The fields on the card should be in the same order

INFORMATION REQUIRED FOR PROCESSING AND REPORT PREPARATION	FIELD SIZE				LOCATION IN OTHER CARDS	SEQUENCE ON SOURCE DOCUMENT	REMARKS
	TRIAL	TRIAL	TRIAL	FINAL			
Type Room	1	1	1	1	13	2	
Admission Date	6	6	5	5		8	
Insurance Plan 1	4	4	4	4	19-22	4	
Name	20	20	20	20		6	
M. L.	1	1	1	1		12	
Sex	1	1	1	1		10	
F. C.	1	1	1	1		16	
Charity Code	4	4	4	4		17	
State Code	2	2	2	2		18	
W. C. Code	3	3	3	3		15	
Room Rate	4	4	4	4		7	
Age	2	2	2	2		9	
Class	3	3	3	3		14	
Attending Physician	4	4	4	4		13	
Admission Number	8	8	6	6	7-12	1	
Card Code	1	1	1	1			
Storage Address	5	5	5	5			Should be in card columns 1-5.
Room Number	6	6	5	5		3	
Insurance Plan 2	4	4	4	4	23-26	5	
Religion	1	1	1	1		11	
Responsible Party Name	20						Place in another card
Street Address	18						Place in another card
City	16						Place in another card
State	4						Place in another card
	139	81	77	77			

CARD DESIGN WORK SHEET

CARD NAME: Patient Card   DESIGNER: H. E. Morrow

FIG. 6.11 Card design worksheet

that the data is normally found on the source document—going from top to bottom or left to right as one would normally read the source document. When the keypunch operator has to look at the top of the source document for the first item, at the bottom for the second item, near the middle for the third, and back near the top for the fourth, it takes longer and gives greater chance for error. The order in which the data is arranged on the punched card is not so important: the machines that process the cards can be set accordingly.

When the fields of a card do not use the entire card, the extra blank spaces can be at the end of the card or they can be distributed between the fields. The arrangement of fields on a card is the card format. It is not necessary to have any blank column or columns between fields of data.

When a company has set up a card format for a particular job, it usually has cards printed with these fields marked by vertical lines, as shown in Fig. 6.10. Special forms can be used when designing the card format. The card design worksheet shown in Fig. 6.11 is used to ensure that you do not assign more than 80 columns. If more data are needed, another card must be used. The card layout form in Fig. 6.12

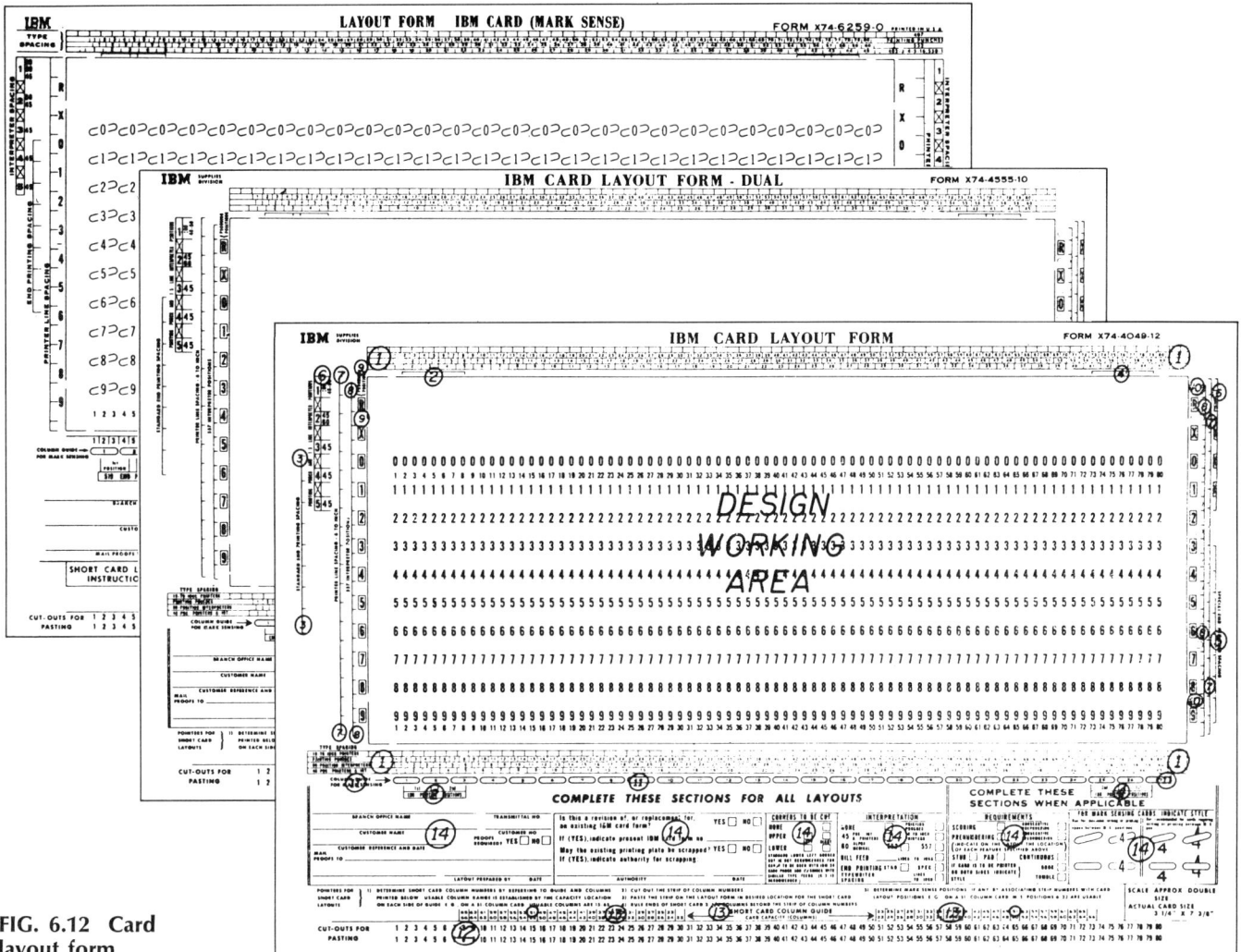

FIG. 6.12 Card
layout form

is used to mark a sample card before having copies printed. The bottom section allows space for information needed when the cards are to be printed. For example, the color of the cards desired and which corner, if any, is to be notched can be indicated. If the card is to contain a section for mark-sensing, this can also be indicated easily.

USES OF PUNCHED CARDS

Punched cards are used for all types of data that must be processed in a company or in a school. There are faster ways of processing data than using punched cards. Remember that these faster media use computers and are frequently more expensive. Also, there are special machines that can read characters printed by hand and record the data on punched cards or on tape. At the present time, these machines are very expensive and can be used efficiently only in specific limited situations. In years to come, we will certainly see increased use of these machines. Computers and these specialized machines will be discussed in the computer section.

SPECIAL TYPES OF PUNCHED CARDS

Numerous types of special IBM cards can be purchased for specific purposes. The more common ones are the porta-punch card, tumbler card, mark-sensed card, check card, stub card, and microfilm card.

On *porta-punch cards* each punching position is perforated so that data can be punched out easily by hand, as shown in Fig. 6.13. These can be used by students to answer multiple-choice tests and question-

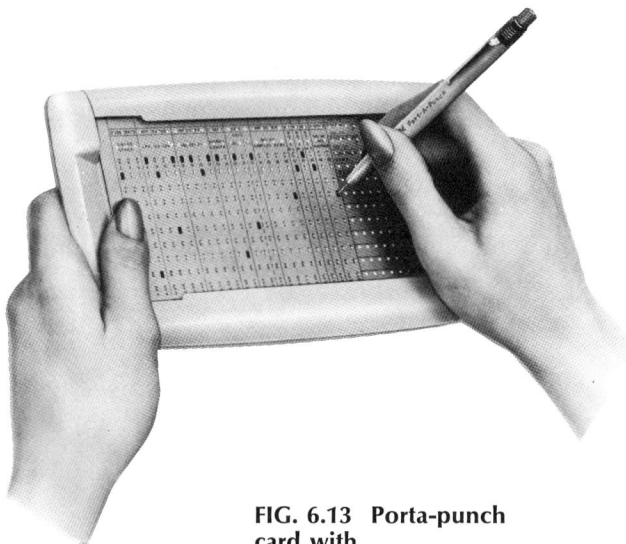

FIG. 6.13 Porta-punch card with perforated holes

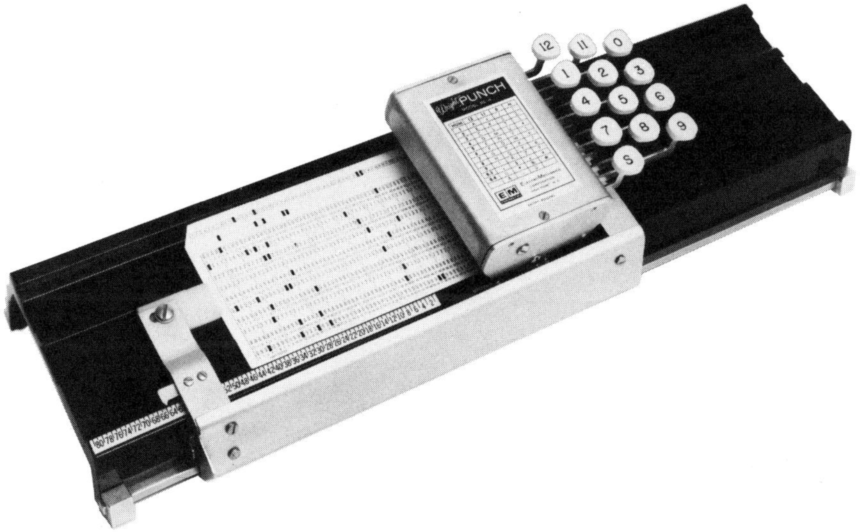

FIG. 6.14 Data punch machine

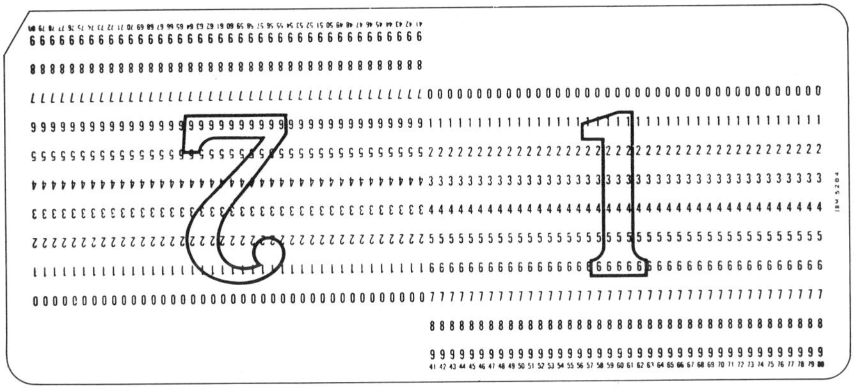

FIG. 6.15 Tumbler card

naires. Another type of porta-punch card does not have perforations. It is used in the hand-operated machine shown in Fig. 6.14.

A *tumbler card* can be used two times. When the data takes 40 columns or less, this is an economical procedure. Turned to one end, card columns 1 through 40 can be used. When this data is no longer needed, the card can be turned around and columns 1 through 40 on the other end can be used. This is sometimes called a double card; a sample is shown in Fig. 6.15.

A *mark-sensed card* can be one of two types. It can allow for marking marks to resemble the Hollerith coding system, as shown in

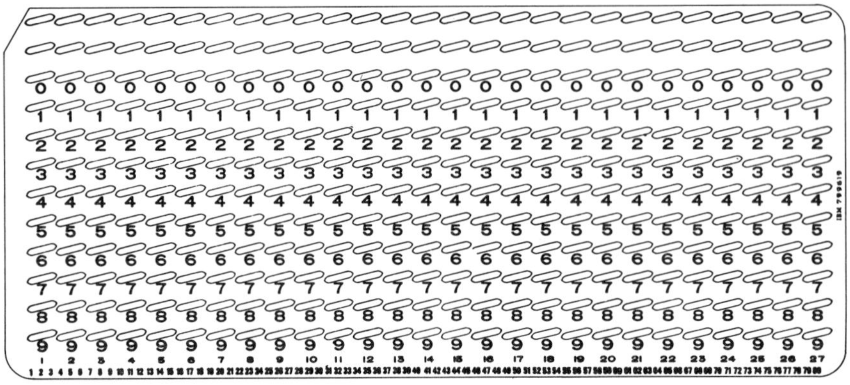

FIG. 6.16 Mark
sense card

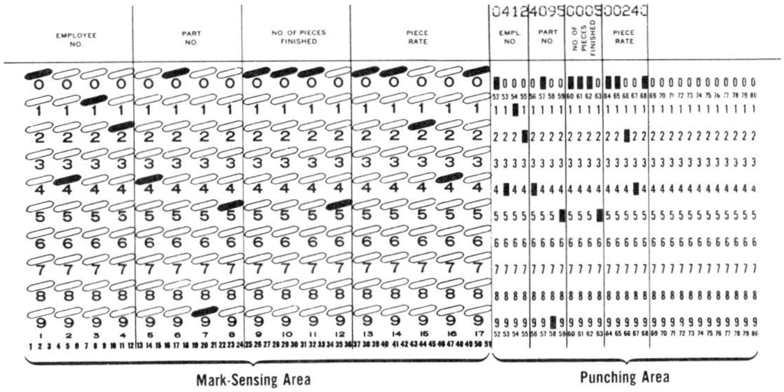

Mark-Sensing Area   Punching Area

FIG. 6.17 Mark sense
card with special
positions punched
and printed

Fig. 6.16. Or it can allow for making other marks according to the
printing on the card. For example, Fig. 6.17 shows a card that employees use to mark the quantity of each item completed. They indicate each item of data required on the card: employee number, part
number, number of pieces finished, and piece rate. These cards are
carefully planned so that the places where pencil marks can be made
are between the rows where punches are. Special machines can read
these pencil marks and automatically punch the correct data in the
correct columns. Pencils with special electrographic lead are used to
make the marks on these cards.

A *check card* is a standard-sized IBM card, as shown in Fig. 6.18.
The data have been punched and printed on it. After the check has
been cashed and returned to the company from its bank, the company

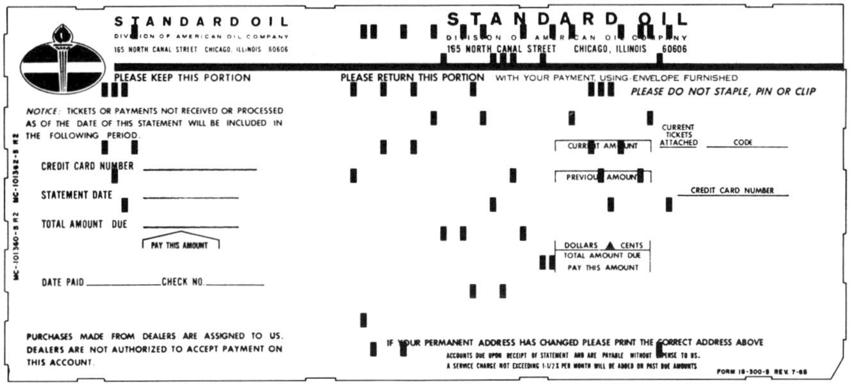

FIG. 6.18   Check card

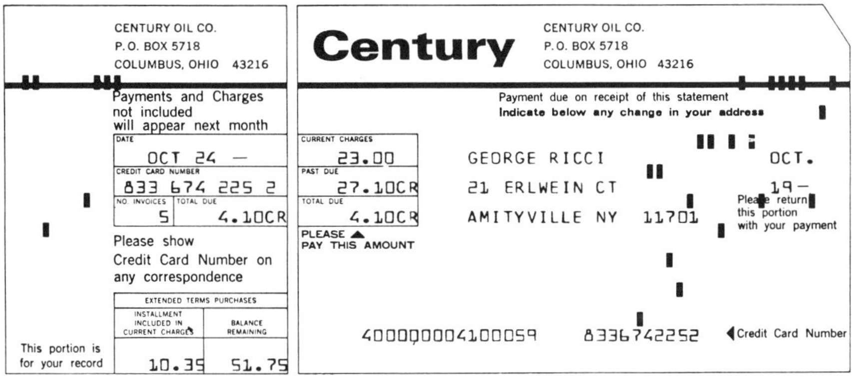

FIG. 6.19   Stub card

can put the checks back in numerical or alphabetical order by machine unless the cards have been torn or bent.

A *stub card* is a standard-sized IBM card with a perforated line such as shown in Fig. 6.19. It is frequently used as a bill. When the person receives his bill with holes punched and data printed on it, he tears the card at the perforation. He keeps one part for his records and returns the other part with his payment. When the company receives the partial card and payment, it can have a special machine read the partial card punches and punch a new full-sized card from it. This is much faster than having a keypunch operator punch another card with the same data.

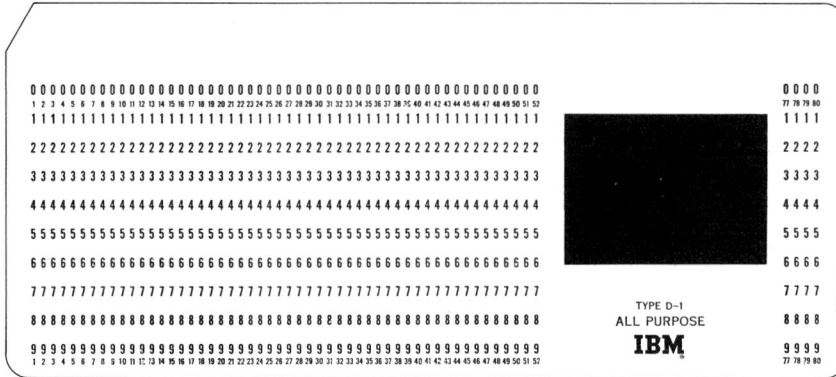

FIG. 6.20 Microfilm card

A *microfilm card* can have data punched on it and a microfilmed picture mounted on it as in Fig. 6.20. The microfilm can be a picture of an 8½" × 11" sheets of paper or one even larger. It can be used for important files that must be saved, such as medical and legal files. It saves space, but it is expensive. A special machine can enlarge the microfilmed data when it is needed, and another special machine can make a paper copy of it. The card which is used for filing purposes can be punched with pertinent data about the microfilmed report.

There are also many other special cards that have been designed to meet the needs of specific companies. Those illustrated are merely the more common types of special cards.

THE REMINGTON RAND CODE—UNIVAC

This type of coding system is still used by the older Remington Rand equipment, so we will discuss it briefly. It is frequently referred to as the Univac code because Univac is the brand name of the Remington Rand equipment.

The card that it uses is the same size as the IBM card. The card layout is quite different, however. The card is divided into two sections, a top half and a bottom half. Each section contains six rows and 45 columns. The top half contains columns 1 through 45 and the bottom half contains columns 46 through 90. Therefore, each card can contain 90 characters. The punches are round, and the coding system is not nearly so easy to learn as the Hollerith coding system because it is not in a logical pattern. See Fig. 6.21. Fields of data are

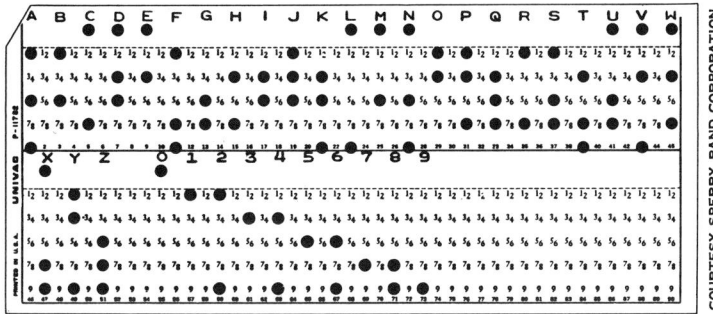

FIG. 6.21   Univac card

FIG. 6.22   New 96-column IBM card compared to Standard 80-column IBM card

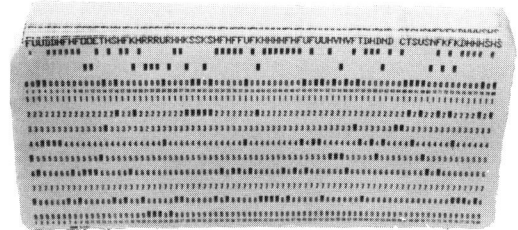

planned in much the same way as they are for the IBM c.
main differences are the coding system and the layout of the
and rows.

THE NEW IBM PUNCHED CARD

The new IBM card represents a significant advance in data processing. As we noted, it is 3¼″ × 2⅝″, approximately one-third of the size of the 80-column card shown in Fig. 6.22. The smaller card, however, can hold 96 characters, 20 percent more than the larger card.

The new card is divided into two main sections. The top section takes up slightly more than one-third of the card; this is used for printing the characters. This printing section consists of 4 lines, each with 32 positions; making a total of 128 possible printing positions. The bottom section is used for punching the data. It consists of three rows called tiers, each with 32 punching positions. Therefore, it contains 96 possible punching positions. The 32 extra printing positions allow for flexibility in planning the printing positions and allowing extra spaces between items. Although the keypunch machine usually prints the characters in the numbered position in which they are punched, other machines can be used to print the data in different positions and provide extra blank spaces in the print section. The punched holes are round and much smaller than the rectangular holes on the larger card. This new IBM card is usually referred to as the *96-column card* since it contains 96 punching positions, or sometimes as the *3-tier card* since it contains three rows of punching positions.

This new development permits the use of new card-handling techniques and equipment. The result has been the development of smaller and simpler equipment and a correspondingly lower cost. Although this card was developed for use with the System/3 desk-sized computer, several machines used with this system are similar and comparable to the unit record machines used with the 80-column card.

CODING SYSTEM OF THE 96-COLUMN CARD

This 96-column card uses the 6-bit coding system, which means that there are six possible punching positions per column rather than 12 as on the 80-column card. The basic principle of the Hollerith code is used, but is converted into 6 bits or positions. The rows are labeled on each side of the card, as shown in Fig. 6.23. The rows labeled 1, 2, 4, and 8 are used to represent the numbers. Using these numeric values, it is easy to understand the code: A punch is placed in the correct row or rows to add up to the numeric value desired. For example, the number 1 is represented by a punch in the row labeled 1. The number 5 is represented by a punch in the rows labeled 4 and 1 (4 + 1 = 5). Since there is no row labeled 0, it is represented by a punch in the A-row. Other than this use of the A-row, the A- and B-rows are not used in the numeric codes. See Fig. 6.23.

Notice that the 0 is printed with a line through it so that it cannot be confused with the letter O. This feature is merely to aid in visually reading the printed characters. There is no confusion when processing data by the machines because the punching codes for the two characters are different.

Using a combination of the numbers 1, 2, 4, and 8 can also result in numbers from 10 through 15, but such combinations are not used. The 8-column is necessary to represent the numbers 8 and 9. When processing data by punched cards, only one digit can be in a column. Also the keypunch machines have only the numbers 0 through 9 on their keys.

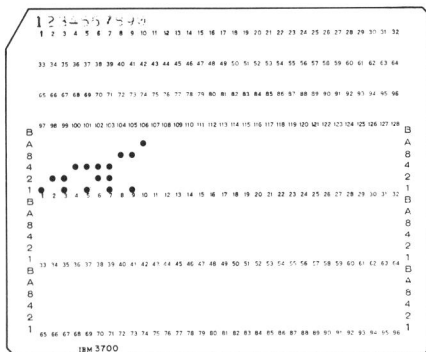

FIG. 6.23 Number code with 6-bit coding system

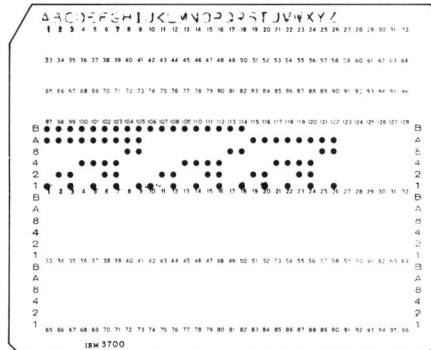

FIG. 6.24 Alphabetic code with 6-bit coding system

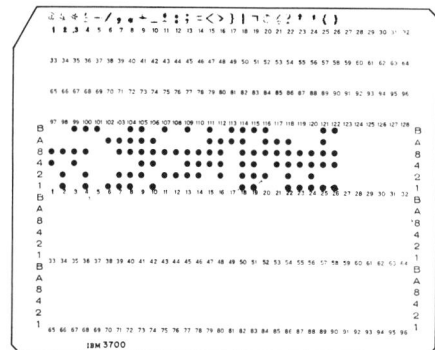

FIG. 6.25 Symbols with 6-bit coding system

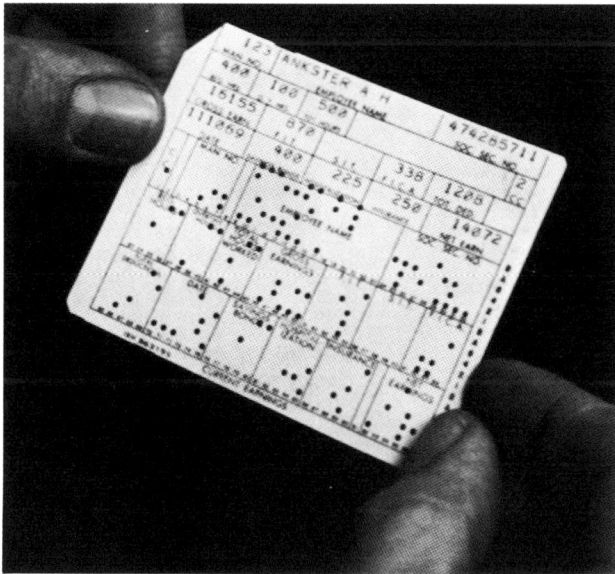

FIG. 6.26 Fields marked on a 96-column card

The columns labeled A and B are used to represent the three zone punches from the Hollerith coding system. The 12-zone (A-I) is a punch in both the A and B rows; the 11-zone (J-R) is a punch in the B row; and the 0-zone (S-Z) is a punch in the A row. For example, in the Hollerith coding system, the letter R is represented by an 11-zone and number 9 punch. In 6-bit coding, R is represented by punches in the B, 8, and I rows. The B represents the 11-zone, and the numbers 8 and 1 represent the number 9. See Fig. 6.24. Some of the special symbol codes are shown in Fig. 6.25.

The fields are planned in a manner similar to that for the 80-column card, but are marked differently, as shown in Fig. 6.26. This difference is necessary because the print position is not directly above the punching position—other rows separate them. Also 32 extra printing positions are available. As a result, the printing section and the punching section must have the fields marked separately.

OTHER RECORDING MEDIA

There are several other recording media such as paper tape, magnetic tape, and magnetic discs. They are commonly used with computers, not with punched card equipment. These media will be explained when we begin to study computers.

HANDLING AND CARE OF CARDS

Cards can be damaged enough rather easily so that they will not go through the machines. They are ruined if they are torn, bent, or badly warped. Sometimes warped cards can be straightened by bending them in the opposite direction. Otherwise, badly warped, bent, and torn cards have to be punched again. Anyone who handles cards should always be very careful. Damaged cards waste time by getting jammed in a machine and causing it to stop, and of course it takes time to make a new card.

Several precautions should be taken to help keep cards from being damaged.

1. When handling cards, be careful not to bend or drop them.
2. Put a blank card at the bottom and top of a stack before using a rubber band. If any damage is done, it will be to the blank card.
3. Place the rubber band to the left or right of the center. If it is always placed right in the center, some cards will gradually become nicked or slightly bent at the edge after repeated use.
4. Never use paper clips or staples on cards.
5. To avoid their warping, do not store cards where it is very warm or damp.
6. If possible, store cards in tightly-closed boxes. This will protect them from humidity and help to prevent warping.

7. When you finish using cards, return them to their proper storage place immediately, to avoid loss or damage.

Occasionally a duplicate of each card in a file is made for one of several reasons:

1. To provide replacement if cards are lost.
2. To save time of repunching immediately if a specific card is damaged.
3. To store in another place to prevent any chance of loss by fire.
4. To replace worn-out cards immediately.

QUESTIONS AND PROBLEMS

1. What is the form of the input and output of the unit record machines?
2. Can machines other than unit record machines use punched cards?
3. What two terms are used to refer to both input and output?
4. Why do punched cards need to be thicker than ordinary paper?
5. What are the standard sizes of IBM punched cards?
6. Why was the newer small size punched card developed?
7. What is the standard punched card coding system?
8. Why is it advantageous for all manufacturers to use standard sized cards with the same coding system?
9. Describe an IBM card, standard size.
10. What is the highest number that can be in one column of a card?
11. How many columns would the number 3,679 take?
12. How are the numbers represented in the Hollerith coding system?
13. How many punches are in each column for alphabetic data?
14. What kind of punches are the 0-row, 11-row, and 12-row for alphabetic data?
15. What letters are represented by the following punches using the Hollerith coding system?

    12 zone 7 digit   0 zone 2 digit
    11 zone 4 digit   11 zone 5 digit
     0 zone 9 digit   12 zone 1 digit

16. Does the Hollerith coding system distinguish between small and capital letters?
17. How many punches are in each column for special characters in the Hollerith coding system?

18. Are the $-sign and decimal point usually punched on cards in representing amounts of money?

19. Why must each type of data be in specific columns of each card?

20. When planning the fields on a card, what major consideration must be kept in mind?

21. List the steps to follow when planning the fields of a card.

22. What is the most important consideration in placing the fields of data on the card?   Why?

23. When the fields of a punched card do not take up the entire card, where is it best to leave the blank spaces?

24. Describe briefly six special types of IBM cards.

25. Briefly describe the layout of the older Univac punched card.

26. Briefly describe the layout of the new small IBM card.

27. Compare the punching capacity of the standard IBM punched card and the new IBM punched card.

28. What principle is used in the new IBM punched card coding system?

29. List the six row labels, going from top to bottom of the new IBM card.

30. How is each Hollerith code zone represented on the new IBM punched card?

31. What does each of the following combinations of punches represent on the new IBM card code?

    8, 1   A B 8 1   A 8 1
    4, 2, 1   A B 4   A 4 2
    2, 1   B 4 2   A 2
    1   B 1

32. How can warped cards be made usable?

33. List seven precautions that can help keep punched cards from being damaged.

In the past, unit record equipment was used quite extensively in business. In the late 1960's this was already changing as larger companies converted their record-keeping systems to computers and as smaller companies began to use time-sharing and service bureaus where they could rent computer time. Then at the beginning of the 1970's a new development was introduced which immediately affected the use of unit record equipment. This was the introduction of the desk-size computer. Its cost is comparable to that for installing unit record equipment; it is faster and more efficient; and it has more uses. It will probably continue to reduce the demand for unit record equipment. However, some companies will continue to need unit record equipment, especially to use along with their computer systems. So we still need to understand the functions of these machines in modern business data processing.

USES OF PUNCHED CARD MACHINES WITH COMPUTERS

Punched card machines have been used extensively and independently of computers. The punched card calculator and punched card accounting machines were essential to most complete data processing cycles to perform the calculations and provide their results. Many of the computer systems, however, use to advantage some punched card machines as an adjunct, especially the smaller computer systems. These punched card machines include the keypunch machine, sorter, collator, interpreter, and printer. After we discuss these machines, we will explain briefly the punched card calculator and punched card accounting machine.

RECORDING DATA ON PUNCHED CARDS

Before any functions can be performed with punched card equipment, the data must be made comparable, accessible, and punched on the cards. The basic machine which performs this function of recording is the keypunch machine. Several other machines that are important   **89**

FIG. 7.1 IBM Model
26 keypunch

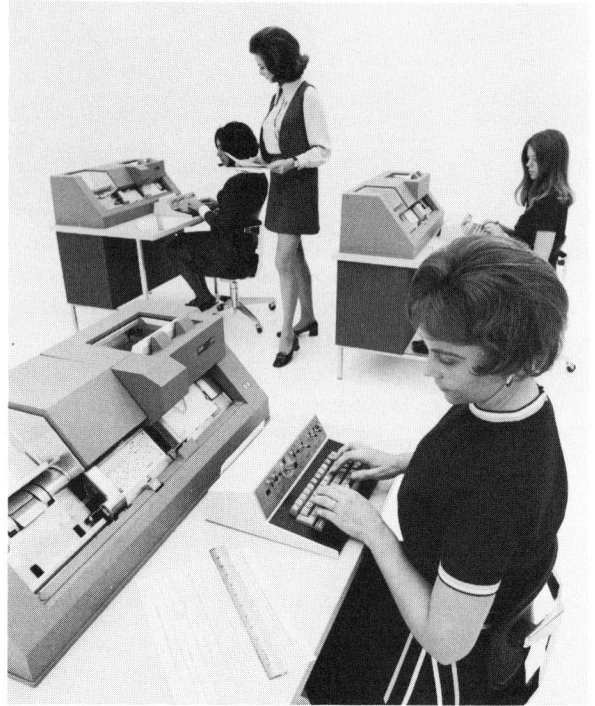

FIG. 7.2 IBM Model
129 keypunch
in operation

in the recording function for punched cards are the verifier which
checks for mistakes on punched cards, the interpreter which prints
on the cards the characters that have been punched on them, the reproducer which makes duplicate copies of cards, and various scanning
machines which read marks on paper or cards and convert them to
punches on cards.

KEYPUNCH MACHINE

The keypunch machine is a recording machine which puts the data
on the cards in the form of punched holes. It is an important machine
in punched card data processing. Figures 7.1 and 7.2 show two models

FIG. 7.3 Alpha-numeric keyboard

of keypunch machines that are currently in use. Most keypunch machines also print the data at the top of the card.

The keypunch operator uses the machine very much as you would a typewriter. Keypunch machines are electric. Figure 7.3 shows the standard alpha-numeric keyboard. Alpha-numeric means that it contains both the alphabetic characters and the numbers. The alphabet or the letters are in the same positions as they are on a standard typewriter keyboard, but the numbers are different. The numbers are positioned so that the keys can be depressed with the forefinger, second and third fingers of the right hand. In this way, the fingers do not have to reach so far, only one hand is used, and fewer errors are made. A large majority of the data punched onto cards is numeric data; for this reason a keyboard different from the one on the typewriter was developed. The symbols are in different positions, too. Some symbols are omitted and different ones are added. For example, there is no comma because sentences are not normally punched onto cards, and the commas are not placed in large numbers. The special symbols that do not look familiar are used for specific and special machine operations.

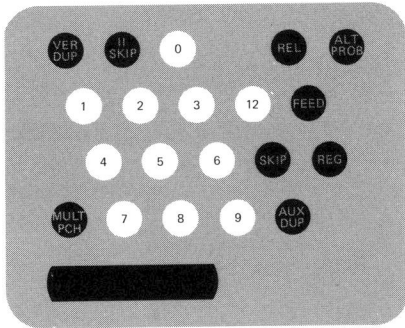

FIG. 7.4 Keyboard for special keypunch machine

On a punched card, there is no need to distinguish between capital and lower case letters because only capital letters are used. Therefore, rather than having a capital shift key, there is a numeric shift key for numbers and an alphabetic shift key for letters. When no shift key is depressed, the machine automatically punches the letters or alphabetic characters. The numeric shift key must be depressed and held down while punching all numbers unless a program card is being used (to be explained later). Remember that each letter is represented by two punches; the machine automatically punches them both at the same time when a letter key is depressed on the keyboard.

Special keypunch machines are available with just the numbers and some special symbols when no alphabetic characters have to be used (see Fig. 7.4). The keyboard is similar to a 10-key adding machine but the top and bottom rows are in the opposite order.

Most keypunch machines can also print the characters at the top of the card at the same time that the character is being punched. The character is printed above the same column that is being punched. If it is desired to have the data printed, a keypunch machine with this added feature is used. In this way, the data can be quickly read by a person when necessary without his having to decode the punches. The papers or forms from which the keypunch operator copies the data are called source documents.

Newer keypunch machines are available with a memory. This improvement saves the time previously spent repunching a card when the keypunch operator makes a mistake. As the operator depresses the keys, the characters enter the "memory" of the machine; they are not punched directly on the card. This enables the operator to backspace to correct mistakes that are immediately realized. When all the data for a card have been keyed, the card is punched. The operator may begin keying in the data for the next card before the card is in position. The keypunch machine in Fig. 7.2 has this monolithic-circuit memory.

PROGRAM CONTROL

A special device on the keypunch machine makes it easier and faster for the keypunch operator to do the job. This is the program control unit which contains a replaceable program card. A specially made program card can be inserted for each type of job the keypunch operator must perform. The program card makes it possible for the machine to

1. Shift automatically to alphabetic or numeric characters without the operator's having to use the shift keys,

2. Tabulate or skip to a specific column automatically, and/or

3. Duplicate specific standard data automatically.

The program unit of the keypunch machine contains a program drum which is cylindrical in shape. The program card is placed on the drum shown in Fig. 7.5 and into the unit of the keypunch machine. Keypunch machines are usually used with a program card, a regular card with special codes punched on it. A card can wear out after hard use or it can tear. Therefore, we frequently use metal cards the same size and shape as regular punched cards. When the program is not in use, a blank card should be put on the program drum.

The most frequently used codes on program cards are for punching alphabetic data, for punching numeric data, for duplicating alphabetic or numeric data, and for automatically skipping to the beginning of a new field. We can list these codes as follows:

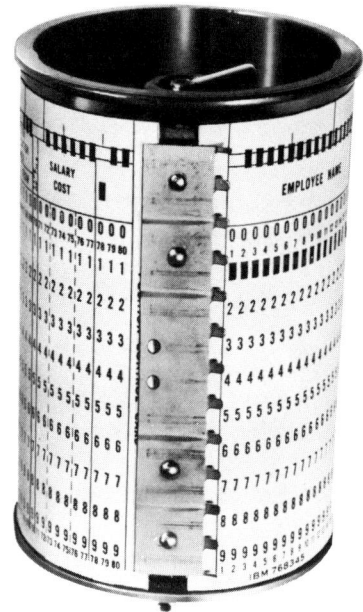

FIG. 7.5 Program drum of the keypunch machine

Purpose	First Column/Code	Rest of Field/Code
Punching numeric data	Blank	&-sign
Punching alphabetic data	1	A
Duplicating numeric data	0	&-sign
Duplicating alphabetic data	0 and 1	A
Skipping a field	—	&-sign

PRACTICE MACHINES

For students to learn the basic skill of keypunching, some schools use IBM Selectric Typewriters with a special keyboard comparable to the alpha-numeric keypunch keyboard. Although it prints the characters on paper and does not use punched cards, it does give a person practice in using the keyboard. The numbers are used with the shift key or shift lock depressed. This machine can also be used for ordinary typing. A Royal typewriter model adaptable for this practice is shown in Fig. 7.6. It has a regular typewriter keyboard with a "tandem" trainer attached for practicing the numbers.

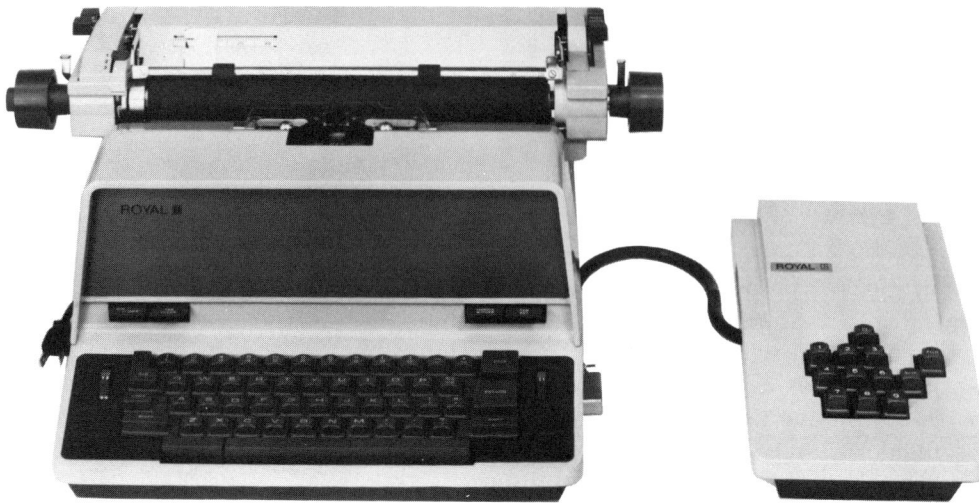

FIG. 7.6 Keypunch with tandem trainer

JOBS AVAILABLE FOR KEYPUNCH OPERATORS

The great demand for keypunch operators is gradually decreasing because numerous other devices for recording original data have been developed, such as the various types of scanners. A knowledge of typing is not necessary for many keypunch jobs, particularly if the duties require punching mostly numeric data. A person who is not very successful at typing numbers on a typewriter should not fear learning to operate a keypunch machine—remember that the numbers are in a different position which makes recording them easier. Keypunch operator jobs which require the punching of some alphabetic characters might require a basic typewriting ability as a qualification for the job. Some companies hire people without previous experience and train them on the job. .

Accuracy is very important. If a mistake is made, the entire card must be repunched. The efficiency of a keypunch operator is usually measured in terms of the average number of characters punched an hour, such as 5400 strokes an hour.

Most keypunch operators are women, but men should be able to use the machines if they have jobs operating other machines or even

**FIG. 7.7 Mark
scoring reader**

in connection with computers. If a card is lost, torn, or bent and a man
needs it immediately, he can save time and trouble by being able to
operate the keypunch machine himself.

OTHER RECORDING DEVICES FOR PUNCHED CARDS

Numerous other methods are used for recording data on punched
cards, some simpler and others more complex than the keypunch machine, some of which we discussed in Chapter 6. One method is by
a small hand-operated mechanism. The A-M Data Punch is sometimes
used. The IBM Porta-Punch uses special cards that have perforated
rectangular holes which fall out when they are punched with a pen-
like tool.

Another method utilizes a special machine that can read pencil
marks that have been made on the cards. The mark-sensing machine
operates on the principle that graphite conducts electricity and can

control circuits to actuate the punching mechanisms. Data marked on cards with electrographic lead is automatically converted to punched holes in the desired card columns. A mark-sensing machine can punch as many as 100 cards a minute.

An optical Mark Scoring Reader (Fig. 7.7) can score specially designed 8½″ by 11″ answer sheets. It does not put a check mark to indicate the wrong answers; instead it accumulates the number of right answers and prints the total in the margin of the answer sheet. If the person's identification number is on the answer sheet, the scoring reader can also punch a card with his score indicated. This type of machine can handle as many as 1200 answer sheets an hour.

Another method is a special Optical Character Reader (OCR) machine, sometimes called an optical reader card punch. It can read printed (not written) letters and numbers from special forms or punched cards and punch the data onto cards. This method is used on the charge cards of some gasoline companies, for example. When you purchase gas and give your credit card to the attendant, he uses a special machine to make an impression on the paper of whatever is on your charge plate. Then he inserts the amount charged and you sign it. He gives you a copy of it, he keeps a copy, and he sends a copy to the main office of the gasoline company where your monthly bill is processed. There an OCR machine reads the data from this paper and punches cards or records it on magnetic tape so that the items can be used in preparing your monthly bill. This machine is usually used with computer installations, not with unit record installations. It can punch as many as 200 cards a minute, to reduce the need for keypunching. Similar OCR machines are used by the United States Postal Service in several large cities. They read the bottom line of the addresses on envelopes, but do not punch or in any other way record the data. After reading the 5-digit zip code, these OCR machines direct each envelope to a specific stacker, thus sorting the envelopes by areas to which they are addressed.

VERIFIER

Verifying is checking the accuracy of cards that have been punched. If we do it visually, we could call it proofreading, especially if the characters are printed at the top of each card. Going through this step might at first seem very time-consuming, expensive, and unnecessary. However, accuracy on punched cards is so important that this step is definitely necessary in some punched card systems. If there is an error

**FIG. 7.8 IBM
59 card verifier**

on a card, all further processing of that data will be wrong, and the
work will have to be done again. The special machine called the
verifier is used to check the accuracy of cards that have been punched.

The verifier, as shown in Fig. 7.8, is similar to the keypunch machine; the only major difference is that it does not punch the characters on the cards. It merely checks to see that the required holes have
been punched in each column. The operator of the verifier goes
through the same motions as does the keypunch operator. A program
card is in the machine and the verifier depresses the correct keys reading from the same source documents that the keypunch operator used.
As the card that the keypunch operator punched goes through the
verifier, each column is checked as the operator depresses the key
for that column. If there are no errors, a notch is placed in the right-
hand edge of the card to indicate that it has been verified and is correct (see Fig. 7.9). If there is an error, the card is not notched at the

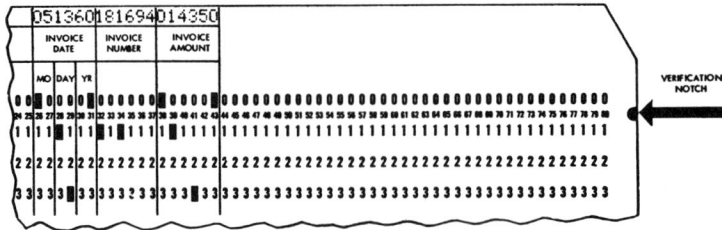

FIG. 7.9 Verification notch made by the verifier (no error)

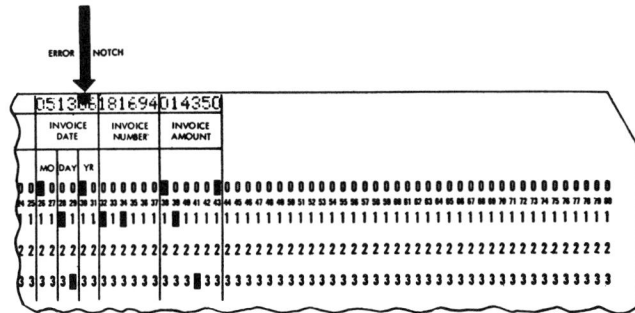

FIG. 7.10 Error notch made by the verifier

side; it is notched above the column of the error and must be re-punched and reverified, as in Fig. 7.10.

A card which has been verified might still contain an error, but only if both the keypunch operator and the verifier operator made the same mistake. This rarely happens if different people do the key-punching and the verifying jobs. It is never good practice to have a person verify his own work—if he frequently mixes up the numbers 6 and 9, he might do the same when keypunching and when verifying.

When the information in one or more fields of the cards is not important enough to warrant verifying, as is frequently the case, then one verifier operator can process as many cards as two or three key-punch operators. Another reason that the verifier operator can fre-quently work faster is that the source documents are in a neat and orderly arrangement when the keypunch operator gives them to the verifier, whereas they may not have been in such a neat order when the keypunch operator received them—some might have been upside down, sideways, or even folded. Employment offices usually advertise for keypunch operators even if the person needed is actually going to operate a verifying machine.

FIG. 7.11   Reproducing punch

INTERPRETING OR DUPLICATING

Duplicating the data that is already punched in cards can be done in either of two ways. The data can be printed on the card in which it is already punched or it can be reproduced. Printing the data on the card in which it is already punched is called interpreting and is done on a machine called an *Interpreter*. This process does not result in another form or document, but it does convert the data into an easily readable form, which is sometimes necessary, particularly if the key-punch machine does no printing.

Making a duplicate card of information already punched is done on a Reproducer like the one shown in Fig. 7.11. This machine can reproduce as many as 100 punched cards a minute, but it does not print the characters on the cards. If only one duplicate of each card is made, the process is merely called *reproducing* or sometimes called *one-for-one reproducing*. If many duplicates of each card are being made, this procedure is usually called *gang punching*.

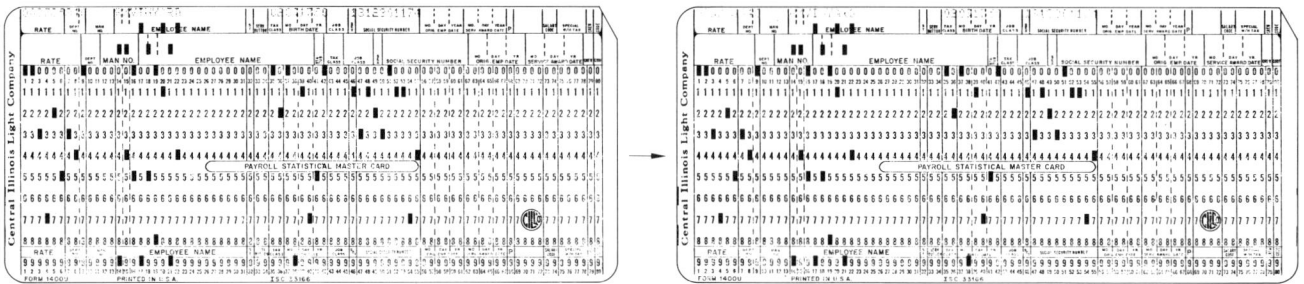

FIG. 7.12   80–80 reproducing

Cards may be reproduced

1. By making one or more duplicates. Since each column is reproduced exactly as it was on the original card, this is called *80–80 reproducing* (see Fig. 7.12).

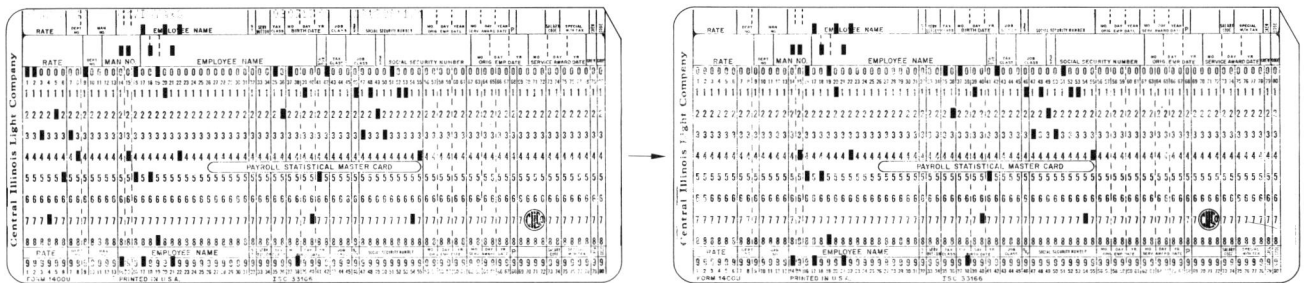

FIG. 7.13   Partial reproducing

2. With some of the data left out; in other words, only parts of the punched data are reproduced. This is called *partial reproducing* (see Fig. 7.13).

3. With some additional data added. This procedure is called *emitted reproducing* (see Fig. 7.14).

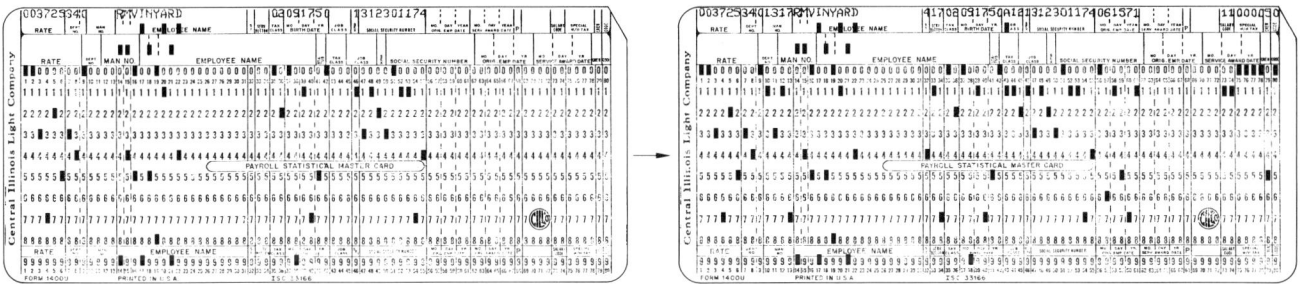

FIG. 7.14   Emitted reproducing

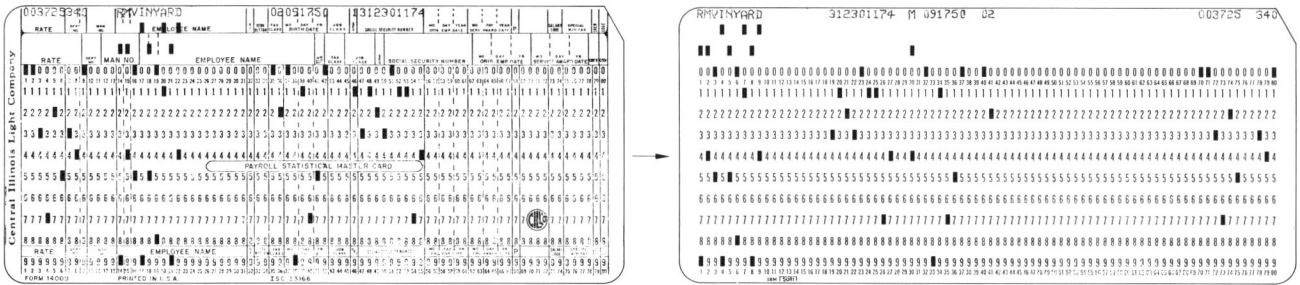

FIG. 7.15   Rearranged reproducing

4. With all the same data as the original card, but in a different sequence or order on the new card. This is called *rearranged reproducing* (see Fig. 7.15).

More than one of these possibilities can be used at the same time; it is possible, for example, to rearrange the order and leave out some of the data on the new card.

   To illustrate gang punching we might take, for example, a stack of cards, one card for each sale made during a certain day. Each card would contain all the needed information except the date. If we want to have the date placed in specific columns on each card, we make a master or header card with just the date in those specific columns. Then we place this card on top of the stack of cards and put the

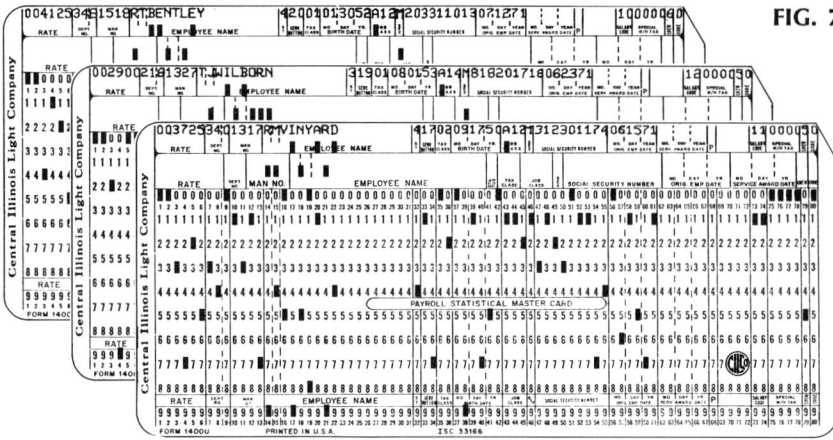

FIG. 7.16

(a) Original cards without date

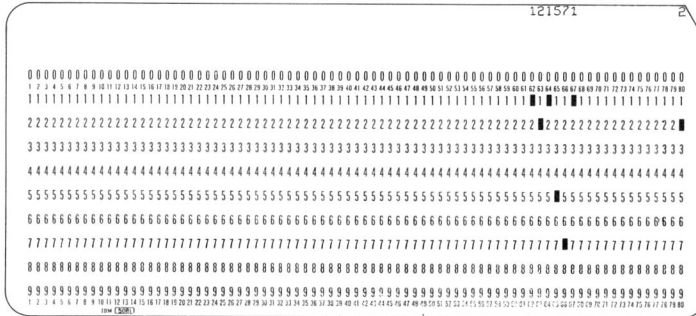

(b) Header card with date and code

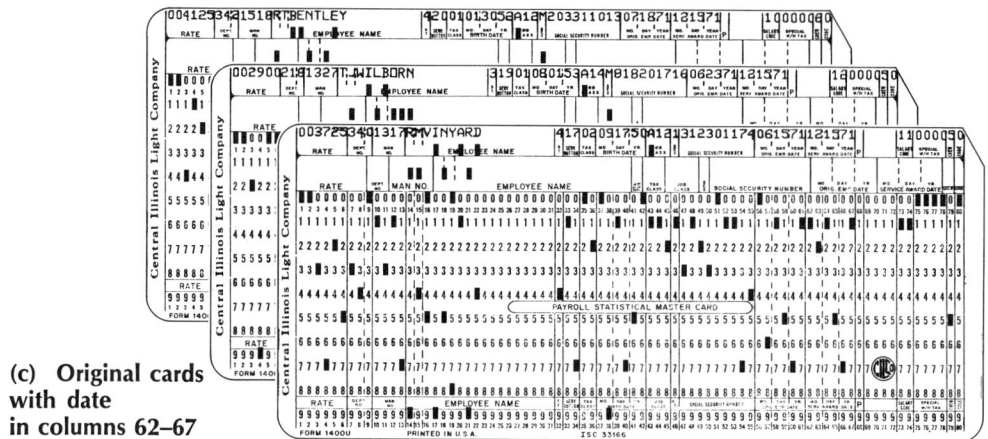

(c) Original cards with date in columns 62–67

entire stack into the reproducing machine. The data on this header card can then be reproduced on each other card in the stack (see Fig. 7.16).

A more complicated method of gang punching is *interspersed gang punching.* An appropriate header card is placed before each group of cards in order to have different data reproduced on the cards in that group. For example, we might have a stack of cards for the sales made by each salesman and a header card with each salesman's identification number in the appropriate columns. Directly above the sales report cards for each salesman we would have a header card with his identification number. Each header card contains special punches that represent a code to the machine to tell it that this is a new header card.

INTRODUCTION TO THE CONTROL PANEL

In order for the reproducer to read the desired columns in a punched card and to punch the data in the desired columns on the blank card, the reproducer must be told what columns to read and to punch. Remember that not all operations using this machine reproduce the cards exactly as they are originally punched. In fact, relatively few jobs are done in this manner. Most jobs for the reproducer require the partial, emitted, or rearranged process, or a combination of these. This varies for each specific job. The possibilities are too complicated and variable for the machine to have keys or buttons to depress in order to give the machine specific instructions for each job. Therefore, we use a *wired board* or *panel,* or a plug board. It is called a *control board* or a *control panel* because it does control the operation of the machine. The reproducer cannot operate without a wired board. Figure 7.17 shows a wired board with some wires inserted.

In some companies, unit record data processing machine operators are expected to be able to wire the control panels, but in other companies wiring is a separate job. In some companies, the person receives a completed diagram that someone else has made and merely inserts the wires as illustrated on the diagram. This type of wiring job is not very difficult and does not require an in-depth understanding of the machines. In other companies, a person who does wiring merely receives written details concerning the job; this include a description of the input and the required output. He makes up a wiring diagram

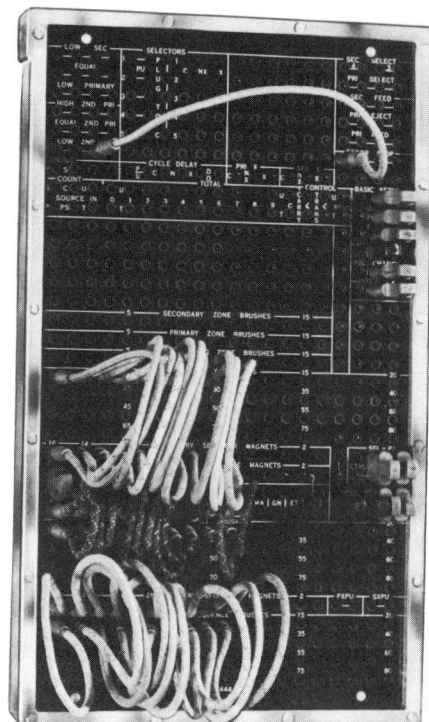

FIG. 7.17 Wired control panel

and then does the actual wiring. This type of person must have a thorough understanding of the functions of the machine. Most people who do wiring are able to wire all the punched card machines and are able to operate them.

Once a panel has been wired and checked to see that it is accurate, it is labeled for the specific job and saved so that it can be used each time the same job must be performed. This saves rewiring the board each time the job is to be repeated. If the same job will not be done again, the wires are removed so that the board can be used for another job. If the wiring of a specific job is relatively easy and quick to do and the job is only performed infrequently, the wired panel might not be saved; it might be rewired each time it is needed.

INTERPRETER

The interpreter (shown in Fig. 7.18) reads the holes that are already punched on a card and prints the characters on the same card. The size of print is larger than that produced by a keypunch machine. Therefore, the characters cannot be directly above the column in which the data are punched, and not all 80 characters can be printed across one line of a card. Since they are larger, however, they are much easier to read.

Interpreting is frequently done across the top of the card so that it can be seen more easily in a file. It is also possible to print characters between the lines where the punches are. For example, this type of printing is done on pay checks that are actually punched cards that have some holes already punched along with the printed data. Some of the information is printed by other printing machines (such as the name of the company and the name of the bank) and some data are printed with an interpreter (such as the name and amount of the check which are also punched on the card).

Interpreting can be done in several forms, similar to reproducing. Printing all 80 characters that are punched is *80–80 interpretation;* even if not all 80 columns contain punches, they could and would be interpreted if they did contain punches. Printing only some of the characters that have been punched on the card is *partial interpretation.* Adding other characters that were not punched on the card is *emitted interpretation;* this might be adding a dollar sign before the numbers. Changing the order of the data that is punched on the card is *rear-*

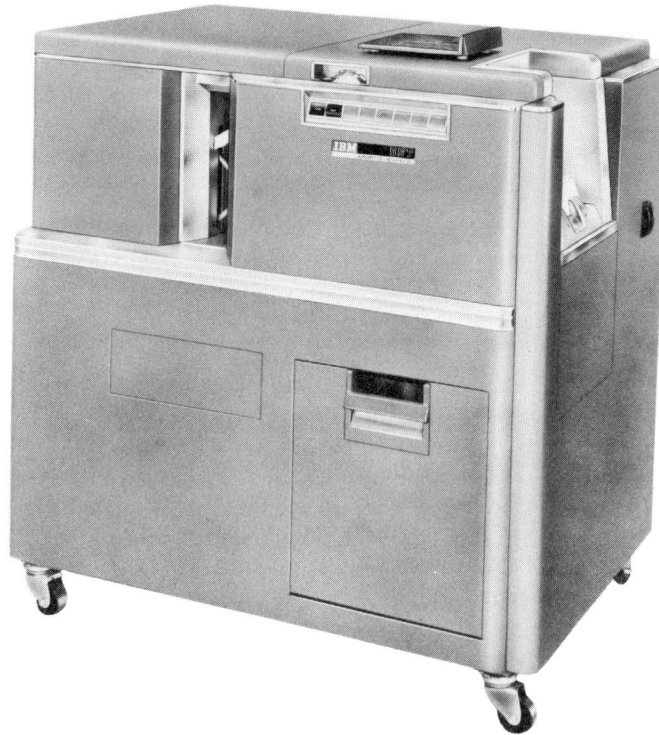

FIG. 7.18 Interpreter

ranged interpretation. Each of these types of interpreting can be used by itself, or several can be used together. Altering the placement of the printing can make the cards useful for many different purposes. The person's name and address can be placed so that it will show for mailing in an envelope that has a window. Or you might receive an advertisement with a card on which to place an order for the item being advertised. When the company receives the card you have signed as your order, the same card can be used to make up a bill that is sent to you telling you how much you owe. If you bent or tore the card, another card would have to be made. The federal Income Tax refund checks are sent on punched cards, but were prepared by computers not by unit record machines.

Only 60 characters can be printed across one line of a punched card when using the interpreter. In order to interpret all 80 columns of a card, it must pass through the machine at least twice. Some interpreters can print only two lines at the top of the card; others can print as many as 25 lines, one at a time. These machines can be instructed to print one or several asterisks directly to the left of the amount on checks, for protection. Most interpreters can process from 60 to 100 cards a minute.

With the interpreter, as with the reproducer, numerous variations are possible through careful wiring of the control panel. The reproducer contains a punching mechanism, whereas the interpreter contains a printing mechanism.

JOBS AVAILABLE AS OPERATORS OF REPRODUCERS OR INTERPRETERS

A person does not obtain a job merely as an operator of a reproducer or of an interpreter. However, these are two of the machines he must be able to use when he works as an operator of a unit record data processing machine or a punched card machine. As already mentioned, the person who wires the control panels is frequently not the person who operates the punched card machines. The wirer usually can wire all the machines that use control panels and must have a very good understanding of the operations of each machine.

READING A CARD BY THE MACHINES

Most punched card machines must read the data punched on the cards. The reading mechanism contains brushes or a brush. The card passes between the brushes and a contact roller as shown in Fig. 7.19. Where there is a hole in the card, the brush contacts the roller and completes a circuit for an electrical impulse. Some of the punched card machines read all 80 columns at the same time and contain 80 reading brushes, one per card column, as shown in Fig. 7.19. Other punched card machines read only one column at a time and contain one brush that reads the specified column from bottom to top of the card; or they contain one brush per punching position (12 brushes) and read one column at the same time. On some of the machines, such as the sorter, you can see the reading brush rather easily. On other punched card machines, the reading brushes are inside the machine. Some of the newer machines use no brushes, but contain reading devices that are photoelectric in principle.

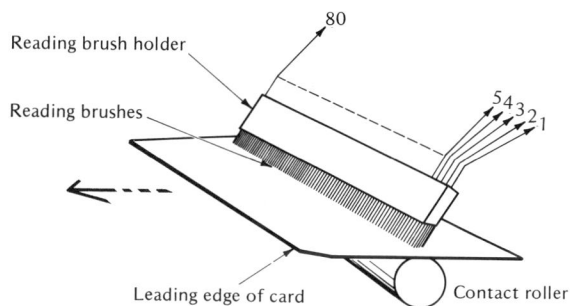

FIG. 7.19 Reading mechanism

Reading brush holder

Reading brushes

80

5 4 3 2 1

Leading edge of card

Contact roller

FIG. 7.20 IBM System/3, with multifunction unit in the center

RECORDING DATA ON THE 96-COLUMN CARD

Since the 96-column card was designed for use with the System/3 desk-size computer, the recording functions are performed on machines that are not separate but are actually attached to the computer. The multi-function card unit, shown as a part of the System/3 in Fig. 7.20, punches cards, interprets cards, and reproduces cards performing the functions in ways similar to those of the various unit record machines already explained. When originally punching cards, the operator punches only one character at a time, and the character can

FIG. 7.21 IBM 5496 data recorder for System/3

be printed simultaneously in the corresponding position at the top of the card. When interpreting cards, the System/3 can print the data on 120 cards a minute. When reproducing cards, it can punch 120 cards a minute.

Separate from the System/3 is a Data Recorder which can also be used to reproduce and print data. It reads 20 columns per second; this means all three tiers, or 60 characters are read per second. See Fig. 7.21.

QUESTIONS AND PROBLEMS

1. Why is there less demand for unit record equipment now than there has been in the past?

2. What is the basic machine that is used to punch data onto cards?

3. What unit record machines are used much less than they were before the introduction of the new smaller computers?

4. What unit record machines are most frequently still used with the computer?

5. What is the basic purpose of the Verifier? The Interpreter? The Reproducer? The Scanner?

6. Do all keypunch machines also print the data at the top of the card?

7. What term is used to refer to both alphabetic and numeric characters?

8. Why are the numbers in a different position on the keypunch machine keyboard than on the typewriter keyboard?

9. What type of data is punched most often onto cards?

10. Why does the keypunch machine keyboard not have a comma?

11. For what purpose are the shift keys used?

12. When no shift key is used, what does the machine automatically punch when the program unit is not being used?

13. Where is each character printed on the punched card?

14. What name is given to the papers or forms from which the keypunch operator copies?

15. What functions can a program card perform?

16. What are keypunch practice machines?

17. Why is a knowledge of typewriting not always necessary for a keypunch operator?

18. What must be done if the keypunch operator makes a mistake punching a card?

19. Why is it helpful for men to learn how to use a keypunch machine?

20. Why has the demand for keypunch operators not been increasing so much in recent years?

21. How does a mark-sensing machine operate?

22. Why and how are OCR machines used in the United States Postal Service?

23. The verifier is very similar to what other punched card machine?

24. If there are no errors on a card, what does the verifier do?

25. If there is an error on a card, what does the verifier do?

26. Explain the ways that a card with a "no-error" notch could still have an error.
27. Why does the entire card not always have to be verified?
28. List two reasons explaining why a verifier operator can usually work faster than a keypunch operator.
29. What are two ways that data on punched cards can be duplicated?
30. What name is given to the process of punching the same data onto another card?
31. What name is given to the process of printing the data on the card in which it is already punched?
32. What is one-for-one reproducing?
33. What is gang punching?
34. Briefly describe the four forms of reproducing cards.
35. How is interspersed gang punching accomplished?
36. What controls the functioning of the reproducer?
37. Why are wired control panels frequently saved?
38. In what ways is the printing done by the interpreter different from the printing done by the keypunch machine?
39. How many times must each card pass through the interpreter in order to have all 80 columns interpreted?
40. What is the advantage of printing one or more asterisks directly to the left of the amount on checks?
41. Describe briefly how most punched card machines read punched cards.
42. What advantage is there to the reproducing function on the new 96-column IBM card?

OPERATIONS WITH PUNCHED CARDS | Part 1

CHAPTER 8

Cards that have been punched are used immediately or are filed for future use. The processing steps frequently include putting the cards in some specific order, performing calculations, and presenting the results in a report. The unit record machines (Fig. 8.1) used to put the cards in a specific order are the sorters and collators; those used to perform the calculations and provide the results are the calculators, accounting machines, and printers. With a computer installation, sorters and collators are sometimes needed as an adjunct, but the punched card calculator and accounting machine are seldom needed.

FIG. 8.1 IBM Unit record installation

FIG. 8.2 Filing cabinets

FILING NEEDS FOR PUNCHED CARDS

Punched cards, whether to be used immediately or kept for future use, are usually put in some logical order first. Like other documents, cards are stored in filing cabinets. Since they are so much smaller than standard documents, special filing cabinets are used. They come in many sizes, ranging from a one-drawer file to floor cabinets with many drawers. Several of the punched card filing cabinets are shown in Fig. 8.2.

Cards are filed in a specific order, so that if one or more cards are needed from the file, they can be found easily. If only a few cards are needed, they can be retrieved manually if the data is also printed on the cards. If many cards are needed, machines handle the job more quickly, of course. When the complete file of cards must be used again, they are frequently checked to make sure that all the cards are in order.

SPACE REQUIRED FOR PUNCHED CARDS

Transferring data to punched cards saves space if the original documents that contained the same data were larger. It is particularly important to record the data carefully because the original documents are usually destroyed; saving them would require additional filing space. Also, the data should be recorded consistently; the card format must be carefully planned so the cards can be efficiently used.

The punched card that contains a microfilm duplicate of a sheet of paper is a storing method that saves a great deal of space. Another advantage to this method is that the microfilmed document can be filed and retrieved with the sorter and collator rather than manually because the film and the punched data are on the same card.

SORTING PUNCHED CARDS

As we have already noted, the punched cards must frequently be rearranged in some specific order before they are further processed. The machine used is the sorter. The sorter can put a group of cards in a specific sequence, either alphabetic or numeric. For example, alphabetic sorting would place the cards containing the names of all the employees into alphabetic order, whereas numeric sorting would put the cards containing the employee numbers of all the employees into order by the employee numbers.

Punched cards can be arranged with the sorter by sequencing, grouping, or selecting. *Sequencing* is arranging the punched cards in a specific logical order, usually alphabetically or numerically. *Grouping* is putting together in one group or stack all the cards that contain the same or similar data. Code numbers or letters are usually used for this operation. For example, if the cards with all the employees' names and numbers also contain a code to represent the department (1 = office, 2 = factory, 3 = maintenance, 4 = custodial, 5 = executive), the cards can be grouped into these five separate classifications using the sorter. *Selecting* is taking from a stack only the cards that contain certain data. This is usually done by code number also. If just the custodial employees' names are needed, they can be taken from the stack of cards for all the employees without grouping each of the other classifications separately.

The sorter can read only one column of a card at a time. For 1-digit codes, they have to go through the machine only once. However, if cards are to be sorted by 5-digit identification numbers, they must go through the machine five times.

FIG. 8.3   IBM 084 Sorter

The older sorter models read the holes with a brush and can process up to 1000 cards a minute. Newer models, as shown in Fig. 8.3, sense the holes photoelectrically; they can process as many as 2000 cards a minute.

Across the front of the sorter are 13 pockets or bins which the cards fall into after the machine reads the specific column (see Fig. 8.3). There is a pocket for each of the 12 rows on the card and a reject pocket for the cards that do not have anything punched into the specific column. From left to right, the pockets are: 9, 8, 7, 6, 5, 4, 3, 2, 1, 0, 11, 12, R. The pockets are sometimes referred to as stackers.

Numeric Sorting

Pockets 0–9 are used for numeric sorting. If a card has a number punch in a specific column being read, the card falls into that pocket. If nothing is punched in that column, the card goes into the reject pocket. Remember that only one column can be read by the sorter at a time. The units column is sorted first—we always begin at the right end of the number. Figure 8.4 shows a sample of a 3-digit numeric sorting operation. At the right are the cards before they are sorted. The pockets show where the cards would fall during the first run-through. At the left are the cards after they have been properly taken from the pockets. This stack is then put back in the card hopper in this order for sorting by the next column to the left. Remember that the cards are face down.

After the first sort, the units are in the correct order (right-hand column); after the second sort the units and tens are in the correct order; after the third sort, the units, tens and hundreds are in the

STACKED CARDS   FEED
AFTER SORT   HOPPER

789													789
218													086
908													643
086													090
795													444
745													218
444													421
643													908
421													500
321													795
090		218			795				421	090			745
500	789	908		086	745	444	643		321	500			321

| 9 | 8 | 7 | 6 | 5 | 4 | 3 | 2 | 1 | 0 | 11 | 12 | R |

(a) First sort

STACKED CARDS   FEED
AFTER SORT   HOPPER

795													789
090													218
789													908
086													086
745													795
444													745
643													444
421													643
321													421
218					745								321
908	795	789			444		421		908				090
500	090	086			643		321	218	500				500

| 9 | 8 | 7 | 6 | 5 | 4 | 3 | 2 | 1 | 0 | 11 | 12 | R |

(b) Second sort

FIG. 8.4 Three-digit numeric sorting

FIG. 8.4 (cont.)

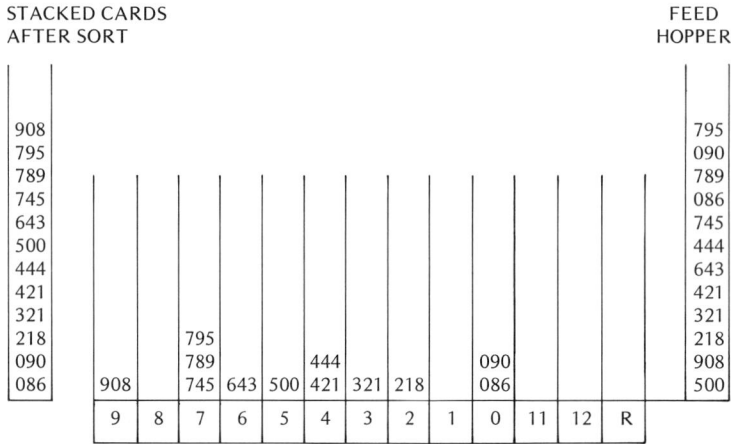

(c) **Third sort**

correct order. After each sort, the cards are taken out of the pockets from right to left, with each succeeding stack placed on top of the cards already taken out of the pockets. All cards are upside-down as they are processed by the sorter.

Alphabetic Sorting

Sorting cards alphabetically takes twice as long as doing so numerically because each column must be sorted twice. The first time each column is sorted the machine reads only the number punch in the column, so the cards fall into pockets 1 through 9; the second time the column is sorted, the machine reads only the zone punch in the same column, so the cards fall into pockets 0, 11, and 12.

Figure 8.5 shows a sample of a 1-column alphabetic sorting operation. At the right are the cards before they are sorted. The pockets show how the cards fall into the number pockets. The stacked cards at the left show the cards after they have been removed from right to left. Each stack is placed on top of the previous cards as they are picked up. The second sort shows how the cards fall into the zone pockets and are then stacked in the correct order. Figure 8.6 shows a sample of a 2-column alphabetic sorting operation. The cards are sorted one column at a time, from right to left. After the first two sorts, the cards are in correct alphabetic order going by the right-hand letter. After the second two sorts, the cards are in correct order by both letters.

STACKED CARDS
AFTER SORT

FEED
HOPPER

Stacked cards (left, top to bottom): I H Q X O E U T S B J A

Feed hopper (right, top to bottom): J H S U A T B E O X Q I

Pockets (left to right):
9	8	7	6	5	4	3	2	1	0	11	12	R
I	H	X	O	E	U	T	S	J				
	Q						B	A				

(a) First sort

STACKED CARDS
AFTER SORT

FEED
HOPPER

Stacked cards (left, top to bottom): X U Y S Q O J I H E B A

Feed hopper (right, top to bottom): I H Q X O E U T S B J A

Pockets (left to right):
9	8	7	6	5	4	3	2	1	0	11	12	R
									X	Q	I	
									U	O	H	
									T	J	E	
									S		B	
											A	

(b) Second sort

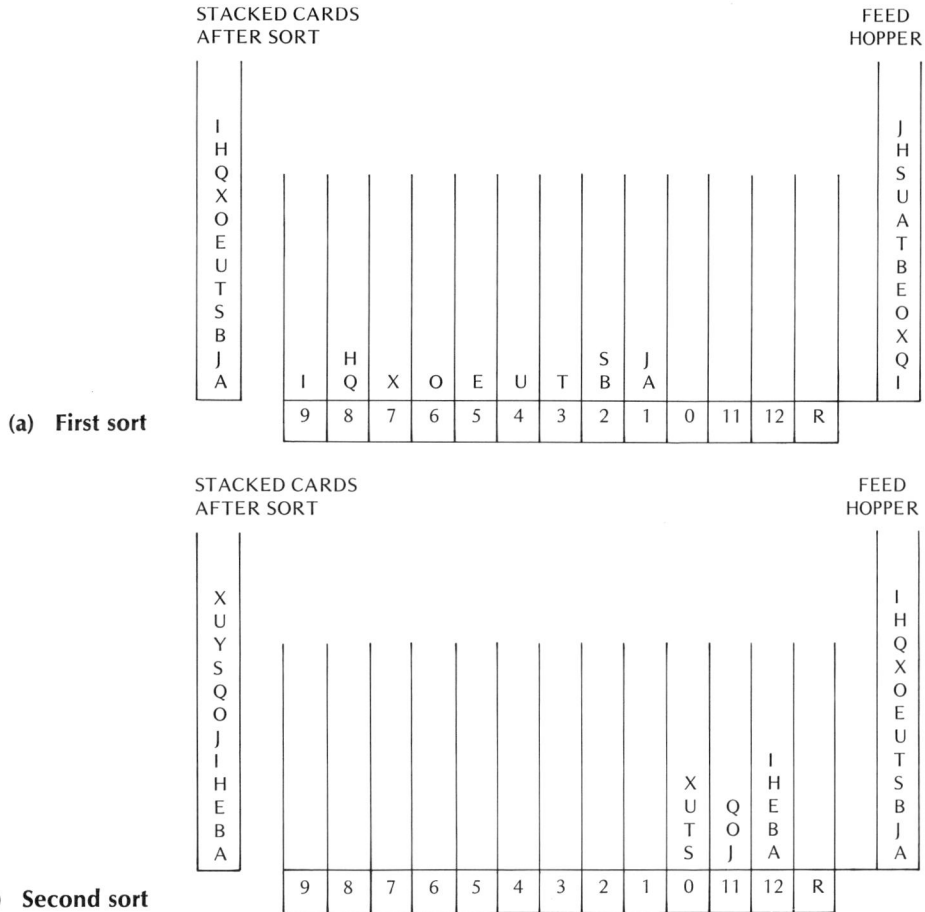

FIG. 8.5 One-column alphabetic sorting

Other Methods of Sorting

Since grouping is sorting by a code number, we simply use the column selector for the column in which the code is punched. The cards fall into the appropriate pockets depending on their code number. If it is a two-digit code, the cards must be sorted twice, but frequently this type of code number is limited to one digit.

Selecting is taking only specific cards out of a group of cards, so the sort selector is set for the number or letter desired and the

STACKED CARDS   FEED
AFTER SORT   HOPPER

				MZ										
MZ															MZ
TO															IT
NO															ON
SF															BB
ON															YE
YE															TO
AN															NO
EV															OC
TM															AN
IT					ON										SF
OC			TO	YE											EV
BB			NO	AN		IT	BB								US
US	MZ		SF	EV	TM	OC	US								TM

9	8	7	6	5	4	3	2	1	0	11	12	R

(a) First sort

STACKED CARDS   FEED
AFTER SORT   HOPPER

MZ															MZ
EV															TO
IT															NO
US															SF
TO															ON
NO															YE
ON															AN
AN															EV
TM										TO					TM
SF									MZ	NO	SF				IT
YE									EV	ON	YE				OC
OC									IT	AN	OC				BB
BB									US	TM	BB				US

9	8	7	6	5	4	3	2	1	0	11	12	R

(b) Second sort

FIG. 8.6 Two-column alphabetic sorting sequence

column indicator is set for the correct column. The desired cards fall
into the appropriate pocket, depending on the code number desired,
and all other cards go into the reject pocket. In this way, all the cards
not wanted remain in their original order or sequence. This can be
an advantage in a situation like this: Let's assume the cards with the
names and addresses of all students in the college are in alphabetic
order. We want to mail the graduation details only to the seniors.
We can use the selecting method so that the cards for all seniors go
into the 4-pocket (4 is the senior code number). These cards remain

STACKED CARDS
AFTER SORT

FEED
HOPPER

```
IT                                                    MZ
YE                                                    EV
ON                                                    IT
OC                                                    US
EV                                                    TO
NO                                                    NO
MZ                                                    ON
US                                                    AN
TO                                                    TM
TM                                                    SF
SF                                                    YE
BB              ON  EV  MZ  TO  SF                     OC
AN      IT  YE  OC  NO  US  TM  BB  AN                 BB
        9   8   7   6   5   4   3   2   1   0   11  12  R
```

(c) Third sort

STACKED CARDS
AFTER SORT

FEED
HOPPER

```
YE                                                    IT
US                                                    YE
TO                                                    ON
TM                                                    OC
SF                                                    EV
ON                                                    NO
OC                                                    MZ
NO                                                    US
MZ                              YE                     TO
IT                              US  ON  IT             TM
EV                              TO  OC  EV             SF
BB                              TM  NO  BB             BB
AN                              SF  MZ  AN             AN
        9   8   7   6   5   4   3   2   1   0   11  12  R
```

(d) Fourth sort

Fig. 8.6 (cont.)

in alphabetic order as they go into this pocket. All other cards go into the reject pocket, also remaining in alphabetic order. If regular numeric sorting had been used, there would now be 5 stacks of cards: one for freshmen, one for sophomores, one for juniors, one for seniors, and one for unclassified students, each in alphabetic order. Obviously, putting all the cards back into the original alphabetic order will take less time if there are only two stacks to be combined. With these two stacks, each in alphabetic order, the next machine, the collator, can now be used to put the cards back into one alphabetic stack.

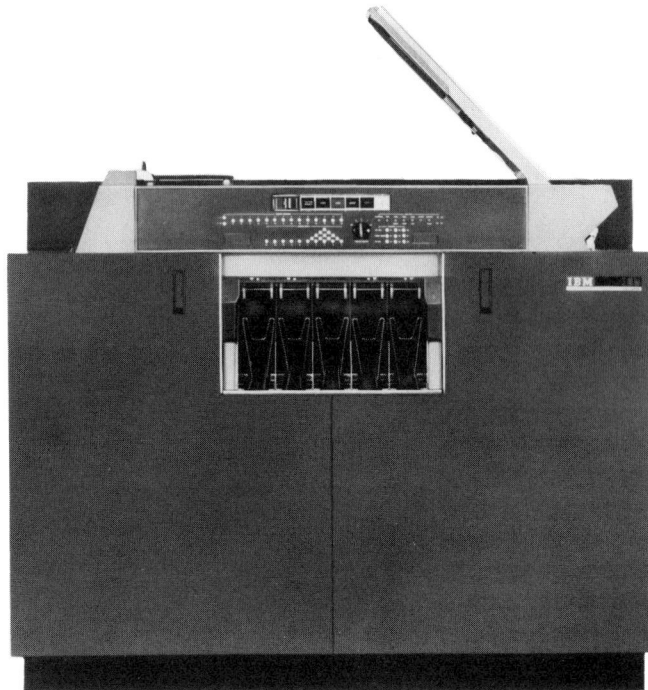

FIG. 8.7   IBM 188 collator

Control of the Sorter

The sorter is one of the few unit record machines that does not require the use of a control panel. A dial indicator is used to specify the sorting operation desired, and a column indicator is moved to the correct column number.

COLLATING PUNCHED CARDS

Storing records and being able to find them when they are needed are two functions which are extremely time-consuming with manual and mechanical data processing methods. As we have seen, using punched cards and the punched card equipment helps to solve this problem; so, too, does the use of the collator. The collator can perform several operations necessary in retrieving cards from files so that we can use the data in other machines. It can combine two stacks or files of cards that are already in the correct order into one stack in the correct order; this is called *merging*. It can compare two stacks or files of cards to see whether they both contain comparable cards; this is called *matching*. It can take specific cards that are required out of a stack or file of cards; this is called *selection*. It can check one stack of cards to see whether any cards are out of their correct order; this is called *sequence checking*. Each operation can be performed with the use of the control panel properly wired. Without a collator, all the cards would have to be sorted again to accomplish some of these jobs, which would obviously take more time.

Basically, in Fig. 8.7 the collator functions by comparing the data punched into specific columns of two cards, one from each of the two stacks of input cards. The older collators have brushes that detect the holes and can process from 250 to 500 cards a minute. Newer transistorized, solid-state models can process as many as 1300 cards a minute.

SEQUENCE CHECKING

When the collator finds a card out of its correct numeric or alphabetic order, an error light goes on and the machine stops. The operator examines the card or cards that are out of order, puts them in correct order by hand, and starts the machine again. When the collator is checking the cards (Fig. 8.8), it stops when it compares the cards with the numbers 1008 and 1005 because the first card has a higher number than the second card.

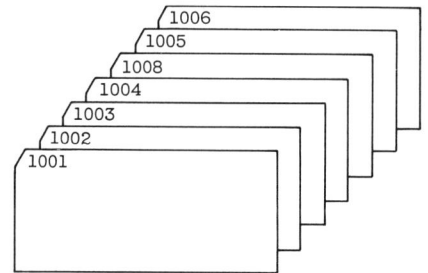

FIG. 8.8 Sequence-checking with the collator

If a company has cards with each employee's name, home address, and employee number, the employee numbers are assigned in a manner to correspond with the name so that when the cards are in numeric sequence, they are also in alphabetic order. In this way, each time any of the cards must be sorted, they can be sorted numerically rather than alphabetically, a less time-consuming operation. Each time an employee reports a change in his home address, his card is removed from the file drawer by hand, a new card is punched with the new address, and the card is returned to the file by hand. Since this filing is done by hand, errors can easily be made. Occasionally the cards should be checked to determine whether they are in the correct order, and mistakes should be corrected. This is a sample of sequence checking where the employee number is used. If the company does not have a collator, the cards must be completely sorted again, which of course, would take more time than sequence checking.

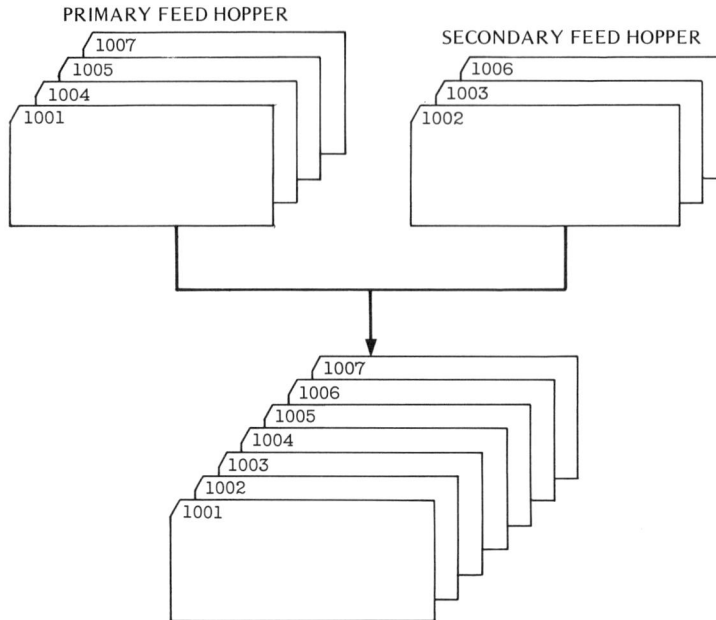

FIG. 8.9 Merging with the collator

MERGING OPERATION

Merging is combining two stacks of cards that are already in correct order into one stack in the correct order. As the cards, one from each stack, are compared, the one with the lower number goes to the card stacker as output. The card that remains is then compared to the next card in the other stack. This comparing operation continues until all the cards have been processed. The results are illustrated in Fig. 8.9.

MATCHING OPERATION

Matching is comparing two stacks of punched cards to determine whether both stacks contain comparable cards. The cards are compared, in a process similar to merging, but they are kept in their two separate stacks by being directed into different card stackers. If there is a card in one stack that does not match one in the other stack, it goes into a special card stacker designated for such "rejects." Figure 8.10 shows an example of matching. The matched cards go into card Stackers 2 and 3. The unmatched cards from one group of cards go into Stacker 1, and those from the other group go into Stacker 4.

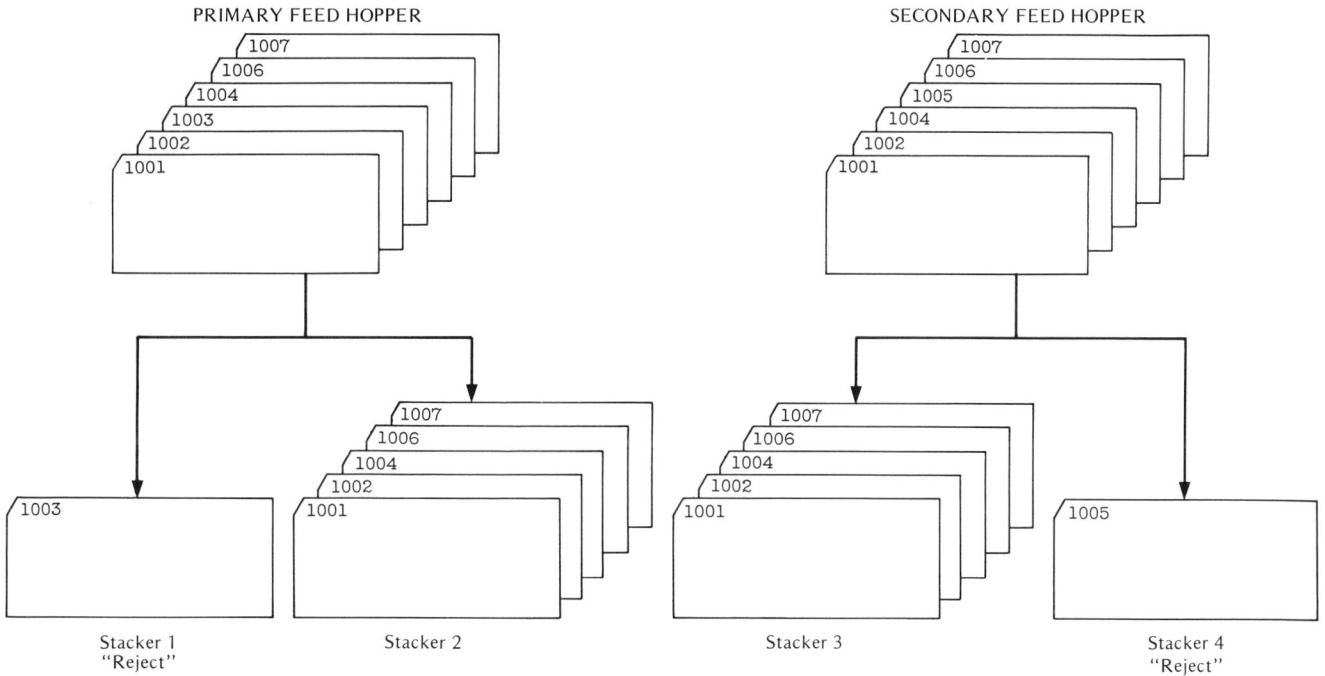

FIG. 8.10 Matching with the collator

SELECTING OPERATION

Card selection is taking just the required cards out of a stack or file of punched cards. The two stacks of cards being compared consist of the complete file from which some specific cards are required and a stack of cards comparable to those needed. Figure 8.11 illustrates the selecting operation which makes use of the collator. The cards from the complete file go into Stacker 3 if they are the required cards and into Stacker 4 if they are not the required cards. The cards from the smaller stack that represent the required cards can go into Stacker 2 if their match is found, and Stacker 1 if their match is not found.

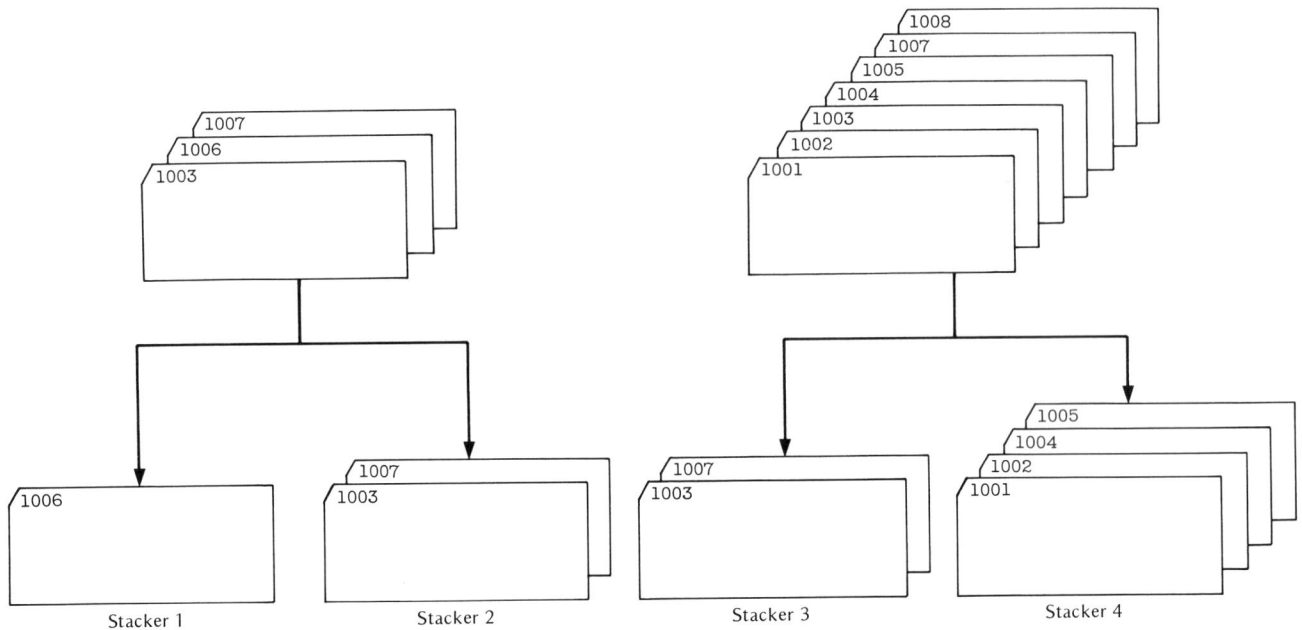

Fig. 8.11 Selecting with the collator

The examples that have been given for the use of the collator represent only basic applications. With correct wiring of the control panel, numerous variations can be performed. Some collators can work only with numeric data; others can work with both alphabetic and numeric data. An understanding of both the sorter and the collator is essential. You can save a great deal of time by using the correct machine for each specific application. For many applications, either the sorter or the collator could be used, but one would make the job faster and easier than the other. For example,

1. If a few cards are out of order, you can find the errors by using the collator. This is simpler than completely re-sorting them with the sorter, one column at a time.

2. If selection is being done with just one column, the sorter is faster. If several columns are used, the collator is faster.

The collator is frequently faster for a particular job because it can work with more than one column at a time; the sorter can work with only one column at a time.

QUESTIONS AND PROBLEMS

1. What unit record machines can be used to put punched cards into a specific order?

2. What unit record machines can be used to perform calculations and provide results?

3. Why would a sorter and collator possibly be needed along with a computer?

4. Why would a calculator and accounting machine not be needed along with a computer?

5. Even if punched cards are to be filed immediately after they are punched, what is frequently done before they are filed?

6. Why is it important to file punched cards in a specific order?

7. Into what sequences can a sorter put a group of punched cards?

8. Briefly describe the sorting methods of sequencing, grouping, and selecting.

9. How many columns can be sorted at a time?

10. How are the pockets numbered, going from left to right?

11. If a card does not have anything punched in the column being sorted, what happens to the card?

12. What column of a numeric field is sorted first?

13. How are the cards placed into the feed hopper of the sorter?

14. Consider cards with the following numbers being sorted: 101, 764, 382, 987, 361. Which cards are in the
    0-pocket after the first sort?
    1-pocket after the first sort?
    0-pocket after the second sort?
    6-pocket after the second sort?
    3-pocket after the third sort?
    7-pocket after the third sort?
    8-pocket after the third sort?

15. Given that 9999 is the highest number in a group of cards. How many times would the cards have to be sorted?

16. If $99.99 were the highest amount on the cards, how many times would they have to be sorted?

17. Why does alphabetic sorting take twice as long as numeric sorting?

18. Which punch is read in the first sort for alphabetic data?

19. Cards with what letters fall into each of the following zone punches: 12-zone? 11-zone? 0-zone?

20. After the first sort, into which pocket would a card go if each of the following characters were in the column being sorted?

    A   S   J
    H   Y   P
    N   D   V

21. After the second sort, into which pocket would a card go if each of the following characters were in the column being sorted?

    A   J   S
    D   H   Y
    V   P   N

22. How many times would cards with three alphabetic characters have to be sorted in order for them to be in correct order?

23. Which character is sorted first in alphabetic sorting?

24. If 3-character alphabetic codes are in Columns 7–9, what column is sorted first, second, and last?

25. Where do the unwanted cards go during the selecting operation with the sorter?

26. What is the advantage of using the selecting operation?

27. Does the sorter require a control panel?

28. Briefly describe each of the functions of the collator.

29. Does the collator require a control panel?

30. When sequence checking, what does the collator do when it finds a card out of order?

31. How does the comparing operation work with the collator?

32. When the collator is set up for matching, what happens to a card that does not match?

33. What important point must be remembered before you can expect the collator to perform any of its operations correctly?

34. If you know that only a relatively few cards are out of order, should you use the sorter or the collator?

35. If you know that a relatively large number of the cards are out of order, should you use the sorter or the collator?

36. If selection is being done with several columns, should the sorter or collator be used?

37. Make illustrations like Fig. 8.4 to show the sorting sequence for cards with these two-digit numbers: 01   28   30   38   63   07   45   92   51   91   74   42; for cards with these 2 letter codes: DO   AN   BE   ON   GX   MJ   SO   AT   CO   FH   IT   ME.

PUNCHED CARD CALCULATION

Calculation may involve one or more of the mathematical processes of addition, subtraction, multiplication, and division. One form of calculator is a punched card machine. The data must first be placed on cards, frequently the cards must be reproduced, and usually they must be placed in a definite order or sequence. Calculators may be used in schools, for example, to calculate student grade point averages or in business to determine employees' earnings per week.

CALCULATOR OPERATIONS

The calculator can perform any combination of mathematical operations in any order. This is accomplished through the wiring in the control panel. The basic types of calculations it can perform are basic calculation, group calculation, and totaling calculation.

The calculator reads the data that has been punched on the cards, performs the necessary calculations, and punches the answers on the same card it is reading. Some models of calculators contain the reading section, calculating section, and punching section all within the one machine, as in Fig. 9.1. Its speed depends on the complexity of the problem and the number of digits being used; for example, a multiplying operation that involves a five-digit multiplier and punching up to 15 columns averages about 1700 cards an hour, or nearly 30 cards a minute. Other models of calculators consist of two separate units: the unit that reads and punches the cards, *the read-punch unit,* and the unit that performs the calculations, *the calculating unit.* They are connected by a cable.

Basic calculation is performing the required mathematical operations when all the necessary data are on the input card. The result is punched on the same card.

127

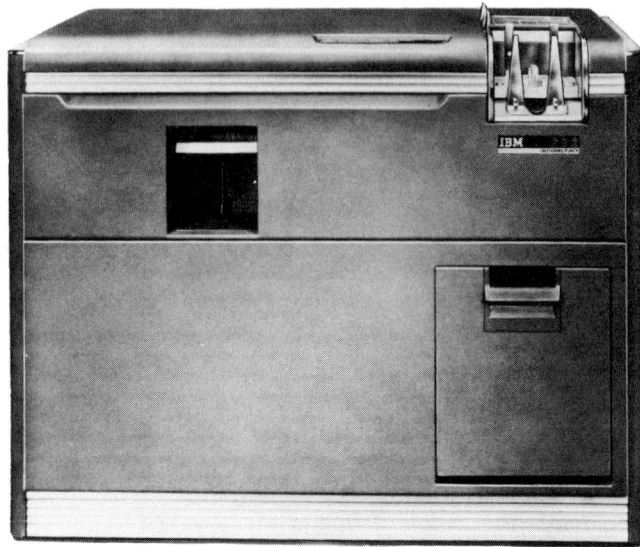

FIG. 9.1   IBM 602 calculating punch

Group calculation is used when all the required data for the calculation are not on each input card. Before processing the cards, some standard data that are the same for all the cards are punched on a separate card; this card is inserted first. For example, if each input card contains four items and the average of the amounts or numbers on each card is required, the first card would contain the number 4 so that the sum for each card would be divided by 4 to obtain the average.

Accumulated total calculation means that the *total* of each card is added, providing a running total of all the cards as they are processed.

PUNCHED CARD ACCOUNTING MACHINE

Summarizing, or *reporting,* includes the printing of the required results—all the other data processing functions have helped prepare the cards and data for this step. This summarizing or reporting is an extremely important function in a punched card system. For example, your name, social security number, hours worked, hourly rate, gross earnings, deductions, and net earnings for each week's work are of no use to you if they are merely punched on a card each week and

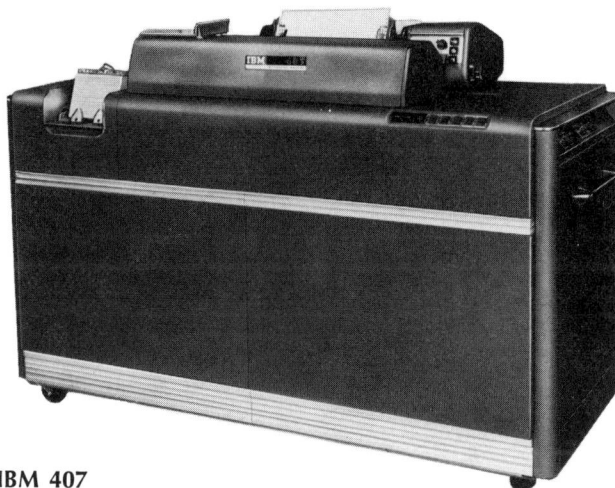

**FIG. 9.2 IBM 407
accounting machine**

placed in the company payroll files unless a check is printed after the calculations are made.

The machines that perform two functions, summarizing and reporting, are called tabulating machines. The machine commonly used for this purpose is the accounting machine as shown in Fig. 9.2. It reads the data punched on cards, adds and subtracts totals, and prints data. It can process from 50 to more than 150 cards a minute, depending on the operations required; it can print 150 lines a minute.

The printing operations of the accounting machine are classified as detail printing and group printing. *Detail printing* is sometimes called *listing* because it is actually printing or listing all the data that is on the punched card. There are several variations of detail printing, corresponding to the types of cards on the reproducer. We may have, for example,

80–80 printing: Printing on one line all the data from the punched card and printing it in the same order.

Partial printing: Leaving out part of the data from the punched card.

Rearranged printing: Changing the order of the data from that on
                             the punched card when printing.

Emitted printing: Adding data not on the punched cards, such
                             as dollar signs.

Group printing accumulates numbers and then prints the resulting total. It utilizes the capacity of the accounting machine to add and subtract. You can set it to count the number of cards being processed and then print the total after the last card has been processed. If you know the exact number of cards that should have been processed, you know immediately whether any cards are missing. You can also set it to add and subtract amounts on the cards and print only totals rather than individual amounts.

PRINTING ON A FORM

The accounting machine automatically prints in the correct position of the form and advances to a new form at the correct time. This is made possible by the use of standard forms that are attached to each other (continuous forms) with holes on both sides of the form. These holes fit over protruding parts of the cylinder which are called pins. This device makes the paper move evenly through the machine.

A special tape is used to control the forms so that they will be so positioned that the printing will be done on the correct line of each form. Each control tape is the same length as the form to be printed. Although its holes are in the center rather than on each side, it goes through the machine smoothly because it is narrow. Figure 9.3 shows the relationship between a form and the tape. Each horizontal line on the tape represents a place where a line can be printed on the form. When the last line of a form has been printed, the form and the tape move simultaneously until the tape gets to the code for a first line. The tape keeps rotating in the circular manner and is used with each form that is printed. This machine can use tapes of different lengths. Frequently several (two, three or four) tapes are placed together so that each one is not used so frequently and thus does not wear out so soon and have to be made again.

A convenient punching machine can be used to code the tape. The tape is guided so that it is in the correct position by the pin and index mark. A dial is used to indicate the column in which a punch should be placed. The punch is made by merely depressing the top of the machine just as you would in operating a stapler.

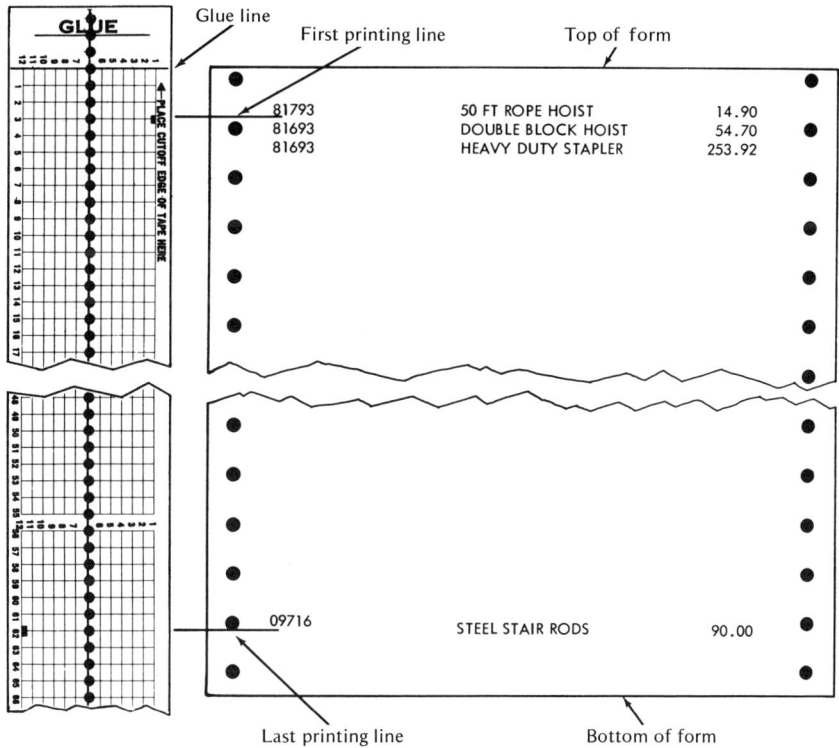

FIG. 9.3 Control tape coded to correspond to the required form

Labels in figure:
- GLUE
- Glue line
- First printing line
- Top of form
- PLACE CUTOFF EDGE OF TAPE HERE
- 81793 50 FT ROPE HOIST 14.90
- 81693 DOUBLE BLOCK HOIST 54.70
- 81693 HEAVY DUTY STAPLER 253.92
- 09716 STEEL STAIR RODS 90.00
- Last printing line
- Bottom of form

PRINTING MECHANISM

There is a print wheel containing all the letters, numbers, and special characters for each printing position on a line of a paper or form. If the machine has a maximum of 120 characters that can be printed on each line, there are 120 print wheels. Each print wheel needed to print the particular line is rotated to the correct position and the complete line is printed at one time. Each print wheel contains the 10 digits (0 through 9), the 26 alphabetic characters, and 11 special characters or symbols. The forms can be a maximum of 12 inches wide, with 120 characters; 10 characters can be printed per inch.

OTHER CALCULATING AND SUMMARIZING MACHINES

A computing-accounting machine is basically an accounting machine with a built-in computing device (so that it can multiply and divide as well as add and subtract). This machine combines the special abilities

FIG. 9.4 IBM electronic statistical machine

of both machines into one more efficient machine. The cards do not have to be processed by two separate machines when it is necessary to add, subtract, multiply, or divide and to also accumulate totals and prepare a summarized report. The calculator punches answers on the same card the input was on, but it does not print reports.

An electronic statistical machine, as shown in Fig. 9.4, combines some of the abilities of the sorter, collator, calculator, and accounting machine into one machine. It can sort, check the sequence, select, edit, count, accumulate totals, and print at a rate of 450 cards a minute.

**FIG. 9.5 IBM
5486 sorter**

PROCESSING THE 96-COLUMN CARD

The major processing of data with the 96-column card is performed by the central processing unit which is a computer and will be explained in the computer section. There is, however, a sorter available to put the cards in alphabetic or numeric order. It is a small unit which sits on a table top, as shown in Fig. 9.5. Its sorting speed is from 1000 to 1500 cards a minute, due to its photoelectric sensing device for reading the holes. Since it has only 6 stackers, it sorts the cards in a different sequence than does the 80-column card sorter. For example, in numeric sorting half of the cards go to stackers 1–5

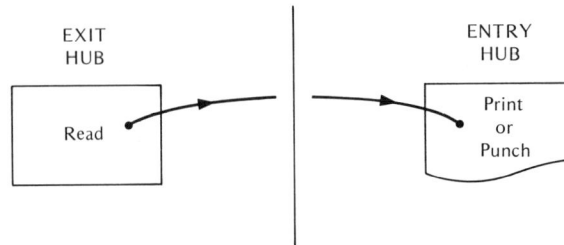

FIG. 9.6   Exit hub and entry hub

and the other half go to the 6th stacker. The cards are removed and the ones from the sixth stacker go into the individual stackers. In this way part of the cards are sorted one time, and part are sorted two times. Because the sorter operates at such a fast speed, this is still a relatively fast process.

MORE ON CONTROL PANELS

The control panel is sometimes called the *wiring board* or a *plug board*. The panel consists of rows of holes, each of which has a specific function. Each end of various wires is inserted into appropriate holes to make connections that will tell the machine specifically what to do. Wires are purchased in different lengths, such as 2", 3", 4", and even 12". Each length is a different color. If two holes in the board to be connected are close together, a short wire is used to avoid having extra wire in the way. The length of the wire and the color have no effect on the operation of the machine. They merely aid the person who is doing the wiring.

Each hole in the board is called a hub, either an exit hub or an entry hub. Exit hubs refer to the card that is being read. Entry hubs refer to the card that is being punched or paper that is being printed. An easy way to remember this is that data that are being read from a card are exiting from that card (exit hub), and data that are being punched or printed are entering that card or paper (entry hub). See Fig. 9.6. Technically, these terms refer to the fact that electrical current is received from the machine by the exit hub and sent through the wire to the entry hub and back into the machine.

The only IBM punched card machines that do not use a control panel are the keypunch machine, verifier, and sorter. Even these machines of some other manufacturers usually require a small amount of wiring.

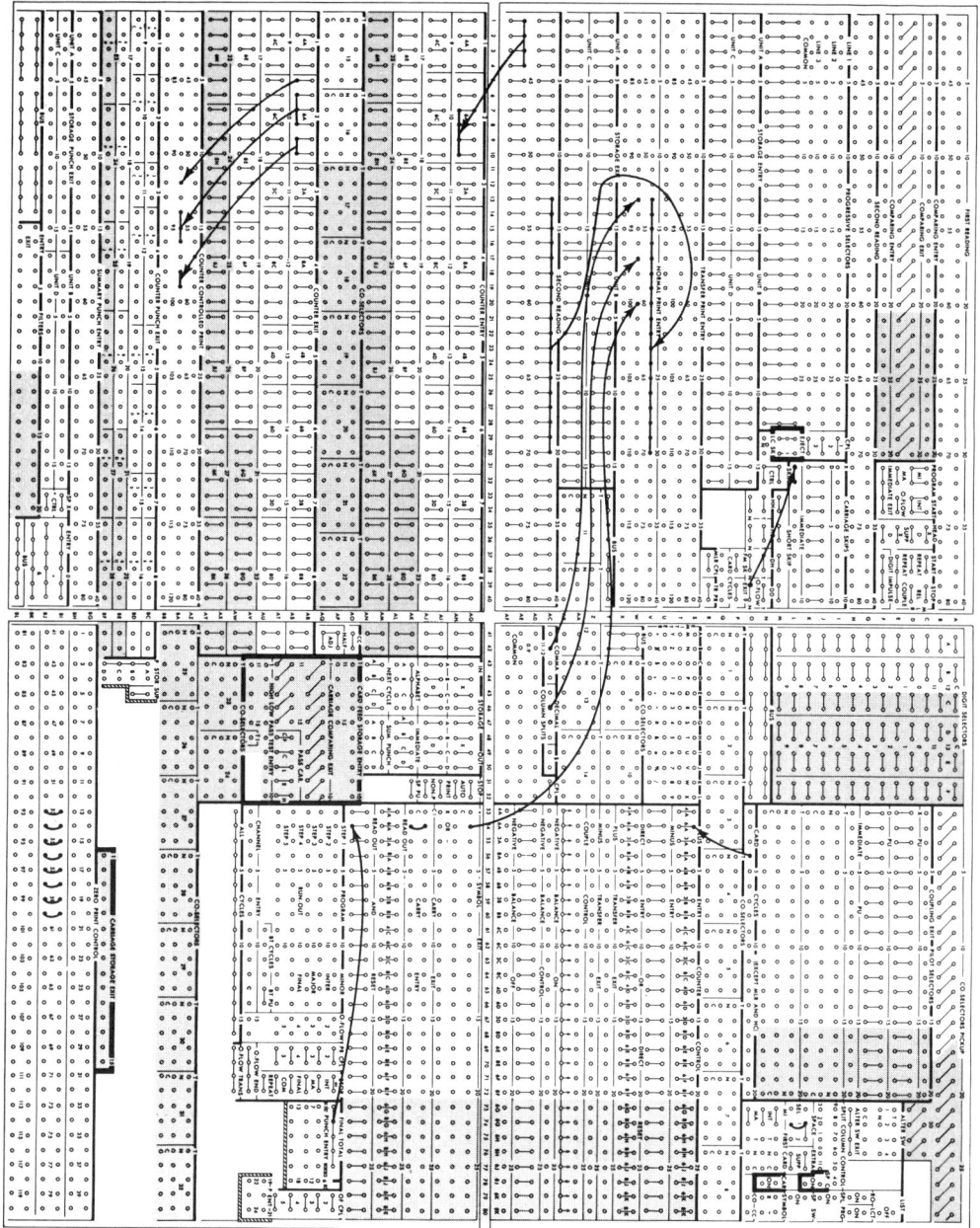

FIG. 9.7 Diagram for IBM 407 accounting machine

FIG. 9.8 Wired control panels IBM

Steps in Wiring

Wiring is difficult and is usually a separate job. The wirer must understand all the capabilities or functions of the specific machine, understand the job or problem to be wired, and be able to insert the wires at the correct places. Most wirers are able to wire several of the punched card machines.

Since each punched card machine has different functions, the details concerning the wiring are different. When planning the wiring of any machine, the person must consider three basic factors:

1. The original location of the data.
2. What is to be done with the data.
3. Where the results are to be punched and/or printed.

The person who does the wiring first plans how he will do it, using a diagram form that resembles the actual control panel, as in Fig. 9.7. This shows a part of an accounting machine job diagrammed. Figure 9.8 shows control panels for different unit record machines. The control panels for each type of punched card machine are of different sizes with the exit hubs and entry hubs labeled appropriately for the specific functions the machine can perform. Wiring diagrams are available for each control panel.

QUESTIONS AND PROBLEMS

1. Where does the punched card calculator place the answer to each problem?
2. When is basic calculation used?
3. When is group calculation used?
4. Why is summarizing such an important function in a data processing system?
5. What is the name of the commonly used tabulating machine?
6. What three basic things can the accounting machine do?
7. What is detail printing?
8. What is group printing?
9. How is the accounting machine's counting ability useful?
10. What controls the position of the forms?
11. If 120 characters can be printed on a line, how many print wheels are there?
12. What functions can an electronic statistical machine perform?
13. Why can the 96-column card sorter work so fast?
14. How many times does each column have to be sorted if numeric data is on the 96-column card?
15. What is the purpose of a control panel?
16. What other names are sometimes used rather than control panel?

17. What is the significance of the color of the wire?

18. What are the holes of the control panel called?

19. Which hubs refer to the cards that are being read?

20. Which hubs refer to the cards that are to be punched or paper being printed?

21. What IBM unit record machines do not need a control panel?

22. In order to prepare a control panel, what three things must a person understand?

23. When planning the wiring of a control panel, what three basic factors must you consider?

UNIT
RECORD
DATA
PROCESSING
SYSTEMS

CHAPTER 10

The IBM unit record data processing machines in use today (Fig. 10.1) far outnumber comparable machines made by all other manufacturers combined. Enough other equipment is in use, however, so that we should be familiar with it. We do not want to have the wrong impression—that IBM is the only manufacturer of unit record data processing machines. The larger of the other manufacturers of unit record data processing equipment are Sperry Rand and National Cash Register (NCR). With the exception of IBM, most other unit record manufacturers produce only the unit record equipment that is usually used along with their computers or other special machines.

FIG. 10.1 IBM
Unit record
installation

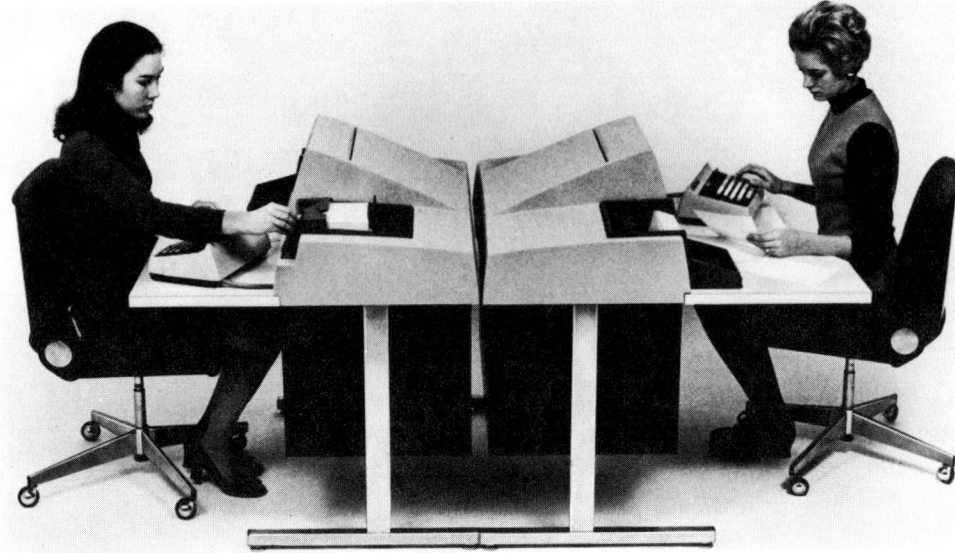

FIG. 10.2 Univac
keypunch machines

UNIVAC DIVISION OF SPERRY RAND

James Powers designed the first Univac unit record data processing equipment to use the 90-column card with round holes. The machines that were made to process these cards included a keypunch, verifier, sorter, collator, interpreter, reproducer, and accounting machine. So that the Univac machines could be used by companies that also used IBM and other equipment, Univac introduced a new series of machines in 1966 to process cards identical to IBM cards using the Hollerith coding system. This was a tremendous step forward toward standardization of punched cards. The 90-column card machines are now gradually being replaced by the new Univac unit record data processing machines that use the 80-column card with the Hollerith coding system.

Each Univac machine produces the same results as its comparable IBM machine, but some of the machines operate in a somewhat different way. Not only is each punched card a unit record to be used for further processing and producing reports, but card format and flowcharting of the entire job are determined in the same manner. Let us examine further the more important differences and similarities.

Univac 1501 Keypunch Machine

The operation of the Univac keypunch machine, shown in Fig. 10.2, is significantly different from that of the IBM keypunch. As you will recall,

On the IBM keypunch: Each character is punched onto the card as soon as the operator strikes the key.

On the Univac keypunch: All keys are depressed and the information is placed in the machine's electronic memory or *core storage*. After all the data have been inserted through the keyboard, the entire card is punched.

In the latter system, if the operator is aware of the fact that he has struck the wrong key, he can correct the mistake before the card is punched and ruined. He has only to backspace and depress the correct key. The Univac keypunch cannot print characters on the card, however.

Univac 1150-Verifier

The Univac Verifier, shown in Fig. 10.3, operates exactly like the Univac keypunch machine. After putting the punched cards into the machine, the operator depresses the keys so that each character transfers into the core storage. When all the data for one card have been inserted, the complete card is checked. If a card has no error, a notch is placed in the right-hand edge of the card. If there is an error, a notch is placed above the column containing the error.

Univac 2001 Sorter

The operation of the Univac sorter, shown in Fig. 10.4, is significantly different from that of the IBM sorter, but it performs the same functions. The Univac has a *connection panel*. The connection panel is permanent, but the wiring can be altered to sort specific column positions, specific codes, and specify the card stacker into which the cards will fall.* The Univac sorter contains 14 stackers rather than 13. The

---

* On the IBM sorter, the card stackers into which the cards fall cannot be altered.

FIG. 10.3   Univac
verifier

FIG. 10.4   Univac
sorter

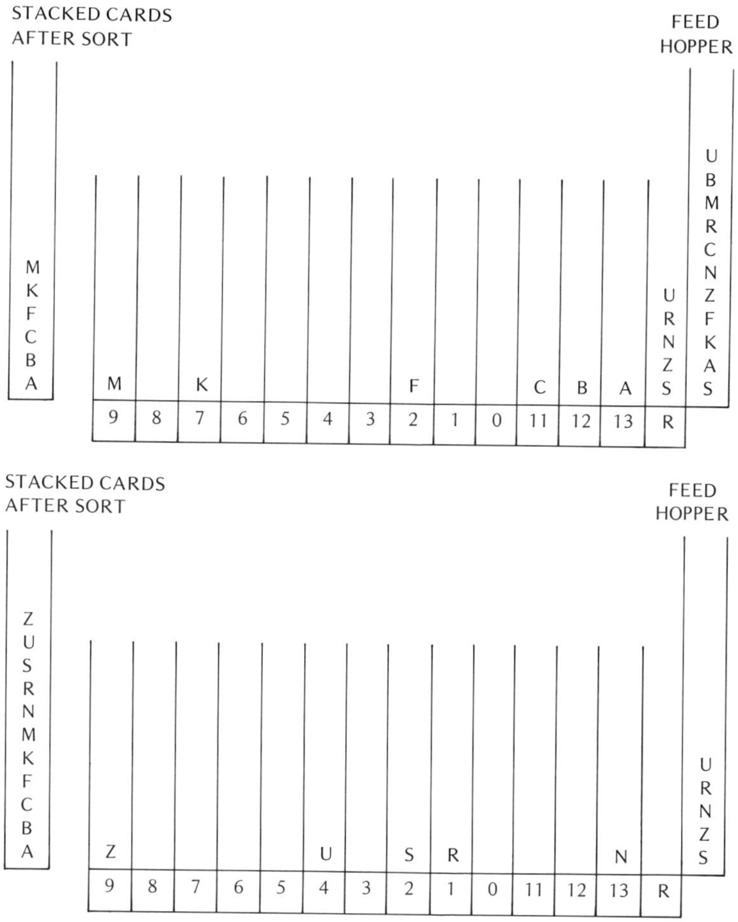

(a) AM button depressed

(b) NZ button depressed

FIG. 10.5 Alphabetic sorting by UNIVAC sorter

extra one is the number 13 just before the Reject stacker. It is used in alphabetic sorting.

   With numeric sorting, each card passes through the machine one time per column, just as it does on the IBM sorters. Cards with no punch or with two punches in the column being sorted go to the Reject stacker. A column indicator is used in a similar manner to indicate which column is to be sorted.

   In alphabetic sorting, the cards pass through the machine twice, but in a much different manner than in the IBM sorters. For the first

FIG. 10.6   Univac
interpreter

pass, Button AM on the control panel is depressed. Cards with the A code fall into Stacker 13, cards with the B code fall into Stacker 12, and so on until cards with the M code fall into Stacker 9. All cards with the N–Z codes fall into the Reject stacker. The cards in all stackers except the Reject stacker are removed in correct order and set aside. The Reject cards are sorted with the NZ button depressed. Cards with the N code fall into Stacker 13, cards with the 0 code fall into Stacker 12, and so on until cards with the Z code fall into Stacker 9. These cards are removed in correct order and placed with the A–M cards. As you see, only half the cards go through the machine more than once. Follow the steps in Fig. 10.5, sorting by just one letter so that you will understand how this sorter functions. As with the IBM sorters, sorting is done from right to left within the field being sorted.

Univac 2102 Interpreter

The Univac interpreter, shown in Fig. 10.6, operates very much like the IBM interpreters. The major difference is that it can print only one line across the top of the card, as in Fig. 10.7, whereas the IBM interpreters can print more than one line on the card. The Univac inter-

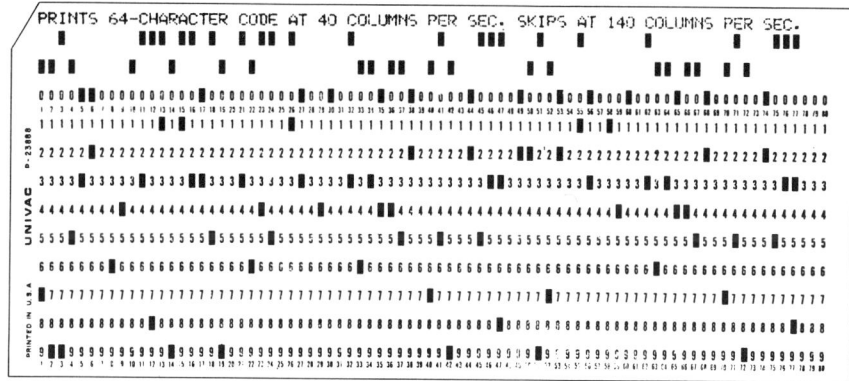

FIG. 10.7 Univac
interpreted card

preter is more important to its system than the IBM interpreter because it is the only way the characters can be printed—remember that
the Univac keypunch does not print.

Like the IBM interpreters, the Univac interpreter can be wired to
print only specified columns and also to insert symbols such as the
dollar-sign that were not punched.

NATIONAL CASH REGISTER PUNCHED CARD MACHINES

Although the National Cash Register Company (NCR) is best known
for cash registers, it also manufactures several punched card machines.
The most important punched card machines are the accounting machines; but the company produces other punched card machines that
frequently are needed along with the accounting machines—a keypunch and a sorter. These punched card machines are sold under the
NCR name but are actually produced by the Bull Company, the largest
French manufacturer of this type of equipment.

NCR Accounting Machines

NCR manufactures numerous types of accounting machines, each one
for a different type of user. The NCR electronic data processing system shown in Fig. 10.8 is one of its newer models. It consists of an
accounting machine (to the right) and a keypunch machine (to the
left). After the cards have been punched, they are read by the mechanism at the far right-hand side of the accounting machine. The operator can key in additional data on the accounting machine keyboard.
The results are automatically printed on the forms in the accounting

FIG. 10.8   NCR electronic data processing system

FIG. 10.9   NCR sorter

machine carriage and are automatically punched on the keypunch machine.

This machine is controlled by tape which is similar to paper tape but durable enough so that it can be used many times without tearing or wearing out. The tape reader controls the machine at a millisecond speed comparable to the speed of many computers. This accounting machine system processes data electronically rather than by mechanical or electro-mechanical means. This means that it stores and manipulates data in binary codes, and is operated by electrical impulses rather than actual moving machine parts. Although the machine uses an electronic means of processing data, similar to computers, it is considered a unit record or punched card machine because it uses punched cards as its input and part of its output.

NCR Keypunch Machine

The NCR keypunch machine (Fig. 10.8) can be operated separately from the accounting machine. It can print the characters, uses a program card, and in operation is similar to the IBM models.

NCR Sorter

The NCR sorter, shown in Fig. 10.9, sorts cards numerically and alphabetically, and, like the IBM sorter, requires two sorts per column. The major difference is that the pockets are in reverse order. Since the Reject pocket is at the left, the operator must remove the cards from left to right. The machine can sort as many as 550 cards a minute.

SPECIAL COMBINATIONS OF MACHINES

The various manufacturers of unit record equipment occasionally combine several machines into a special unit or system for a specific type of use. Such a system is the *billing system* which consists of an electric typewriter, a 10-key numeric keyboard, a calculating unit, and a card punch unit, as shown in Fig. 10.10. The operator types the customer data and the descriptions of the items purchased from a source document; then she inserts the prices and quantities on the 10-key numeric keyboard; the calculating unit performs the required calculations and automatically directs the typewriter to print the answer on the form. At the same time, the necessary data is being punched onto a card as a permanent record.

FIG. 10.10   IBM billing system

A data transmission system provides a method for transmitting data over the telephone lines. The sending station consists of a punched card reader, a numeric keyboard, and a telephone. The receiving station consists of a modified keypunch machine attached directly to the telephone lines. The person at the sending station dials the correct number and puts the punched cards through the punched card reading unit. He can also key in additional numbers using the numeric keyboard. The punched card code is converted into sounds that are transmitted through the telephone lines. No operator is needed at the receiving station. The machine automatically punches the required cards. This process is actually similar to the one used in reproducing punched cards, but the reproduced cards are in a different room, city, or state from the original cards. Data can be transmitted at a rate of about 12–15 characters a second.

PLANNING SYSTEMS

Each unit record machine performs one function or several variations of that function. Not one of these machines by itself can complete a job. The keypunch machine by itself is useless without other machines to process the punched cards; other machines cannot use cards unless they have been punched. These machines, then, are inter-related. The complete system must be planned very carefully in order to use the components efficiently and get the required results quickly and accurately.

Briefly stated, the steps you must follow in using unit record machines are:

1. Understand the problem completely.
2. Plan the solution to the problem.
3. Plan the format of the cards.
4. Work out the wiring diagrams.
5. Test the plan.
6. Check the test run.
7. Make any necessary changes or corrections.
8. Put the plan into operation.

Understanding the problem is extremely important. Be sure that you have a clear understanding of all the required results. If you begin using a plan that has not been studied carefully enough, some details may have been overlooked and the results may be incomplete or completely unusable.

When you plan the solution to the problem, you decide what machines should be used. Testing the plan is usually done with sample data, and the results are checked to see whether they are correct and whether they are complete. If any changes have to be made, the new plan should be tested and checked. Only after the plan has been perfected should the actual data be processed.

Functions Required in a Unit Record System

Each unit record data processing machine is used to perform one or more of the following operations:

Classifying	Duplicating	Calculating	Communicating
Recording	Sorting	Summarizing	Storing

Source data is usually *classified* by a code number assigned by a person. *Recording* of data is usually performed with the keypunch machine, although other methods such as optical scanning machines are beginning to be used. *Duplicating* data is done by using the interpreter or reproducer, depending on the required form of the duplicated data. A duplicate of a card can also be made on the keypunch machine immediately after the original card is punched, although this is a slower process.

Sorting of data on punched cards makes use of the sorter and/or the collator. Understanding the various operations of each of these two machines helps a person determine which one is more efficient for each particular job. Data is usually sorted before it is either filed or processed so that it is in some specific order. *Calculating* is performed with data recorded on punched cards by either the punched card calculator or the accounting machine. The machine to be used is determined by the requirements of each specific job. The ordinary accounting machine only adds and subtracts, although a special attachment can be used with it so that it can also multiply and divide.

For *summarizing* we use the accounting machine which condenses the data and gives us totals that we need. The machines themselves do not actually *communicate,* of course, but they do provide the data that are transferred to the people who will use it.

Storing is done in cabinets, drawers, and files specially designed for the punched cards. Several of the unit record machines, such as the sorter and collator, help get the data ready for storing or filing and help retrieve data when they are needed.

FLOWCHARTING

A graphic method has been developed for planning each application that uses unit record data processing equipment. The graphic method of illustrating the procedures in a data processing problem is flowcharting. It includes all steps in the complete operation, including the manual and mechanical.

Figure 10.11 shows the more common symbols and their uses. These symbols are used to identify the input, processing, and output. Their use makes it easier to read the chart and decreases the amount of writing or printing needed. The complete system can be easily seen and interpreted. Special symbols indicate the input-output media to

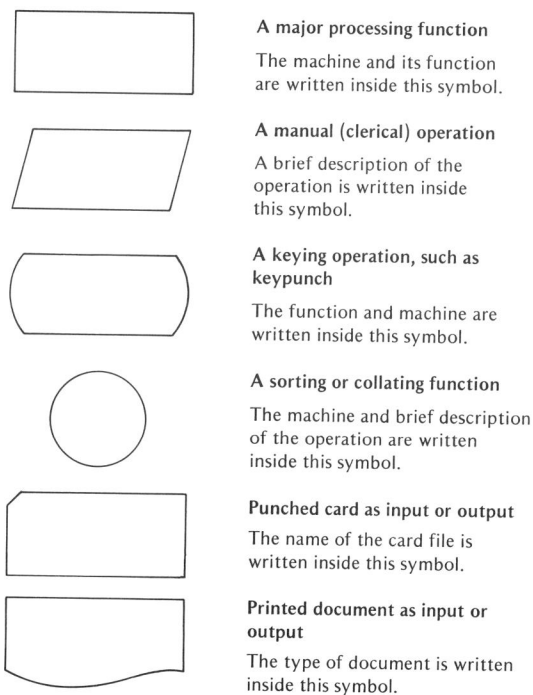

A major processing function

The machine and its function are written inside this symbol.

A manual (clerical) operation

A brief description of the operation is written inside this symbol.

A keying operation, such as keypunch

The function and machine are written inside this symbol.

A sorting or collating function

The machine and brief description of the operation are written inside this symbol.

Punched card as input or output

The name of the card file is written inside this symbol.

Printed document as input or output

The type of document is written inside this symbol.

FIG. 10.11 Flowchart symbols

be used; no words are necessary. Words have to be placed inside one of these symbols only to indicate the exact file, the format, or other details.

There are more symbols, but these are the only ones needed for most basic unit record applications. It does not take long to draw them because templates are used, as shown in Fig. 10.12. Many of the additional symbols shown on this template will be used when flow-charting computer problems. Most manufacturers use these standard-ized symbols and provide these plastic templates with the equipment.

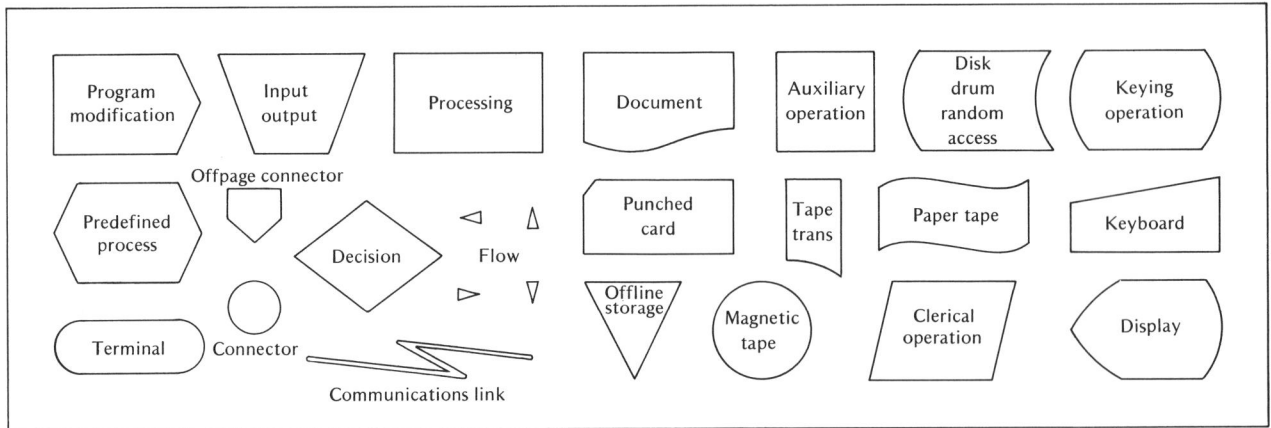

FIG. 10.12   Flowchart template

A Sample Flowchart

To illustrate that a flowchart is actually a chart of how one would ordinarily think through a problem, follow the arrows in the flowchart of Fig. 10.13. It shows the steps you would take in solving a math problem, working with and without a desk calculator.

The symbols in a flowchart are connected by arrows to show the direction to follow. The sample flowchart in Fig. 10.14 shows the machines used to prepare the bill to be sent to each customer who made a purchase. Although this flowchart does not show it, a calculation step would be needed if customers purchased more than one item.

The use of flowcharts also helps determine which of several methods is quicker. You can analyze each step and estimate how long the operation will take. The sum of the length of time each step will take for alternative flowchart solutions to the same problem will help you determine which flowchart to use. The fact that one flowchart contains fewer steps does not necessarily mean that it is the quickest method. Each step might take so long that another flowchart with more steps would actually represent the more efficient solution.

After the flowchart has been finalized, the details must be worked out. The format of each type of punched card must be determined very carefully so that the card can be used efficiently by each necessary machine. Each machine that uses a control panel must be wired and labeled so that it can be used each time this job is performed. If mistakes show up when the system is tested, each detail must be checked to determine where the error is; it may result, for example, from poor card format, wrong wiring, incorrect order of flowchart, or one of many other faults. After the error is found, you must determine whether less time and confusion would result if the existing procedures were modified or whether a completely new procedure should be planned.

Connector Symbols

Many flowcharts are rather long and do not fit on one column going down the sheet of paper. Connectors (see Fig. 10.15) are used to show where to continue. The round connector symbol is used when it re-

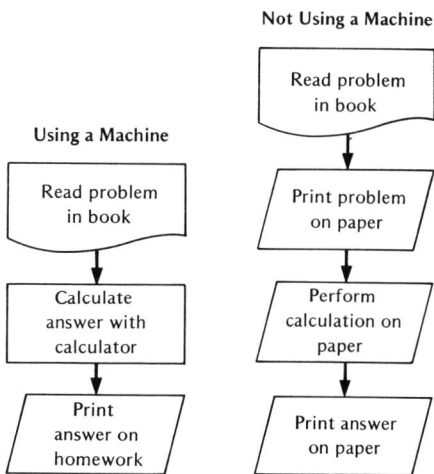

Not Using a Machine

Read problem
in book

↓

Print problem
on paper

↓

Perform
calculation on
paper

↓

Print answer
on paper

Using a Machine

Read problem
in book

↓

Calculate
answer with
calculator

↓

Print
answer on
homework

**FIG. 10.13 Flowchart
of math problem**

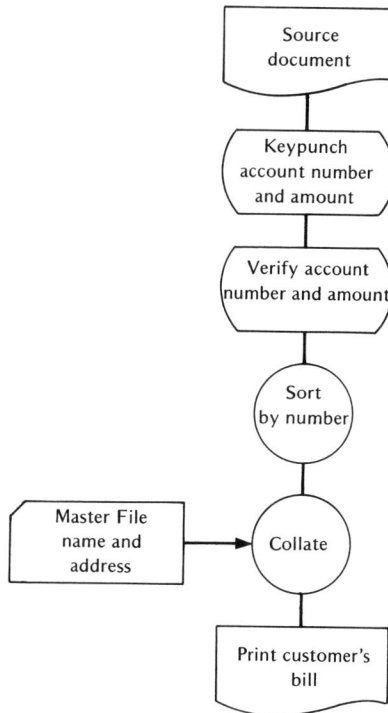

Source
document

↓

Keypunch
account number
and amount

↓

Verify account
number and amount

↓

Sort
by number

Master File
name and
address → Collate

↓

Print customer's
bill

**FIG. 10.14 Flowchart
of a business
problem**

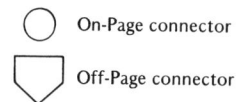

○ On-Page connector

▽ Off-Page connector

FIG. 10.15 Connectors

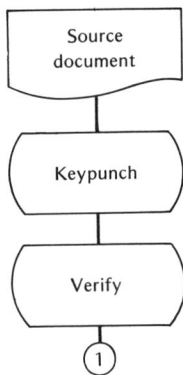

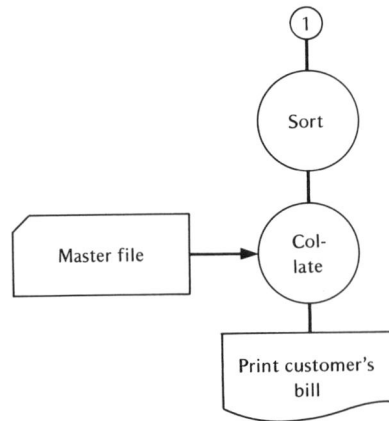

FIG. 10.16 Flowchart with a connector symbol

fers to another place on the same sheet of paper. The pointed connector is usually used to refer to another sheet of paper. The same number is used in each symbol to show which symbols connect to each other. Figure 10.16 shows an on-page connector. Sometimes letters are used rather than numbers inside these symbols. These symbols are especially helpful when we do more complex and longer computer flowcharts.

Types of Flowcharts

These flowcharts are called *systems flowcharts*. A systems flowchart shows the machines and other means used to process the data, beginning with the original source document and ending with the desired final results. It shows the flow of data through all the machines in the system. It specifies the order in which each machine must be used.

A *program flowchart* illustrates what must take place within a specific machine. It can be made and used for wiring some of the unit record data processing machines, but its most common use is with computer programming. A program flowchart is much more detailed and is sometimes referred to as a *technique flowchart*.

Jobs Available in Flowcharting

The person who designs the systems flowcharts for using unit record data processing machines is a *systems analyst*. He must have a complete understanding of the capabilities of each unit record data proc-

IBM — INTERNATIONAL BUSINESS MACHINES CORPORATION

JOB INSTRUCTIONS

FORM X 24-6298-1 — PRINTED IN U.S.A.

JOB NAME	JOB NO.	FREQUENCY	DUE IN	DUE OUT
Invoice Register	1	☐ Daily ☐ Monthly ■ Weekly ☐ Quarterly ☐ Bi-Weekly ☐ Annual ☐ Semi-Monthly ☐ Other	TIME 8:00 DATE Mon.	TIME 9:00 DATE Tues.

OPER. NO.	MACH. TYPE	ESTIMATED VOLUME	ESTIMATED TIME	DESCRIPTION
1.	26	1000	4.2	Key punch and verify sales cards from invoices. Invoice
	56	1000	4.0	No.: c.c. 1-5, Date: 6-10, Customer #: c.c. 11-15,
				Salesman #: 16-18, City: 19-21, State: 22-23, Item #:
				24-26, Quantity: 29-32, Sales Amount: 33-38, X in 39.
				File invoices after verifying.
2.	83	1000	.1	Sort cards on invoice number, c.c. 1-5.
3.	407	1000	.1	Prepare a detailed printed report - Invoice Register
4.	-	-	.1	Balance invoice register to batch total tapes of sales
				orders and post to control sheet.

Date: _____   Section ___1___   Page ___1___

640215MSP

FIG. 10.17 Job instruction sheet

essing machine and an understanding of all aspects of the problem that must be solved.

A few examples show why the systems analyst must know the special advantages of each of the unit record data processing machines.

1. The problem might be to decide whether to use the sorter or the collator to put stacks of cards in order. Let's assume two stacks al-

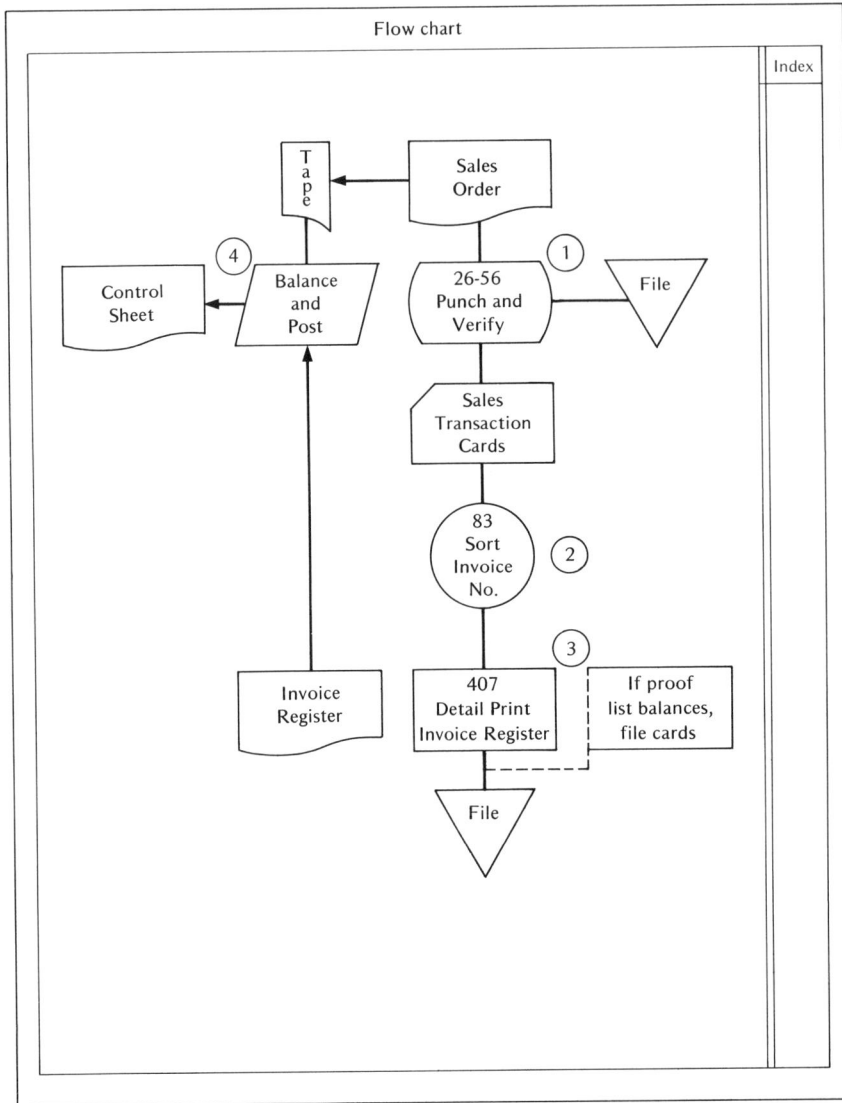

FIG. 10.18 Flowchart sheet

ready in order must be merged. In this case, the collator should be used since it would take less time. If it were known, however, that some of the cards were out of order, then it would probably take less time to use the sorter.

2. As we have seen, either the reproducer or the keypunch machine can be used to duplicate cards. Several points must be considered in deciding which to use. If the originals have already been punched, it would probably be easier to use the reproducer. However, if only a few are needed, it might be quicker to use the keypunch than to wire the control panel for the reproducer.

The person who schedules the people and the unit record machines is the *manager of data processing operations*. In smaller installations, he also performs the duties of a systems analyst. His first step usually is to complete a Job Instruction Sheet, as shown in Fig. 10.17, and to place the completed flowchart on a Flowchart Form as shown in Fig. 10.18. Note the details at the top of the Job Instruction Sheet; they assist the machine operators. Especially important is the "Due Out" so that the time when the job must be completed is clearly stated. As we have seen, the Estimated Time column at the left is helpful to the person who must decide among several methods, and, once the decision has been made, helps the person who schedules the workers and the machines.

QUESTIONS AND PROBLEMS

1. In addition to IBM, what other large manufacturers of unit record machines are there?
2. Why did Univac introduce a new series of unit record machines in 1966?
3. In what ways is the Univac keypunch machine different from the IBM keypunch machines?
4. Why is the way the Univac keypunch punches data for the entire card all at once an advantage?
5. What functions does the Univac sorter connection panel serve?
6. Does the Univac sorter operate differently from the IBM sorter for numeric sorting? If so, explain briefly.
7. Does the Univac sorter operate differently from the IBM sorter for alphabetic sorting? If so, explain briefly.
8. What is the major difference between the Univac interpreter and the IBM interpreter?
9. Why is the Univac interpreter so important?
10. What company produces the NCR unit record machines?
11. What is the most important NCR unit record machine?

12. What is the major difference between the NCR sorter and the IBM sorter?

13. Can any unit record machine by itself perform a job useful to business?

14. List the basic steps that must be followed when planning each application, using unit record machines.

15. List the unit record machine or machines that can be used to perform each of the following data processing functions:

    Classifying   Calculating
    Recording   Summarizing
    Duplicating   Communicating
    Sorting   Storage

16. Draw the flowchart symbol used for each of the following functions:

    Keying operation   Sorting or collating
    Major processing   A manual (clerical) operation
    Punched card as I/0   Printed document as I/0

17. In what ways does the use of these flowchart symbols help?

18. How do we indicate the direction to follow on a flowchart?

19. Does the fact that one flowchart contains fewer symbols than another flowchart for the same problem mean that it is the quicker method? Explain your answer.

20. What must be determined when an error is found in a system?

21. What is the purpose of connector symbols on flowcharts?

22. What is a systems flowchart?

23. What is a program flowchart?

24. What is the title of the person who designs systems flowcharts both for unit record and computer systems?

25. What is the title of the person who schedules the people and the unit record machines?

26. What are two uses of the Estimated Time column on the Job Instruction Sheet?

PART III

ELECTRONIC DATA PROCESSING: THE COMPUTER

INTRODUCTION
TO
COMPUTER
DATA
PROCESSING

CHAPTER 11

The oldest computer is not much older than the average high-school or college student. The study of computers is a relatively new addition to the curricula of schools and colleges. Teaching is further complicated because many minute and detailed operations of the computers are constantly being improved and changed. Most of the fundamentals which we will study remain essentially the same, however.

We might begin by defining the computer as a device that is capable of processing data by executing a predetermined sequence of instructions; the processing includes performing mathematical operations, manipulating input and output devices, editing, and making decisions. All the unit record machines that we have been studying can process data by executing a predetermined sequence of instruction. For the unit record equipment, this sequence of instructions was communicated to the machine by the wired control panel, buttons, and dials. So far the unit record equipment fits the first part of the definition of a computer. However, we find the difference in the second part of the explanation: that the computer's processing includes mathematical operations, manipulating input and output devices, editing, and making decisions. Using a combination of unit record machines, we could accomplish these functions, but we would have to move the punched cards from machine to machine. The computer performs all these operations automatically.

COMPUTER SYSTEM

When using the word computer, we are actually referring to a computer system, several machines that automatically work together. The three basic units of the computer are

1. An *input unit* which feeds data into the computer,

FIG. 11.1 IBM computer room scene

2. A *processing unit* which both stores data and instructions and converts the data into the required results, and

3. An *output unit* which records the results.

The input unit can be one that reads punched cards, tape, or even printed words on paper. Since more than one input method can be used, more than one input machine might be needed in a computer system.

The processing unit, called the *central processor* (computer itself), performs several functions. It receives the instructions and the data from the input unit and keeps them until they are needed. It uses the instructions to direct itself in performing the required mathematical calculations on the data. It also directs the required results to the output unit.

The instructions which control the operation of a computer are called the *program*. A computer program consists of many individual steps which must be followed in correct order to obtain the required results. Each step is designated by a code symbol the machine can utilize. The computer keeps the program in its storage, or memory,

FIG. 11.2 IBM system/360 Model 20

section. One instruction at a time is used by the control unit. The control section interprets the individual instructions and directs what is to be done by one of the units. It might tell the input unit to accept some new data, it might tell the computation section to make a computation, or it might tell the output unit to record some data. When each instruction has been carried out, the computer interprets the next instruction and so on until the entire job has been completed.

The output unit can be one that records the data on paper, cards, or tape. As with the input, more than one output method can be used, so more than one output machine might be needed (Fig. 11.2). One machine can handle both the reading and the punching of cards since it functions as both an input and output unit. The printer can function only as an output unit.

In the computer system shown in Fig. 11.2, there are actually four machines: a card reader-punch, a central processor, a printer, and a magnetic tape machine. In this system two input methods are used: punched cards and magnetic tape. Three output methods are used: punched cards, magnetic tape, and printed forms. A computer system can have other input and output media, such as magnetic disks. The disk storage might be substituted in place of the magnetic tape device, but seldom does a computer system not have a card reader and/or a printer. The input/output units are connected to the central processing unit by means of cables under the floor, so that they are not hazardous to people walking in the area.

Since a computer is operated electronically, it is frequently called an *electronic computer,* and processing data with a computer is called *electronic data processing.* In mechanical and unit record data processing machines, moving parts perform the calculations and other functions. The electronic impulses used by the electronic computers are much faster than moving mechanisms. Consequently the computer processes data much faster than punched card machines. In the computer the input media reads the data, converts the source material to electronic impulses, and stores and processes it in the central processing unit of the computer.

COMPUTER HARDWARE, SOFTWARE, AND PEOPLEWARE

The basic elements of a computer system include its equipment, its procedures, its programs of instruction, and the personnel. A system is actually a combination of equipment and procedures which will produce a desired result efficiently and economically.

The computer hardware consists of the physical equipment, the mechanical, magnetic, electrical, and electronic devices. *Computer hardware* performs the operations of data preparation, data input, data storage, data control and computation, and data output. With the exception of data preparation, these operations are performed by the input and output devices and the central processing unit. The data preparation is usually performed by equipment not attached to the central processing unit and is referred to as *off-line equipment;* all components attached to and controlled by the central processing unit are referred to as *on-line equipment.*

The *computer software* consists of the programs and routines associated with a computer (compilers, library routines) and all the documents associated with a computer (manuals, circuit diagrams). It is through proper preparation and use of the computer software that the computer user is able to take full advantage of its capabilities. The computer manufacturer provides some programs for certain general types of tasks needed by many of its users. Most programs are written by the specific user for his various projects.

The *computer peopleware* consist primarily of the computer operators, programmers, and systems analysts. Although other personnel are also important to the entire system, these are the ones who are directly responsible for achieving the desired results from the computer.

BASE 2 MATH SYSTEM

The coding system for representing letters, numbers, and symbols within the computer is different from the one used by the processors of punched cards. Since the computer functions by means of electronic charges, it is possible to turn the power for each storage cell off or on, just as you would an electric light bulb. If one storage cell's power is not turned on, it represents the value "zero"; if it is turned on, it represents the value "one." The base 2 numbering system consists of two digits, the zero and one, so it is the basic storage method used by the computer. It will be explained in greater detail in Chapter 14.

FLOW OF DATA

Data flow through a computer system as shown in Fig. 11.3. Follow the arrows carefully. An input device reads the data and passes information to the control section of the central processing unit. The control section directs the data to the correct storage locations. When specific data are needed, the control section gets the information from storage and directs it to the processing section. The control section also directs the processing section to perform the correct calculations. Then the control section directs the results of the processing back to the correct storage locations. When some data are to be recorded on one of the output devices, the control section directs the correct data out of storage and to the output unit.

This seems like a slow process, but today's newer computers can perform each step in a program at a speed so fast that it is measured in nanoseconds. A *nanosecond* is a billionth of a second. Proportion-

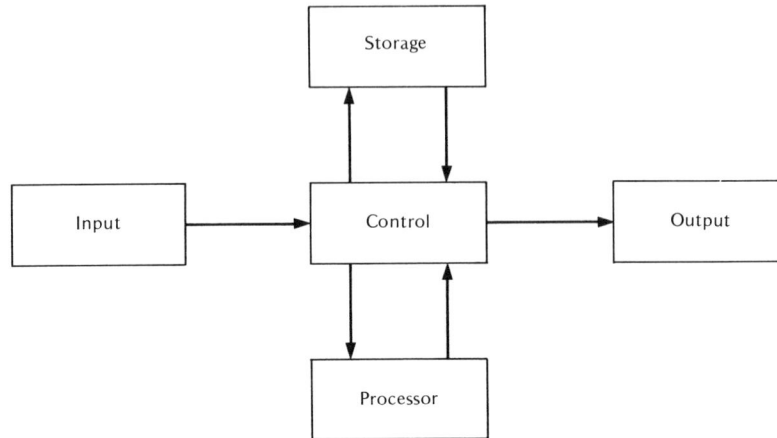

FIG. 11.3 Flow of data through a computer system

ately, a nanosecond is to a second as a second is to about 11,574 days, or almost 32 years.

TYPES OF COMPUTERS

The digital and the analog are the two basic types of electronic computers. An analog computer measures physical qualities such as pressure, temperature, voltage, or current, and converts them into measurable numeric quantities (just as a thermometer converts temperature into degrees designated by a number). Computations are performed by combining these quantities; simple circuits are built to add, subtract, multiply, divide, and in other ways combine these quantities electrically. Networks of these circuits solve very complex mathematical expressions. Analog computers are best suited for problems where the inputs and outputs are complex functions, and in problems where a system being studied is producing the inputs as a direct result and reaction to its previous outputs. This type of computer is used primarily for scientific and engineering work. An analog computer can change the course of a missile by interpreting the results of measuring its speed, the air resistance, and other factors. The accuracy of an analog computer is limited to the precision with which voltage can be measured; accuracy of greater than .001 is difficult.

The greater accuracy possible with the digital computer makes it advantageous for business applications. It counts with numbers to represent specific quantities such as dollars, cents, and hours. Its input is definite numeric values, rather than measurements. A digital computer can work to any required accuracy, such as .00001 and greater, by merely using as many digits as needed. It can be programmed to carry the solutions to as many decimal places as necessary.

Not all digital computers are used for business applications, however. Some are used to solve complex formulas for engineering and research. A programmer for problems of this kind must have a good mathematical and scientific background. The scientist or engineer must sometimes do this programming himself because the problems are so highly technical. A digital computer can be made to act as an analog computer by equipping it with devices to convert the analog input to a digital form and convert the digital output back to its analog form.

A third type of computer is actually a combination of the analog and the digital computer. This *hybrid* computer combines the best features of an analog and of a digital computer. It is not designed to take the place of either the analog or the digital computer, but for a newer and rapidly increasing number of applications for which neither the analog nor the digital computer is practical. The hybrid computer solves problems with greater accuracy than the analog computer and with more speed than the digital computer. It combines the advantageous speed of the analog computer and the accuracy of the digital computer; the capabilities of one system compensate for the limitations of the other. Many engineering and scientific problems are best solved with a hybrid computer system. In the past, such problems were solved by running some parts on an analog computer and other parts, on a digital. The hybrid gives accurate results in the most economical way. Many problems now being handled by the hybrid computer presented obstacles previously because they were too complex for the analog computer and too time-consuming for the digital computer.

DIGITAL COMPUTERS

A digital computer that is used in solving business problems is used in a different way for scientific problems. The differences frequently lie in the

1. number of times the program is used,

2. importance of speed of the program,

3. quantity of input,

4. amount of processing, and

5. quantity of output.

A scientific program might be used once to solve one series of problems and not be needed again; or it might be used many times. Most
business programs, however, are used frequently—every day, week, or
month—over and over again. For example, the same instructions are
followed to compute each student's grade point average or every employee's earnings and record the results of each computation.

As we have seen, there are numerous procedures that could be
followed to solve any one problem. It is particularly important to
select the best for business use, since this program will be used so
many times. If one procedure completes each student's grade report
in 4 seconds and another procedure completes it in 5 seconds, the
shorter method takes 50 minutes less if there are 3000 students. If a
large company has several thousand employees' pay checks to process
each week, a small saving per unit is important.

A large quantity of input is usually needed for business problems
—such as each student's report card data. Fast methods of input are
needed, and frequently two or more input media are needed. For
scientific problems, a much smaller quantity of input is usually needed
—just the technical data for solving one problem.

Once the input has been accepted by the computer, the processing of a business problem requires very few math computations for
each person's data, but the same computations must be made over
and over again for the large number of persons involved. The processing of a scientific problem, by contrast, often requires extensive computations to produce the required results.

A large amount of output is required for a business problem, such
as a permanent record on magnetic tape and a printed check for each
person's data. For a scientific problem, the output is usually just a
printed answer to the problem showing all the calculations that were
done by the computer.

The reasons for business and scientific uses of digital computers
are apparent now. Most business problems are not very difficult for
a person to perform manually or mechanically. In fact, they are
handled this way in very small business firms. When the problem must
be performed many times in a large business firm, it can be done much

more rapidly and accurately by computer. Modern scientific problems present complications and formulas that would be extremely difficult for a person to solve manually or mechanically. The computer does this work not only more quickly, but also more accurately.

Some of the largest banks, utility companies, and insurance companies have more than a million customers. Two important advantages of using computers can certainly be realized in such cases. Magnetic tape storage devices eliminate the need for a building full of storage cabinets and individual records, and each account can be updated in less than a second rather in the several minutes it would take for a person to do the same work.

CLASSIFICATIONS OF COMPUTERS

Computers are frequently classified as either general purpose or special purpose computers. General purpose computers are basically similar in their arrangement and their logical design although they differ in some details. They can perform a variety of jobs as programmed. Because they are manufactured on a large scale, they cost less than special purpose computers and have had more extensive testing during their design and production to eliminate "bugs." Both analog and digital computers can be general purpose machines.

Although a special purpose computer is designed and built for a specific operation, it incorporates many of the features of a general purpose computer. It usually lacks the flexibility of a general purpose machine, and, of course, the special designing costs and custom production make it relatively expensive. Special purpose computers are used to advantage by public utility companies for preparing customer bills and by the telephone system for direct dialing. In recent years they have been put into use for air traffic control and airline reservation systems; they have also been adapted to serve as a clearinghouse system for processing checks.

Although these examples of special purpose computers are digital computers, analog computers can also be made for special purposes. Some are advantageously used in manufacturing operations such as steel making and oil refining. At the present time, most hybrid computers are special purpose machines. They can be designed to simulate testing situations to avoid the time and expense of testing under actual conditions. They have been useful, for example, in projects designed to improve rubber production. In a water pollution study, the simulation was able to show in 1 second what would actually happen in 12 hours. When the speed of the computer was moved from "slow" to "fast," the computer took only 1/500 of a second to show what would happen in 12 hours.

PROGRAMMING REQUIRED

The computer is not a mysterious "genius" as some people seem to think. If it is not programmed correctly, the results are meaningless and can cause much confusion and wasted time. It cannot answer a question like "Should the company be dissolved?" It can merely show the figures that report operating figures for past years or project such figures for future periods. A person using such figures must answer the question. Before the computer can even produce these figures, it must be given raw data and told exactly how to treat the information—told in a step-by-step procedure. This, too, is the job of a person, the computer programmer. Not only must the programmer have a complete understanding of the problem and required results, but he must also have a general understanding of how the computer works.

QUESTIONS AND PROBLEMS

1. What is a computer?
2. Basically, how do computers differ from unit record machines?
3. List the three basic units of a computer system.
4. List the functions performed by the processing unit.
5. Where does the computer keep the program of instructions?
6. Why are the cables connecting the units of the computer together under the floor?
7. Why is processing data with a computer frequently called electronic data processing?
8. Why are computers so much faster than mechanical and unit record machines?
9. What comprises computer hardware?
10. What does the term "on-line" mean?
11. Basically, what does computer "software" comprise?
12. What do we mean by "computer peopleware"?
13. List six ways the control section directs the data in the computer.

14. What is a nanosecond? How does it compare to a second?

15. Explain the basic differences between an analog and a digital computer.

16. Which type of computer is most appropriate for business applications?

17. Briefly explain the differences that frequently exist between the business and scientific applications of digital computers.

18. How can a digital computer be made to act like an analog computer?

19. What is the basic purpose of the hybrid computer?

20. What types of problems are frequently solved best with a hybrid computer?

21. Why is the computer advantageous for business problems?

22. Why is the computer advantageous for scientific problems?

23. What is the job classification of the person who makes up the step-by-step procedures for the computer to follow?

24. List the advantages of the general purpose computer.

25. What are the primary disadvantages of the special purpose computer?

26. When is it advantageous to have a special purpose computer?

DEVELOPMENT
OF
COMPUTERS

CHAPTER 12

As you recall, data processing was developed to speed up the handling of data. During and after World War II the demand grew as a result of increased manufacturing, increased government demands for reports, and increased demands from research and development. By the 1940's, most of the machines that process punched cards had been introduced. The limitations of the punched card machines led to figuring out ways of improving the handling of data and solving of complex problems. Obviously, having one set of controls operate all the functions would be an advantage over having to take the cards to separate machines to have each specific function performed. Some of the important developments are still credited to one person employed by a company, but others are credited only to the company, largely because several people worked on the idea together.

The first important development was a machine designed to improve upon punched card machines that could perform only one operation at a time. This marked the beginning of the evolution of the stored-program concept. The machine was merely named the IBM Model 604. The program was determined by wiring a plug board, necessitating a different board for each program. To solve this wiring problem, IBM's Card-Programmed Calculator (CPC) was designed to use a deck of punched cards to determine the sequence of operations. A code on each card directed the machine to perform a specific operation. This development eliminated the need for a different plug board for each problem.

Having the program on punched cards helped Aiken complete the first programmed computer to operate successfully. In 1944 he completed the Mark I at Harvard University with the help of IBM. It could read instructions on punched paper tape, refer to any tables stored in it, and extract data necessary for solving a problem. It could be adapted to solve problems for engineers and mathematicians. The calculating elements consisted of mechanical counters driven through

172

FIG. 12.1 Portion of Babbage's analytical engine (front view) Courtesy British Crown Copyright Science Museum, London

electromagnetic clutches controlled by electro-mechanical relay circuits. It was the first machine to solve a long series of arithmetic and logical functions.

The next development was the completion in 1946 of the Eniac (Electronic Numerical Integerator and Calculator) by Mauchly and Eckert. At that time, the press referred to it as the "mechanical brain" because it was so fast in working out long calculations. Although it did not greatly improve upon the Mark I, it used vacuum tubes and was the first electronic computer. Its proponents experienced many difficulties, but it was successful. At that time vacuum tubes were not very reliable. The machine used more than 18,000 of these tubes, and all of them had to be working for the machine to function properly. This machine was needed during World War II to produce the mathematical tables that were required for firing projectiles. It was completed rather late to do much good for this purpose, but it did represent an advancement in computer technology. Many wires had to be plugged in manually to make each unit perform its operations.

Then Neumann, a well-known mathematician, introduced a central control for this machine, which eliminated the need for special wiring for each program. Codes could be stored in its memory, and Eniac became the first stored program machine. A stored program means that the instructions, or detailed steps for solving a problem, are kept inside the computer's memory unit. This capability allows a computer to work faster than previous models for which each instruction had to be read from a punched card or from punched paper tape.

In 1946 Eckert and Mauchly started the Eckert Mauchly Corporation and started to develop Univac. Their company later became a division of Sperry Rand Corporation. Sperry-Rand completed the Universal Automatic Computer (Univac). The Univac I, introduced in the mid 1950's, was the first computer system designed for commercial business problems. Shortly thereafter, IBM introduced its model 650 for business problems. Thus began the more widespread use of business computers.

Several of the early foreign computers were the Madam (Manchester Automatic Digital Machine) which was constructed at the University of Manchester in England; and the Sec (Simple Electronic Computer) which was constructed at the University of London.

By 1960 more than 60 different models of computers were available for business problems. By 1965 more than 20,000 computers were being used to perform data processing operations in business in the United States. By 1968 more than 47,000 computers had been installed in offices, hospitals, and schools. In 1970 some 60,000 to 70,000 computers were in use solving business problems. Remember that the first business computer was introduced as late as 1954.

COMPUTER GENERATIONS

The use of computers grew at a relatively slow rate during their beginning years; now this growth continues at a rapidly accelerating rate. As advances take place in computer technology, each major change is classified as a new generation of computers. Since their slow beginning in the 1940's and 1950's, three distinct generations have already been seen.

The first generation of computers used vacuum tubes and relays. These components resulted in very large machines which required great amounts of air conditioning to keep them cool enough to function. Their operating speed was measured in thousandths of a second (milliseconds), which seems relatively slow now. (A millisecond is to a second as a second is to about 17 minutes.)

The second generation of computers used transistors rather than vacuum tubes and relays. This development had several advantages: The computers could be smaller, required less air conditioning, had a faster operating speed, and required less maintenance. Most of these computers worked at a speed measured in millionths of a second (microseconds). (A microsecond is to a second as a second is to about 278 hours, or 11½ days.)

The third generation of computers began to be used in the mid-1960's. They used monolithic circuit techniques which had been developed in the United States space programs. This resulted in another increase in speed, and the work is measured now in billionths of a second (nanoseconds). They also provide greater accuracy and reliability. (A nanosecond is to a second as a second is to about 11,574 days, or almost 32 years.)

SIZES OF COMPUTERS

Computer systems are classified as either large-scale, medium-scale, or small-scale, depending on how fast they can handle data and the variety of operations they can perform. Large-scale computers are extremely fast and can handle a variety of operations; their rental ranges from about $50,000 to more than $100,000 a month. Medium-scale computers are not so fast and cannot handle quite so many operations; their rental ranges from about $12,000 to $50,000 a month. The small-scale computers are somewhat limited in the operations that they can handle and are the slowest; their monthly rental ranges from slightly less than $1,000 to about $8,000 a month. Figures 12.2 through 12.8 show samples of each general size category of computers. The size of the storage capacity in the central processing unit also helps to determine the classification and monthly rental cost of a computer.

The size categories of special purpose computers are determined by their speed and storage capacity, not by the varieties of operations they can perform, since each type is made for a specified purpose or reason.

FIG. 12.2 New small-scale computer — Honeywell Systems Model 115/2

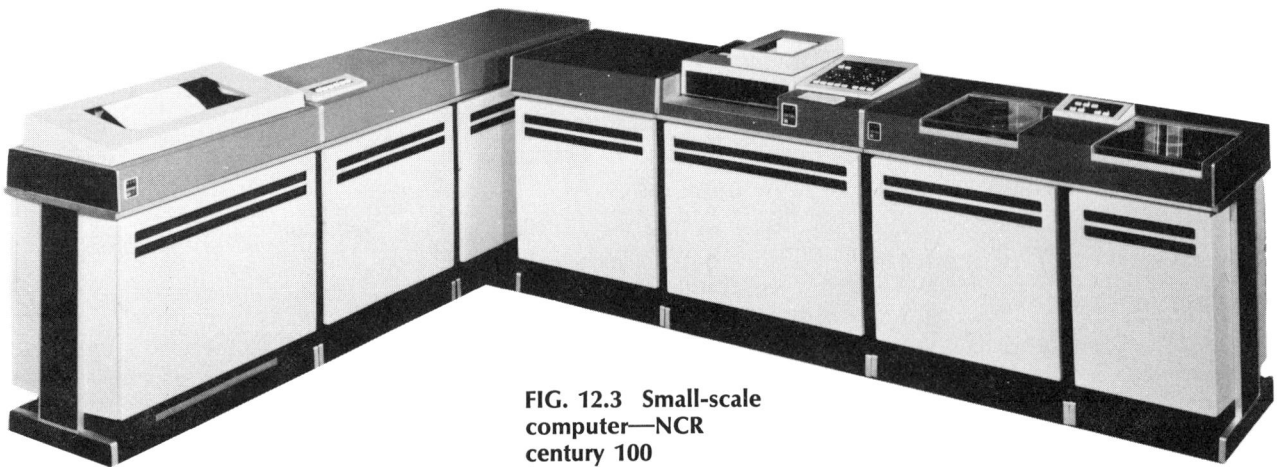

FIG. 12.3 Small-scale computer—NCR century 100

FIG. 12.4 Medium-scale computer—NCR century 300

FIG. 12.5 Medium-scale computer—IBM systems S/360 model 30 (with peripheral units)

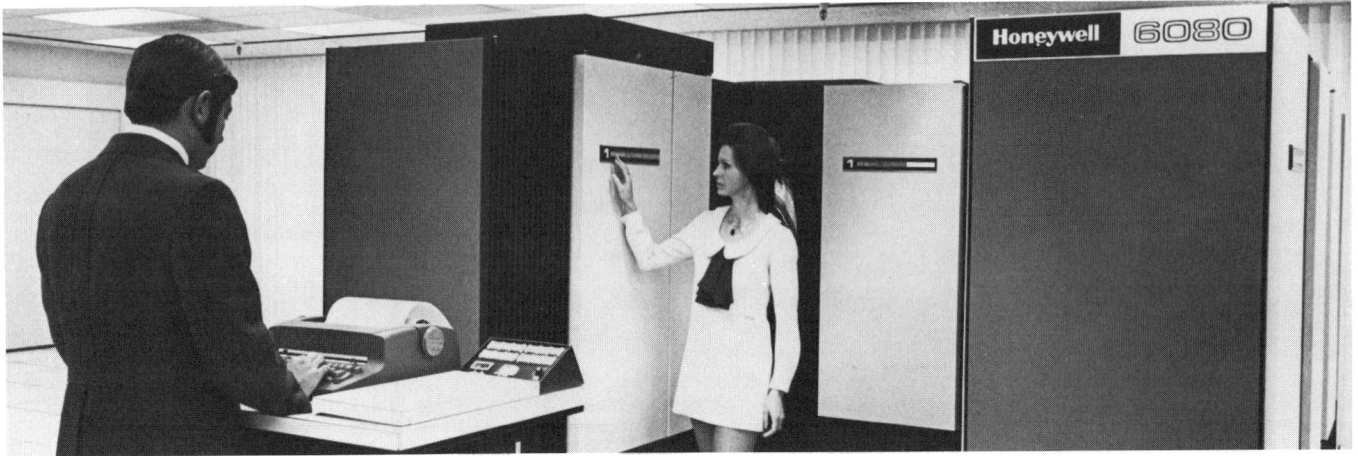

FIG. 12.6   Multi-dimensional processing—Honeywell

FIG. 12.7   IBM System/3 96-column card

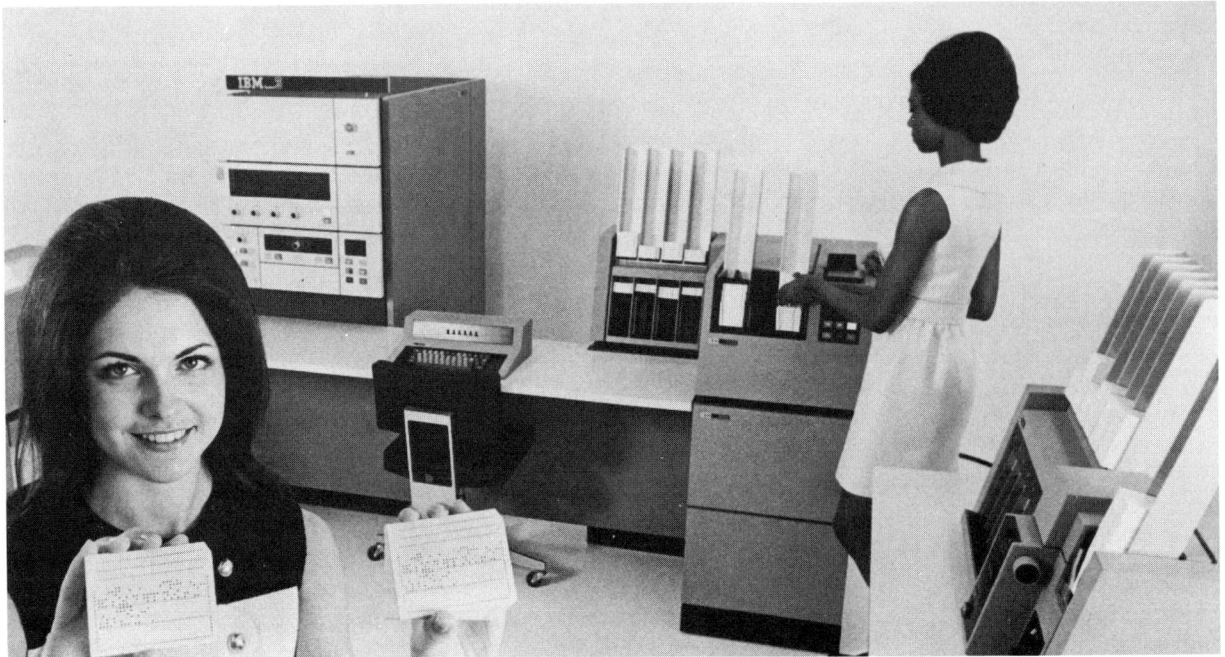

FIG. 12.8 Information system—G. E. Honeywell

RENTING VERSUS BUYING A COMPUTER

In general, computers are rented rather than purchased. There are several advantages in renting. If a company decides that it selected the wrong computer for its purposes, it is easier to exchange rented equipment than to try to find a buyer who wants exactly the equipment you no longer need. Furthermore, when your equipment becomes outdated and you want newer and faster machines, you would have the same trouble in finding a buyer for your used equipment.

And you would probably have to sell it for a much lower price than it was really worth since many other organizations would also be trying to sell their old computers in order to buy the new models. A rental contract can include repair services. Although monthly rental prices sound high, purchase would frequently prove to be even more expensive. When the manufacturer receives old equipment, he can sometimes incorporate some of the component parts in newer models.

COMPUTER COMPANIES

In addition to IBM the larger companies that make computers include Control Data Corporation, Sperry Rand, Honeywell, Burroughs, National Cash Register, Philco, General Electric, and RCA. In addition to these companies that manufacture computers, many smaller companies make special supplies and components. So many accessories are needed with a computer installation that it would be nearly impossible for one company to make them all in addition to manufacturing the computers. Supplies, for example, include cards, tape, and many forms; accessory equipment includes filing devices, other storage methods, and some specialized machines.

QUESTIONS AND PROBLEMS

1. What caused the need for improved methods of processing data during and after World War II?
2. What did people trying to improve upon punched card methods realize as a basic problem with the punched card data processing methods?
3. Briefly describe the improvements made by the IBM Model 604.
4. Briefly describe the advances IBM made with its CPC.
5. Briefly describe the advances made by the Mark I.
6. Who developed the Mark I?
7. Briefly describe the improvements made by the Eniac.
8. What was the chief weakness of the Eniac?
9. How did Neumann improve the Eniac?
10. What does "stored program" mean?
11. What is the major advantage of the stored program concept?
12. What is the significance of the Univac I?
13. Who developed the Univac I?

14. What characteristics distinguish the first generation of computers?
15. What characteristics distinguish the second generation of computers?
16. What characteristics distinguish the third generation of computers?
17. Compare each of the following parts of a second to a second.
    millisecond   microsecond   nanosecond
18. How can general purpose computers be used?
19. How can special purpose computers be used?
20. What factors determine whether a computer system is a small-, a medium-, or a large-scale computer?
21. List two advantages of renting a computer.
22. List several computer manufacturers.

COMPUTER
INPUT/OUTPUT

CHAPTER 13

A computer can take in data from several sources. The input data, frequently referred to merely as *input,* can be in the form of punched cards, punched paper tape, magnetic tape, magnetic characters printed on paper, ordinary characters printed on paper, or can be transferred by a light pen or by a keyboard. By one method or another the numbers and letters are converted into electronic impulses that the computer can interpret and utilize.

After processing by the computer, the output data, frequently referred to merely as *output,* are recorded by means of punched cards, punched paper tape, magnetic tape, print on paper, drawings on paper, or even by an electronic display that resembles a television screen. Each method converts the electronic impulses that the computer develops into a coding system or letters and numbers, depending on the output media in use. Frequently the output data must be printed as a report and recorded on tape or cards for future reference.

Besides the special data to be processed, other types of data are put into the computer. The computer program consisting of the step-by-step instructions is, of course, of first importance. Facts and other material that may be needed, such as income tax withholding charts, are also stored so that they will be available for use.

INPUT-OUTPUT MEDIA COMBINED

Since some of the machines can be used as both an input and an output device, the two terms are frequently used together and written as input/output or abbreviated as I/O. Any combination of separate input/output devices can be used. The fact that punched cards and magnetic tape are used as input does not mean that these same two output devices must be used. It is possible that the output might be print on paper and magnetic tape. The types of I/O devices used with a computer depend on the jobs it performs and the needs of these jobs. An extra input or output device can be added to the system if needed after the computer system has already been in use.

FIG. 13.1   Univac

A particular input or output machine must be hooked to the central processing unit of the computer for each kind of input or output the machine needs to handle. Some of these machines function as both input and output devices. For example, a card read-punch machine can read cards for input and punch cards for output. These I/O machines are attached to the computer by cables that run under the floor.

PUNCHED CARDS

Punched cards are used frequently for input but less frequently as output. We find them so often as input because they represent a simple method and are common in unit record data processing. Smaller computers usually use them. Sometimes it is advantageous to punch the data on cards and arrange them in some special order before using the data as input for the computer.

Three classifications of punched card machines are used as input-output media for the computer. These are machines that

1. only read cards for the computer input of data,
2. only punch cards for the computer output of data,
3. both read and punch cards for the computer input and output of data.

FIG. 13.2 Card read-punch unit—IBM V20–9281

A machine that only reads cards, the *card reader,* can read cards faster than can unit record machines. Its average speed is about 500 cards a minute. If each card contains 80 characters, this would be about 40,000 characters a minute. Cards are seldom completely filled, however. Whether the cards are completely filled or not, the machine can read the cards at about the same rate. Some models can read more than 1000 cards a minute.

A machine that only punches cards, the *card punch,* can handle between 100 and 250 cards a minute, although some are capable of doing 500 cards a minute.

The machine that reads and punches cards, the *card read-punch unit,* is shown in Fig. 13.2. One section of the machine operates like the separate card reader; the other, like the card punch machine.

Some special card reader machines convert the data from punched cards to magnetic tape and other faster input media. These machines are separate from the computer. Having the data recorded on the faster input media saves time in getting the data into the memory section of the computer. Similarly, faster output media can be used by the computer; later, these data can be transferred to punched cards by another machine, if punched cards are needed. Machines of this kind are called *data converters.* Like the unit record reading devices, these machines read the cards either by a brush on the top of the card which makes contact with a roller beneath the card wherever a hole is detected, or by a light from the top of the card which shines through each hole to contact photoelectric cells beneath the card. The light sensing method is faster and causes fewer mistakes. The brushes gradually wear out the cards, and they sometimes catch, causing the cards to jam.

The card punch machine contains a punching station and a reading station so that each card column can be checked for accuracy after it is punched. Since these card reading and punching machines are mechanical in design, they operate at a very limited speed; this greatly restricts their effectiveness compared to other computer input/output media.

PAPER TAPE

Paper tape contains round holes for its code. It is usually about an inch wide, but the exact size depends on the manufacturer of the machines and the coding system used. Two coding systems are common, one with 5 rows and one with 8 rows for the punches. The rows are called channels. Since these codes are difficult to read by eye and these machines never print the characters, the primary use for the tape is for computer input. It is seldom used for output.

The 5-channel tape is shown in Fig. 13.3, with each channel labeled. The small holes in the center are used simply to feed the tape into the machine. The columns are not numbered on the tape because, unlike the punched card, it has no specific length for each record. The amount of data is not limited to 80 characters, as it is on the punched card. Each group of data is called a "record" rather than a unit record, because each unit is not on a separate, detached form.

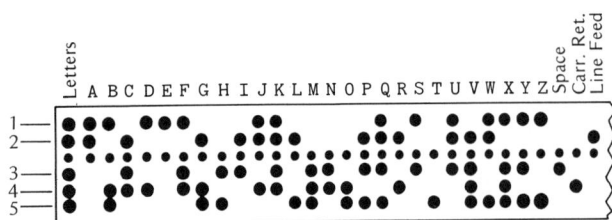

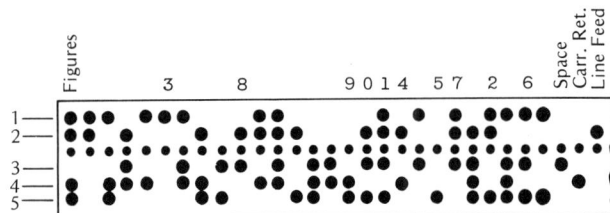

FIG. 13.3 Five-Channel paper tape code

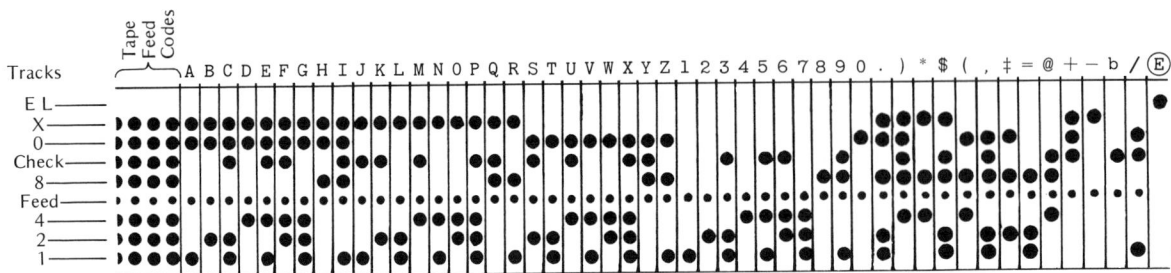

FIG. 13.4 Eight-Channel paper tape code

When a record contains fewer than 80 characters, it is not necessary to leave blank columns as it would be on a punched card. There is, at the end of each individual record, a special symbol. The next record begins in the next column. The tapes are wound on reels, each of which contains many individual records. These reels are referred to as *files*. Each individual record on the reel of tape must be recorded in the same format as is used in the fields of the punched cards. As you can see in the illustration, some letters and numbers use the same code, such as the number 3 and the letter E. Therefore, at the beginning of each field is a code to specify whether it contains letters or numbers.

The 8-column coding for paper tape is somewhat easier to decode by eye, but the characters are never printed on it, either. As in Fig. 13.4, the rows are called *tracks,* and this system uses the base 2 math system in its coding. This system will be explained in greater detail in the next chapter. Briefly, the numbers are represented by holes in rows so that their value adds up to the number represented. The values of the rows from bottom to top are 1, 2, 4, and 8. The number 5 has punches in the rows with the values of 4 and 1 to total 5. The

FIG. 13.5 Teletype paper tape machine

check row is used automatically by the machine to point out some errors. For each column where the code contains an even number of punches, the code automatically puts a punch in the "check" track, or row, so that each column always contains an odd number of punches. If the machine by mistake punches an extra punch or one less punch in a column when transferring data, the error would be caught by the checking device. This is called an *odd parity check*. Some codes use an even parity check and put a punch in each column for which the code originally has an odd number of punches so that all columns contain an even number of punches.

The coding system on the 8-column paper tape for the letters and numbers is similar to the Hollerith code for punched cards. The number punch for each letter is the same. The letter A has a 1-punch in the Hollerith coding system; the letter I has a 9-punch (8 and 1). There are 2 zones rather than 3, and they are labeled the X- and the 0-zone. No punches are in these rows for the numbers. The Hollerith 12-zone is equal to the X and 0 punched. The 11-zone is equal to the X punched. The 0-zone is equal to the 0 punched. The check punch is used to make all columns have either an odd number of punches or an even number of punches. The parity check cannot determine whether you inserted a wrong character or whether the machine punched correctly.

Tape can be punched by using a typewriter that has a special attachment for punching tape, as in Fig. 13.5. In this way, the printed copy can be used for proofreading. A special code can be used to correct mistakes. You do not have to begin the entire tape again. A similar mechanism can be attached to a cash register to record the data on paper tape in addition to the printed paper used as a customer receipt. These tapes later can be read by a paper tape reader as input for the computer, as in Fig. 13.6. A computer paper tape punch can be used as an output media from the computer. This machine functions similarly to one that reads and punches cards.

The tape method of recording data has one important advantage over using punched cards: It provides the computer with faster input and output so that the computer uses less operating time. The tape reader can read about 1000 characters a second, which is more than double the speed of most punched card readers. It can punch about 300 characters a second, which is from slightly faster to double the speed of the different models of card punches. However, although paper tape provides much faster input and output for the computer, it has several important disadvantages. It cannot double as a readable file as the cards can. The order of the individual records on a file cannot be easily changed. It has limited use as an output media—it can be used only as later input again.

MAGNETIC TAPE

Magnetic tape is actually plastic tape that is coated on one side with metallic oxide. It is coded on the metallic side with small magnetic

FIG. 13.6 NCR 660–101 paper tape reader

**FIG. 13.7 IBM reel of
magnetic tape**

charges. A person cannot see these charges on the tape; they can be
read only by special machines. In Fig. 13.8, lines are used to represent
the magnetic charges.

Magnetic tape is usually $\frac{1}{2}$-inch wide and purchased on reels with
either 1200 or 2400 feet of tape, as shown in Fig. 13.7. With this
method of recording the codes, the coded characters can be very
close together; it is possible to have from 200 to more than 3000
characters per inch. The most common magnetic tape for medium-
and large-sized computer systems is designed for 1600 characters per

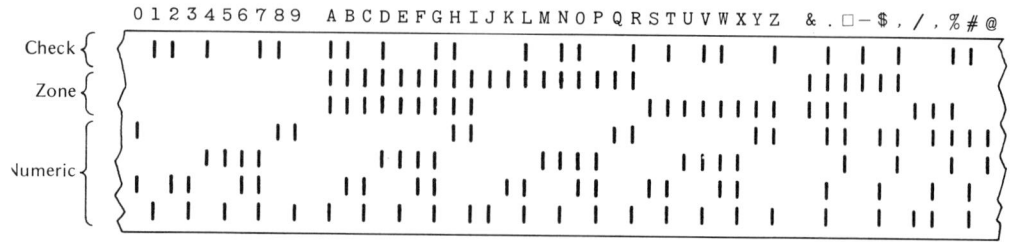

FIG. 13.8 Seven-chanel magnetic tape code

Character	EBCDIC Configuration	Bit Representation
0	1111	0000
1	1111	0001
2	1111	0010
3	1111	0011
4	1111	0100
5	1111	0101
6	1111	0110
7	1111	0111
8	1111	1000
9	1111	1001
A	1100	0001
B	1100	0010
C	1100	0011
D	1100	0100
E	1100	0101
F	1100	0110
G	1100	0111
H	1100	1000
I	1100	1001
J	1101	0001
K	1101	0010
L	1101	0011
M	1101	0100
N	1101	0101
O	1101	0110
P	1101	0111
Q	1101	1000
R	1101	1001
S	1110	0010
T	1110	0011
U	1110	0100
V	1110	0101
W	1110	0110
X	1110	0111
Y	1110	1000
Z	1110	1001

FIG. 13.9 EBCDIC code

inch. Tape has successfully been tested to hold 3200 characters per inch, but is not practical because of the current limitations of the recording and sensing devices. The number of characters per inch a tape holds is referred to as its density. A 2400-foot tape comes on a reel about 12 inches in diameter. It can hold 28,800,000 characters even if it has only 1000 characters per inch. This would be equivalent to 360,000 punched cards if every column of every card contained a character. Moreover, since most cards are not completely filled, this would be comparable to an even larger number of cards. A stack an inch high contains no more than 150 punched cards. You can see, then, that a reel of tape holds as much information as a 2400-inch stack of cards which would be 200 feet high, about equal in height to a 16-story building.

The coding system of 7-channel magnetic tape contains 7 rows which are comparable to 7 of the 8 rows on 8-track paper tape. Rather than being called rows or tracks, they are sometimes called *channels* and are labeled as in Fig. 13.8. The lower 4 channels represent the numbers coded like the base 2 math system. The next 2 channels represent the zones, and the top one is used for the parity check.

An extensively used magnetic tape is the 9-track tape which utilizes 8 tracks for the EBCDIC (Extended Binary Coded Decimal Interchange Code) shown in Fig. 13.9. Each of the 9 positions is called a bit, and the 8 bits (omitting the parity check) is called a byte. Since any number 0–9 can be recorded in the binary system with no more than 4 bits, every byte can be divided into 2 sections plus the parity check. In this way, 2 numbers can be recorded in each byte, as shown in Fig. 13.10. This is called "packing" of numeric data and doubles the capacity of the magnetic tape. It also saves core space inside the memory of the computer. When operating in "pack" mode, you cannot use alphabetic and symbolic data. We do not have to actually work with this coding system. It is used on magnetic tape and in computer core storage. The computer converts these data to and from the Hollerith code and the print in the English language.

Rather than having a special code to represent the end of each record, magnetic tape uses a blank space, between $\frac{1}{2}''$ and $\frac{3}{4}''$ long, called the *inter-record gap,* or IRG (see Fig. 13.11). Each record is set up consistently by fields as we found was done on cards and paper tape. In this way the programmer can instruct the machine to read one record at a time just as he instructs it to read one card at a time.

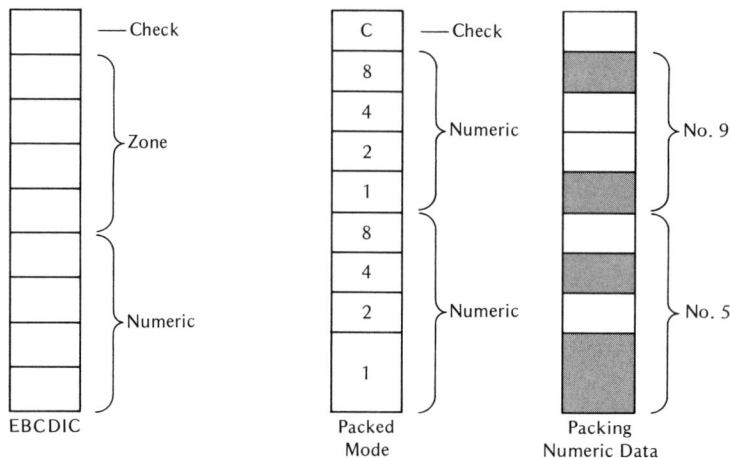

FIG. 13.10 Packing numeric data

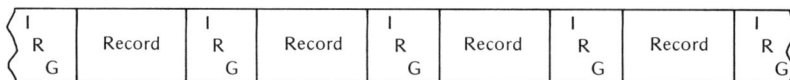

FIG. 13.11 Magnetic tape illustration of inter-record gap (IRG)

The input tape drive is used to put data into the computer, and the output tape drive is used to record data that have been processed. These can be two separate machines, but are usually all in one machine like that shown in Fig. 13.12. The input section contains an input mounting reel for the reel of tape to be read or recorded, an erase head to erase old data from the tape, a write head to be used for the output; it also contains a take-up reel on which the tape is wound after it has been read or recorded. If the machine is being used to read, the erase head and write head are not working. When tape is being recorded or being written, the reel may contain blank tape or tape with old data no longer needed. The erase head is always in operation during the writing operation to insure clean tape. The write head records the data one column at a time but can do this very fast.

Old data no longer needed can be erased and new data recorded on a tape, so each magnetic tape can be used numerous times. Threading the tape each time it is inserted into the unit does wear out the end of the tape, so some of the newer tapes have automatic loading

FIG. 13.12   Four IBM 3420 magnetic tape units w/ 3840 control unit (right)

and threading with a wraparound cartridge. In this way, a person just touches the outer cartridge around the edge of each reel of tape and does not handle either the reel or the tape. A suction pulls the tape to thread it. Magnetic tape reels are usually 8½″ or 10½″ in diameter. Smaller reels are called *mini reels*.

The magnetic tape reader can read from about 20″ to more than 150″ per second, depending on the machine model. If it reads 100″ per second and contains 1600 characters per inch, this would be reading about 160,000 characters per second. This is about the average rate, but rates do range from 8000 characters to more than 240,000 characters per second. At 160,000 characters per second, this would be comparable to 2000 completely filled punched cards, and this is per second *not* per minute. When numeric data are packed, the reader can handle twice as many characters per second. Magnetic tape media can usually record at the same rate that they read.

Usually, the original magnetic tape is output from the computer; then the next time it is used as input, and a new updated tape is the new output. Data recorded on punched cards or paper tape can be

FIG. 13.13   Magnetic tape inscriber—Honeywell

transferred to magnetic tape by a data converter. Also, data can be originally recorded on magnetic tape by a Magnetic Tape Inscriber, as in Fig. 13.13. The operator uses a keyboard similar to a keypunch machine to record data from a source document. The tape density is usually about only 20 characters per inch. If the tape input reads only 50″ of tape per second, this is 1000 characters per second, which is still much faster than processing with card readers as computer input.

Magnetic tape devices are naturally quite expensive, but really necessary if a company wants to take full advantage of the faster computers and process more data each hour. Punched cards and paper tape cannot feed data into the computer and take it out of the computer nearly so fast as the computer can process the data. The greater speed of magnetic tape has helped, but some computers can process data even faster than this input-output method can function.

Some smaller computer systems do not use magnetic tape because this great speed is not needed and costs are high, and because either the input or output must be punched cards so that they can be used on unit record equipment. However, magnetic tape cartridge units are rapidly becoming more popular and are now inexpensive enough to be used with *small* computer systems.

PRINTER

A printer, as shown in Fig. 13.14, can be used only as an output device, not as input. The coding system used is our English letters and numbers so that it can be used to print students' report cards, payroll checks, address labels, or customers' bills. Using this output medium along with another output medium, such as tape or punched cards, is common. In this way, both a permanent record and a form for the student, employee, or customer are obtained.

Models that can print both capital and small letters contain print chains that contain both capital letters and small letters. Some models of high-speed printers can print from 1000 to 1500 lines per minute (LPM). This provides a maximum of 216,000 characters per minute, which is comparable to the amount the faster magnetic tape units can record *per second*.

A special printer with a keyboard can be used for input and output. It uses a Selectric typewriter and is used only when variable input is required, because it can print only about 15 characters per second. It can be advantageously used when variable job parameters are needed, such as calculation factors for scientific problems, and when data are needed directly and quickly from disk storage, such as the current account balances of specific customers.

Special form paper is put into the printer, and the line of print is controlled with a carriage tape similar to that used by the accounting machines. Forms can even be printed with carbon copies. Each line of print can contain up to 144 characters, but complete lines are seldom printed. The various models of printers have different maximum-line lengths, including 100 characters per line, 120 characters per line, 132 characters per line, and 144 characters per line. The most common is 132 characters per line. The printer that can print only capital letters contains a single print chain. The chain contains each letter,

**FIG. 13.14 IBM
1403 printer**

number, and special character several times around the chain. The chain is constantly spinning around its path with small hammers hitting the characters through a ribbon to make impressions on the paper. It prints one character at a time but does this so rapidly that it almost looks as though it is printing a complete line at a time.

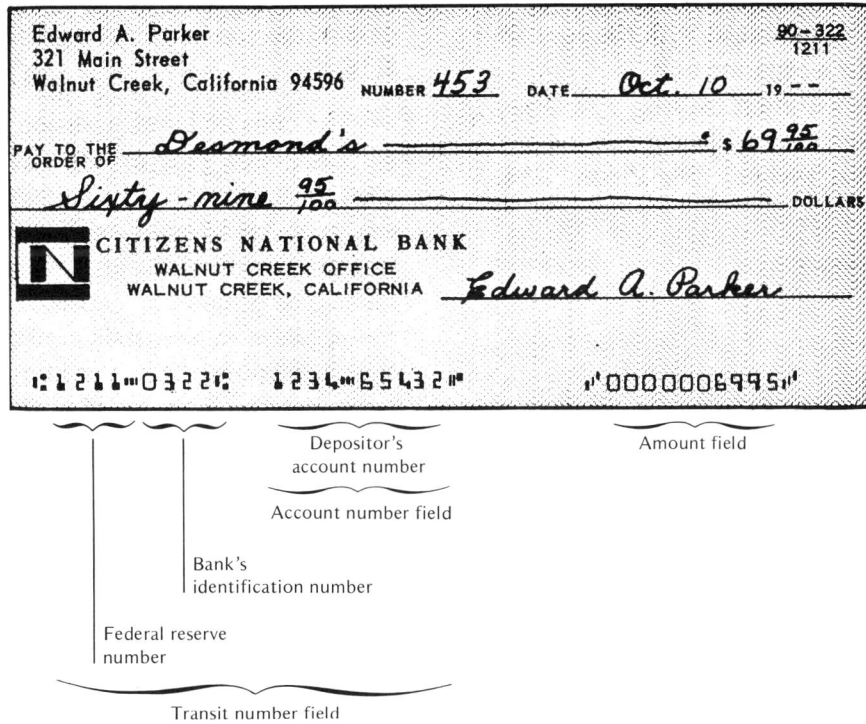

FIG. 13.15 Magnetic ink
characters on a
check (NCR)

OPTICAL READERS AND MAGNETIC SCANNERS

Optical readers and magnetic scanners can be used only as input devices; their only function is to read and interpret marks, letters, and numbers from paper. The machines that read ordinary printed characters are generally referred to as *optical readers*. The machines that read magnetized characters and marks are generally referred to as *scanners*. A magnetic scanner can interpret only documents printed with special ink and characters, such as the characters printed on many bank checks (see Fig. 13.15). The magnetic scanner translates this code into a code the computer can use. When a check is received by the bank for processing, the bank can use a magnetic recording machine to stamp the amount of the check on it so that the check itself can be used for processing. This eliminates the necessity for

FIG. 13.16 Magnetic ink scanner and sorter—NCR

transferring this data to another medium, such as punched cards. This system is helpful to the larger banks and to clearinghouses where checks are collected and routed to the banks on which they were drawn. The magnetic ink scanner in Fig. 13.16 also sorts the documents.

The other type of scanner is called an optical scanner because it works as the eye does. It can read typed and printed letters and numbers that are not magnetized. It is frequently called an *optical character reader* (OCR). The primary difference between these devices is that the magnetic scanners can interpret only magnetized marks and characters, whereas the optical readers can interpret nonmagnetized marks and characters. Although the optical readers are relatively new, several different types are already available. Some can read only typed or machine-printed characters; others can read hand-printed characters.

FIG. 13.17   OCR unit

At the present time relatively few of these machines are in use, but they are of great interest. The earlier ones used in the late 1960's can read one or two lines as a document passes through them; others can read an entire page on one pass through the machine. Those which can read one or two lines are ideal for handling small forms having only a limited amount of data. The maximum line length can vary from 32 characters to 150 characters. Some OCR machines can

FIG. 3.18 Computer console—Honeywell

read numbers only or letters only; others can read both letters and numbers. They can also read some special characters, depending on the model of the machine.

The OCR machine can be used as input into the computer. It can also be used to produce other media such as punched cards and printed pages. It is much faster to use these machines than to have a keypunch operator punch the cards. As these machines are perfected, they will undoubtedly replace some keypunch operators. However, they are too expensive for some types of use.

OCR machines can be made to accept special sizes of forms. They can also sort the forms into several stackers after reading them. The optical character reader in Fig. 13.17 has three stackers. Other models have anywhere from 1 to 21 stackers. The data must be recorded in the same position on each form, the forms must be clean and have a dull surface, and the paper must have at least a certain amount of stiffness.

One type of optical character reader can read the numbers of journal tapes from cash registers and adding machines at a rate of more than 3000 lines a minute, with up to 10 characters per line. Another machine can read a full page of print at a time, which greatly simplifies and speeds up the handling of source documents. The optical mark page reader can read marks on 8½″ x 11″ data sheets, and the marks do not have to be magnetized or made with an electrographic pencil. These machines transfer the data directly to the computer without first having to convert the data to magnetic tape or punched cards.

One application of these devices is illustrated in the use of oil company charge accounts. When a customer purchases gas, the attendant prints the amount of his purchase, and a special device imprints the data from his charge card onto the form. A copy of the form can be read by such an optical scanner to produce the customer's monthly statement and to produce the company's permanent records.

CONSOLE TYPEWRITER

The console of the computer is the part that contains indicator lights, switches, buttons, and other mechanisms, including a typewriter, as shown in Fig. 13.18. It is used by the computer operator to communicate directly with the computer. This is actually used as a part of the control function and will be explained in greater detail later. The typewriter, which is a part of the console, can be used for input into the computer. Because it can provide input only as fast as the person can type accurately, it is not used for input of data to be processed. It is used for giving the central processing unit additional instructions not in the program of instructions.

The console also provides a type of output. The lights that go on and off tell the computer operator about the internal operations of the computer and can point out some troubles during processing.

VISUAL DISPLAY UNIT

The operator of the visual display unit uses the keyboard for input, as shown in Fig. 13.19. The requested data are shown on the cathode-ray tube as output taken from the computer storage. A photocopy process can also be used to make a permanent copy of the data on the screen. The operator can use a light pen to change the data displayed on the screen, and the data are then changed immediately in the memory of

FIG. 13.19 IBM 2260
visual display
units

the computer. Many of these units can be connected to one computer at the same time. They provide direct and immediate communication with the computer.

A sample of the use of this type of equipment is provided by a
company that has a very large mail-order business. As each charge
account mail order is received, the operator uses this unit to check
the person's credit rating in order to determine whether or not this
order should be sent to him. In such a case, there is no need to also
make a photocopy of the data flashed on the screen. The operator
merely places the individual's order either in the stack of approved
credit ratings so that the order will be processed and sent, in the
stack for further checking, or in the stack for sending the person a
letter telling them his account is already overdue. Similar equipment
is also used at the larger airports.

FIG. 13.20 IBM 2250 display unit with light pen

A light pen is a pointer with a light at its pointer end. The operator of the unit holds it in his hand and uses it to put data directly into the computer. For example, several alternatives might be shown on the screen. The operator touches the light pen against the screen to record the desired response. The position at which the light pen point touches the screen is converted to a coded response and entered into the computer. Similar devices without lights are also used and are frequently called *sense probes*.

The visual display unit that can use a light pen or a sense probe is useful in many applications, such as entering patient data for hospital information systems, entering insurance claim data and new policy data by insurance companies, and specialized ordering in manufacturing operations and planning. In many of these situations, the data could be entered by the keyboard rather than by the light pen or sense probe.

Figures 13.20 and 13.21 show a graphic display unit which charts a graph or diagram, in addition to showing letters and numbers. It is sometimes called a "plotter" and is used for drawing construction designs, for work-flow charts of manufacturing projects, and for other types of diagrams.

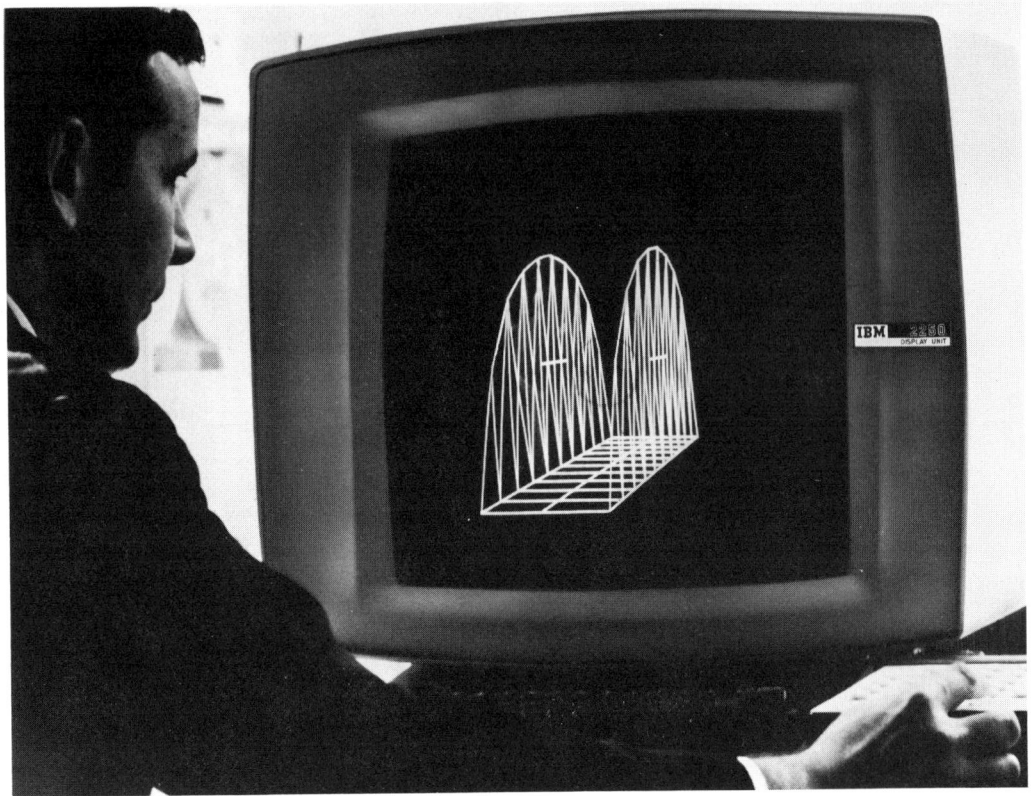

FIG. 13.21   IBM 2250 graphic display unit

A new means of communicating with a computer is by spoken words. The person speaks at the telephone station which is connected to the audio response unit, as shown in Fig. 13.22. This unit converts the data into codes and transmits them to the computer central processing unit. The computer composes a reply and returns the message to the audio response unit for reply to the inquirer. Vocabulary storage in the unit shown in Fig. 13.22 is limited to 100 words at the present time. These are words chosen from the most frequently used words associated with the specific industry application. By program control, inquiries can be limited to authorized personnel only.

FIG. 13.22 IBM 7770 audio response unit

REMOTE TERMINALS

It is frequently desirable to transmit data into a computer from a location away from the computer, either from a different part of the same building or from another building location. The time it would take to physically transport the punched cards, magnetic tape, or other input can be eliminated. Numerous types of remote terminals perform this function—provide computer input and output from a location away from the computer. The I/O terminals are attached to a Transmission Control Unit which performs all the necessary data conversion. More than 100 communication lines can be attached to one control unit and operate simultaneously. The data can be transmitted over common carrier switched telephone lines, common carrier switched teletypewriter exchange (TWX) networks, leased private line telephone and telegraph services, Western Union channels, and private communication systems.

A combination of I/O media operating as remote terminals is called a Data Communication System. A system might include a printer, display unit, and a keyboard, or it might include any combination of the following:

card reader	magnetic character reader	printer
card punch	magnetic tape reader	display station
paper tape reader	magnetic tape recorder	magnetic data inscriber
paper tape punch	optical character reader	keyboard

Display stations are being used more and more as remote terminals for such information as inquiry about customer accounts. Various types of terminals are used with time-sharing systems. The terminal is connected to a computer located elsewhere, and payment for its use is calculated by the amount of computer time required to process the requested data.

Schools might use a terminal of this type connected to a computer at a larger university so that the students could run their own programs. Companies that have a limited need for a computer might also use the time-sharing method. A basic terminal of this type could consist merely of a keyboard for input and a printer for output, or a paper-tape reader punch could be attached to this equipment. Computer programmers can use a display unit when working with programs. Several instructions can be shown on a screen at one time. A light pen can be used to modify or correct program instructions.

Special terminals have been designed for use by tellers in banks and in savings and loan associations, as shown in Fig. 13.23. The teller can use the terminal to process deposit and withdrawal transactions, post passbooks, and print checks or receipts at the teller's window. Transaction data are transmitted to the computer system, and the new balance or account status information is immediately available.

Numerous additional input and output devices are made specially for specific applications. Even more varieties of these types of machines will be available in the next few years. Faster input/output units are still needed to keep pace with the speed of computers.

FIG. 13.23   Bank teller terminal—NCR

INPUT/OUTPUT MEDIA COMPARED

The speed with which the input and the output can be handled is becoming of increasing importance as the computer CPU's (Central Processing Units) are functioning at greater speeds than in past years. The input units transfer either human language or a machine language to the CPU where it is retained until needed. The output units transfer the processed results from the CPU to make them available to the user or to make them available to another machine for further processing. The CPU cannot be processing the data while it is being manipulated as input or output. Therefore, it is important that the input and output operations be completed as quickly as possible so that the CPU is free to carry out the faster processing steps as efficiently as possible. The blank spaces in the CPU in Fig. 13.24 are of primary importance

Input (punched card reader)	Step 1	No activity	No activity	Step 1	No activity	No activity
Processing (CDU)	No activity	Step 2	No activity	No activity	Step 2	No activity
Output (printer)	No activity	No activity	Step 3	No activity	No activity	Step 3

Process: Read Data (Step 1)
Perform Computations (Step 2)
Output (Step 3)

FIG. 13.24 Central processing unit, illustrating times of "no activity"

and must be kept to a minimum. A method using special programming is available on some computers making it possible for the CPU to actually perform other processing steps on another program while an I/O operation is taking place. Details concerning this special capability, called *multiprogramming,* are described in Chapter 16. Depending on the size and speed of the particular computer system, the I/O media as compared below are important considerations.

Input

Card reader (punched cards)	300–1600 cards/min.
CRT display (cathode ray tube)	250–10,000 chars./sec.
Paper tape reader (paper tape)	350–1000 chars./sec.
Optical scanner (paper tape)	70–2500 chars./sec.
Magnetic tape reader (magnetic tape)	8000–240,000 chars./sec.
Console typewriter (special paper)	6–15 chars./sec.

Output

Card punch	100–200 cards/min.
CTR display	250–10,000 chars./sec.
Paper tape punch	20–150 chars./sec.
Printer	300–1500 lines/min.
Magnetic tape	8000–240,000 chars./sec.
Console typewriter	6–15 chars./sec.

QUESTIONS AND PROBLEMS

1. What is computer input?
2. What is computer output?

3. What additional input does the computer need besides the data to be processed?

4. List several reasons punched cards are frequently used as computer input.

5. List the three classifications of punched card machines used as computer I/O.

6. What is the advantage of having the data on a punched card converted to magnetic tape?

7. Briefly describe the advantage of reading punched cards by photoelectric means rather than by brushes.

8. What is the primary purpose of paper tape?

9. Does the paper tape punch also print the characters?

10. What is the purpose of the small holes in the center of the paper tape?

11. Why are the columns not numbered on paper tape?

12. Why is each record not called a unit record as it is on the punched cards?

13. Why can each field contain only alphabetical or numeric data, but not both?

14. How does the check row work for "odd parity check" on 8-channel tape?

15. How can errors be corrected when using a special typewriter to punch paper tape?

16. List the advantages and disadvantages of using paper tape rather than punched cards.

17. Describe magnetic tape.

18. How many characters can a 2400-foot reel of tape hold if there are 1600 characters per inch?

19. Why has the magnetic tape that holds 3200 characters per inch not yet become practical?

20. What is the primary advantage of the 8-bit coding system?

21. What term is used to describe this "doubling up" of numeric data?

22. How is the end of each record indicated on magnetic tape?

23. What is the name given to this blank space between records?

24. When is old data erased by the magnetic tape unit?

25. What is the advantage to the automatic loading and threading provided by the newer magnetic tape units?

26. Why do some smaller computers not use magnetic tape?

27. What function can a printer serve?

28. Can printers print both capital and small letters?

29. What number of characters per line of print is the most common?

30. What function can optical readers and magnetic scanners serve?

31. What are scanners?

32. What are optical readers?

33. Explain one actual application of optical character readers.

34. Why is there great current interest in scanning and optical reading machines?

35. Approximately how fast can each of the following I/O machines work?
    Punched card reader   Paper tape punch
    Punched card punch   Magnetic tape reader
    Paper tape reader   Printer

36. What is the purpose of the computer console?

37. Why is the console typewriter not generally used for input of data to be processed?

38. How can the data on a display screen be changed?

39. Briefly describe a use of display screens in business.

40. What is a sense probe?

41. What is the limiting factor to "talking" to a computer?

42. What functions do remote terminals serve?

43. How are the data transmitted to and from remote terminals?

44. List input media that can be used at remote terminals.

45. List output media that can be used at remote terminals.

46. List four advantageous uses of terminals.

47. Why are faster I/O media needed?

CENTRAL PROCESSING UNIT OF THE COMPUTER

CHAPTER 14

We have seen how the data get into and out of the computer system. Before we can program the computer, we must learn how information is stored inside the computer, how calculations are handled, and how all of the various functions are controlled. As you will recall, the computer system consists of three basic units: input unit, central processing unit, and output unit. The central processing unit consists of three components:

1. the storage or memory section,
2. the computation section, and
3. the control section.

The central processing unit of the computer system is actually the computer. However, the computer cannot work by itself. The input/output machines are hooked to the central processing unit so that it can function. Obviously we need the entire computer system.

STORAGE SECTION

The storage section of the computer is where the data are placed when the unit reads the input; it is also where the instructions are kept until needed. After the central processing unit uses each, it is not destroyed or lost; it remains in storage so that it can be used again. The data to be processed consist primarily of numbers that are to be used in calculations. After the programmed calculations have been made, the results are placed in storage until they are ready to be used as output by the output unit. Data that are no longer needed are erased or cleared from storage in one of two ways:

1. The programmer includes an instruction telling the machine to erase some specific data.

2. The programmer includes an instruction telling the machine to place some new data where some other data were stored. Old data are automatically eliminated and new data take their place.

The data can include more than the numbers for use in calculations. Data can include people's names and other words so that the computer's output unit can print each student's report card after his grade point average is calculated, or so that each employee's pay check can be printed. The data can also include charts and tables such as the ones used in calculating federal withholding taxes.

STORAGE LOCATIONS

Each storage location can usually hold one character and is comparable to one column on a punched card or one column on tape. These storage locations have to be identified so that the computer programmer can write the instructions that the computer can interpret. If the instructions merely told the computer to get from storage the number of absences during the first school term, the computer would not know where to find this number; it must be told where the number is located. Therefore, each storage location is identified by a number called an *address*. The address number merely identifies the storage location; it tells you nothing about what is in that storage location. This is comparable to your home address number. If your address is 1121 River Road, the number 1121 identifies the specific house but does not automatically tell the name of the family or how many people live there.

The total number of storage locations is usually designated in thousands of characters or words, and "thousands" is represented by the capital letter K. If a computer has a storage capacity of 10,000 characters, we express its capacity as 10K. One with a memory of 1500 characters would be referred to as having 1.5K characters. The storage capacities of most computers range from as small as 2K to 32,000K and even higher. If the storage capacity of a computer becomes too small as the computer is used for more and more different applications, additional storage modules can be attached to the com-

C	O	M	P	U	T	E	R		I
01	02	03	04	05	06	07	08	09	10

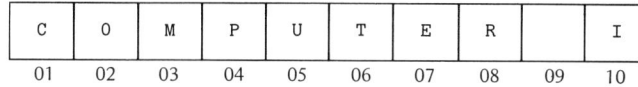

FIG. 14.1 Single position address system

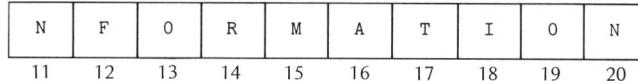

N	F	O	R	M	A	T	I	O	N
11	12	13	14	15	16	17	18	19	20

FIG. 14.2 Multiple-position address system with 10 positions per address

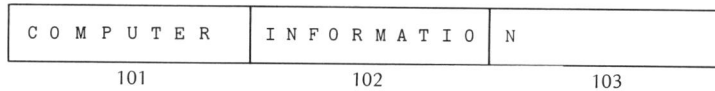

C O M P U T E R	I N F O R M A T I O	N	
101	102	103	

puter (up to a certain limit). These additional storage locations are numbered and called addresses.

> *Data stored in a computer are referred to as computer words, whether they are numbers or alphabetic words.* If the word is data that is to be processed, it is a *data word;* if it is an instruction in a computer program, it is an *instruction word.*

Two different addressing systems are used to identify the specific storage locations. One is the *single position address system.* In this system, one character can be placed in each address. Each word can consume as many addresses as necessary. Then the next word begins at the next address, as in Fig. 14.1. Since each word can be as long as necessary, this system is said to have variable word lengths. The beginning of each new word or field must be identified by a special character to separate it from the previous word. This character is usually called a *word mark* or a *flag.*

The other is called the *multiple position address system.* Since a specified number of characters can be placed in each address, it is said to have a *fixed word length.* Each word begins at the first storage location for that address. If the word is shorter than the number of storage locations in each address, the remaining locations are left blank. If the word is longer than the number of storage locations in that address, the remaining characters are either omitted or two addresses are used. See Fig. 14.2 which allows 10 storage locations at each address. The specific addresses to be used are determined when the programmer writes the instructions and decides whether or not the complete words are needed. If the word is for the person's last name and must be printed on customer bills or pay checks, then two

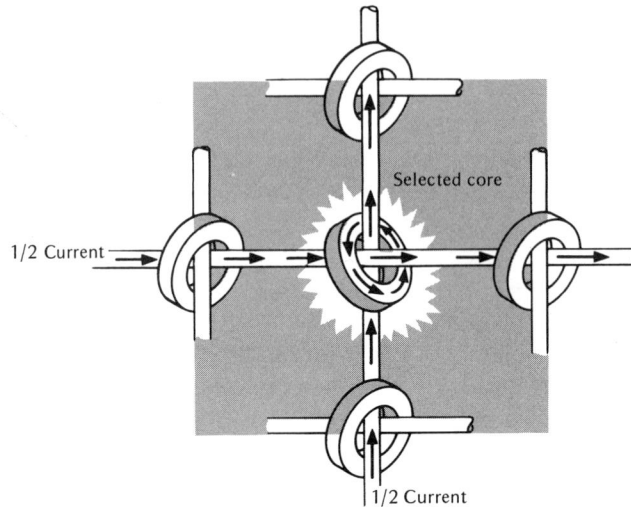

FIG. 14.3 Five magnetic cores with one being turned on

addresses must be used, since some people's last names contain more than 10 characters. If each address contains 10 storage locations and there are 1000 addresses, then the storage capacity of the computer is 10,000 characters, or 1000 words. Since each word has a specified maximum size, this system is said to have a fixed word length. Most modern computers have a fixed word length because this method permits the computer to operate faster. Computer storage is usually available in increments of 1024, 4096, 8192, 16,384, 32,768, etc. Therefore, each K actually refers to 1024 words rather than 1000 words.

INTERNAL STORAGE

Storage of data in the CPU is referred to as *internal storage* because the data are being stored inside the computer. The internal storage of most computers is composed of magnetic cores. Several newer methods being used in some computers utilize magnetic thin film, lasers, and bubble memory. Some of these are still in the experimental stage. In the past, magnetic drums were used as internal storage; however, they are more commonly used as external storage devices now.

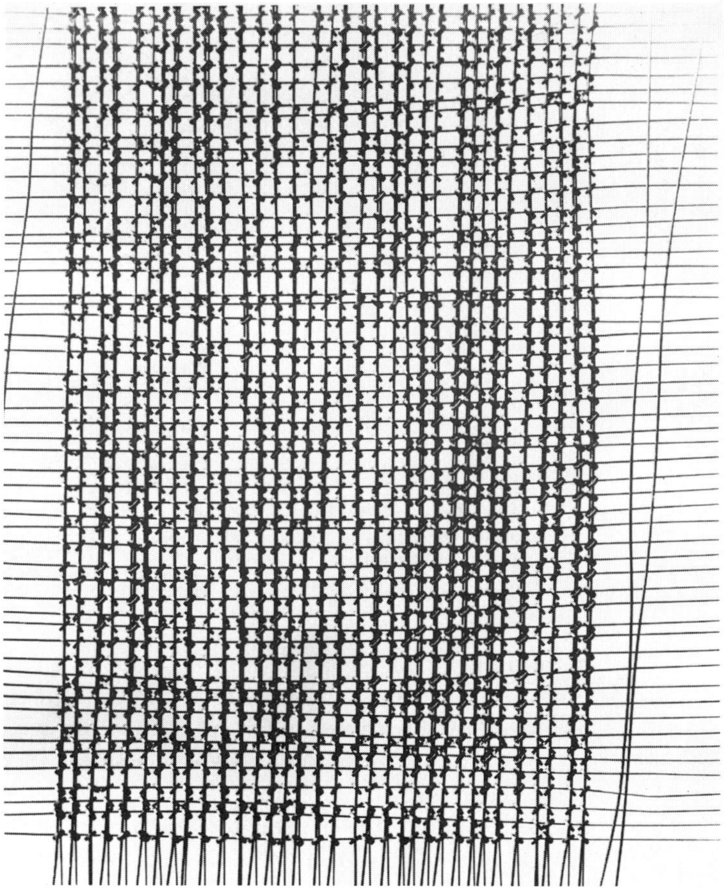

FIG. 14.4 Magnetic core plane IBM

Magnetic Core Storage

The storage method that is used in most computers today is the magnetic core. Each core is doughnut shaped and has wires running through it, as in Fig. 14.3. Each core is only about 1/16″ in diameter; they are arranged in groups. When electrical current goes through a wire, it contains half the amount of power needed to turn on a core. When two wires that are turned on meet, there is enough power to turn on the core, as shown in Fig. 14.3. All other cores remain off. Each core that should be turned on is turned on separately, but the

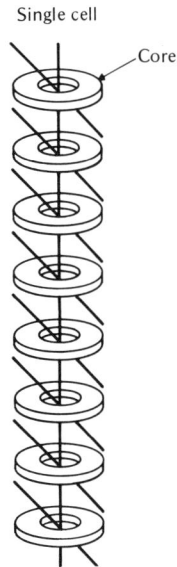

FIG. 14.5 Eight cores make up one storage location

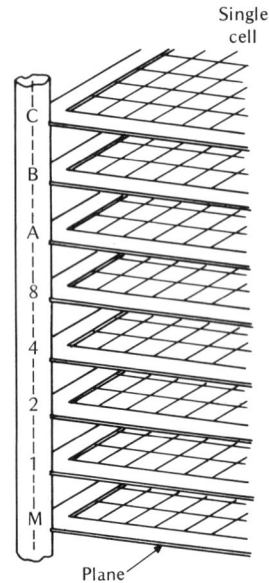

FIG. 14.6 Eight planes allow for many storage locations

computer does this so fast that it seems as though they are all turned on at once. If the current were going the opposite direction than that indicated by the arrows in Fig. 14.3, the core would remain in the "off" state. Although not shown, there is a third wire passing through each core, called a *sense wire,* for reading the core's direction of polarity or magnetization. This is used to indicate to the computer whether the core is on or off. Cores are arranged in groups to make up addresses. The number of cores needed at each address varies with the type of coded data representation used by the computer.

Inside the central processing unit the cores are arranged in groups called planes, as shown in Fig. 14.4. For the 8-bit representation, 8 planes are needed for each storage location or address (see Fig. 14.5). However, each group of 8 planes contains many storage locations, as shown in Fig. 14.6. A completely assembled storage unit consists of a stack of many planes.

Binary Number System

Since the computer uses the binary number system, we should learn about it. This knowledge will help us understand the use of the cores

Position	5	4	3	2	1
	10^4	10^3	10^2	10^1	10^0
Value	10,000	1,000	100	10	1

FIG. 14.7 Base 10 or Decimal number system

for storage. Let us start by stating that each core has two possible states: "on" and "off," just as an electric light bulb can be either on or off.

The binary system is also called the *base 2 system*. This is comparable to calling the decimal system the base 10 system. The base 10 system contains 10 numbers: 0 through 9. The base 2 system contains 2 numbers: 0 and 1. This means that the base 2 system does not use the numbers 2 through 9, just 0 and 1, yet it can still represent any number. The value of a 1 in each position of a decimal, or base 10, number uses the number 10 to each power as shown in Fig. 14.7.

Position 1 is 10 to the 0 power. Any number to the 0 power is equal to 1. Therefore, a number 1 in this column has the value of 1.

Position 2 is 10 to the first power. Any number to the first power is the number itself. Therefore, a number 1 in this column has the value of 10.

Position 3 is 10 to the second power. This means 10 squared (10 × 10). Therefore, a number 1 in this column has the value of 100.

Position 4 is 10 to the third power. This means 10 cubed (10 × 10 × 10). Therefore, a number 1 in this column has the value of 1000.

Position 5 is 10 to the fourth power. This means (10 × 10 × 10 × 10). Therefore, a number 1 in this column has the value of 10,000.

To understand the base 2 method, substitute the number 2 rather than the number 10 in the chart (see Fig. 14.8). Determine the value of the number 2 to each indicated power.

Position	5	4	3	2	1
	2^4	2^3	2^2	2^1	2^0
Value	16	8	4	2	1

FIG. 14.8 Base 2 or Binary number system

Position 1 is 2 to the 0 power. Any number to the 0 power is equal to the number 1. Therefore, a number 1 in this column has the value 1.

Position 2 is 2 to the first power. Any number to the first power is the number itself. Therefore, a number 1 in this column has the value of 2.

Position 3 is 2 to the second power. This means 2 squared (2×2). Therefore, a number 1 in this column has the value of 4.

Position 4 is 2 to the third power. This means 2 cubed ($2 \times 2 \times 2$). Therefore, a number 1 in this column has the value of 8.

Position 5 is 2 to the fourth power. This means ($2 \times 2 \times 2 \times 2$). Therefore, a number 1 in this column has the value of 16.

The next positions would be 2^5 (32), 2^6 (64), 2^7 (128), 2^8 (264), and so on.

We are very slow in translating a number from the base 2 system because we must make the following computations. The problem is to read the number: 1011101. (Remember, we are moving from right to left.)

Solution

A number 1 in position 1 is equal to 1.	1
A number 0 has no value.	0
A number 1 in position 3 is equal to 4.	4
A number 1 in position 4 is equal to 8.	8
A number 1 in position 5 is equal to 16.	16
A number 0 has no value.	0
A number 1 in position 7 is equal to 64.	64
The number is	93

The easiest way to write a number in the base 2 system when you are not very familiar with it is to label the columns as follows. Problem: Write the number 45 in the base 2 system. (Now we will be working from left to right.)

Solution (see illustration below)

Step 1   Since the number is 45, the highest value that can be used is 32, so place a number 1 in this column.

Step 2   Since $32 + 16 = 48$ is higher than the number we need (45), we cannot use the 16 column, so place a 0 here.

Step 3   Since $32 + 8 = 40$ is not larger than the number we need (45), place a number 1 in this column. We now have the number 40 $(32 + 8)$.

Step 4   Since $40 + 4$ is not larger than the number we need (45), place a number 1 in this column. We now have the number 44 $(32 + 8 + 4)$.

Step 5   Since $44 + 2 = 46$ is larger than the number we need (45), place a number 0 here.

Step 6   Since $44 + 1 = 45$ is the number we need, place a number 1 in this column. We now have the number 45 as required $(32 + 8 + 4 + 1)$.

	64	32	16	8	4	2	1
Step 1		1					
Step 2		1	0				
Step 3		1	0	1			
Step 4		1	0	1	1		
Step 5		1	0	1	1	0	
Step 6		1	0	1	1	0	1

The answer is 101101

As you see, we can represent any number in the base 2 system, but it takes longer since we are not so familiar with the system. This is the base on which the computer performs calculations because it is the way it stores data. But the computer can handle this math system much more efficiently than we can. We will take the mathematician's word for the fact that it is possible to add, subtract, multiply, divide, and find square roots using the base 2 system. It is interesting to see how it is done, but is not necessary for us to understand the details since the computer does this automatically. The programmer does not have to explain these steps.

Binary Coded Decimal (BCD) System

Computers are designed so that they can accept data with the numbers written in the decimal system since it is the system we use. Then the numbers are converted to the binary code for storage and for computations. They are again converted to the decimal numbers for output. Since both decimal and binary numbers are used, this system of storage is called the *binary coded decimal system* and is abbreviated the BCD system. Each storage location can receive as input any number from 0 through 9 in the decimal system. Therefore, the highest binary number it needs to store is the number 9 which is converted to 1001. This means that only 4 cores are needed in each storage address to represent each digit.

Extended Binary Coded Decimal Interchange Code (EBCDIC)

Many third-generation computers, such as the IBM 360 series, use the EBCDIC, an 8-bit code. As we have already learned, each group of 8 bits can represent a character in storage and is called a byte. In this 8-bit byte, four bits are required to represent a number 0–9, and four bits are required to represent a zone for the alphabetic and special characters. As shown in Fig. 14.9, the four bits that represent the numbers are labeled "BIT Representation," and the 4 bits that represent the zones are labeled "EBCDIC Configuration." Corresponding to the Hollerith code, the 12-zone is 1100, the 11-zone is 1101, and the 0-zone is 1110 in EBCDIC. Special characters are represented in a similar manner.

The use of the 8 bits in this manner allows us to have a maximum of 256 different characters. This makes it possible to represent many special characters and to represent both upper-case and lower-case alphabetic characters. The ability to have more special characters permits added control codes which are especially useful if we are using remote control terminals.

American Standard Code for Information Interchange (ASCII)

The American Standards Association, now called the American National Standards Institute, accepted a code similar to the EBCDIC with

Character	EBCDIC Code		ASCII-8 Code	
	EBCDII Configuration	Bit Representation	ASCII-8 Configuration	Bit Representation
0	1111	0000	0101	0000
1	1111	0001	0101	0001
2	1111	0010	0101	0010
3	1111	0011	0101	0011
4	1111	0100	0101	0100
5	1111	0101	0101	0101
6	1111	0110	0101	0110
7	1111	0111	0101	0111
8	1111	1000	0101	1000
9	1111	1001	0101	1001
A	1100	0001	1010	0001
B	1100	0010	1010	0010
C	1100	0011	1010	0011
D	1100	0100	1010	0100
E	1100	0101	1010	0101
F	1100	0110	1010	0110
G	1100	0111	1010	0111
H	1100	1000	1010	1000
I	1100	1001	1010	1001
J	1101	0001	1010	1010
K	1101	0010	1010	1011
L	1101	0011	1010	1100
M	1101	0100	1010	1101
N	1101	0101	1010	1110
O	1101	0110	1010	1111
P	1101	0111	1011	0000
Q	1101	1000	1011	0001
R	1101	1001	1011	0010
S	1110	0010	1011	0011
T	1110	0011	1011	0100
U	1110	0100	1011	0101
V	1110	0101	1011	0110
W	1110	0110	1011	0111
X	1110	0111	1011	1000
Y	1110	1000	1011	1001
Z	1110	1001	1011	1010

FIG. 14.9 EBCDIC Code and ASCII-8 Code for alphabetic characters and numbers.

8 bits to a byte. The code is known as the *American Standard Code for Information Interchange* and is abbreviated ASCII. Its general format and advantages are like those of the EBCDIC, but its specific codes are different. The zones are different, and the bit representation is different beginning with the letter J so that it does not completely correspond to the Hollerith code. The ASCII code is also shown in Fig. 14.9.

When data are accepted by the input media, remember that they are on punched cards, paper tape, or magnetic tape. The computer automatically changes the input into these codes based on the binary system. Also, the computer automatically changes these codes back to the proper characters or codes for the output media being used. You do not have to work with these codes at all, but you will have a better understanding of the computer if you know how the coding system works.

New Internal Memory Devices

Several new internal memory storage devices have been developed, and others are being developed. *Thin film memory* consists of a thin plate of glass with ferrite rectangles taking the place of ferrite cores strung on wires, as shown in Fig. 14.10. One of the newer thin film memory devices is a glass plate, 2.7″ by 1.7″. It has room for 768 nickel ferrite rectangles, each of which represents one bit. Each plane is comparable to 128 characters in memory, since we are using the 6-bit coding system. Memory actually consists of stacks of these planes. Initially, thin film planes were very expensive to make, but new techniques of vacuum depositing have recently brought the cost of thin film memory into a practical price range. It would be desirable, however, if these planes were even smaller.

Photo-digital memory, as its name implies, involves the developing of films. An electron beam is used to record binary data on pieces of film that are 1.3″ by 2.7″. An internal automated film laboratory develops the film; it is then in plastic cells which are taken through a series of pneumatic tubes to be filed for later use. Data recorded on a film are read with a flying spot scanner. This memory system was designed by IBM for the United States Atomic Energy Commission. It is still very expensive and is in the research and development stage.

Cryogenic memory is another new development which is still too expensive to be competitively marketed, although it is exceptionally

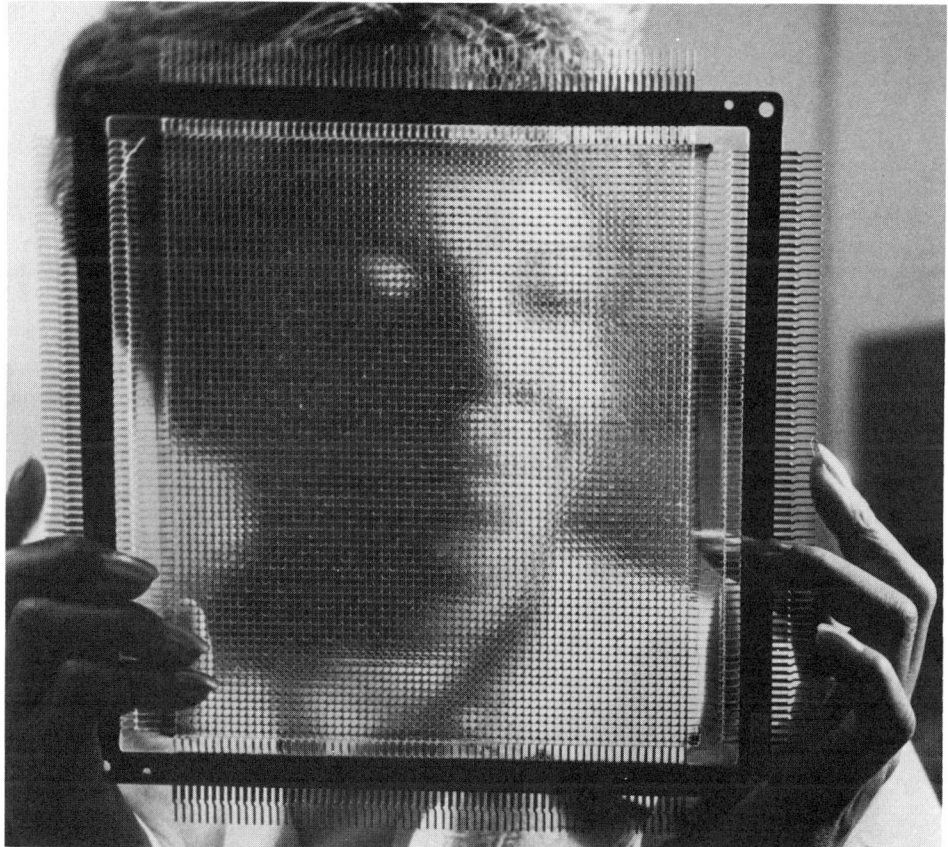

FIG.14.10 Memory plane of unique National Cash Register Century Series

fast and small. The term cryogenic is derived from a term which relates to cold temperatures; a cryogenic memory is a superconducting memory that operates only at a very low temperature. Bell Laboratories are still experimenting with *bubble memory;* they have developed a method whereby magnetized spots are in the form of minute bubbles.

A new *rod memory* device is also in use. It consists of tiny rods automatically placed in solenoids—coils of two interwoven wires—with inner diameters of only 10 mils. After assembly, the planes are coated with plastic and stacked to form memory modules.

These new internal storage devices and others not yet developed will pave the way toward more powerful computers in the future—with faster and more storage capacity at realistic prices.

EXTERNAL STORAGE

Storage of data anywhere except inside the central processing unit of the computer is, of course, external storage. It is frequently called *auxiliary storage.* The limited storage capacity makes it necessary to store some data outside the computer. For example, the balance on each individual savings account in a savings and loan association cannot be stored inside the computer. It is not necessary for all these data to be inside the computer anyway. For example, when the individual amounts for all savings account deposits and withdrawals for the day have been punched onto cards, these cards are used as input into the computer. A card containing a person's savings account number and the amount of his deposit is read into the computer. The computer must find the old balance of that particular account, make the necessary calculation, and record the new balance. The program of instructions tells the computer the exact steps to follow in doing this. But if the old balance for all accounts cannot be stored inside the computer, where does the computer get the needed information?

Connected to the computer are other machines that contain files of data recorded on magnetic tape, magnetic discs, magnetic drums, or data cells. When the computer is instructed to obtain some data from one of these storage devices, it can do so very fast in one of two ways. The computer can *direct access* or *sequential access.* By direct access the external storage device can obtain a specific record without having to read all records from the beginning of the file. External storage devices with this capacity are the magnetic drum, magnetic disk, and data cell. Direct access is sometimes referred to as *random access.* High-speed access to data storage locations provided by direct-access processing permits the user to maintain up-to-date files and to make frequent direct reference to the stored data. Sequential access means that all the records from the beginning have to be read in order to obtain a specific record. The external storage device that operates in this manner is magnetic tape. When a record is needed from external storage, it must be located, transferred to internal storage, processed, and transferred back to the external storage device to update the file.

The time it takes the computer to locate the required data and transfer them to or from storage is called *access time*. Since so many references must be made to external storage in most data processing operations, the access time has a direct bearing on the efficiency of the entire system. For example,

1. *Core storage,* an internal storage method, is the most expensive storage device in terms of cost per storage location. However, it also provides the fastest access time; therefore, it may be the most economical in terms of cost per machine calculation.

2. *Drum storage,* an external storage method, has a lower direct cost and slower speed; it is more economical when speed is not so important.

3. Most *disk storage* devices are slower than the drum storage ones, but offer the advantage of a capacity in the millions of digits and cost less than either core or drum devices.

External storage is used when there are many accounts and only part of them must be referred to each time some of the accounts are being updated. On charge accounts, for example, not all the customers make a purchase or a payment each day; on savings accounts, not all receive deposits or withdrawals each day. Therefore, this kind of data is stored externally, and only the necessary accounts are obtained by the computer each day. The more commonly used external storage methods are magnetic drums, magnetic disks, and disk packs.

Magnetic Drums

Magnetic drums were once used as internal storage devices, but were replaced by magnetic cores. Magnetic drums are now used as external storage devices. They are not so fast as some of the other external storage devices, but neither are they so expensive. A magnetic drum unit is shown in Fig. 14.11. It would be connected by cable to the central processing unit of the computer system.

Figure 14.12 represents part of a magnetic drum showing that each storage location has an address and that it has a coding system like that of the 7-channel magnetic tape. Data are recorded by means of magnetic charges; each location is either ON (charged) or OFF. Data can be erased from the magnetic drum, and new data can be placed on it; so it is reusable. The read-write head remains stationary, and

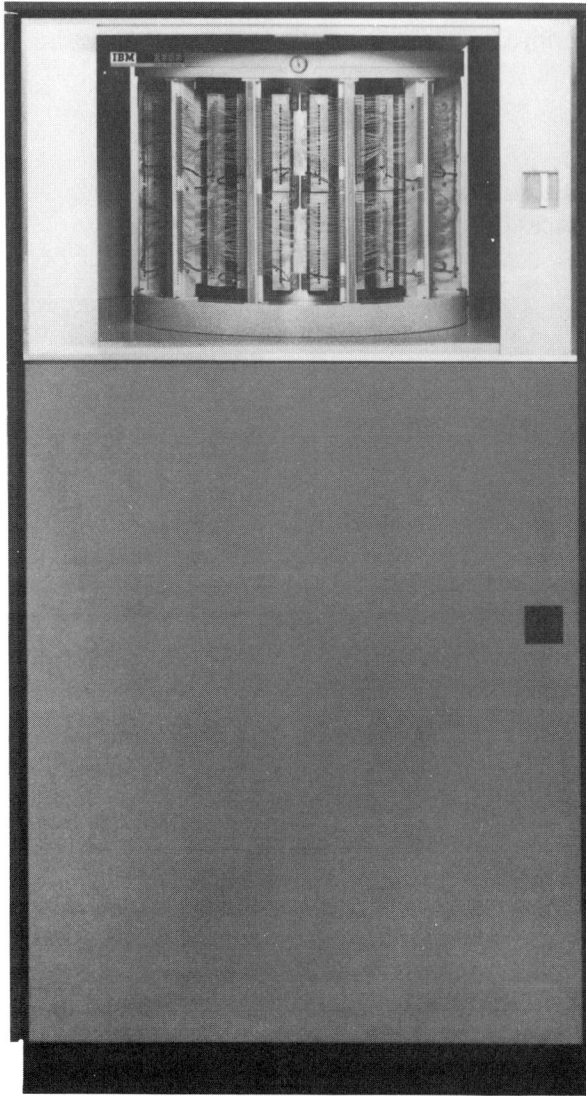

FIG. 14.11 IBM 2302 Drum storage

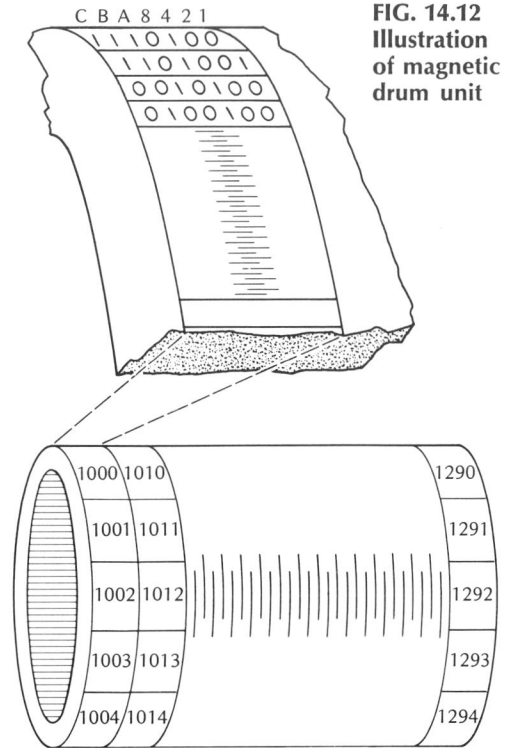

FIG. 14.12 Illustration of magnetic drum unit

the drum rotates as it is being read or as data are being recorded on it. Numerous read-write heads extend across the surface of the drum.

When data are read from a magnetic drum, the information is transferred to the internal storage of the computer so that it can be processed. After processing has taken place, the results can be recorded on the magnetic drum as a permanent record for future use.

**FIG. 14.13
Magnetic
disk IBM**

Magnetic drum storage currently is used in three ways:

1. For the storage of data that are referred to repeatedly throughout the computing operation (such as logarithmic tables, tax charts, and actuarial tables);

2. As a supplementary storage for the main or internal storage, for which its high capacity and intermediate access time make it appropriate; and

3. To provide program storage and program modification data.

Magnetic Disks

A magnetic disk is a thin metal disk with a coating on each side so that each side can be magnetized and made to hold data. A disk looks like a phonograph record without grooves (see Fig. 14.13). A group of disks is *a disk module;* two modules are a *disk unit* (see Fig. 14.14).

Read and write heads are attached to arms that can move very fast to any part of the disk. The arms move away from the edge to read or write as the disk is spinning, and then move back to the edge, ready

FIG. 14.14 Small computer handles big jobs — Honeywell

to be used again. They can read from or write on any location designated.

Each disk surface contains tracks on which the data are recorded.
One model contains 492 tracks per disk surface. Recorded data may
be read as often as necessary. However, if new information is re-

FIG. 14.15   655-102
Dual-spindle
disk unit

corded on a track, the old material is automatically erased. This feature
makes it possible to use the disk surface over and over again.

Magnetic disks used for external storage are also referred to as a
random access device because a specific item can be obtained directly.
It is not necessary for the device to read all the data before the needed
information is extracted.

Disk Pack

A *disk pack unit* is similar to a disk unit, but has a few differences
which provide advantages for some users. A disk pack unit, as shown
in Fig. 14.15, can hold one disk pack; the disk pack shown in Fig. 14.16

FIG. 14.16 NCR 955-1 disk pack

consists of six disks. Each one is like the magnetic disk just described, but is smaller and has fewer tracks on each surface. Only one disk pack fits into the disk pack unit, but the disk pack can be removed and another pack inserted. The magnetic disks previously described are permanent, but many more are in the unit.

Since these disk packs can be removed, nothing is recorded on the top of the first disk or the bottom of the last one because these surfaces can be scratched too easily in handling. The result is that we have only ten surfaces for recording data. A disk pack that contains 14″ diameter disks can hold up to 7.5 million characters of information. Some disk packs contain 11 disks rather than 6; they have 20 surfaces for recording data and can store up to 29.18 million characters (bytes) of information.

The most important advantage to a disk pack unit is that one disk pack can be removed from the unit and another inserted without having to have another complete unit for the additional disk pack. When using a regular disk unit, you have to get a new complete unit when one unit is used to capacity.

FIG. 14.17 IBM data cell

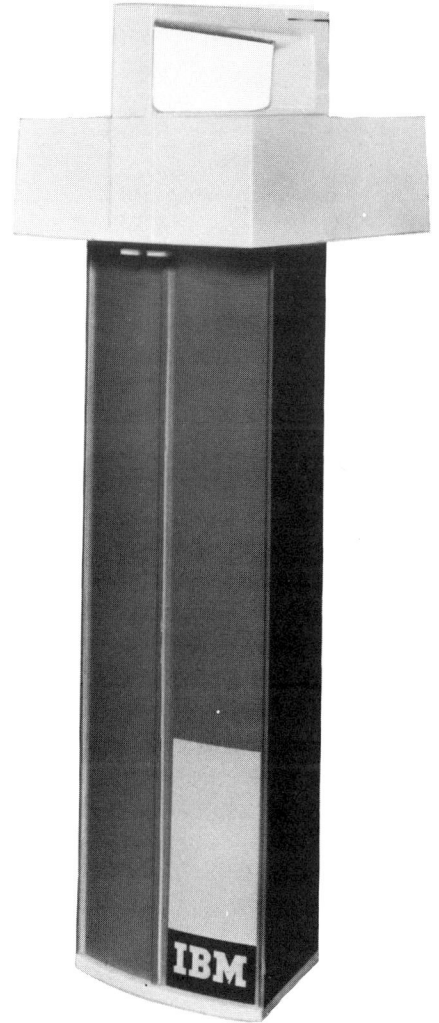

Data Cell Storage

A data cell, as shown in Fig. 14.17, stores several hundred strips of magnetic film, each of which is approximately 2″ wide and 12″ long. One side of each strip has a magnetically sensitive coating on which data can be stored in 200 tracks. Ten of these strips grouped together form a subcell; twenty subcells make up one data cell. The cell drive unit can hold up to 10 data cells. Furthermore, cells can be removed and replaced with others containing different files of information.

Any individual strip can be retrieved. The cell drive positions the selected cell under the retrieval mechanism, and the array of cells rotates until the subcell containing the strip to be processed is under a drum. The selected strip is removed from the subcell and wrapped around the drum. The read/write heads are actuated to read or record the required data. Then the strip is dropped back into its position in the subcell.

The data cell (Fig. 14.18) drive extends direct access or random access storage capabilities to a volume beyond that of the other storage devices. Each drive (10 cells) can hold 400 million characters of data. The data cell storage has slower access time than magnetic disk storage, but it allows direct access to large amounts of data at a relatively low cost.

The NCR Card Random Access Memory (CRAM) consists of a removable cartridge containing 256 magnetic cards made of a material similar to magnetic tape. Since each cartridge can store 5.6 million characters, the CRAM, with a capacity of 16 cartridges, can retain more than 89 million characters at a time. It operates much like the IBM data cells (see Fig. 14.19).

In summary, then, direct access devices are important because the internal or primary storage cannot hold all the data possibly needed for effective utilization of a computer. When selecting the devices to use, a business firm must keep in mind the relationship between the storage volume required and the unit cost of the various devices available. These direct access devices have disadvantages compared to magnetic tape due to the method of control and higher cost in rela-

FIG. 14.18 IBM 2321 Data cell drive

tion to the storage capacity. As the cost of direct access devices is reduced and their speed and capacity increased, they will become increasingly useful.

COMPUTATION SECTION

The computation section contains the circuitry needed to perform the arithmetic and logical operations. The arithmetic portion performs the basic functions of addition, subtraction, multiplication, and division under the direction of the control unit. It also shifts numbers, rounds, sets the algebraic sign of results, and compares. The logical portion carries out the decision-making operations to change the sequence of instruction execution.

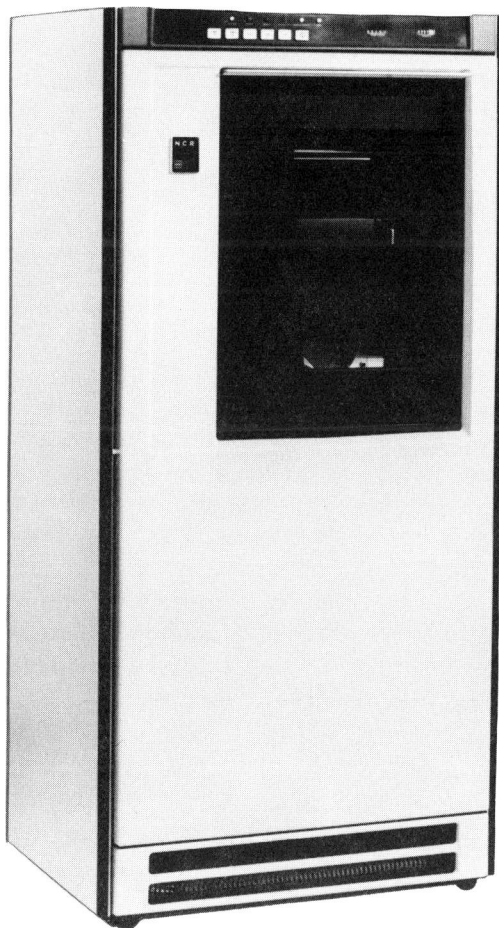

**FIG. 14.19   NCR
653-101 card random
access memory file**

The functional units of the computation section include registers, counters, and an adder. A register receives information, holds it, and transfers it as directed by control circuits. Several types of registers are needed. The accumulator is a register needed during arithmetic operations. In the addition of two numbers, the first one is stored in the accumulator. The next number is added to the contents of the accumulator which then contains the sum. An adder receives data from two or more sources, performs the addition, and sends the results to the accumulator register. When the final total is reached, it is directed back to the computer memory.

An instruction register holds each instruction until it is executed. Then the next instruction is placed in it, ready for the control section to interpret. A sequence register controls the sequence of instructions by referring to the location of each instruction as it is used. This means that it contains the memory address of the next instruction to be read into the instruction register.

A counter is used to keep track of the number of occurrences of an event. It is closely related to a register and may perform some of the same functions. Its contents can be increased, such as beginning with 0 and counting upward to 20, for example, to indicate when a sequence has occurred 20 times or it can be decreased beginning with, for example, 20 and counting downward to 0 to indicate when a sequence has occurred 20 times.

The computer performs multiplication by means of repeated addition. For example, to multiply 798×31, the computer adds 798 to itself 31 times; the computer can do this much faster than we can multiply the two numbers. Subtraction involves complementing the subtrahend (lower number) and adding the complement to the minuend (upper number). Using the nine's complement method, we can illustrate how the results are obtained.

Problem: 4431
            − 813
           _____

1. Add sufficient 0's to the left of the lower number so it contains the same number of digits as the upper number.
   813 becomes 0813.

2. Change 0813 (lower number) to its 9's complement, remembering that a number plus its complement equals 9. You can use the following chart.

Number	0	1	2	3	4	5	6	7	8	9
Complement	9	8	7	6	5	4	3	2	1	0

   0813 becomes 9186.

3. Add the upper number to the 9's complement of the lower number.

   4431
   +9186
   _____
   1 3617

4. Now the end number (end-around carry) is added to the low order digit,

1 3617
   +1
———
3618 which is the answer.

The computer divides by repeated subtraction but, again, does this at a phenomenal speed. Although the example above showed the arithmetic being done in the base 10, or decimal, system, remember that the computer does this in base 2.

We will not consider the internal functioning of the computer's parts in calculation nor how characters are moved from one location to another.

The computation section also performs the logic function of the computer. When instructed, it can compare two numbers to determine whether they are equal, whether the first is larger than the second, or whether the first is smaller than the second. It can also compare two letters or words to determine whether or not they are the same. Depending on the answer to this comparison, it follows appropriate steps.

CONTROL SECTION

According to the stored program, the control section automatically directs all units of the computer so that each unit does the correct thing at the correct time. The program details the steps that the computer must follow. As we have already noted, these individual instructions are recorded on punched cards or tape and are used as input. Since they are kept in the storage section of the computer, the program is called a stored program. As each step is to be executed, the control section interprets the instructions and directs the correct unit to perform properly. Then it reads the next step and continues until it has completed all the steps of the program. Finally, the program is returned to the storage section so that it can be used again. For many kinds of work, the same steps are used over and over again. For example, in computing students' grade point averages and printing their report cards, the same steps are followed until the data for all students have been processed. Then the computer stops. The console buttons are used for giving some instructions to the computer, among them telling it to "start" accepting the input or to "stop" for some reason before it has completed the job.

QUESTIONS AND PROBLEMS

1. What are the three basic units of the computer?
2. What are the three component sections of the CPU?
3. What is the storage section of the computer?
4. What types of data are kept in the storage section?
5. How can information that is no longer needed be erased?
6. What is the storage capacity of a computer designated as 5K?
7. Briefly explain the two addressing systems for computer storage.
8. What is the customary internal storage method currently used in computers?
9. Briefly describe a magnetic core.
10. Why is the binary arithmetic system used by the computer?
11. What is the value of each of the first seven positions in the binary number system?
12. What is the decimal equivalent of the number 100110 in the binary system?
13. What is the binary equivalent of the number 76 in the decimal system?
14. What is the name given to a system that uses both decimal and binary numbers?
15. What is the highest number needed in any one storage location of the computer?
16. How many cores in storage are needed in order to represent any number 0–9?
17. What coding system do most third-generation computers use?
18. How many bits are needed to represent a character using EBCDIC?
19. What are the advantages of the EBCDIC system?
20. What code is accepted currently by the ANSI (American National Standards Institute)?
21. In what ways is ASCII similar to EBCDIC?
22. How is ASCII different from EBCDIC?
23. What is thin film memory?
24. Basically, how does photo-digital memory work?
25. What does external storage mean?
26. Why is external storage usually needed?
27. What are the external storage methods?
28. What is the difference between direct access and sequential access?

29. What external storage devices operate by the direct access method?

30. What external storage device operates by the sequential access method?

31. How does the access time correspond to the efficiency of the computer system?

32. When are old data no longer needed erased from most of these storage devices?

33. What are the three general uses of magnetic drums?

34. Why is magnetic drum storage sometimes advantageous for supplementary storage to main storage?

35. In what ways does a disk pack unit differ from a disk unit?

36. Describe the basic structure of a data cell.

37. Compare data cell storage to magnetic disk storage.

38. Why are direct access devices so important to the computer system?

39. What operations take place in the computation section of the computer?

40. Briefly describe each of the functional units of the computation section.

41. How does the computer perform all arithmetic computations?

42. What is the 9's complement of the number 7612?

43. Why might the computer be instructed to compare two words?

44. What does the control section use to direct the computer functions?

SAMPLES
OF
TYPICAL
COMPUTER
SYSTEMS
IN
USE
TODAY

CHAPTER 15

Now that we have discussed the components of a computer system in some detail, let's look at various ways businesses combine them to make up useful computer systems. Systems are conveniently classified as small-scale, medium-scale, and large-scale, depending upon their storage capacity, internal speed, and overall functioning. The categories are given here merely to indicate a general classification as a good starting point. The smallest systems are rented for as little as $1,000 a month; the largest systems, for more than $100,000 a month. Many of the actual computer systems in use do not easily fall into any one of the three size categories because of the numerous alternatives available within each computer system.

SMALL-SCALE COMPUTER SYSTEMS

Small-scale computer systems are relatively new developments in computers. They are basically card-oriented and are slower than the larger computers. They use some of the unit record techniques such as sorting and collating. Many of them can use data files stored on magnetic tape or magnetic disks. Comparing magnetic tapes and disks, we find that using magnetic tape devices is less expensive for storing and for processing, but requires that the input data (usually punched cards) be in the same sequence as the master file on the magnetic tape. Magnetic disk devices are more expensive but permit random access. They are sometimes referred to as "mini" computers.

An example of a user of a small computer system would be a department store or even a small chain of stores with charge account customers. The customer records are maintained on magnetic tape or magnetic disks in alphabetic order or customer account number order. Each new transaction, whether a purchase or a payment on account, is recorded on a punched card and used as computer input. The magnetic tape or magnetic disk files are then updated by the computer.

These small computers have been designed for users whose volume of data or whose financial resources do not warrant the use of a larger computer system, but who can benefit from the techniques of automated data processing. In the past, these users were limited to the use of the unit record equipment. These newer small-scale computer systems are more efficient at about the same cost, and wider acceptance will undoubtedly further decrease the use of unit record equipment in the future.

NCR Century 100 (National Cash Register)

The National Cash Register (NCR) Century 100 computer system uses a magnetic file system and is designed for batch processing, random access, and real time processing. The basic system consists of four units, as shown in Fig. 15.1: the central processing unit, a card or tape reader, a disk unit, and a printer. Two additional input/output devices can be attached to expand the basic system as desired.

The CPU has a capacity of 16K and can be expanded up to 32K with an access time of 800 nanoseconds. The CPU contains the circuits for basic arithmetic, logic, internal memory, and I/O control. The I/O control handles input/output operations and communication between the CPU and peripherals.

The operator's console is the functioning control center for system operation. It is located physically on the processor. Indicator lights, option switches, and other control switches provide communication between the operator and the processor.

The basic magnetic memory element in the NCR Century 100 computers is a rod .110 inches long and .006 inches in diameter. Rods are made by depositing a thin film of nickel-iron and a protective urethane coating on a length of beryllium-copper wire. Individual rods are inserted into windings of prewired planes which are in turn wired together to form stacks. Two stacks make up an NCR Century

FIG. 15.1   Small-scale computer—NCR century 100

memory module capable of storing 16,384 characters of information. The basic NCR Century 100 system has one memory module of 16,384 characters (or 16K) and may be increased to 32,768 characters (or 32K).

Each rod stores one bit by being polarized in one of two directions. As we have already noted, eight bits, considered as a single character of information, constitute a byte. This is the smallest addressable unit of information in an NCR Century system. A ninth (odd parity) bit is generated for each stored character, but it is not accessible to the program.

Data are stored in binary form. A character may be any 8-bit character symbol, or it may be two 4-bit binary coded decimal numbers. Any character in memory can be addressed directly. Numerical data are represented in one of three forms: unsigned binary, unsigned binary-coded decimal, or signed packed binary-coded decimal.

The Century 100's basic system contains either a punched card reader or a paper tape reader and a printer. It can also use two additional input/output media such as an I/O writer to provide programmer communication with the system, magnetic tape encoders, and optical character readers particularly useful with journal tape from NCR cash registers and accounting machines.

The Century 100 basic system consists of one disk unit with an 8.4 million character capacity and can have a second unit attached to double this capacity. It can transfer data at a rate of 108,000 characters per second. A magnetic tape handler can also be added to the basic system to read and record magnetic tape. Another storage device is the card random access memory (CRAM) with a high capacity random access method. With the CRAM unit, data are recorded on oxide-coated mylar cards. Each card is notched with an individual binary configuration that permits the processor to select only that card containing the required information. Up to eight CRAM units can be connected to the common trunk through each controller for immediate access to approximately 1 billion characters per trunk position.

The programming languages available for the Century 100 are COBOL, FORTRAN, and NEAT/3. NEAT/3 was designed for the NCR series of computers to be used for all general business applications. It uses near-English commands, similar to other programming languages, and has preprogrammed many common processing operations.

The Century 200 is similar to the Century 100, but is a medium-scale computer with larger internal memory and faster processing; it also allows for more peripheral devices.

IBM System/3 Computer (International Business Machines)

The IBM System/3 is an electronic, stored-program computer that offers direct access storage capabilities to small business firms and branch and suboffice locations of larger companies. Comparable direct access storage was previously available (from IBM) only with substantially higher cost computer systems.

The basic System/3 computer consists of a central processing unit, a multi-function card unit, a printer, and a disk storage, as shown in Fig. 15.2. Also shown is an off-line sorter.

The central processing unit has a capacity ranging from 8192 to 32,768 bytes with an access time of 1.52 microseconds. Primary storage uses magnetic cores and the EBCDIC code. The CPU consists of arithmetic and logic units, primary storage, a control system, and a

FIG. 15.2   Small-scale computer—IBM System/3 with card units

console for control. Optional is a dual program feature for running two programs concurrently; when one program is performing an input or output function, the CPU can be processing part of the other program rather than be idle.

The input/output devices include the multi-function card unit (MFCU) and a printer. The MFCU can read, punch, print, sort, and collate along one path avoiding unnecessary handling of the cards. The new, smaller size of IBM card is used. The printer is a relatively fast output for the system. The keyboard of the MFCU can be used to communicate directly with the computer for entering special data and can also be used as a second printer. However, a data converter is available to convert data on 80-column cards to 96-column cards, and a card reader is now available to read data from 80-column cards directly into the computer.

FIG. 15.3   Partial program RPGII for System/3 ▶

```
                H008   008
0001    FCARDS    IPEAF        96              MFCU1
0002    FMASTER   ISEAF        96              MFCU2
0003    FREPORT  O    F       120      OV      PRINTER
        I*    DATE CARD
0004    IMASTER   AA    01     1 C*
0005    I                                           2   19 DATEX
0006    I                                          20   23 NBR
0007    I          BB    02   80 C1
0008    I                                           1    3 CLT1
0009    I                                          46   73 TITLE
0010    I                                          74   76 GEN1   L1
0011    I                                          77   79 DTAL1  L1
0012    I                                          74   74 XTEST  L3
0013    I                                          74   79 ACC1      M1
0014    ICARDS    CC    03   80 C4
0015    I                                          25  322MACTY
0016    I                                          46  552DEBIT            40
0017    I                                          63  722CREDIT
0018    I                                          74   76 GEN2   L1
0019    I                                          77   79 DTAL2  L1
0020    I                                          74  740TEST   L3
0021    I                                          74  750XXTST  L2
0022    I                                          74   79 ACC2      M1
0023    C    L2               SETOF                          88
0024    C    L2               Z-ADD0      T1
0025    C    L1               SETOF                          6065
0026    C    L1               Z-ADD0      ITOT1
0027    C    L1               Z-ADD0      ITOT2
0028    C    01               MOVE '******'  ASTRIC 12
0029    C    01               MOVEL'******'  ASTRIC
0030    C    03 71    12       COMP XXTST                    313332
0031    C    03       2        COMP TEST                     717372
0032    C    03 71N40DEBIT     ADD  ITOT1      ITOT1 102
0033    C    03 71 40ITOT1     SUB  CREDIT     ITOT1
0034    C    03N71 40CREDIT    ADD  ITOT2      ITOT2 102
0035    C    03N71N40ITOT2     SUB  DEBIT      ITOT2
0036    CL1          ITOT1     COMP 0                         60
0037    CL1          ITOT2     COMP 0                         65
0038    CL1N60 65 71ITOT1     ADD  SASST      SASST 102
0039    CL1N60 65 71ITOT1     ADD  ASSETS     ASSETS 102
0040    CL1 60N65 72ITOT2     ADD  LIB        LIB   102
0041    CL1 60N65 73ITOT2     ADD  WORTH      WORTH 102
0042    CL1          1         ADD  T1         T1     20
0043    CL1          1         COMP T1                        88
0044    CLR          LIB       ADD  WORTH      LAW   102
0045    CLR          LAW       COMP ASSETS                    90
0046    CLRN90       ASSETS    SUB  LAW        DIFF   82
0047    OREPORT  D    01   OV
0048    O         OR         01
0049    O                                         39 'B A L A N C E'
0050    O                                         54 'S H E E T'
0051    O         D 2        OV
```

The basic external storage is a disk storage unit made up of one removable disk cartridge and one stationary disk cartridge. They provide a 2.45 million character capacity with an access time of 153 milliseconds. Optional units are available also with two disk cartridges but double the capacity, with three disk cartridges (one stationary and two removable) having a capacity of 7.35 million characters, or with four disks (two stationary and two removable) having a capacity of 9.8 million characters. All the larger units have 269 millisecond access time. Disk storage makes the system particularly useful for applications requiring large storage capacity and fast access to data on file.

In addition to the basic System/3, there are off-line devices that had to be specially made for the system to accommodate the new card size. The sorter uses photoelectric sensing elements and can sort both alphabetic and numeric data. The magnetic character reader is designed to process up to 500 checks and other related banking documents per minute.

The System/3 uses a special programming language called RPG II. It is a modified version of Report Program Generator I (RPG I). It uses English-like statements and should be printed on special program sheets. Standard programs available as software with the System/3 computer include a sort program, a system control program, and a utility program. A partial program written in RPG II is shown in Fig. 15.3. It is used in a company's preparation of its balance sheet. FORTRAN and COBOL can also be used with the System/3.

MEDIUM-SCALE COMPUTER SYSTEMS

Medium-scale computer systems have wide use and many options available, especially in the peripheral devices. Because of their faster processing speed, they do not use punched cards for input or output unless absolutely necessary. When punched cards are necessary for input or output, they are usually transferred with data converters separate from the actual computer. Data on punched cards can be transferred to magnetic tape, and then the magnetic tape can be used as computer input to reduce the input time required. These computers take advantage of operating systems in order to be more efficient.

Univac 9400 System

The Univac 9400 system is a magnetic tape or disk-oriented system with a basic storage capacity of 24,576 bytes and a cycle time of 600 nanoseconds. Internal storage consists of a plated wire memory.

FIG. 15.4 Medium-scale computer—Univac 9400 system

This Univac series of computers also includes a Univac 9200 and a Univac 9300, which would be classified as small-scale computer systems. The Univac 9200 computer is a small, card-oriented data processing system with a basic internal storage capacity of 8192 bytes. This system can be easily expanded to the higher performance card- or tape-oriented Univac 9300 system. From this system, it is easy to make the transition to the still more powerful Univac 9400 system.

The applications with the Univac 9400 system are broadly classified as

1. random and sequential batch processing, and

2. communications-oriented processing.

Programs can be performed concurrently while sharing access to all facilities of the system. A Univac 9400 system is shown in Fig. 15.4.

Central Processing Unit

Main storage, control, arithmetic, and input/output sections represent the major parts of the central processing unit. The main storage of the Univac 9400 System is contained in freestanding units with a 600 nanosecond cycle rate for each halfword (two bytes). The individually addressable units of main storage are called bytes. Each byte contains eight bits plus one bit for parity or checking accuracy. Parity is such that the total number of ones in the byte, including the parity bit, is odd. The parity bit is generated automatically when data are written into storage. Because the parity bit cannot be accessed by the program, a byte is considered in terms of the eight accessible bits when discussed further.

The low-order (512) bytes of main storage have been reserved to contain specific operating information. The data stored in these locations are accessed by the hardware and the operating system during the execution of the appropriate functions. The operating system provides for loading and protecting the appropriate data in these locations.

The control section controls the sequence in which instructions are executed, and it interprets and controls the execution of each individual instruction. The cycling of main storage is initiated by this section, as well as all the hardware aspects of interrupt handling, error checking, and protection. The control section also maintains the instruction address counter and provides for the different processor modes of operation.

The arithmetic section performs all data manipulations including logical and numerical arithmetic, data comparisons, and shifting. This section also performs single or double indexing of operand addresses. The adder in this section performs arithmetic in two's complement form. There are three classes of arithmetic operations as follows:

Binary (fixed-point arithmetic),
Logical operations,
Decimal arithmetic.

Input/Output Section

The input/output section of the Univac 9400 central processor initiates, directs, and monitors the transfer of data between storage and the peripheral subsystems. After an I/O instruction has been transferred to the control unit from the control section, the data transfer is performed concurrently with other central processor functions. The multiplexer channel enables many input/output devices to transfer data concurrently to and from the central processor at a rate of 85,000 bytes per second. Two selector channels are available with the system to provide a combined data exchange capability of 666,000 bytes per second.

The I/O devices available for use with this computer system include a card reader, card punch, line printer, and a visual communication terminal. The external storage devices are classified as subsystems and include magnetic tape units, paper tape units, and magnetic disk units.

Operating System Supervisor

The supervisor within the operating system of the Univac 9400 system is responsible for the administration of control commands to the computer system. The supervisor coordinates all I/O activity and other services provided by components of the operating system. It schedules processing time to the many jobs in a multi-programming environment, then supervises the execution of these jobs.

The major unit of work in the Univac 9400 system is considered a job; each job can be subdivided into job steps, or individual programs. The supervisor exercises a series control over the job steps and at the same time applies a parallel control to the various jobs so that they can be executed concurrently.

The supervisor is designed in such a way that it is easy to use in any data processing situation, provides maximum utilization of the computer's facilities, and handles problems directly, efficiently, and promptly with the major portion of time allotted to the user's program.

The supervisor permits concurrent processing of user programs with system functions. In disk-oriented systems, a supervisor can be generated to control from one to five problem programs being executed concurrently in the computing system. In tape-oriented systems, a supervisor can be generated to control one or more symbiont programs in addition to the execution of one main problem program. Many supervisor functions in both disk-oriented and tape-oriented systems are designed as autonomous activities that can be executed as independent programs.

The multiprogramming technique employed in this system involves the distribution of processing time to programs based on program priorities, time allocation, and input/output utilization.

Programming

Language processors are provided to allow the user of the Univac 9400 System flexibility in preparing programs. Programs may be written in assembly language, COBOL, and FORTRAN, or through the facilities provided by the report program generator. The symbolic language of the assembler provides a simple and convenient method of writing programs through the use of mnemonic instruction codes, assembler directives, data generation instructions, assembly time modification instructions, and the powerful macro generation calls.

The report program generator provides for the automatic preparation of accurate report programs. The user describes the input records, the calculations to be performed, and the output records. The report program generator produces an object program that will prepare the desired report.

Service and utility programs are provided to remove the burden from the user for accomplishing common functions in operating the Univac 9400 System. Some of these functions include sorting data according to a specified order and merging data to facilitate processing, maintaining files on magnetic tape and/or direct access storage, and linking output modules of language processors into a single executable program.

The Univac 9400 System software includes two program testing aids: a dynamic (snapshot) dump, and a terminal (postmortem) dump. The *snapshot dump* is used primarily as a program debugging aid. It provides, by user specification, a listing of register contents, control information, or the contents of any range of addresses in the user's program. It permits the program to be continued after the specified information is listed. The *postmortem dump* is used when a program is terminated through an error or abort condition by the Supervisor. This dump provides complete listings of all aspects of the user's program. In this case the program must be reloaded before it can be restarted.

IBM 360 Computers

The IBM 360 computer systems are so widely used and have so many optional peripheral equipment available that few users have exactly the same combination of equipment. The IBM 360 series of computers encompass a wide range of equipment designed for program compatibility among the various models. A company can change to a larger model with little trouble. The models of the IBM System 360 computers differ not only in their main storage capacity and speed, but also in the number and variety of peripheral devices attached to the basic units. The larger models are faster and have a larger main storage

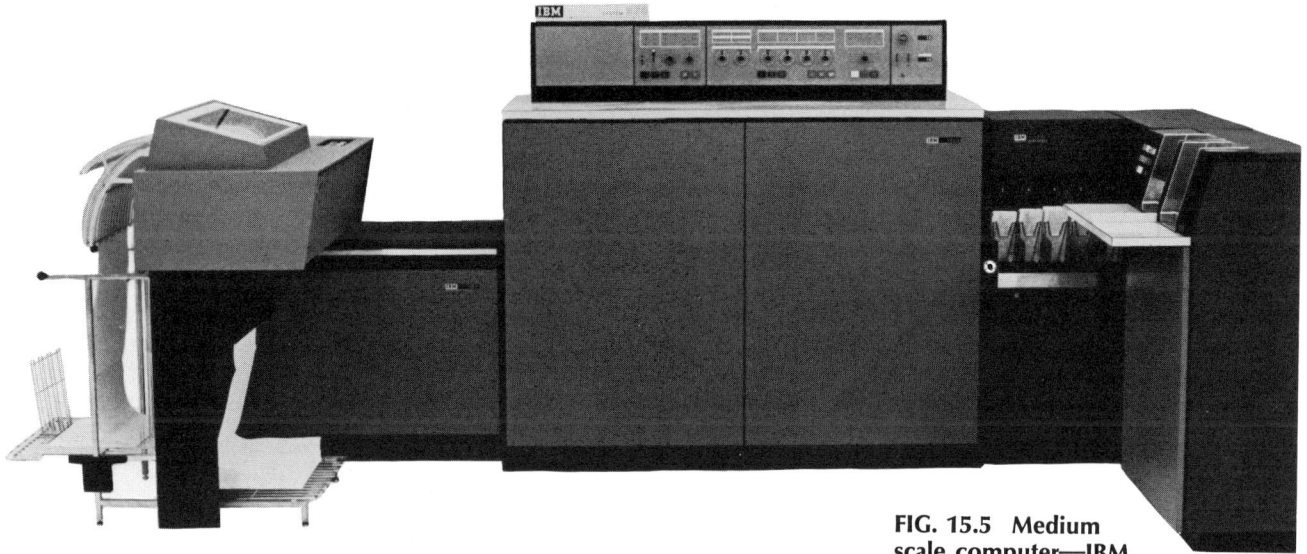

FIG. 15.5 Medium
scale computer—IBM
system/360
Model 20

capacity. The System 360/20 and System 360/25 are usually classified
as medium-scale computers, while the System 360/40 and higher ones
are classified as large-scale computers. The number refers to the size
of the main storage capacity. This general description of the functional
characteristics of the System 360 applies to all System 360 computers.
Fig. 15.5 is an IBM 360/20.

Central Processing Unit

The main storage of the IBM System 360 is arranged into bytes, each
consisting of 8 bits. Each byte has an address and can hold one number, letter or special character, or two numbers when operating in
"packed" mode. The capacity of main storage ranges from 8192 bytes
in the smaller models to 524,288 bytes and even more in some of the
larger models. Arithmetic can be performed in three different number representations: binary integer, floating point, and decimal. The
CPU actually determines the size of the specific System 360 computer.
The various CPU models are listed in Chart 1.

Chart 1   IBM Model 360 Computers

CPU Model	Computer System	Storage Capacity
2020	System/360–20	4,096– 16,384 chars.
2030	System/360-30	8,192– 65,536 chars.
2040	System/360-40	16,384– 262,144 chars.
2044	System/360-44	32,768– 262,144 chars.
2050	System/360-50	65,536– 524,288 chars.
2065	System/360-65	131,072–1,048,576 chars.
2075	System/360-75	262,144–1,048,576 chars.

I/O and External Storage

The IBM System 360 computers have one or more input and output channels; several devices can be attached to each channel. There are two types of channels: the *selector* and *multiplexor*. A computer can have one or more selector channels. These channels are used for high-speed devices such as magnetic tape units, magnetic disk drives, and magnetic drums. At the same time, one device on each selector channel can be active for transmission of data. A multiplexor channel is used for slower-speed devices such as the card reader, card punch, printer, pen-and-ink plotter, or typewriter console. A multiplexor channel is capable of simultaneously transmitting data to and from several of these slow-speed devices.

Programming

Compilers are available for the System/360 computers for most programming languages, the most commonly used being COBOL, FORTRAN, and PL/1. A wide range of utility programs is also available for use with these computers.

Operating System

The operating system of the IBM System/360 is a series of programs provided by IBM and designed to aid and supervise both the internal activities of the computer and its input and output. Such an operating system has the twofold purpose of helping users utilize the complex and sophisticated features of the hardware, and making such use efficient by means of careful planning and overlapping of activities. To ensure efficient computer use, the operating system provides for a high degree of concurrency: several input and output operations can be performed at the same time that instructions are being executed in the central processing unit. For this concurrency to be possible, the computer must have some sophisticated features; the operating system makes use of these features in ways that individual programs would find terribly burdensome. Thus, by means of the operating system, services can be provided in a comprehensive and consistent manner, relieving the individual programmer of many laborious chores.

Concurrency of operations means that often the output for one job, internal processing for a second job, and input for a third job are being performed simultaneously. Immediately after the processing for one job is finished, processing for another job begins. Still more sophisticated operating systems allow time-sharing, under which programs and data for several jobs are in the computer at the same time, taking turns at execution. In such environments, which are necessary for the efficient use of computers, the data of one job must be protected from destruction by the data of another job. The operating system provides this protection.

When the computer is running, it may be in one of two states: the *problem state* or the *supervisor state*. The computer is in the problem state when a user's program is running; it is in the supervisor state only when the supervisor is running. One of the hardware features that helps the supervisor (the part of the operating system) perform its functions is the privileged nature of certain instructions. Input and output instructions, among others, are privileged, which means they can be executed only when the computer is in the supervisor state. Therefore, a user's program must ask the supervisor to do any input and output required.

The supervisor can also make use of the interrupt feature of the IBM System/360. Certain conditions, such as errors, requests from the user's program, and input or output terminations can cause interruption of the user's program and transfer of control to the supervisor. The supervisor may start new input or output transmission, honor requests for service by the user's program, analyze and correct errors— any or all of these—before returning control of the user's program. The interrupt feature thus allows the supervisor to operate input and output devices in a sophisticated and efficient manner and to retain firm control over the activities of the user's program.

Other Features

A consideration in the system's design was to facilitate the newer application approaches to computing, such as communications and multiprogramming. Communications applications include time-sharing, message switching, and the whole area of teleprocessing. Time-sharing, or the *conversational mode,* refers to the use of a number of remote terminals, each of which has access to the computer. Here each terminal may be regarded as a personal computer, and all the independent users have access to a single computer virtually simultaneously because of ultra-high processing and switching speeds.

Message switching involves a telecommunications network where messages from remote points are sent to a central location for routing to their destination. A common teleprocessing application is the processing of inquiries from remote terminals. Any terminal user may introduce data to the system, and programs residing in the system can be activated to perform whatever processing is required. The message may be a query that can be answered by information stored within the system, or it may be data to be entered and processed, with or without the request for an answer.

The program that handles the messages is called the *foreground program.* Other processing may take place between the servicing of messages. This "background" program is interrupted, and the "foreground" program assumes control upon the receipt of a message. When the message is processed and no other messages are held pending, the foreground program relinquishes control to the background program.

Maximum utilization of system resources becomes particularly vital to a communication, or teleprocessing, system (a) if input is unscheduled, (b) if jobs are stacked (where series of jobs are run under the control of a supervisory program with a minimum of operator intervention), and (c) in multiprogramming.

In applications involving multiprogramming, optimum use is made of all facilities by having the system operate upon multiple programs or routines (tasks). While one task awaits data from an I/O device, another task utilizes the processing unit, and still other tasks utilize other I/O devices. As soon as a task utilizing the processing unit must wait for an I/O operation, it relinquishes control of the processing unit, and a waiting task assumes control. The size, speed, and configuration of the system determine whether multiprogramming is practicable.

LARGE-SCALE COMPUTER SYSTEMS

Large-scale computer systems vary greatly because so many different applications are required by the various users. Some are even specially designed, or special-purpose computers.

CDC Model 7600 (Control Data Corporation)

The CDC 7600 is one of the largest computer systems commercially available at the present time. It has significant functional differences compared to most other computer systems. These differences include its peripheral processing units (PPU) in addition to the usual central processing unit (CPU), its two internal core memories, called large core memory (LCM) and small core memory (SCM), and its programming languages.

Central and Peripheral Processing Units

The 7600 system contains a central processing unit (CPU) and a number of peripheral processing units (PPU). Some of the PPU are physically located with the CPU; others may be remotely located. The PPU communicate with the CPU over high-speed data links. The data are buffered at the CPU end of the data link. The PPU provide a communication message switching function between the CPU and individual peripheral equipment controllers. Each PPU has a number of high speed data links to individual peripheral equipment controllers in addition to the data link to the CPU. The PPU share the data link to the CPU among the peripheral equipment controllers on a record-by-record basis.

The PPU serve to gather input data from these peripheral equipment controllers for delivery to the CPU for processing and distribute processed data to these equipment controllers for output devices. A maximum of 15 PPU may be connected directly to the CPU, and all 15 of these CPU input-output channels may be in operation at the same time.

The CPU is a single, integrated data processing unit. It consists of a computation section, small-core memory, large-core memory, and input-output section. These sections are all contained in one main frame cabinet and operate in a tightly synchronous mode with a clock period of 27.5 nanoseconds.

Internal Memory

The CPU contains two types of internal core memory: small-core memory (SCM) and large-core memory (LCM). SCM is arranged in 32 banks of 2K words each, with words of 60-bit length. This provides a capacity of 65,536 words (K = 1024), or about 650,000 characters. The SCM performs certain basic functions in the system which the LCM cannot perform effectively. These functions are ones that require rapid random access to unrelated sections of data. Most of SCM is used for fields of program code and fields of data being processed by the current program.

The LCM is arranged in 8 banks of 64K words each, with the words of 60-bit length. This provides a capacity of 512,000 words (K = 1000), or about 5 million characters. The LCM provides the basic working storage for the CPU. All object programs are assembled here for execution in the SCM. All data files are buffered through LCM for the object programs. Small object programs are usually run to completion in SCM with the complete input file in LCM at the beginning of execution and the complete output files in LCM at the end of execution. The low-order addresses in LCM are reserved for tables, monitor programs, and compilers. The remainder of LCM is divided into two parts, each holding a program. A duplicate of one of the programs is in SCM and is being executed. The other program is waiting to be executed.

The monitor program, as mentioned above, is a CPU program loaded on the machine with the operating system; it remains in the CPU as long as the operating system is used.

System Operation

Job execution proceeds through the system in three phases. In the first phase, the input file is generated on a disk pack, tape unit, or disk file. In the second phase, the input is copied into a job field in LCM. To prepare the job for execution, the control cards from the input file are interpreted by the monitor program, and the necessary compiler or library routines are read from outside the LCM. When ready for execution, the program code is transferred to SCM. If the program and associated data are too large to fit entirely in SCM, a portion of the data is retained in LCM and directly addressed there. One program is executed at a time in SCM. If the amount of input and output is small enough, the entire job may be run in one execution interval. If the job execution is delayed because data have to be transferred, another job uses SCM while the data for the first job are being transferred. This second phase is complete when the output data are delivered to the output file in LCM and then to a system mass storage unit. The third phase consists of copying the output data from the mass storage to an operating station. During this phase, the LCM job field has already been released for another job.

Peripheral Equipment

External storage usually consists of magnetic disks and drums combined in a disk/drum subsystem. The disk file can hold a maximum of more than 5 billion bits. The drum unit can hold a maximum of nearly 160 million bits.

The I/O section contains 15 channels for I/O hookup. The I/O devices available include card readers and punches, tape transports, line printers, removable disk storage drives, and CRT displays.

Programming

The CDC 7600 can use several programming languages including FORTRAN, COBOL, and COMPASS. FORTRAN can be used for mathematical and scientific problems, and COBOL for business problems. COMPASS is an assembly language that provides a symbolic programming language which uses the computer's ability efficiently. The wideband export/import programs allow batch processing from remote locations by way of wide-band communication links.

ANALOG COMPUTERS

The TR-20 as shown in Fig. 15.6 is a desk-size analog computer. With an accuracy up to .05%, it is capable of performing the mathematical operations of summation, integration, sign changing, multiplication, division, and function generation; these are the operations required in the solution of most routine engineering problems. Differential equations, basic to most engineering problems, can be solved with surprising rapidity on this computer. Even if an engineer has never used a computer before, he can learn to use a small desk-size computer as easily as he learned to use a slide rule. A turn of a knob feeds in design parameters. The computer then provides an instant-by-instant dynamic picture of the effect of each change. The relationships of heat, pressure, flow, vibration, torque, or any other variables can be studied.

FIG. 15.6   Desk-size analog computer—EAI (Electronic Associates, Inc.)

A desk-size analog computer has several advantages to an engineer, such as:

1. He can carry it to his desk to solve day-to-day problems, thus eliminating repetitive hand calculations.

2. He can experiment with new ideas that would otherwise be too costly or time-consuming to try.

3. He can perfect new designs and work out the "bugs" in the design before building models or prototypes.

4. Even though the company has large analog computers, he can use a small one to solve smaller problems. This eliminates tie-ups and excessive waiting time for the larger equipment.

Steps in Using This Analog Computer

The routine engineering problems require five steps for their completion with a small desk-size computer such as the TR-20. Some of the steps are shown in Fig. 15.7 and the procedure for obtaining a problem solution is briefly explained here:

Step 1   Problem Analysis. The problem is translated into a mathematical description using algebraic and differential equations.

Step 2   Programming. An information flow sheet is prepared using a block diagram to represent the various computer elements and their interconnections.

Step 3   Patching. Following this diagram, the patch cord connections are made between the various computer elements.

Step 4   Insertion of Problem Parameters. Coefficient potentiometers are adjusted to provide design parameter inputs.

Step 5   Solution. The computer solution is performed in the exact manner prescribed by the mathematical equations. Solutions are presented on an *X-Y* plotter, strip chart recorder, or repetitive operation display unit.

Console

The console of the TR-20 analog computer is divided into four basic areas. They are the attenuator row, the nonlinear row, the amplifier row, and the control panel. In these portions of the console, the plug-in computing components are interchangeable to provide flexi-

**FIG. 15.7 EAI—
Analog computer
problem steps**

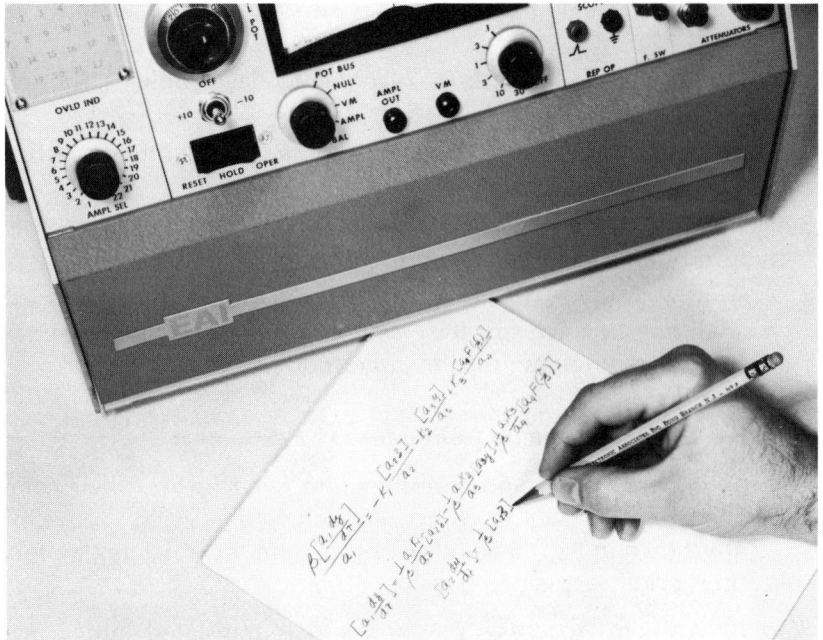

**Step 1,
problem analysis**

Step 3, patching

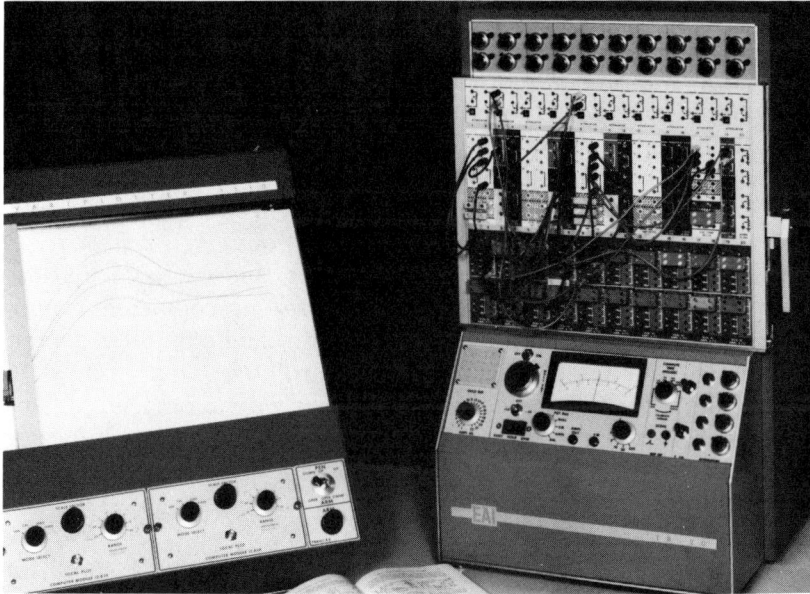

Step 5,
solution plotted

bility and expansion. These solid-state, plug-in standardized computing components all plug into the console from the front of the computer. The computer patch panel is automatically formed by the color-coded patching module on the front of each component. This feature and the ability to place different types of computing components into the same console position provide flexibility in arranging the different equipment complements.

The attenuator row is the top row of the computing components on the console. It is wired to accept up to a maximum of 10 dual coefficient setting potentiometer plug-in modules. These modules are used for setting problem coefficients and boundary conditions, as well as for problem inputs.

The nonlinear row is the middle row of computing components. It is wired to accept a variety of interchangeable linear and nonlinear computing components. Examples of the computing components include integrator networks that make possible the mathematical operation of integration, multipliers that electronically multiply two variables of either sign (positive or negative), several diode function generators that permit special computations such as squares and square roots, a reference panel that makes available accurate reference voltage required for problem solution, and comparators that compare a variable input voltage to a predetermined voltage.

The amplifier row is the bottom row of computing components and is just above the control panel. It is wired to hold up to 10 dual operational amplifier modules. These amplifiers are used for addition, subtraction, integration, and inversion. With other components, they also perform a variety of nonlinear operations.

The control panel contains knobs, buttons, and switches that are clearly marked. This control panel is used in setting coefficient potentiometers, reading out problem variables, controlling computer operating mode (i.e.,—hold—operate—reset), controlling primary power to computer and periodic manual balancing of operational amplifiers. An important feature of the panel is the individual overload indicator on the left-hand side which immediately identifies any amplifier that is in an overload condition so that programming errors can be located with minimum delay.

A null meter is built into TR-20 control panel; it is designed for precise measurement of fixed voltages. A precision potentiometer is provided with the nulling system whereby output signals can be read to three-place accuracy (0.1%). The null meter is also used for setting coefficient potentiometers to an accuracy of 0.1%.

External Read-Out Equipment

Both a plotter and a display unit can be used with the TR-20 to provide the computer's output. The plotter is the larger unit with white paper. It is called an *X-Y* plotter because it provides the recording of any two problem variables (called *X* and *Y*) with one a function of (dependent on) the other. Comparative studies can be made by using different parameter values (by changing the value of *X* or *Y*) and then comparing the resulting graphs. The output lines that comprise the graphs are recorded on paper so that they are permanent records.

The display unit shows results similar to the *X-Y* plotter, but projects the lines on a screen. It can display up to four outputs (plotted lines) simultaneously.

Sample Problems

The TR-20 analog computer is capable of solving both linear problems and non-linear problems. Figures 15.8 and 15.9 show a sample of

PROBLEM

Solve the second order linear differential equation:

$$\frac{1}{\omega_n^2}\frac{d^2x}{dt^2} + \frac{2\zeta}{\omega_n}\frac{dx}{dt} + x = k(t) \qquad 1)$$

with the initial conditions $(t = 0)$

$$\frac{dx}{dt} = \dot{x}_0 = +2.5\omega_n, \quad x = x_0 = -4.0$$

and parameters

$$\zeta = 0.3,\ 0.6,\ 1.2$$
$$\omega_n = 1.0,\ 2.0,\ 3.0$$
$$k = 2.0,\ \text{a constant.}$$

For computer solution it is appropriate to write the equation in the form:

$$\frac{1}{\omega_n}\frac{d^2x}{dt^2} = k\omega_n - 2\zeta\omega_n\left(\frac{1}{\omega_n}\frac{dx}{dt}\right) - \omega_n x \qquad 2)$$

The problem variables, x and its derivatives, are represented on the computer by voltages, amplitude scaled within the ±10 volt allowable range by including a suitable scale factor . . .

$$\frac{\text{max. allowable voltage}}{\text{max. value of variable}} = \text{scale factor (volts/unit)}$$

scale factor x variable = scaled voltage

variable	estimated max. value	scale factor	scaled voltage
x	5	2	$[2x]$
$\frac{1}{\omega_n}\frac{dx}{dt}$	5	2	$\left[\frac{2}{\omega_n}\frac{dx}{dt}\right]$

Substituting the scaled voltages into eq (2) and adjusting the coefficients to maintain equality . . .

$$\left[\frac{2}{\omega_n}\frac{d^2x}{dt^2}\right] = 2\omega_n k - 2\zeta\omega_n\left[\frac{2}{\omega_n}\frac{dx}{dt}\right] - \omega_n[2x] \qquad 3)$$

Further adjustment of coefficients enables each term to be expressed as a product of integrator gain, potentiometer coefficient setting and scaled computer voltage . . .

$$\left[\frac{2}{\omega_n}\frac{d^2x}{dt^2}\right]' = 10\left(\frac{2k\omega_n}{10\cdot10}\right)[10] - 10\left(\frac{2\zeta\omega_n}{10}\right)\left[\frac{2}{\omega_n}\frac{dx}{dt}\right] - 10\left(\frac{\omega_n}{10}\right)[2x] \qquad 4)$$

In this equation the terms inside the square brackets represent voltage outputs from the computer components, such as the output of an amplifier or from the reference source. The terms inside the parenthesis represent pot settings, and the factors without parenthesis or brackets indicate the required input gain to the first integrator.

COMPUTER PROGRAM

The computer circuit diagram is obtained by

1) Integrating the highest derivative (L.H.S. of eq.4) twice to produce $\frac{2}{\omega_n}\frac{dx}{dt}$ and $2x$
2) Instrumenting the R.H.S. of eq.4 to complete the loops.
3) Providing a time-base generator by integrating a constant voltage in integrator 4.

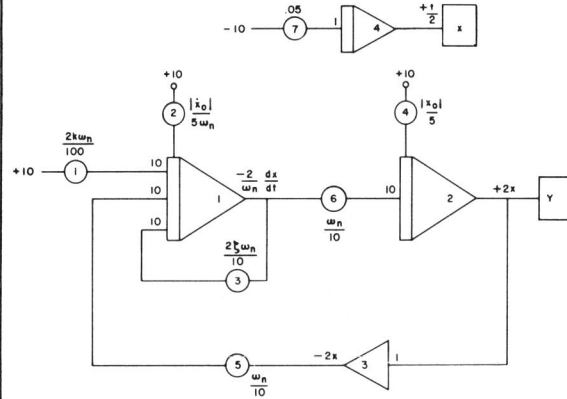

SOLUTION

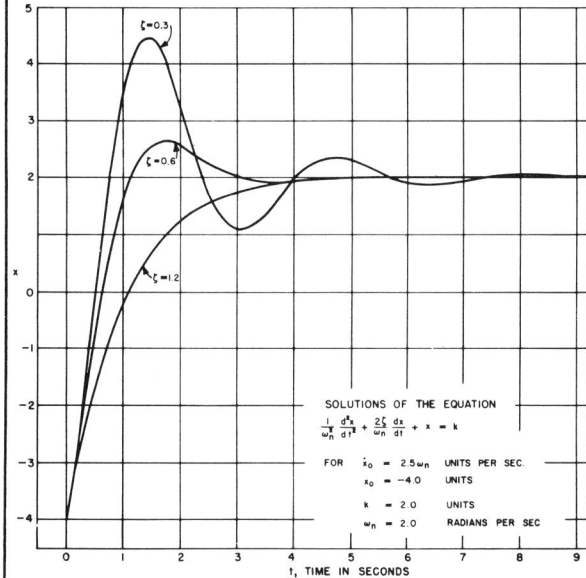

SOLUTIONS OF THE EQUATION
$$\frac{1}{\omega_n^2}\frac{d^2x}{dt^2} + \frac{2\zeta}{\omega_n}\frac{dx}{dt} + x = k$$

FOR	$\dot{x}_0 = 2.5\omega_n$	UNITS PER SEC.
	$x_0 = -4.0$	UNITS
	$k = 2.0$	UNITS
	$\omega_n = 2.0$	RADIANS PER SEC

t, TIME IN SECONDS

FIG. 15.8 Basic TR-20

PROBLEM

Solve the normalized form of Van der Pol's equation:

$$\frac{d^2x}{dt^2} - \lambda(1-x^2)\frac{dx}{dt} + x = 0 \qquad 1)$$

for initial conditions ($t = 0$)

$$\frac{dx}{dt} = \dot{x}_0 \qquad -5 < \dot{x}_0 < +5$$
$$x = x_0 \qquad -5 < x_0 < +5$$

and values of λ

$$0.1 < \lambda \leq 2.$$

Plot a phase plane diagram.

The problem variables, x and dx/dt, are amplitude scaled within the ±10 volt allowable range by including a suitable scale factor...

$$\frac{\text{max. allowable voltage}}{\text{max. value of variable}} = \text{scale factor (volts/unit)}$$

$$\text{variable} \times \text{scale factor} = \text{scaled voltage}$$

variable	estimated max. value	scale factor	scaled voltage
x	5	2	$[2x]$
$\frac{dx}{dt}$	10	1	$\left[\frac{dx}{dt}\right]$

Solving for the highest derivative...

$$\frac{d^2x}{dt^2} = \lambda\frac{dx}{dt} - \lambda x^2\frac{dx}{dt} - x \qquad 2)$$

Substituting the scaled voltages into eq.2 and adjusting the coefficients to maintain equality...

$$\left[\frac{d^2x}{dt^2}\right] = \lambda\left[\frac{dx}{dt}\right] - \frac{100\lambda}{4}\left[\frac{\frac{[2x]^2}{10}\left[\frac{dx}{dt}\right]}{10}\right] - \frac{1}{2}[2x] \qquad 3)$$

Factors of 10 are included in the nonlinear term for they are produced automatically in the computer voltage representing this term.

COMPUTER PROGRAM

The circuit diagram shows the computer mechanization of eq.3

A time scale factor β is included in all the inputs to all the integrators to permit changes in the speed with which the solution is produced.

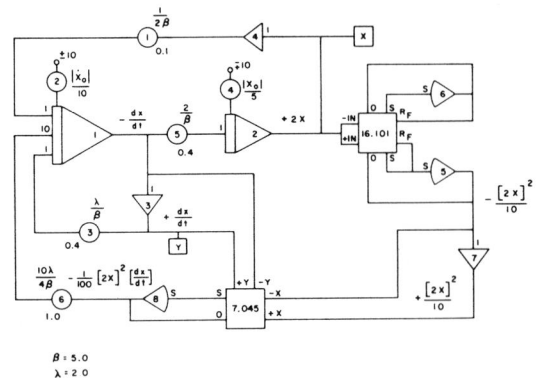

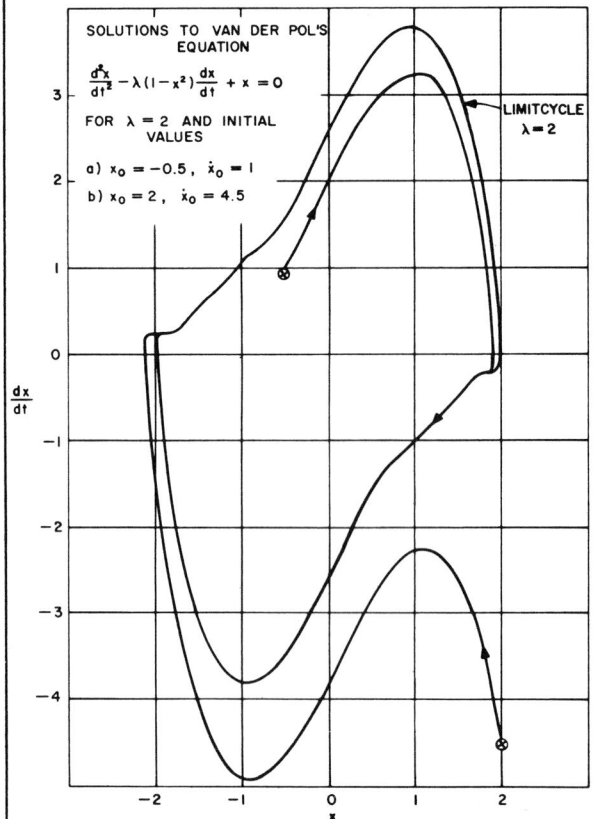

FIG. 15.9 Basic TR-20—Nonlinear problem

each, first stating the problem in detail, then showing the computer program as a circuit diagram, and finally showing the graphed or plotted solution to the problem.

LARGER DESK-SIZE ANALOG COMPUTERS

Larger desk-size analog computers are available for solving more sophisticated problems such as ones that require high-speed repetitive operations and iterative techniques; they are actually comparable in their capabilities to many console computing systems. Typical applications include: system optimization, boundary value problems, model building—including portions of the anatomy for biomedical investigations—rapid determination of stability of control systems, approximate computation and display of integral transforms, statistical studies requiring many solutions, and a wide variety of routine computational problems requiring multiple solutions.

By adding a digital expansion system, the analog computer has digital-logic capabilities for "hybrid" problems.

QUESTIONS AND PROBLEMS

1. What factors determine whether a computer is a small-, medium-, or large-scale computer?
2. Why do many computers not fall definitely into a size category?
3. Why have small-scale computers had an effect on the use of unit record equipment?
4. What are the advantages of magnetic disks over magnetic tape?
5. What is the internal memory device of the NCR Century computers?
6. What I/O media can be used with the NCR Century computers?
7. What is a CRAM unit and how does it work?
8. What are the basic components of the System/3 computer?
9. What is the primary storage of the System/3?
10. How does the dual program feature work?
11. What functions can the multifunctional card unit perform?
12. Under what conditions is disk storage helpful for the System/3?
13. What general type of options are important with medium-scale computer systems?
14. How are punched cards usually used with the medium-scale computers?
15. What internal storage does the Univac 9400 computer system use?

16. What is a byte?
17. What function does the multiplexer channel serve?
18. What does the Univac 9400 supervisor do?
19. What are the advantages of this supervisor?
20. What programming languages can be used with the NCR series?
21. List samples of the service and utility programs available with the NCR series.
22. How is the snapshot "dump" used?
23. What does program compatibility permit?
24. What do the various model numbers of IBM 360 computers refer to?
25. What are selector channels?
26. List several slower-speed I/O devices for the 360 computers.
27. Basically, how do the operating system programs aid in the use of the computer?
28. What type of concurrency is possible?
29. What types of communication applications are possible with the IBM 360 computers?
30. What is "message switching"?
31. What are the primary differences between the CDC 7600 computer system and most other computer systems?
32. What types of functions do the SCM perform?
33. Which memory is the basic storage for the CPU?
34. What are the three phases of job execution in the CDC?
35. What is the function of wide-band export/import programs?
36. What mathematical operations can the TR-20 perform?
37. What type of computer is the TR-20?
38. In what ways is the TR-20 advantageous to an engineer?
39. Briefly list the five steps in solving problems you would take in using an analog computer.
40. Briefly explain the purpose of each of the four basic areas of the analog computer console.

PART IV

COMPUTER
PROGRAMMING
AND
SYSTEMS
DESIGN

People who have no understanding of how a computer works think that it is a genius that knows everything and can answer any question. Once we have learned something about the way a computer works and what it can and cannot do, we realize that we must tell it exactly what to do. What is amazing, however, is the speed at which it can operate. However, a different program must be prepared for each different type of job the computer is to process. For example, a company would need different programs for computing the payroll, for keeping the inventory up to date, and for handling customers' charge accounts, although the same computer could be used for all these jobs.

We will discuss further the following steps which one or more human beings must take to prepare a computer program. It is necessary to

1. Understand and analyze the problem.
2. Prepare a flowchart of the solution to the problem.
3. Write the program.
4. Assemble or compile the object program.
5. Test and correct the program.
6. Prepare the program for actual use.

A programmer does not usually perform all these steps. A person classified as a systems analyst analyzes the problem and usually prepares the flowchart. Then the programmer uses this program flowchart to write the program, assemble or compile the object program, and test the program. The programmer must frequently consult with the systems analyst when correcting the program, especially if the changes involve modifying the flowchart. The programmer then prepares the program for actual use. If the same person performs all these duties, he is usually functioning as both a systems analyst and a programmer. The person who uses this program and operates the computer is a computer operator. A programmer might want to operate the computer himself when he is testing his program, but after he has perfected the program, someone else takes over this job.

1. UNDERSTAND AND ANALYZE THE PROBLEM

The importance of this first step in the development of a computer program cannot be overemphasized. If a mistake is made here or if some fact is overlooked, all the time spent in planning the program can be wasted. You must completely understand the input available. Plan the fields of data very carefully. You must have a good understanding of *all* the output required. A printed bill to the customer is not enough; permanent records are equally important. You must also understand the logical and computational procedures that are needed to solve the problem. Understanding all these aspects of a problem to be solved by a computer naturally means that the systems analyst is very familiar with the computer and the advantages and disadvantages of all available accessory devices. He must frequently consult with the heads of the departments that supply the input data and with those that need the output data.

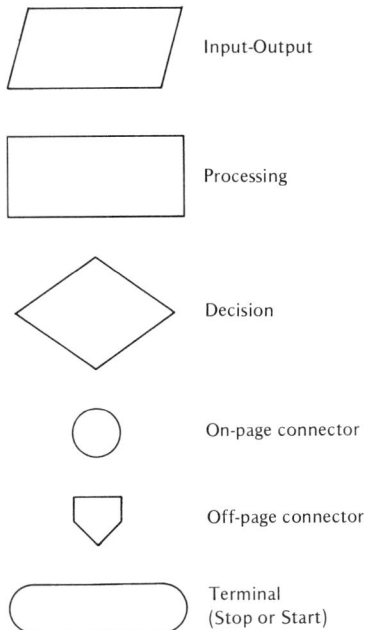

2. PREPARE A FLOWCHART OF THE SOLUTION TO THE PROBLEM

The steps for solving a problem can be written out in detail. Usually, however, a flowchart is used; it is a graphic illustration of the steps the computer is to follow. The advantages of making a flowchart rather than just listing the steps are that it is

1. Precise, like an outline.
2. Definite and cannot be easily misinterpreted.
3. Easy to follow because of its graphic form.
4. Easier to use as a means of comparing several different solutions to the problem.
5. Easier to use when making changes or corrections.

   Flowcharts are often made so that you read the symbols from left to right across the paper, and from the top to bottom of the paper. Arrows are usually used to connect the symbols so that the order cannot be confused.

   A few common symbols that are most frequently used to make a computer flowchart are shown in Fig. 16.1. There are others, but these

Input-Output

Processing

Decision

On-page connector

Off-page connector

Terminal
(Stop or Start)

FIG. 16.1 Common flowchart symbols

are the basic ones we will be using. The template is used to make these symbols consistently the same size. These symbols are frequently referred to as *blocks,* so the flowchart is often called a *block diagram.*

The diamond-shaped symbol is used when the computer must make a decision. Remember that this programming utilizes the logic capacity of the computer. The decisions the computer can make are whether or not

The first number is equal to the second,
The first number is larger than the second,
The first number is smaller than the second,
Alphabetic characters are the same, and
The last record has been processed.

The on-page connector and off-page connector are used just as they are on unit record data processing flowcharts—to indicate the continuity on the flowchart. We based the flowchart in Fig. 16.2 on an activity with which we are all familiar—studying—in order to illustrate the logical order in which a flowchart must be made. The flowchart begins and ends with the terminal symbol. Frequently the start symbol is omitted. Arrows are used to indicate direction, but are sometimes omitted when it is obvious. Rectangles indicate processes such as opening the book and reading a page. The diamond-shaped symbols indicate decisions that must be made; inside the symbol is the question that can be answered by Yes or No. An arrow indicates the path to follow for each answer.

At the bottom of the first column is a small circle with the number 1 inside it. A circle is an on-page connector which means that the flowchart continues at another place on the same sheet of paper. You find another circle with the number 1 at the top of the next column, so this is where to continue the problem.

When the flowchart indicates that you go back to repeat a previous step, a loop is formed. A loop results when you get to a question involving a decision, "Is it 12 p.m. yet?" If the answer is No, you watch TV a while; then you see the arrow going upward and back to the step "Look at watch" again. Each time the answer to the question, "Is it 12 p.m. yet?" is No, you go through this loop again. When it is 12 p.m. or later, then the answer is Yes, and you follow the arrow downward to turn off the TV and go to bed.

A business problem using some of the same symbols is shown in Fig. 16.3, which shows the flowchart of a payroll problem. Because

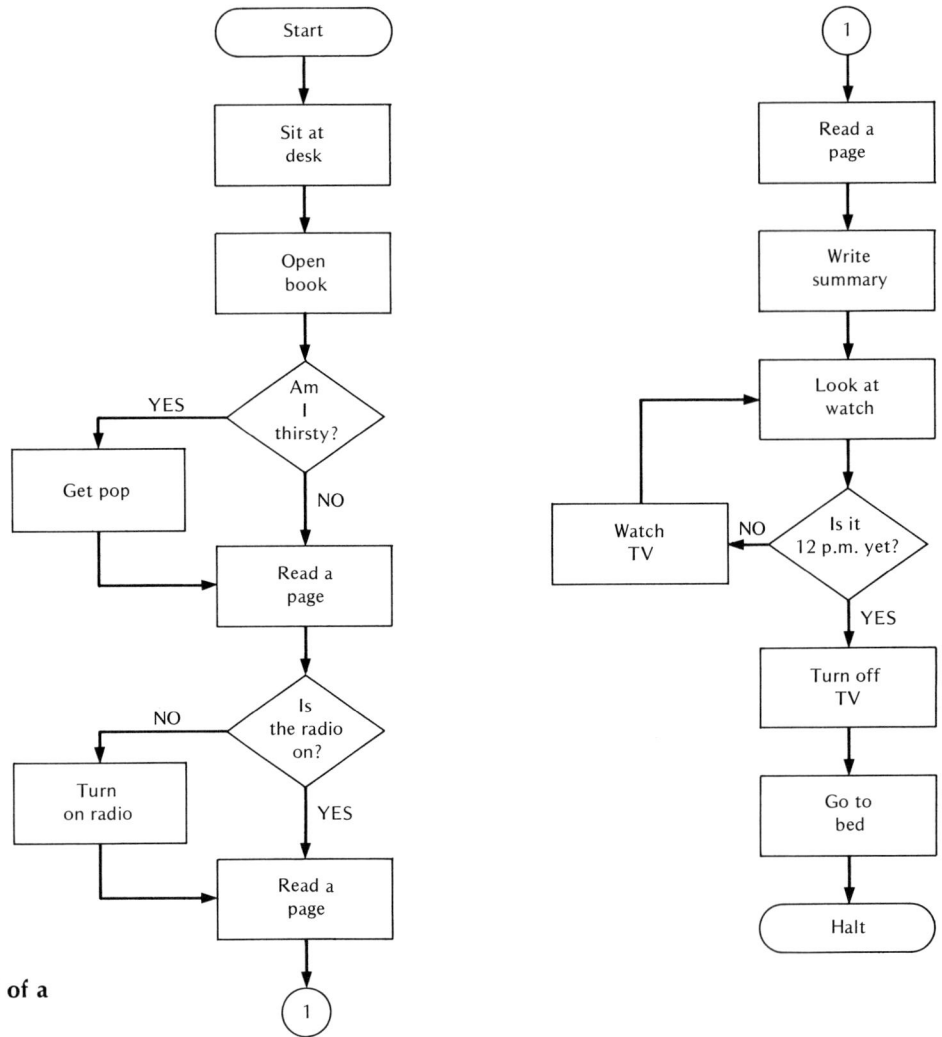

FIG. 16.2 Flowchart of a common activity

the chart is very general and does not state the detailed steps involved in each calculation, it is considered a *general flowchart*. A flowchart which contains the detailed steps is considered a *program flowchart*, sometimes called a *block diagram*. Figure 16.4 illustrates just a section of a program flowchart—the part that would be substituted for the "Calculate gross pay" rectangle of the general flowchart in Fig. 16.3.

This partial flowchart shows the steps necessary for calculating gross pay. The difficulty is that any time over 40 hours a week is con-

FIG. 16.3 General flowchart of a business problem

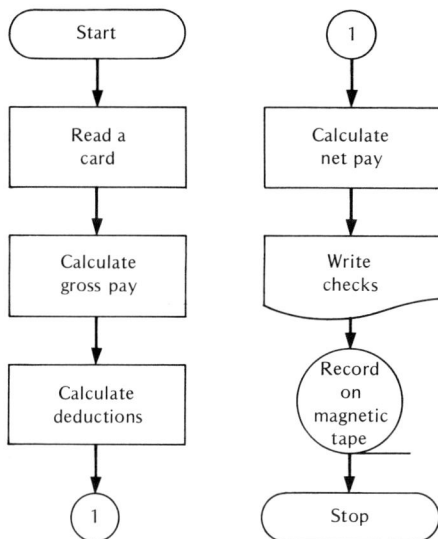

FIG. 16.4 Program flowchart of a portion of a general flowchart

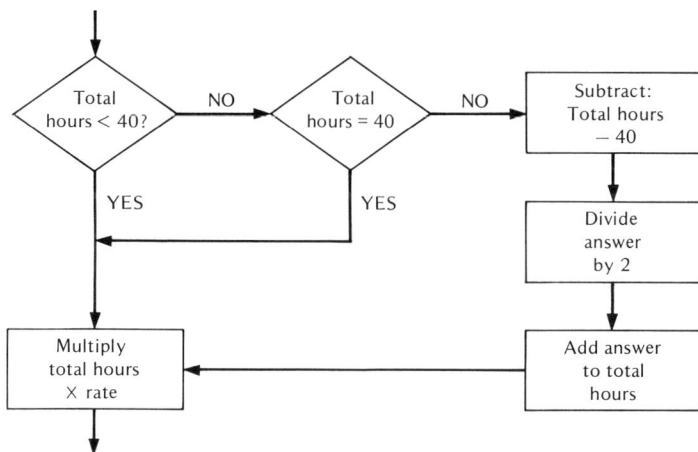

sidered as overtime, and employees receive a bonus for working overtime. The bonus is equal to half of their hourly rate; for each overtime hour they get one and a half times their regular hourly rate.

The first question asks whether the person worked less than 40 hours. If the answer is Yes, it is obvious that the person did not work overtime, so the next step is to multiply the total hours by the hourly rate. If the total hours is not less than 40, there are still two possibilities: exactly 40 hours and over 40 hours. Therefore, another decision must be made; the question is "Do the total hours equal 40?" If the answer is Yes, the person did not work overtime, so the next step is to multiply the total hours by the hourly rate, as indicated by following the arrow. If the answer to the question, "Do total hours equal 40?" is No, then it is apparent that the person worked more than 40 hours (remember that those with less than 40 hours never even reach this decision). For those with more than 40 hours, three steps are followed to determine the total hours to multiply by the hourly rate. We will use an example to make these steps clearer. Assume that the person worked 43 hours during the week. The steps following this section of the program flowchart are:

1. Subtract: total hours − 40	$43 - 40 = 3$
2. Divide the answer by 2	$3 \div 2 = 1.5$
3. Add the answer to total hours worked	$43 + 1.5 = 44.5$

This calculation adds the overtime bonus for the 3 hours to the total hours worked. The total 44.5 hours is actually 40 hours of regular pay plus 3 hours of $1\frac{1}{2}$ times the regular pay ($4\frac{1}{2}$ hours).

The section of the general flowchart that is labeled "Calculate deductions" would be much more complicated on a program flowchart, of course, because numerous deductions would have to be made including those for federal income tax, social security, state income tax, union dues, and possibly even family insurance payments or the purchase of a savings bond. A *program flowchart* with its greater details is obviously much longer than a *general flowchart* of the same problem. The program flowchart is the one the programmer uses to write the step-by-step instructions.

Another type of flowchart is the *systems flowchart* which represents the flow of data through the entire system. The complete procedure of preparing the employees' pay checks as shown in Figs. 16.3 and 16.4 would occupy just one rectangle in a complete systems flowchart. So a systems flowchart is a very general diagram showing the order in which the various functions are to be performed in the complete data processing cycle.

3. WRITE THE PROGRAM

Several different means are available for actually writing the program of computer instructions, depending partly on the computer being used. Most programs are first written in a symbolic language that is

A Cobol coding sheet

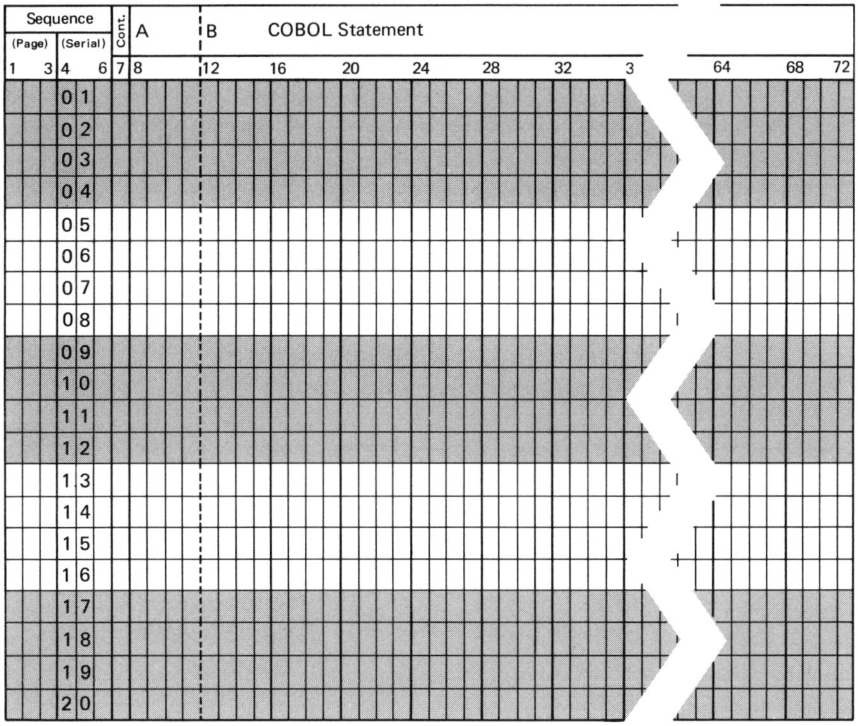

FIG. 16.5   A COBOL coding sheet

easy for the programmer but one that the computer cannot understand. Figure 16.5 shows a coding sheet that is used by the programmer to write a program in a language called *COBOL*. The programmer prints the words and symbols on this form (see Fig. 16.6). Since the instructions as written on this sheet cannot be used directly by the computer, we prepare these symbolic instructions so that they can be changed into instructions the computer can understand.

1. These symbolic instructions are punched on cards, one line on one card because each line is a separate instruction. After the instructions are on the cards, the result is frequently called the *source program*.

2. *Proofread* the punched cards in one of these ways:

   Read the characters at the top of the cards if the keypunch machine printed them,

Coding:

Sequence		Cont.	A	B	COBOL Statement							
(Page)	(Serial)											
1 3	4 6	7	8 12	16	20	24	28	32	36	40	44	48
	0 1		IDENTIFICATION DIVISION.									
	0 2		PROGRAM-ID. 'PAYROLL'.									
	0 3		ENVIRONMENT DIVISION.									
	0 4		DATA DIVISION.									
	0 5		WORKING-STORAGE SECTION.									
	0 6		01 WORKER PICTURE X(24).									
	0 7		01 RATE PICTURE 9(5)V999.									
	0 8		01 TIME PICTURE 9(5)V999.									
	0 9		01 PAY PICTURE 9(5)V999.									
	1 0		PROCEDURE DIVISION.									
	1 1		THIS-MUST-BE-THE-PLACE. ACCEPT RATE.									
	1 2		IF RATE IS EQUAL TO 0									
	1 3		STOP RUN.									
	1 4		ACCEPT WORKER.									
	1 5		ACCEPT TIME.									
	1 6		MULTIPLY RATE BY TIME GIVING PAY.									
	1 7		DISPLAY WORKER.									
	1 8		DISPLAY PAY.									
	1 9		GO TO THIS-MUST-BE-THE-PLACE.									

FIG. 16.6 COBOL statement

Run the cards through the interpreter and read the printed characters, or

Run the cards through a printer to print a line on paper for each instruction and then check that.

Now these instructions are ready to be changed into instructions the computer can understand.

4. ASSEMBLE OR COMPILE THE OBJECT PROGRAM

The program of instructions that is written in a language, or in a code, that the computer can use is called the *object program*. The language, or codes, used are referred to as *machine language,* as previously explained.

The computer changes the source program into the object program (machine language) by means of a *processor program.* The man-

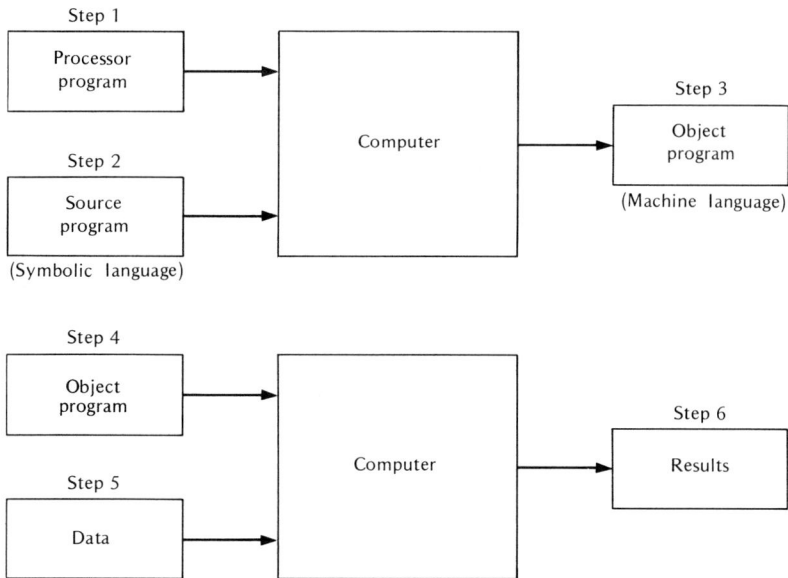

FIG. 16.7 Steps in preparing the object program

ufacturer of the computer prepares the processor program to convert symbolic instruction into machine language instruction. Let us follow the steps diagrammed in Fig. 16.7.

1. The processor program is usually recorded on punched cards, magnetic tape, or a magnetic disk and is read into the computer.

2. The source program is read into the computer. The processor automatically translates each instruction into machine language to become the object program.

3. The object program is the output usually recorded on punched cards, a disk, or magnetic tape, so that it can be used over and over again as input.

4. This object program is then read into the computer, and the processor program is erased from the computer memory. The object program is used to process the actual data.

5. Actual data are used as input and are processed.

5. TEST AND CORRECT THE PROGRAM

The object program is read into the computer, and some sample data are processed with these instructions. The output is checked very carefully. The sample data are prepared by the programmer so that they include every possible condition that can occur in the data that will eventually be processed by this program. Errors in the program are usually caused by incorrect input or the computer's stopping due to an impossible instruction sequence.

If the computer stops because of an error, the computer console can be used to instruct it to print the data that were being processed at the time it stopped along with the instruction it was trying to follow. This capacity is a great help to the programmer who is trying to find and correct the error. A term frequently used to refer to this step in program preparation is *debugging*. It is detecting, locating, and removing mistakes in programs. If the program fails after it has been in successful operation for a while, it is probably because a condition is present in the input data being processed that was not anticipated when the program was originally written, or a phase that was not tested when the program was being tested. This emphasizes the fact that the programmer must foresee all possible conditions that can occur in the data to be processed.

6. PREPARE THE PROGRAM FOR ACTUAL USE

This is the final step for the programmer in preparing the program for use. He prepares an operating instruction sheet to tell the computer operator what he should do and what the computer is expected to do. These notes should be made in the correct order for the operator to follow. Even a new operator who begins working for the company after the program has been in use a while does not have to bother the programmer with numerous questions.

The data that should be included on the operating instruction sheet include:

1. The input and where it is kept.

2. The output required and what should be done with it.

3. Halt instructions telling the operator what to do when the computer stops at specific places in the program.

PROGRAMMING THE COMPUTER

The programmer uses the flowchart of the problem and makes up the instructions in one of several methods that have been designed. To be of greater use to the users, the coding steps in writing instructions have been greatly simplified over the years. We will briefly trace this progress.

Machine Language Instructions

Detailed coded instructions are required before the computer can process data. The earliest electronic computers could be used only by experts who understood the complete internal functioning of the computer, because the instructions for the computer had to be stated in special codes the computer could understand, called machine language. This type of programming is referred to as *machine-oriented* since it is easily usable by the computer, but difficult and very time-consuming for the programmer. Now computers use special machine language programs that convert instructions written by programmers in other languages into machine language; these are called *processor programs*. What evolved was the development of programming languages that are easier to use than the machine languages.

Programming Languages

All programming languages that are not machine languages can be called user-oriented languages because they were developed to make the job of the person doing the programming easier. These user-oriented languages have gradually improved over the last fifteen to twenty years. The first of these nonmachine languages was called a *symbolic language,* or an *assembly language.* It contains one line of coding for each required machine instruction and is sometimes called a *one-for-one language.* A program written in any language that is not machine language is called a *source program.* As we have seen, a specially-designed program used by the computer to change a source program into a machine language program is called a *processor program.*

After the programmer writes the instructions, they are usually punched on cards. A processor program is read into the computer, as we saw in Fig. 16.7, and then the source program is read into the computer. The processor program changes each symbolic language instruction into a complete machine language instruction. These machine language instructions make up the program the computer can use, the object program; they are frequently printed as output. The punched cards for output are then used as input before the actual data can be processed.

An advantage of using a symbolic language over a machine language is the fact that the programmer can use codes similar to the English language rather than symbols. These codes suggest the functions to be performed, such as Add, Subt, and Halt. In this way, each instruction can be written somewhat easier. The major drawback, however, is that some sequences of instructions are repetitive; nevertheless, each instruction has to be rewritten each time the symbolic language requires three separate instructions: one to get the first number, one to add the second number to the first number, and one to store the answer. Since this is a frequently used sequence, along with numerous other sequences, a new concept in programming was developed to aid the programmer. This involved the addition of new codes that actually represent several machine language instructions in one symbolic language instruction. They are called *macro codes,* or *macros.* When one of these codes is used in the source program, the processor program interprets it and produces the several required machine language instructions. The comparison of one macro instruction and several one-for-one instructions can be shown as follows.

Symbolic-Macro Instruction	Symbolic One-for-One Equivalent
Move X, Y (Move the word at X to Y	Cladd X Store Y
Accum A, B, C (Add values in A and B; store their sum in C)	Cladd A Add B Store C

Each programming language development has enabled the programmer to write his programs more quickly with less chance for errors. The idea of macro instructions helped lead the way to the development of numerous new languages.

These languages are referred to as *problem-oriented,* or *procedure-oriented languages,* because they are more suited to the problem and understandable to the programmer than machine languages. Today, it is possible to give directions to the computer by writing sentences or statements in a language that is based on our English language, one that can be read in the same way as the English language.

These languages are problem-oriented languages because they permit the programmer to write convenient equivalents to machine language instructions using the English language. Special problem-oriented languages have been developed for specific needs, since there is a wide variation in the requirements of and terminology familiar to different types of programmers. Therefore, business problems, for example, are usually best programmed with different languages than those most useful for mathematicians, engineers, and scientists.

Problem-Oriented Languages

One of the languages that incorporates the English language is FORTRAN (Mathematical Formula Translating System), which was developed by IBM. This language uses algebraic and English notations and is used for mathematical, scientific, and engineering problems. Programs are written in the form of equations that are automatically compiled by the computer into a machine language computer program. Several FORTRAN languages have been developed, the latest FORTRAN IV.

COBOL is another special language that incorporates the English language. COBOL (Common Business Oriented Language) was developed jointly by computer manufacturers and users of the computer, in cooperation with the United States Department of Defense. It was first presented in 1960. COBOL is problem-oriented to simplify its use by business programmers. It must be converted by the computer into machine language instructions using a processor program. The instructions written by the programmer have little resemblance to machine language, and the programmer has little direct concern with the method by which the COBOL program is translated into machine language.

PL–I (Programming Language) is a special language that also incorporates the English language. It was developed by IBM as a general-purpose language to be used both for business and scientific problems. It combines the features of problem-oriented languages, primarily COBOL and FORTRAN, and has other features. Since it has such extended capabilities, some authorities expect it to become *the* single, most used language in the future. It has not yet been in use long enough to be perfected, or to give real evidence as to whether or not it actually will receive such widespread approval. Like any other high level symbolic language, PL–I instructions must be converted by the computer into machine language instructions through the use of a processor program.

ALGOL (Algorithmic-Oriented Language) is a problem-oriented language which serves similar purposes as FORTRAN, but is not so widely used.

The programming languages used are about as follows.

Business: 80–85%   COBOL
          15–20%   RPG, PL–I, and assembly languages

Science: 80–85%   FORTRAN
          15–20%   ALGOL, special languages assembly languages, PL–I

Processor Programs

The processor programs that are used to convert the source program into the object program are supplied by the computer manufacturers. The terms *compiler* and *assembler* are used when referring to processor programs; their distinction is important. An assembler works only with one-for-one statements; a compiler works with statements that produce groups of statement, or subroutines. A *subroutine* is part of a routine, or a group of statements that make up a specific part of a routine. A *compiler* is usually made up of several parts: First the macro statements are broken down into their one-for-one statements making up the necessary subroutines, and then an assembler changes the statements into machine language and assigns reserved locations. Therefore, a complete complier contains an assembler.

Once a program-oriented language is converted by a processor into a machine language, the resulting machine language can be used indefinitely without having to be converted each time it is used. For example, the machine language instructions can be recorded on punched cards or on magnetic tape and used as input each time the specific program is to be used.

Utility Programs

Many jobs that the computer performs frequently are needed by a variety of different users. For these users, the computer manufacturers have developed sets of what we call *utility programs*. Some of the most common of these are

1. Program loaders which put new programs into the computer storage.

2. Converters which transfer data from one medium to another, such as from tape to printer, card to tape, and tape to card.

3. Duplicators that reproduce records, primarily to make duplicate reels of tape.

4. Print memory programs used to automatically print specified areas of primary storage. Such a program is referred to as *dump* and is frequently used by programmers in the process of "debugging."

The use of these utility programs makes such functions easy to carry out and saves a programmer from writing such programs. Organizations of similar types of computer users maintain libraries of general programs available to their members. Much time can be saved by those who are able to make full use of such facilities.

Operating Systems

As larger and more sophisticated computers are used, it is desirable to reduce the time spent when operators are required to use manual controls. Only in this way can the full speed and potential of the computer be realized. These manual instructions include the starting of each program's loading procedure. The computer manufacturers, therefore, have developed specialized programming systems called *operating systems* that automatically perform many of the functions previously performed by the computer operator. They also perform some routines that were not possible with only manual control. The basic capabilities of the operating system include multi-programming, job stacking, and priority scheduling.

Multi-programming permits more than one program to be executed concurrently. Primary storage is divided into sections, each of which holds a different program. The operating system controls the execution of these programs by switching another program into operation when the previous program is idle while an I/O operation is being performed. Each time a program is idled because of an I/O operation, the operating system switches to another program until all the programs have been completed. This system, in effect, eliminates idle time of the computer caused by time spent manipulating the I/O media.

Job stacking means that the programs to be executed are stacked behind each other in the input device. Manual loading procedures are required only for the first program in the stack; then the succeeding programs are executed in sequence by the operating system.

Priority scheduling allows the operating system to select programs for executing from the direct access secondary storage on a predetermined priority basis. When a high priority program is entered into the computer while other programs are being executed, it is placed ahead of all programs with a lower priority even though they were inserted earlier. These programs are inserted into the computer one at a time and are stored in the direct access secondary storage.

QUESTIONS AND PROBLEMS

1. List the steps for preparing a computer program.
2. Who performs the various steps in preparing a program?
3. Why is Step 1 in preparing a computer program so important?
4. List the advantages of using a flowchart rather than listing the steps in sentence form.
5. In what direction do you usually read the flowchart?
6. Why is a flowchart often called a block diagram?
7. What are the flowchart symbols for
   I/O
   processing
   decision
   connector
   keying operation
   terminal
8. How should a flowchart begin and end?
9. Which type of flowchart would be longer, general or program flowchart?
10. Which flowchart would a programmer need to write the instructions?
11. What does a systems flowchart show?
12. How are programmer-oriented instructions prepared for use as computer instructions?
13. Briefly describe the steps in changing the source program into the object program.
14. Why must the test or sample data be prepared very carefully?
15. Why could the earliest computers be used only by experts who understood the complete internal functioning of the computer?

16. What is an advantage to using a symbolic language rather than a machine language?

17. What was the major problem in using symbolic languages?

18. What is the significance of macro codes?

19. Why are the newer programming languages called problem- or procedure-oriented languages?

20. Why have special problem-oriented languages been developed?

21. Explain the derivation of the following programming language names.
    FORTRAN   COBOL   PL–I   ALGOL

22. Which programming language is most likely to become the one language to be used in the future? Why?

23. Distinguish between a compiler and an assembler.

24. Describe how the usual parts of a compiler work.

25. Briefly describe four common types of utility programs.

26. What is a purpose of dumping?

27. Briefly describe the basic capabilities of an operating system.

28. What is the effect of an operating system?

29. What is the advantage of multi-programming?

30. How is job stacking performed?

31. What is the advantage of priority scheduling?

COBOL

CHAPTER 17

The COBOL programming language was developed in 1961 for programs that involve commercial or business data processing methods. A primary purpose was to have a language that would enable the user to advance from one generation of equipment to another in a rapid and orderly manner with no major reprogramming problems. Like other computer languages, COBOL has had several revisions. The one used here is for the 360 computer systems. Once you learn this version, it is relatively easy to learn the other versions if necessary. Like FORTRAN, COBOL is a high-level programming language. The name is derived from COmmon Business Oriented Language. It is based on the English language and uses words common to business problems. Instructions are written in sentences and paragraph form.

Like any language, COBOL contains letters, numbers, and symbols to represent some commonly used terms. It has a vocabulary and rules of grammar that must be followed. When we have learned these basics, we are able to program the computer in COBOL. To write a program for the computer, the programmer makes up a sequence of statements to indicate the specific steps the computer must follow to process the data. Let us, then, study the basics needed to write a COBOL program.

THE COBOL CHARACTER SET

A character set comprises the symbols that can be used in the programming language. The COBOL character set consists of

1. Alphabetic characters: the capital letters A through Z,
2. Numeric characters: the digits 0 through 9,
3. Punctuation characters: , ; . ' ( ) ,
4. Special characters: — = * + / $ > < ,
5. Blank or space.

These characters are referred to as *legal,* or *valid, characters;* no other characters can be used in COBOL programming. The characters that cannot be used are referred to as illegal, or not valid. All letters are written as capitals.

COBOL WORDS

COBOL words can be made up of the alphabetic, numeric, and one special character, the hyphen, which is frequently used. A COBOL words ends in one of two ways, by either a space or a punctuation symbol. In this way GROSS EARN is not a single COBOL word, but GROSS-EARN is one COBOL word. Whenever words are connected by hyphens, they count together as one COBOL word. Then END-OF-MONTH is one COBOL word. The word must be spelled exactly the same each time it is used, or the computer will interpret it as being two different words. For example, the computer would consider END-OF-MONTH, and ENDOFMONTH, and EDN-OF-MONTH as three different COBOL words.

DATA NAMES

A data name is a COBOL word which the programmer makes up to define some data in the problem. The only restrictions are the following.

1. It must have between one and thirty characters.

2. At least one character must be alphabetic.

3. Neither the first nor last character can be a hyphen.

Remember that a COBOL word cannot have a space within it. Data names could be:

```
E                   12A34
HOURS               EMPLOYEE-NUMBER
YEARTODATE          CURRENT---MONTH
MONTH1MONTH2MONTH3
```

MATHEMATICAL STATEMENTS

A COBOL program consists of a series of statements that give the computer the step-by-step procedure it must follow to solve the problem. The arithmetic operations of addition, subtraction, multiplication, and division are the most basic computer statements. Each statement must follow a definite pattern.

The basic *addition statement* consists of

ADD data-name data-name GIVING data-name.

Two add statements are:

```
ADD A B GIVING C.
ADD PAY OVERTIME GIVING GROSS.
```

The computer has to already have been given the values of PAY and OVERTIME in order to execute this statement. It finds these values, adds them, and stores the sum in the position reserved for GROSS. Notice that we do not add the word "to" between the two data words to be added, as we would naturally do. Each statement ends with a period. Data words in this statement are PAY, OVERTIME, and GROSS. The two standard words are ADD and GIVING and are reserved words. As we learn the other statements, we will find more reserved words. No reserved word can be used as a data word, even if it is not used as a reserved word in that particular program.

The form for the *multiply statement* is:

`MULTIPLY` data-name `BY` data-name `GIVING` data-name.

The reserved words are MULTIPLY, BY, and GIVING, and they tell the computer to multiply two quantities and to store the results. The three data names indicate what two quantities to multiply and where to store the results. The statement MULTIPLY HOURS BY RATE GIVING EARNINGS instructs the computer to calculate the product of HOURS and RATE and store this product in the position reserved for EARNINGS.

The form for the *subtract statement* is:

`SUBTRACT` data-name `FROM` data-name `GIVING` data-name.

The reserved words are SUBTRACT, FROM, and GIVING, and they tell the computer to subtract the first quantity from the second quantity and to store the results. The statement SUBTRACT WITHDRAWAL FROM OLD-BAL GIVING NEW-BAL instructs the computer to calculate the difference between the old balance and the withdrawal and to store this answer in the position reserved for NEW-BAL. Notice the hyphen in the two data words to make what are two words to us become one data word to the computer.

The form of the *divide statement* is:

`DIVIDE` data-name `INTO` data-name `GIVING` data-name.

The reserved words are DIVIDE, INTO, and GIVING, and they tell the computer to divide the second quantity by the first quantity and to store the results. The three data names indicate the two quantities to use and where to store the results. The statement DIVIDE NUMBER INTO TOTAL GIVING AVERAGE instructs the computer to calculate the quotient of the total divided by the number and to store the answer in the position reserved for AVERAGE.

Numeric literals are actual numbers, whether whole numbers or decimals, and can be used in arithmetic statements in place of a data name. If you have already added two numbers and want an average, you can write DIVIDE 2 INTO TOTAL GIVING SCORE. This instructs the computer to divide the total of 2 numbers by 2 to obtain their average score.

EXPANDED ARITHMETIC OPERATIONS

Frequently, it is necessary to make several arithmetic computations to obtain the required answer, such as with the formula I = PRT which means interest = principal × rate × time. Problems of this type cannot usually be written in COBOL with one statement. The following procedure would be necessary for this problem:

```
MULTIPLY P BY R GIVING PARTIAL-PRODUCT.
MULTIPLY PARTIAL-PRODUCT BY T GIVING I.
```

When multiplying and dividing, only one step can be directed at a time. When adding or subtracting, a slight variation is possible. The addition statement can be expanded to include as many data names be to added as necessary, such as

```
ADD A B C D E F G GIVING T.
```

It is frequently necessary to add several quantities, and it is frequently necessary to subtract the sum of two or more quantities from the other quantity. The Subtract statement can be expanded to include any number of data names between the words SUBTRACT and FROM, such as:

```
SUBTRACT COST OVERHEAD FROM SELL-PRICE GIVING PROFIT.
```

The two quantities after the word SUBTRACT are added together and then their sum is subtracted from the quantity indicated by the data name after the word FROM; the answer is stored in the position reserved for the data name after the word GIVING.

MOVE STATEMENT

The Move statement can provide the computer with a specific value for a data name, such as

```
MOVE 1972 TO YEAR.
```

It automatically supplies the number 1972 as the value of YEAR for succeeding statements. This statement can also be used to transfer data, such as

    MOVE NET TO BALANCE-DUE.

Therefore, the move statement contains two reserved words, MOVE and TO; and it contains either two data names or a specific value and one data name.

INPUT/OUTPUT STATEMENTS

The input data are assigned to a data name so that they can be processed with the necessary calculations and then returned to the programmer in the required output form. Although other statements and I/O media are available in the COBOL system, we will use the Read and Write statements and will confine our I/O to punched cards as input and printed pages as output. The Read statement is written in the form of

    READ data-name.

It takes one item of data from a punched card and assigns it to the data name indicated. Since data in COBOL are not limited to numbers, data names can refer to any type of data. If the data referred to by a data name contain both alphabetic characters and numbers, they are called *alphameric data*.

The output statement for printing is:

    WRITE data-name.

This instruction causes the computer to print the data represented by the data name stated.

BRANCHING AND LOOPING

Unless we have a way of telling the computer to repeat the same instructions, we have to write the instruction as many times as it is needed. If a company has 540 employees, the statements for calculating each employee's earnings would have to be written 540 times. Looping solves this problem by permitting the computer to repeat a series of operations and keep repeating them until directed to stop; it is referred to as an *unconditional branch*. Since a loop is continuous, other statements are needed to test whether the loop should be repeated or whether the work the loop was to do is finished. These statements are Conditional Branching statements, since they are followed only when some specified conditions exist concerning the data being processed. Looping and Branching statements are control statements; they permit the normal sequence of processing to be modified.

Each section of the instruction statements in COBOL is identified by a name, to be explained in detail later. This is necessary because it enables us to refer to a specific section in a branch or loop statement. Paragraph names are specifically positioned on the COBOL coding sheet and punched card so they will be four spaces to the left of other statements in our samples, such as:

```
START.
     ACCEPT TOTAL.
COMPUTATION.
     DIVIDE 2 INTO AMOUNT GIVING AVERAGE.
```

A paragraph name can be used only once in a program; a paragraph name may consist of alphabetic, alphameric, or numeric characters. If you have already used both ONE and 1 as paragraph names but need another paragraph name that represents "one," you can use 01, since each appears different to the computer. No reserved word can be used as a paragraph name (such as ADD, GIVING). It is not necessary to have a paragraph name before each COBOL statement, but you do need one before each statement that you may need to refer to in working with a loop or a branch.

The *Go To* statement causes the computer to go to a statement that is not the next one in sequential order. It indicates the paragraph name assigned to the statement needed next, in this form:

```
GO TO paragraph-name.
```

This statement causes the computer to next execute the statement immediately after the indicated paragraph name.

The Go To statement creates an unconditional branch and is often placed at the end of a paragraph, instructing the computer to go to the beginning of the same paragraph again or another paragraph, as shown:

Example 1

```
02.
     ACCEPT HOURS.
     MULTIPLY HOURS BY 2.5 GIVING GROSS.
     WRITE HOURS.
     WRITE GROSS.
     GO TO 01.
```

Example 2

```
001.
     ACCEPT GROSS.
     MULTIPLY GROSS BY X GIVING TAX.
     SUBTRACT TAX FROM GROSS GIVING PAY.
     WRITE GROSS.
     WRITE TAX.
     WRITE PAY.
     GO TO 001.
```

The sequence of Example 2 above would cause the computer to continue looping indefinitely. The computer must be able to **decide** when to get out of the loop, or to "break the loop." One way to avoid this problem is to use a conditional branch statement allowing the computer to decide what path to follow next in relation to the data being processed. This is the *If* statement and is written in this form:

IF condition statement. additional statements.

This statement causes the computer to test the condition following the word IF. If this condition is met or is true, the next statement up to the first period is executed. Then it continues to the next statements. If the condition is not met or is false, it skips the statement immediately after the condition (up to the first period) and continues with the next statement following the first period. The statement immediately after the condition is followed only if the condition is met or is true, so it is frequently called the *true branch of the If statement*. The statement following the first period can be called the false branch since it is the next one used if the condition is not met or is false, even though it might also be used after the true branch. For example:

IF EMPL-HOURS IS GREATER THAN 40 WRITE OVERTIME-MESSAGE. MULTI-
PLY RATE BY TIME GIVING REG-GROSS.

One form of the condition of an If statement is

data-name   relation   numeric value.

The relation may be: IS EQUAL TO, IS GREATER THAN, or IS LESS THAN. It is frequently necessary to instruct the computer to do something entirely different with each possible outcome of the condition. In such situations, the If . . . Else statement is used. Its basic form is:

IF condition statement(s) ELSE statement(s).

The reserved word OTHERWISE may be substituted for the reserved word ELSE. Notice that there is only one period in the entire statement.

For example:

```
IF EMPL-HOURS IS GREATER THAN 40 GO TO 04 OTHERWISE MULTIPLY RATE
BY TIME GIVING GROSS.
```

If the condition is met, the computer will execute the statement(s) between the condition and the word OTHERWISE; then it will skip from the word OTHERWISE to the period and will execute the statement after the period if there is one. If the condition is not met, the computer will skip to the word OTHERWISE and will execute the statement between the word OTHERWISE and the period. If this statement is not a branch, it will then continue with any other statements after the period. Either the true branch or the false branch may contain more than one statement, but no period can be used until the end of the complete instruction. For example:

```
IF EMPL-HOURS IS GREATER THAN 40 WRITE A GO TO 04 OTHERWISE WRITE
B GO TO 05.
```

A and B designate appropriate messages to be printed.

END OF PROGRAM

The computer has to be instructed to stop when all required operations have been performed. The Stop statement is

```
STOP RUN.
```

This tells the computer that it is the last instruction in the program.

ORDER OF STATEMENTS

The order in which COBOL statements are written is very important, because the computer normally performs them in the order in which they are given. A data name must be assigned a value before it can be used in a computational statement.

COBOL CODING SHEET

The COBOL coding sheet, as shown in Fig. 16.5, is helpful since COBOL has some definite restrictions that must be maintained. Using the code sheet makes it easier to keypunch the data in the correct card columns. The coding sheet is divided into six areas:

Columns 1–3 are labeled *page,* but the page number needs to be printed only on the first line of each page. It might be helpful to punch it on every card, especially for longer programs. The number 1 is indicated as 001.

Columns 4–6 are labeled *serial* and are reserved for the line number on the page. They are numbered by tens so that line 01 is labeled 010. In this way, if a line was omitted, you can insert it later without having to rewrite the entire page. These insertions can be made on the unnumbered lines at the bottom of the page. For example, between lines 030 and 040 any number from 031 through 039 can be inserted, so 9 lines could actually be inserted to correct a mistake or insert something that was omitted. After the cards are punched, they can be placed in numeric order. Lines 1–6 make up the sequence, so cards that get mixed up can easily be put back into order. Few actual programs can be written on one page.

Column 7 is used to indicate that a statement is continued onto succeeding lines. If a statement requires more than one line, a dash is placed in Column 7 of each continuing line.

Column 8 is labeled A and is called the *A-margin*. Names of division headers, paragraph names, and section names begin here and extend as far as necessary. Column 12 is labeled B and is called the *B-margin*. Any other items begin here and extend as far as necessary to Column 73. COBOL paragraphs or sentences start here.

As a help to the programmer, columns 73–80 are reserved for identification of the program.

It is important that the COBOL programmer use the coding sheet properly so that the keypunch operator punches the data in the correct columns. If each item is not begun in its correct column, the compiler will usually not be able to function correctly to make the object program.

DIVISIONS OF A COBOL PROGRAM

Every COBOL program must contain four divisions, and each is identified by a title called a *division header*. The division headers, listed in the order in which they must appear in every COBOL program, are:

```
IDENTIFICATION DIVISION.
ENVIRONMENT DIVISION.
DATA DIVISION.
PROCEDURE DIVISION.
```

As shown, each division header must end with a period. COBOL statements are written in paragraph form. Each statement must end with a period and at least one blank space. A paragraph may contain only one line on the code sheet. Each paragraph begins with a paragraph name.

The *Identification Division* must contain at least one paragraph, but it may contain additional paragraphs (not explained in this chapter). The first paragraph begins with the paragraph-name statement, followed by a period and at least one blank space. Next is the name of the program, enclosed in apostrophes, followed by a period, as shown:

```
PROGRAM-ID. 'program-name'.
```

An example of the complete Identification Division is:

```
IDENTIFICATION DIVISION.
PROGRAM IDENTIFICATION. 'EMPDATA'.
```

In addition to this one required paragraph, the Identification Division can contain up to six optional paragraphs, giving, for example, the name of the person who wrote the program, the date it was completed, the date it was compiled, the installation for which it is to be used, and special remarks. Each topic is a separate paragraph and contains a paragraph name such as:

```
AUTHOR.          INSTALLATION.
DATE-WRITTEN.    REMARKS.
DATE-COMPILED.
```

The Environment Division is the second division of every COBOL program. This division describes the physical characteristics of equipment to be used and some aspects of the problem that depend on this equipment. This division consists of two sections: a Configuration Section and an I/O Section.

The Configuration Section heading is used, and then the source-computer and object-computer are stated to identify the computer that will compile the program and the computer that will execute the compiled program. The same computer is usually used for both, and this entire section is optional in the COBOL program. An example is:

```
ENVIRONMENT DIVISION.
CONFIGURATION SECTION.
SOURCE-COMPUTER. IBM 360.
OBJECT-COMPUTER. IBM 360.
```

The second section of the Environment Division is the I/O Section, and it cannot be omitted. It contains a sentence describing each group of input or output, which are called files. Files are explained in the next section, the Data Division. This section contains the section heading INPUT-OUTPUT SECTION, the paragraph heading FILE CONTROL, and the following statement for each file:

SELECT file-name ASSIGN to device-name.

The file name has been determined by the programmer and is used in the program. The device name specifies the input or output device, and its name has been specified by the computer manufacturer. For example:

```
INPUT-OUTPUT SECTION.
    FILE CONTROL. SELECT CARD-PAY ASSIGN TO SYSRDR.
    SELECT PRINT-CHK ASSIGN TO SYSPTR.
```

This means that the input is a file of punched cards referring to payroll data and that a card reader is used; the output is a file of printed paper in the form of pay checks and a printer is used. The device names SYSRDR and SYSPTR are used with the IBM 360 system.

The *Data Division* is the third division of every COBOL program, and it contains all the data required to execute the program. Under the heading DATA DIVISION is an explanation of the data which are input, the data which are output, and the data which are manipulated in the program. This division can contain three sections, each of which can be omitted if it is not needed in a specific program. These sections include the File Section, Working-Storage Section, and Report Section.

The *File Section* describes the contents of the data stored externally on punched cards, on magnetic tape, disks, etc. Each file explanation contains two names, the file name which was referred to in the Select statement of the Environment Division and the record name which first appears here. The form contains several statements, generally including a file description (FD) and one or more record descriptions. The file description section includes several lines. The first line is

FD file-name

which is not followed by a period because it is not considered a complete statement. The letters FD always identify the beginning of a file description. The file name is the same one that was used in the Select statement of the Environment Division. Next are two required lines along with one or more optional lines, as necessary. One required line is:

LABEL RECORDS ARE STANDARD

or

```
    LABEL RECORDS ARE OMITTED
```

If there is only one record, the words RECORD IS would be substituted for RECORDS ARE. This line refers to the type of labels on the file for identification purposes. The other required line is:

```
    DATA RECORD IS record-name.
```

It is usually helpful to include the word RECORD, or REC, in the name of the record, although it is not necessary. All these lines of the FD are expressed in only one complete sentence with just one period, as shown:

```
    DATA DIVISION.
    FILE SECTION.
    FD FILE-I
        LABEL RECORD IS OMITTED
        DATA RECORD IS RECORD-A
```

The file name is FILE-I, with I representing input. There are several optional lines that might become necessary in this section with some specific programs, but they are not mentioned or necessary in our discussion.

The next part of the File Section describes the record named in the last line of the FD (Record-A in the example above). Its first line contains the number 01 and the record name just mentioned, in the form shown:

```
    01 record-name
```

after which, as with the file name, we have no period. Then the desired data structure is described, with one line for each item of data. Each line consists of the following:

```
    02 data-name PICTURE description of the data item.
```

The number 02 is standard. The data name describes the actual data used in the program. The description of the data item is a space-by-space description of the data referred to by this data name. (The more common codes are described in Fig. 17.1.) Each possible position in the field of the card or print must be indicated. For example:

999999	means 6 positions of numeric data.
AAAA	means 4 positions of alphabetic data.
99V9	means 3 positions of numeric data with a decimal before the last position.

Character	Function
A	Represents a character position that contains either an alphabetic character or a space.
S	Indicates the presence of an operation sign (+ or −) and must be the left-most character.
V	Represents the location of the assumed decimal point and may appear only once in a character string.
X	Represents a position that can contain any allowable character from the COBOL character set.
Z	Represents the left-most positions which are to have the zeros replaced by spaces (the zero "suppressed").
9	Represents a position which contains numeric characters.

FIG. 17.1 COBOL codes for describing data

S9999	means a 4-position number with a + or − sign.
ZZ99999	means a 7-position number with zeros to be suppressed in the first two positions.
XX99	means a 4-position field with two positions alphameric and two positions numeric.
A(3)X(3)	means a 6-position field with three positions alphabetic and 3 positions alphameric.

A complete field description could be:

    02 CUST-NO PICTURE AAA9999.

As illustrated, the code can indicate each position individually or state the code once and the number of positions in parentheses. A separate statement is required for each data-name needed.

The *Working Storage Section* contains a descriptive statement of each data name that is used in the program and not described in the File Section. This category includes items that are developed internally and whose values are assigned in the source program. Each data name is described by a separate statement, with the label 02 before it and a period at the end. These descriptions are like those in the File Section, except the number is 02. A sample Working Storage Section is

```
WORKING-STORAGE SECTION.
02 COUNTER PICTURE 9999.
02 ANSWER PICTURE 999V9.
```

Each of the two entries above is independent of the other, and their order is not important. They are called *independent data items,* and they are not members of a larger group of data items. Each independent data item is described in a separate statement and requires the level-number 77.

The second type of data item entry in the Working-Storage Section comprises the grouped data items, and they must be placed in a specific desired order within the group. They are written like the others but have a heading labeled 01 with the data-name descriptions labeled 02. To indicate blank spaces between data-name sections, use this statement:

```
FILLER SIZE IS number of spaces.
```

A sample grouped data entry is

```
01 INPUT-RECORD.
   02 FILLER SIZE 10.
   02 HOURS-REG PICTURE 99V99.
   02 FILLER SIZE IS 10.
   02 HOURS-OT PICTURE 99V99.
```

All independent data items must be listed before any grouped data items in the Working-Storage Section. The statements with the word PICTURE describe data names that refer to data that are variable, that change with each group of input data being processed. The word VALUE is used to assign standard data needed in the program or the initial value of some specific data. The statement has the number 88 preceding it and the form is

```
88 data-name VALUE IS number.
```

For example, the initial value assigned to a counter might be 0 or 1. The standard value assigned to be used for determining the average of a total of five numbers would be 5. The value assigned is called a literal value and may be either a numeric literal with numbers, a sign, and a decimal; or it may be a nonnumeric literal with any characters in the COBOL character set except the quotation marks. The nonnumeric literal is enclosed in quotation marks in the statement. For example,

```
88 NUMI VALUE IS +5.
88 ANS VALUE IS 'NO'.
88 NUM6 VALUE IS 3.1416.
```

THE PROCEDURE DIVISION

The Procedure Division explains the operations necessary to perform the steps in processing the data. After the division heading, PROCEDURE DIVISION, the sections and paragraphs are listed with the statements needed to process the data. The statements consist of three types: Compiler-directing statements, Imperative statements, and Conditional statements. Most of the basic statements of these three types have already been explained, but a few more are needed along with those in the File Section.

The Compiler-directing statements, as the name implies, tell the compiler the specific action to take while the program is being compiled. The only Compiler-directing statement we need to know is the Note statement, and its form is

NOTE character-string.

This statement tells the compiler to print the words referred to by character string on the print-out of the compiler's listing, but not to include the statement in the object program. When a Note statement is placed first in a paragraph, the entire paragraph is the character string that is not processed in the object program. When it is not the first statement in a paragraph, just the one statement is considered the character string, so it is terminated by the first period after the word NOTE. For example:

NOTE THE NEXT PARAGRAPH IS SELDOM USED IN THIS PROGRAM.

The Imperative statements tell the computer the specific action to take and give the computer no alternative, as do Conditional statements. The Imperative statements we have already discussed include the arithmetic statements and several other miscellaneous statements:

```
ADD       SUBTRACT    MULTIPLY
DIVIDE    MOVE        READ
WRITE     GO TO       STOP
```

The additional Imperative statements we need to know include the following:

```
OPEN    CLOSE    PERFORM
```

Before the computer can get data from an input file or print data from an output file, these files have to be opened with an Open statement with the form:

```
OPEN INPUT file-name.
OPEN OUTPUT file-name.
```

The file-names must be exactly as they are stated in the File Section. The Open statement is frequently the first statement in the Procedure Division. A good paragraph name is an abbreviation for the word HOUSEKEEPING (HSKPG), although it is not necessary that this be the paragraph name. Notice in the following example that the I/O Open statement can be combined:

```
PROCEDURE DIVISION.
HSKPG. OPEN INPUT EMPL-REC-FILE, OUTPUT EMPL-CHECK-FILE.
```

The Move statement, previously explained, is normally needed before each line of output is built. For example,

```
MOVE SPACES TO PRINT-EMPL-REC.
```

This instruction clears the entire reserved area of any old data. If this were not done, some old data might still be in the FILLER listed in the structure of the line to be printed, and some extra useless data would be printed. With some of the more advanced programming techniques not presented in this chapter, this use of the Move statement will not be necessary.

At the end of the Procedure Division, it is necessary to have a Close statement for each file that was used in the program. This statement (or statements) can be similar to the Open statement, but for this purpose we substitute the word CLOSE and omit the words INPUT and OUTPUT. For example,

```
CLOSE EMPL-REC-FILE.
CLOSE EMPL-CHECK-FILE.
```

Again, these two statements can be combined. A frequently used paragraph name for this final paragraph is END-OF-JOB, or its abbreviation EOJ. For example,

```
EOJ. CLOSE EMPL-REC-FILE, EMPL-CHECK-FILE.
STOP RUN.
```

The Perform statement can be used to alter the normal sequence of statements to permit the execution of another paragraph or complete section. The computer then returns immediately to the normal sequence. The form of this statement is

    PERFORM paragraph-name.

or

    PERFORM section-name.

Follow these statements:

    PERFORM CALC-YR-TO-DATE.
    GO TO 04.

The computer goes to the paragraph named CALC-YR-TO-DATE when it encounters this Perform statement. Immediately after completing the statement(s) in the CALC-YR-TO-DATE paragraph, it returns to the statement following the Perform statement and goes to the paragraph named 04 in this example.

The Write statement has an added convenience: It can instruct the printer to skip lines before or after printing the designated data. The form of this statement can be:

    WRITE data-name BEFORE ADVANCING (integer or data-name) LINES.
or
    WRITE data-name AFTER ADVANCING (integer or data-name) LINES.

These statements allow the printer to space the required number of lines or the value assigned to the designated data name either before or after printing the required data.

The Conditional statements tell the computer what action is to be taken when specified conditions are met. The Conditional statement we have already discussed in the Branching and Looping section of this chapter is the If statement. Another statement that can be constructed as conditional is the Read statement. An added convenience is this new form of the Read statement which automatically instructs the computer what to do next if the last card has been read. The form is

    READ file-name AT END imperative statement(s).

The reserved words AT END automatically tell the computer to determine whether or not there is another input card to be read. The Imperative statement(s) before the period tell the computer what to do next if there are no more cards to be processed. For example,

    READ INPUT EMPL-REC. FILE AT END GO TO EOJ.

When there are still input cards to be processed, the computer jumps over the rest of this statement and goes to the statement following the period. When there are no more cards to be processed, the computer continues this statement and goes to the EOJ paragraph, which contains the Close statements and the Stop Run statement. An At End statement actually makes the Read statement a Branch statement or a Conditional statement. The EOJ statements could have been placed in the Imperative statement(s) part of the At End statement, but this is seldom done.

QUESTIONS AND PROBLEMS

1. What type of problems are best suited to COBOL?
2. In what form are the COBOL instructions written?
3. What is the complete COBOL character set?
4. How does each COBOL word end?
5. What can COBOL words comprise?
6. What are the restrictions to a data name?
7. What are the most basic statements in the COBOL language?
8. How does each COBOL statement end?
9. State the form of each of the following COBOL statements. Either underscore or use all capitals for standard words.

Add	Divide	Print	End program
Multiply	Move	Unconditional branch	Blanks
Subtract	Read	Conditional branch	

10. How can the addition and subtraction statements be expanded?
11. How do branching and looping statements help in writing a program?
12. What is a paragraph name?
13. Why is the order of the COBOL statements very important?
14. Briefly describe the sections of the COBOL code sheet.
15. Why is it important that each item began in its correct column on the COBOL code sheet?
16. List the four COBOL divisions.
17. Where and how is the name of the program indicated?
18. What are the two sections of the environment division? Briefly explain the purpose of each.
19. What does the Data Division contain?
20. Briefly explain the File Section and the Working Storage Section of the Data Division.

21. Write the following picture descriptions:
    8 positions of numeric data
    3 positions of alphabetic data
    6 positions of numeric data with 3 decimal places
    A 4-position number with a + sign
    An 8-position number with 0's in the first two positions to be suppressed
    A 6-position word with the first 2 characters alphameric and the rest numeric

22. When is the "88" statement used?

23. What is the purpose of the Procedure Division?

24. What is the purpose of each of the following statements?
    Compiler-directing statements
    Imperative statements
    Conditional statements

25. What is the purpose of a Note statement?

26. How does a Perform statement work?

27. Write the general form of the statements that allow the printer to skip lines before or after printing the next line.

28. Write the general form of the statement that tells the computer to read the next card and what to do if the last card has been read.

29. Write the Identification Division for a program named EMPL-REC.

30. Write the computer statement(s) to solve AREA = (L × W)/2. Assume that AREA, L, and W are predefined and consist of 5 characters each.

31. Flowchart and code a program to do the following:
    If A is greater than B, go to STEP-4; otherwise go to STEP-6.

32. Flowchart and code a program for the following:
    If X is greater than Z, add Y to Z and go to subroutine-3.

33. Write a program to calculate weekly gross pay for each employee (gross pay = rate × time). Use only the employee social security number for identification. Hours worked do not exceed 69.99 and rate does not exceed $9.99 for any employee. Print the input and results as one line per employee. (Disregard the possibility of overtime for this problem.) Input is on punched cards.

34. Write the program as above but consider that any hours over 40.00 are considered as overtime and receive 24% extra pay.

The FORTRAN language was developed in 1957 for programs involving mathematical computations. It is especially useful in writing programs for scientific and engineering applications. The name is derived from **FOR**mula **TRAN**slation. This chapter presents the basics of FORTRAN programming without the prerequisite of a reader's knowing higher mathematics or having other advanced scientific knowledge. FORTRAN has been available in several versions; the one used here is FORTRAN IV as it is defined for the 360 computer system. Once you learn FORTRAN IV, it is relatively easy to learn the other versions of FOR-TRAN. Remember that this chapter presents only the basics of FOR-TRAN IV programming, not all the details of the language.

Like any language, FORTRAN contains letters and numbers and has symbols to represent some commonly used terms. It has a vocabulary and rules of grammar that must be followed carefully. When you learn these details, you can program a computer in FORTRAN. To write a program for the computer, the programmer makes up a sequence of statements to indicate the specific steps the computer must perform to solve the problem. Definite rules must be followed when making up these statements.

THE FORTRAN CHARACTER SET

A character set is the symbols that can be used. In FORTRAN it consists of

1. Alphabetic characters: all *capital* letters A through Z.
2. Numeric characters: the decimal digits 0 through 9.
3. Operator characters including:
   +   (addition)
   −   (subtraction)
   *   (multiplication)
   /   (division)
   **   (exponentiation)
   =   (an equals sign indicating the assignment, used to mean "replaced by" in FORTRAN.)

303

4. Grouping characters including:

( )   (parentheses)

,   (comma)

'   (apostrophe)

5. Blank character

These characters are the legal, or valid, characters. No other characters can be used in FORTRAN programming.

THE ASSIGNMENT STATEMENT

The Assignment statement is the most basic statement in FORTRAN and is used when arithmetic calculations are to be performed. Examples of Assignment statements are

```
A = B + C + D
AREA = LENGTH * WIDTH
```

In these examples, A, B, C, D, AREA, LENGTH, and WIDTH are all *identifiers*. Identifiers are words or letters made up to represent quantities in a problem. They may consist of one letter or complete words, although the maximum length is six characters. The first character must be alphabetic, but the other characters may be alphabetic or numeric, called alphameric. Samples of identifiers include: AREA, AREA2, ANSWER, ANS1, and A3. You cannot use 2A as an identifier because the first character is not alphabetic. AREA# cannot be an identifier because # is not a valid FORTRAN character. RESULTS cannot be an identifier because it contains more than six characters.

Each Assignment statement has a left side and a right side because it represents an arithmetic operation and its answer. The left side must be one valid identifier (beginning with a letter), and the right side may be any valid FORTRAN expression. These two sides are separated by an "is replaced by" symbol (=). The result of what the right side directs the computer to do is assigned to the identifier on the left side of the assignment symbol and is stored in the computer. The statement X + Y = Z cannot be used; it must be changed to Z = X +Y in the FORTRAN language. With the Assignment statement, you can instruct the computer to perform the four basic arithmetic operations and assign the answer to an identifier. An identifier cannot contain an operational sign.

EXPONENTIAL NOTATION

In addition to the four basic arithmetic operations, a basic operation
that the computer can perform is exponentiation, or raising a quantity
to a designated power such as its square or cube. Exponents are not
limited to whole numbers. Fractional powers can also be used as the
computer can manipulate them. For example,

$$100^{.5} = 100^{1/2} = \sqrt{100} = 10,$$
$$81^{.25} = 81^{1/4} = \sqrt[4]{81} = 3,$$
$$9^{.75} = 9^{3/4} = \sqrt[4]{9^3} = 3.$$

ORDER OF OPERATIONS

Most expressions require more than one arithmetic operation. The
computer can calculate very complicated expressions, but it performs
only one operation at a time, just as we would do. Therefore, it performs these operations in a very specific order, important to the computer programmer. The order of operations is called the *hierarchy,* and
expressions are scanned from left to right. First, it performs any exponentiation that it finds. Then, it performs any multiplication and/or
division it finds necessary. Last, it performs the addition and/or subtraction. This order must be carefully observed to obtain the correct
results. If given the expression 4 + 7 * 3, the computer would not
perform the arithmetic in the order given. It would multiply 7 * 3 = 21
and then add 4 + 21 = 25.

Parentheses are used as a symbol of grouping to provide greater
flexibility in writing expressions and Assignment statements. The previous example could not be written to indicate to first add without the
use of a grouping symbol. In this way (4 + 7) * 3 can be written so
that the computer adds 4 + 7 = 11 and then multiplies 11 * 3 = 33
to get the desired answer. The computer makes the computations required inside the parentheses before it begins any other operations.
Grouping in parentheses is a way of altering the computer's normal
order of performing the arithmetic operations. This procedure is necessary if we want to deal with an expression such as

$$\frac{A + B}{X}$$

which must be written as $(A + B)/X$. Without grouping by means of the parentheses, the computer would divide before adding, and the result would be incorrect.

All operations within the parentheses are performed according to the order of operations already described. There might be a need for more than one pair of parentheses. In such a case, the computer first computes the expression in the innermost parentheses; then it uses that value to compute the expression in the next outer parentheses. When a pair of parentheses are inside another pair, they are called *nested parentheses*. An example is

    A = ((X+Y) * Z + B).

We would normally use brackets or larger parentheses for the outer parentheses, but only one size is available in the FORTRAN character set.

SEQUENCE OF ASSIGNMENT STATEMENTS

The numerous Assignment statements required to complete a problem must be carefully stated in their correct order. An Assignment statement can be used in ways other than to indicate arithmetic operations. It can be used, and frequently is used, to assign a value to an identifier. For example, X = 1.5 and HEIGHT = 6.2 are valid Assignment statements and would be necessary information for the computer before it could execute the Assignment statement AREA = Height * X. In this case, the computer would then automatically reverse the equation and multiply 6.2 * 1.5 = 9.3 and would assign the value 9.3 to AREA. If the identifier AREA were used in a succeeding expression, the computer would automatically supply 9.3 as the value of AREA.

The computer executes each Assignment statement in two separate steps. First, it performs the computations to the right of the replaced-by sign. Second, it assigns the computed value to the Identifier on the left of the replaced-by sign. The same Identifier usually appears several times in a program. When it appears a second time in one sequence of Assignment statements, the last value is assigned to the Identifier and the previous value is lost, as shown in this example:

    X = 7
    X = X + 1

The first value of 7 is initially assigned to X. After computing X + 1, or 7 + 1 = 8, the new value of 8 is assigned to the Identifier X.

MODES

The computer can function in either whole numbers or decimals. Using whole numbers is called *integer arithmetic* and is processed in *fixed-point mode*. Using numbers with decimals is called *real-number arithmetic* and is processed in *floating-point mode*. Since each mode is stored and processed in a different manner, the computer is limited in its ability to process both types in one expression. In general, the modes cannot be mixed in the same expression, although there are a few exceptions. The computer programmer instructs the computer to function in fixed-point mode by using no decimal point in the constants, such as 14 or 67. He instructs the computer to function in floating-point mode by using a decimal point in each constant, such as 1.4 or 67.0. *Constants used in FORTRAN expressions are actual numbers,* not the symbols, or letters and words, that represent numeric values.

Identifiers must be carefully planned so that they indicate the appropriate mode to the computer. The letters IJKLM and N are reserved to represent fixed-point mode. All other letters represent floating-point mode. If the Identifier consists of more than one letter or consists of letters and numbers, the first letter indicates the mode. Therefore, NUMBER, M, and K would be fixed-point identifiers, and XNUM, A, and SUM would be floating-point Identifiers. If SUM is desired as a fixed-point Identifier, a letter I through N has to be placed before it, such as NSUM. In the same manner, NUM becomes a floating-point Identifier when it is changed to ANUM or XNUM. Perhaps the following chart will make this material easier to remember.

Using	is called	processed in	and identified by
whole numbers	integer arithmetic	fixed-point mode	IJKLMN
numbers with decimals	read number arithmetic	floating-point mode	all other letters

In general, the floating-point mode is used for computations, and the fixed-point mode is used for counting. To represent a whole number in floating-point mode, add a decimal point and a zero or merely a decimal point, such as 2.0 or 2. The expression 1 + X is not valid because it is of mixed modes. Changing it to 1. + X makes it valid.

An exception to the mixed mode rule is with exponents. A fixed-point exponent can be used with either a fixed-point or floating-point base. Both expressions A = X**2 and A = M**2 are valid. A floating-point exponent can be used only with floating-point variables, however; so A = X**.2 is valid, but A = M**.2 is not valid because it is mixed mode.

In FORTRAN, the expressions on the two sides of the replaced-by sign of an Assignment statement do not have to be in the same mode. In a conversion, the expression to the right of the replaced-by sign is evaluated completely (the necessary arithmetic is performed), and the value obtained is assigned in the required mode as designated by the Identifier to the left of the replaced-by sign. Examples of changing from fixed-point to floating-point are Z = 2 and XM = M. Examples of changing from floating-point to fixed-point are I = X and NRATE = 3.15. In NRATE = 3.15, the change is from a decimal to an integer, so the new number assigned to NRATE is merely 3 as a whole number; the fractional part is dropped. It is not rounded off to the nearest whole number. This is referred to as *truncation*.

Fixed-point mode used in division can cause errors because the fraction is dropped. In the example N = 8/3, the answer assigned to N would be 2, not even the nearest whole number, because of truncation.

INPUT/OUTPUT STATEMENTS

The programmer must supply the computer with all the information needed to execute the program. The problem variables have to be gotten into the computer, and the results of the calculations have to be gotten out of the computer. The various I/O statements allow for this transfer of data between the various I/O media and the computer. This transfer of data is called *data transmission*.

The Read statement permits the assignment of new values to Identifiers by reading the new values. The Write statement causes the results, or answers, to be printed on paper. Each of these two statements is followed by two numbers in parentheses separated by a comma. The first number represents the I/O device number, and the second number represents the format statement number. After these two numbers is a list of the variable names. Both numbers in parentheses are whole numbers, or integers. These statements are in this form:

READ (integer, integer) list
WRITE (integer, integer) list

There is a comma between the two integers, but none between the parentheses and the first Identifier in the list. The first number, the I/O media number, is arbitrarily determined for the particular computer installation. We will use the number 1 to represent reading a punched card, 2 to represent punching a card, and 3 to represent printing. The second number represents the instruction number on the programmer's code sheet that indicates the positions of the input or output. This will be explained in the next section, Format Statements. The list contains one or more expressions to identify the required input or output.

FORMAT STATEMENTS

A Format statement tells the computer where on the input media the input data are located or where on the output media to record the results, and it tells whether the values are integers or floating-point mode. The Format statement contains two parts, the word FORMAT and the detailed specifications, in this form:

FORMAT (specifications)

Samples of the two basic Format statements are

FORMAT (I8)
FORMAT (F8.2)

The letter F indicates floating-point; and letter I, integer. The first example above indicates an integer consisting of 8 digits, or columns, on the card or paper. The second example indicates a floating-point number consisting of a total of 8 digits, or columns, with 2 of these 8 digits following a decimal point.

A Format statement is required for each different form of I/O required. In the list of program statements, each statement is numbered so that these Format statements can be referred to in the I/O statements. The same Format statement can be used for both input and output if the required formats are the same. Format statements do not contain any arithmetic process to be performed by the computer and are called *nonexecutable statements;* they may be placed in the program anywhere after the starting statement and before the ending statement.

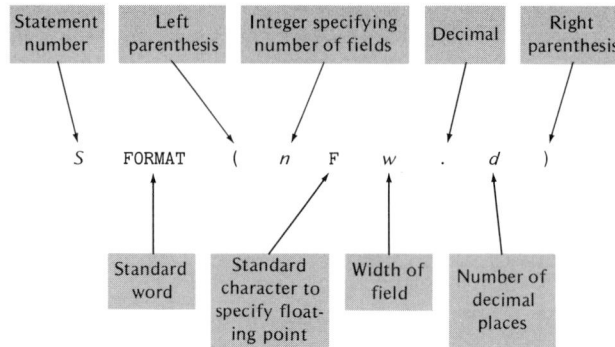

FIG. 18.1 Description of the floating-point format statement

The field allowed for an output number must be large enough to accommodate the largest feasible number it will need. A field that is too large merely leaves blanks to the left of the number. A field that is too small cannot hold the entire number and must drop the left-hand digits and an error message would appear. If a floating-point Identifier is listed in the Read or Write statement, a floating-point field must be provided in the Format statement. The decimal does not have to show on the punched input card. If an integer is listed in the Read or Write statement, a fixed-point field must be provided in the Format statement.

The F-specification refers to the detailed requirements of each floating-point Format statement:

s FORMAT (nF$w.d$)

It is illustrated in Fig. 18.1. When only one field is needed, it is not necessary to put the number 1 before the letter F. The letter F is a constant, always remains the same, to indicate floating-point. The letter w indicates the total number of characters, including decimal places. The decimal point is always the same. The letter d indicates the number of decimal places. It is better to allow a larger field than you think necessary to be assured of avoiding truncation. When too few decimal places are provided, truncation also occurs, as the number is not rounded.

A Format statement

FORMAT (F 2.1, F 4.2)

means that two fields are defined, one with two characters with one digit to the right of the decimal point and one with four characters

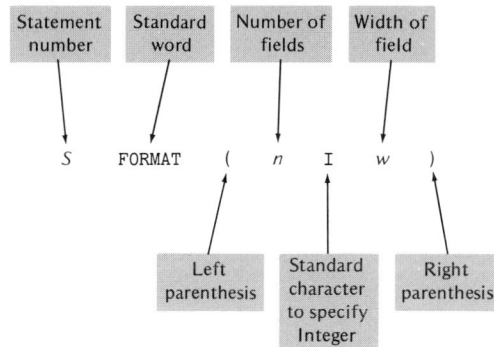

FIG. 18.2 Description of the fixed-point or integer format statement

with two digits to the right of the decimal point. A Format statement

    FORMAT (3F10.4)

means that three fields are defined, each the same with ten characters with four digits to the right of the decimal point.

The I-specification refers to the detailed requirements of each fixed-point, or integer, Format statement:

    s FORMAT (n I w)

It is illustrated in Fig. 18.2. When only one field is needed, it is not necessary to put the number 1 before the letter I. The letter I is a constant, to indicate integer. The letter w indicates the total number of characters in the field. Since there are no decimals, only the number of digits in a whole number have to be considered when planning the field, along with the possibility of a minus sign to indicate a negative number. The Format statement

    FORMAT (2I6)

means that two fields are required, each with a maximum of six characters. The integer output numbers are right-justified within the field.

Both integers and floating-point Identifiers can be in the same Read or Write statement, such as:

    READ (1,20) X, M, Y, N
    20 FORMAT (F8.4, I6, F8.4, I6)

Notice that the letters in the list correspond to the format specifications for integers and floating-point numbers.

The X-specification refers to blanks, or blank fields, as are usually required in an I/O format. This notation is used to skip blank fields and to skip data fields that are not needed from the input card; it is also used to leave blanks in the output punched card or printed line. The format is:

    s   FORMAT (*n* X)

The number of blank spaces is merely placed before the letter X. For example, in the Format statement

    FORMAT (5X, F7.3, 10X, I10),

five blank spaces are at the beginning of the punched card or line of print, and ten blank spaces are between the two data fields.

The carriage control character is the first character in the output image. It is not printed but is used to indicate the kind of spacing down the page. In many computers, if one of the following characters appears in column 1 of an output Format statement, it automatically causes the printer to do the following:

Character	Function
blank	space normally (single)
0	double space
1	skip to a new page
+	do not space—print on the same line as before

Any other number or letter in column 1 of the output Format statement will cause normal reaction. If the statement is

    FORMAT (5X, F10.3),

it will have normal spacing (single), and the first five spaces on the print will be blanks. If the statement is

    FORMAT (I6)

and the number is 142170, the first character is a number 1, and this causes the computer to skip to a new page and print the rest of the number (42170). For this reason, it is best if you always allow for at least one blank at the beginning of each print statement format.

The H-specification is used in cases where some standard alphameric data are desired as output. The letter H reserves a specific amount of space for these data. For example, if it is desirable to print the words GRAND TOTAL on a line alone, the format statement would be:

    10 FORMAT (12H GRAND TOTAL).

The number of characters is placed before the letter H, and the exact characters to be printed are placed after the letter H. To determine the exact number to place before the letter H, count each character, one space between words, and one space after the letter H. Do not count the end parentheses. If a punctuation mark is to be printed at the end, it must be indicated and also counted. If the correct number is not used before the letter H, the entire program will be rejected or an error message will be printed. The Write statement would merely be

```
WRITE (3, 10)
```

with no list following it, since nothing else is to be printed. A Format statement containing the same words along with other data for output is:

```
20 FORMAT (5X, 13H GRAND TOTAL , F10.4)
```

The Write statement would be:

```
20 WRITE (3,20) GRTOT,
```

where GRTOT indicates what is to be printed in reference to F10.4 in the Format statement. Notice that one blank space will appear between the words GRAND TOTAL and the total, since it was allowed for in the format. A space was left before the comma and was counted to get the 13 spaces needed.

The A-specification allows for both reading and printing of alphameric characters. The H-specification allows for only the printing of alphameric characters. Although these data cannot be used for arithmetic operations, they might be needed for clarity of the output. The general format of the A-specification is:

```
s FORMAT (n A w)
```

The letter n indicates the number of times it is to be repeated. The letter A is the constant. The letter w indicates the number of characters to be processed per word of storage. If the characters OHIO are punched in the first four columns of the punched card, the following statements could be used:

```
READ (1, 20) STATE
20 FORMAT (A4)
```

These alphameric data are stored in the computer. They can then be printed by these statements:

```
WRITE (3, 30) STATE
30 FORMAT (1X, A4)
```

In this way, the desired blank space is left so that the computer does not misinterpret anything. The IBM 360 computers can store up to four characters per word in storage. A state name as large as Missouri (eight characters) would require two 4-character words, with the input specifications (2A4). However, most processing that requires state names would now use the standard two-letter abbreviations, which will fit into one 4-character word. FORTRAN programming involves largely numeric data, though, and little alphameric data.

STOP AND END STATEMENTS

The Stop statement consists merely of the word STOP. It indicates the end of the program and tells the computer to cease processing data.

The End statement consists merely of the word END. It indicates to the FORTRAN compiler that the end of a program has been reached. This statement must physically be the last statement in the computer program.

STATEMENT NUMBERS

For convenience, FORTRAN statements can be numbered. They may be assigned any number so long as the same number is not used twice in one program. These numbers are placed to the left of the statement. Not all statements have to be numbered, though; the only ones that require numbers are those that are referred to in other statements, such as Format statements and statements to which a Branch statement refers.

BRANCHING STATEMENTS

In many cases, the program requires some decision-making ability. There are at least two possible paths after each decision. Since the instructions for both cannot be stated directly after the decision statement, it is necessary to use branching to indicate where to find the next instruction to follow. Branching is, therefore, used to vary the flow of the program instructions. To change the normal execution of statements, Control statements are used. The two basic Control statements we will use are the If statement and the Go To statement.

When we use the If statement, three possible conditions may exist, as shown in the flowchart in Fig. 18.3. The expression may be (1) negative, (2) 0, or (3) positive. If it is negative, this means the value is less than 0, so we use the notation < 0 on flowcharts. If the number is 0, the notation $= 0$ is used. If it is positive, the value is greater than 0, and we use the notation > 0 on flowcharts. An If statement has the form:

IF (expression) n_1, n_2, n_3

The expression in parentheses would be the condition being examined. The notations n_1, n_2, n_3 represent the alternative paths the computer

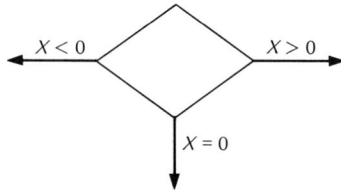

**FIG. 18.3 Flowchart
section showing
the 3-way branch**

can take. The notation n_1 usually represents the path to take if the
condition is negative; n_2 represents the path to take if the condition
is 0; and n_3 represents the path to take if the condition is positive.
Consider the statement:

    IF (A—B) 70,80,90

When the value of A − B is negative, the next statement number to
follow is 70. Notice that there is not a comma after the parentheses
and no spaces are required following the comma. When there is a two-
way branch and, for example, the same statement is repeated whether
the condition evaluated is 0 or positive, then the statement is

    IF (A—B) 70,80,80

A common use of this statement is for comparing two quantities
to determine whether or not they are equal. We do this by writing
the two quantities so that the resulting value is positive, zero, or negative, using the same statements illustrated above. The value of the
expression computed in the If statement is not retained for future use.
It is merely used in making the branching decision. An If statement
must conform to the rules concerning integers and floating-point numbers. Mixed modes cannot be used. The statement

    IF (TOTAL—NUM) 10,12,14

is not a valid statement.

The If statement can be used to bring the computer to the Stop
statement. If the following statements are a part of a computer program when A − B is 0 or positive, the next statement executed is 80,
which is STOP.

        IF (A—B) 70,80,80
    80 STOP

When we use the If statement to branch, we refer to it as a *conditional
branch,* because the exact place where it occurs depends on the condition cited inside the parentheses and therefore is variable. Branching when no alternative exists is an *unconditional branch.*

The unconditional Go To statement is another control statement
that requires branching. It consists merely of the words GO TO and

```
10 Read (1, 30) SIDE
   IF (SIDE) 60, 60, 50
50 AREA = SIDE*SIDE
   WRITE (3, 20) SIDE, AREA              INPUT
   GO TO 10                              Card 1:  number 6.7 in
20 FORMAT (2F10.4)                                columns  6–7.
30 FORMAT (F10.4)                        Card 2:  number 0.0
60 STOP                                           in same posi-
   END                                            tions.
```

FIG. 18.4 Short FORTRAN program illustrating the If and Go To statements

the statement number, for example:

```
GO TO 80
```

This statement usually appears at the end of a series of statements and directs the computer to some other part of the program. Figure 18.4 is a sample program using the If and the Go To statements.

With the designated input and the program in Fig. 18.4, the computer will follow these steps:

1. READ card 1 with SIDE = 6.7 in the format of statement 30.

2. Since the value of SIDE is positive, go to statement 50.

3. Multiply SIDE * SIDE to get AREA = 44.89.

4. Write this answer in the format described in statement 20.

5. Go to statement 10.

6. Read card 2 with SIDE = 0.0 in the format of statement 30.

7. Since the value of SIDE is 0, go to statement 60.

8. Stop.

LOOPING

In many cases, as we have seen, the same steps must be performed several or many times, and looping, or going back to previous instructions, accomplishes this and thus avoids the necessity of our having

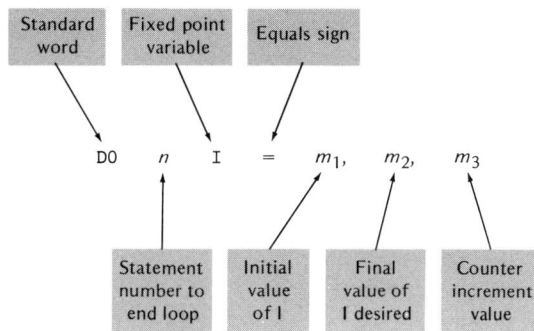

FIG. 18.5 Description
of Do statement

to rewrite the individual statements. In order to instruct the computer
to go through a series of statements more than once, a condition is
tested before the statements are used each time. Control passes to the
next statement following the loop when the required condition has
been met. The Do statement consists of

DO n $i = m_1, m_2, m_3$

The letter n represents the last statement number to be executed and
is located at a later point in the program. The letter i represents an
integer variable which is a counter to be incremented each time the
loop is executed. The m_1 represents the initial value of the counter;
m_2 represents the final value desired for the counter; and m_3 represents
the value by which the counter is to be increased each time the loop
is executed. If m_3 is 1, it does not have to be stated. In the statement

DO 40 I $= 1, 20$

the loop ends with statement 40, and the identifier I to the left of the
replaced-by sign is set to equal 1 (first number to the right of the equal
sign) the first time the loop is executed. Each time the loop is executed, the counter (I) is increased by 1 (assumed, since there is no third
number to the right of the equals sign). When the counter gets to 20
(second number to the right of the equals sign), the loop has been
executed the 20 required times, and the computer goes on to the
next statement after the Do loop.

A loop can contain any FORTRAN statements, but it cannot end
with a control statement such as an If or Go To statement. If a loop
would normally end with one of these statements, an extra dummy

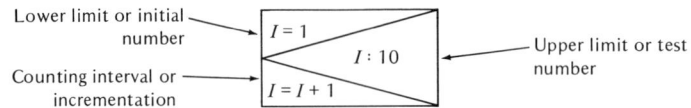

Lower limit or initial number

Counting interval or incrementation

Upper limit or test number

$I = 1$

$I : 10$

$I = I + 1$

DO Statement Illustrated: DO 50 I = 1, 10

FIG. 18.6
Do statement

statement can be added. It is a Continue statement and consists of

   n CONTINUE

The letter *n* represents the statement number. This statement does nothing in the program except to provide the Do statement with a reference number in a loop, as shown below:

```
      DO 50 I = 1, 10
      AREA = I*I
      WRITE (3,3) I, AREA
    3 FORMAT (I10, 10X, F10.4)
   50 CONTINUE
      STOP
      END
```

The set of statements beginning with the Do statement and including all following statements through the statement referred to in the Do loop is called *the range of the Do.* In the example above, the first five statements constitute the range of the Do. When the loop has been executed the required number of times, the index exceeds the value specified by the second quantity to the right of the equals sign, and the loop is said to be satisfied. The flowchart symbol for the Do statement consists of three sections, as shown in Fig. 18.6.

CODING

After making the flowchart of the problem, the programmer translates the steps of the flowchart into FORTRAN language statements. Coding sheets like the one shown in Fig. 18.7 are helpful to indicate the card columns for punching on the program cards. When printing the coding sheets and punching cards, the number of blank spaces inserted between the elements is not important and does not have to be consistent. The following examples are all equivalent:

```
    X = A + B        X=A+B         X   = A +      B
```

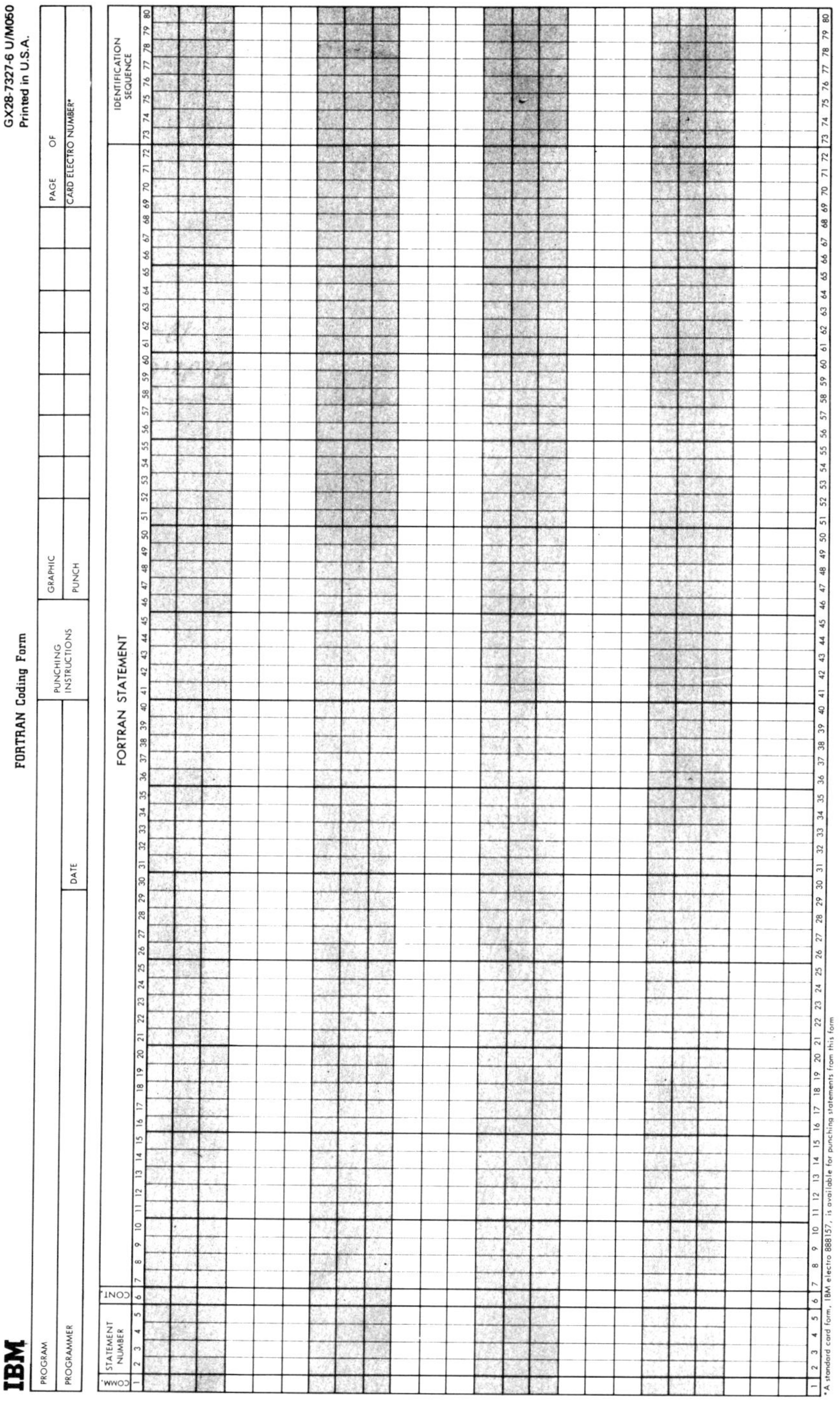

FIG. 18.7
FORTRAN
coding sheet

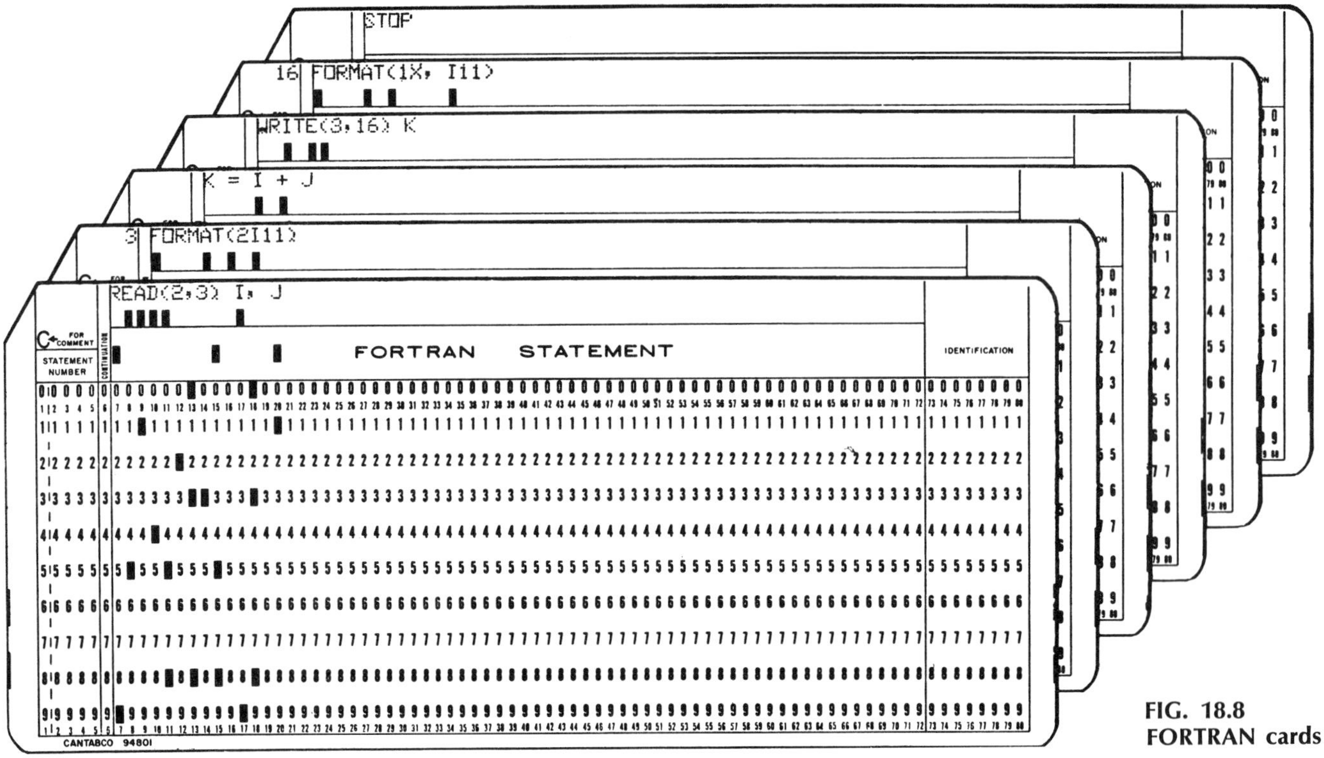

FIG. 18.8
FORTRAN cards

Be careful that you do *not* have blank spaces between digits of numbers, however, because some computers insert 0s. A FORTRAN card is shown in Fig. 18.8, although plain cards can be used. Only columns 1–72 are processed. Information punched into columns 73–80 are merely for the programmer's reference; they are not processed by the computer. Columns 1–5 are reserved for the statement number. These numbers should be right-justified with respect to Column 5, since some compilers provide a 0 in unpunched columns. Column 6 is reserved for a function we have not yet discussed. Columns 7–72 are available for the statements. Data to be processed can be punched anywhere in these columns but have to coincide with the Format statements referring to them in the program.

After the program and input data have been punched on the cards, the program is ready to be compiled. The compiler program is read into the computer, then the source program is read into it. The compiler converts the source language statements into machine language instructions, or the object program. The object program is then used by the computer to process the data.

SAMPLE PROBLEM 1

This problem requires two basic calculations: Compute the diameter and the area of each circle. Each input card contains the radius of a circle with two decimals (in columns 1–5). The value of *pi* to be used will be 3.1416, so the area will contain six decimal places, all to be printed. The line of print is to contain the radius, diameter, and area of the circle, beginning in column 11 and with 10 blanks between numbers. An unknown quantity of cards is to be processed with this program.

```
      TWO = 2
      PI = 3.1416
   10 READ (1, 30) RADIUS
      IF (RADIUS) 50, 50, 20
   20 DIAM = RADIUS * TWO
      AREA = RADIUS ** 2 * PI
      WRITE (3, 40) RADIUS, DIAM, AREA
      GO TO 10
   30 FORMAT (F5.2)
   40 FORMAT (10X, F5.2, 10X, F8.3, 10X, F17.9)
      STOP
   50 END
```

QUESTIONS AND PROBLEMS

1. What types of problems are best suited to FORTRAN?

2. What is the FORTRAN character set?

3. What is the most basic statement in the FORTRAN language?

4. List the limitations of identifiers.

5. Which of the following can be identifiers?
   SUM   SUM1   SUM#   2NUM   SUMS   #SUM

6. What must the left side of each assignment statement be?

7. List the hierarchy of arithmetic operations, first to last.

8. Using the hierarchy above, solve the following two problems.
   ```
   A = 2 + 5 * 6
   X = 3 18/3**2
   ```

9. Write the statement for $X = 3 + 18/3$ so that the addition is done before the division.

10. In what other way can an assignment statement be used to indicate arithmetic operations?

11. How does the computer execute each assignment statement?

12. In this example, what is the final value of X?

```
X = 9
X = X + 3
X = X + 2
```

13. Can modes be mixed in one expression?

14. How does the programmer instruct the computer to function in either floating-point mode or fixed-point mode?

15. How is the mode of an identifier indicated?

16. Indicate the mode of each of the following identifiers:

```
NUM   XNUM   ANS   NANS
```

17. When is each mode generally used?

18. In FORTRAN, do the operations on the both sides of the equals, or "replaced-by," sign have to have the same mode?

19. Explain two situations in which truncation might take place.

20. What do the two numbers in each I/O statement represent?

21. Write Format statements for a

   a) Whole number consisting of a maximum of eight digits.
   b) Decimal number with ten digits, three of which are decimals.

22. What happens when a field is too small for a number?

23. Write the Format statement for the following:

   Three fields, each consisting of a decimal number with a total of seven digits, three of which are decimals.

   Two fields, each consisting of a decimal number, one with a total of six digits, three of which are decimals; and the other with a total of eight digits, four of which are decimals.

   Two fields, each consisting of a whole number with five digits.

   Three fields, each consisting of a whole number, the first with five digits, the second with four digits, and the third with four digits.

   Four fields as follows:

   a) a whole number with four digits.
   b) a decimal number with six digits, three of which are decimals.
   c) a whole number with two digits.
   d) a decimal number with four digits, one of which is a decimal.

Use the previous problems, but provide for three blank spaces after each field.

24. Write the Format statement for the following:

Print the words GRAND TOTAL after allowing eight blank spaces at the beginning of the line. Then allow another eight blank spaces before printing the answer, which is a floating-point with nine digits, three of which are decimals.

25. If the Write statement is WRITE (3,20) ANS, what number must the corresponding Format statement have?

26. What statement must be last in a program?

27. What statements in the program need to be numbered?

28. What are the three possible conditions that may exist when using the If statement?

29. Consider the statement

   IF (A—B) 40, 50, 60.

   a) When would statement 40 be executed next?
   b) When would statement 50 be executed next?
   c) When would statement 60 be executed next?

30. Consider the statement

   IF (X — Y) 70, 80, 80.

   Which statement would be executed next in each situation?

   X = 9 Y = 7   X = 4 Y = 4
   X = 5 Y = 7   X = 0 Y = 1

31. What kind of branch does the If statement provide?

32. Explain each element in the following Do statement.

   DO 40 I = 1, 5

33. What is the range of the Do loop?

34. Are these statements all equivalent in the FORTRAN language?

   C = A + B   C   = A + B   C=A+B

   Why or why not?

35. Write a program to convert each input, which is in years, to days. The maximum input is 999 years, each on a punched card. The required output is one line per input with both the years and days printed.

36. Write the program as above but convert each input that is 99 or less years into days and into hours. Print only inputs over 99 years.

PL/I:
GENERAL
PURPOSE
LANGUAGE

CHAPTER 19

The PL/I programming language was developed by IBM for programs that involve either commercial and business data processing methods or mathematical and scientific problems. As we learned, COBOL was designed specifically for business and commercial data processing problems, and FORTRAN was designed specifically for mathematical and scientific problems. PL/I is a general purpose language that combines the desirable features of both COBOL and FORTRAN and even advances beyond their capabilities in some respects.

One of the advantages of PL/I is the fact that the programmer can write programs for both types of applications. PL/I is a relatively new programming language that has not yet received widespread acceptance. However, because of its potential and possible future use, we will present here the basic concepts. As it gains wider acceptance, its more detailed features will probably undergo numerous modifications.

PL/I CHARACTER SET

A character set is the symbols that can be used in the programming language. The PL/I character set is much larger than that of either COBOL or FORTRAN and consists of the following:

1. Alphabetic characters   the capital letters A through Z.
2. Numeric characters   the decimal digits 0 through 9.
3. Punctuation characters   ,   ;   :   '   (   )
4. Arithmetic symbols   +   −   *   /
5. Comparison symbols   >   <   =
6. Special characters   /   &   %   # $ @   ?   _
7. Blank space

Some of these characters are combined for special meanings, and others have meanings different from the ones their symbols would normally imply.

324

BASIC CONCEPTS OF THE PL/I LANGUAGE

The PL/I language allows the programmer many more options and greater freedom in constructing the program than are available in either COBOL or FORTRAN. Similar to COBOL, though, the programs are made up of statements very much like sentences in the English language. Each statement either states a property of the program or tells the computer to perform some operation or sequence of operations.

Every PL/I statement ends with a semicolon rather than with a period. In our examples, each statement will take a separate line, although this format is not necessary and does not affect the meaning of the program. A long statement might take several lines, whereas several short statements might be placed on one line together.

PL/I WORDS

PL/I words can be made up of the alphabetic and numeric characters and the underbar. The underbar is called the *break character*. Although it looks like a typewriter underscore, it occupies a space by itself and can be used as a hyphen. In the PL/I language, the characters $, @, and # are considered to be letters (alphabetic characters), so they can also be used in PL/I words. PL/I words cannot contain blanks. The first character of a word must be a letter.

PL/I words are divided into two basic categories: identifiers and keywords. Identifiers are used, for example, to name, or identify, variables, functions, the name of the program, and other program parts. Programmers, who determine the identifiers, find it advantageous to make up ones that closely resemble the data they are describing. Here are some samples of PL/I identifiers:

    SUM1   GROSS_SALES   X   ABC   INCOME_$ #SALES

These cannot be used as identifiers:

GROSS SALES	because it contains a blank
2X	because it starts with a number
TOT. SALES	because a period is neither a letter nor a number, and the expression also contains a space.

Keywords are PL/I words that have special meaning due to the way they are used in the program. They are used for identifying specific kinds of statements, for naming other program components, as well as for other purposes. They are actually special identifiers and must conform to all the rules stated for identifiers. Keywords in the PL/I language have fixed meanings similar to reserved words in COBOL. They differ, however, because they are not reserved for one special purpose, but are recognizable as keywords having special meaning only when used in specific positions in statements and in a specific sequence, called a *string of characters*. Therefore, these same words can be used elsewhere in the program as identifiers. Some of the keywords we will be using are:

PROCEDURE	OPTIONS	MAIN
DECLARE	FLOAT	GET
LIST	PUT	SKIP
PAGE	LINE	EDIT
END	GO	IF

There are, however, many more keywords in PL/I. We will study the specific uses of the basic keywords in order to write some relatively simple programs.

VARIABLES AND CONSTANTS IN A PROGRAM

A variable may have different values during the execution of a program. For example, the word HOURS is an identifier that can have a different value for each employee. Therefore, variables must be assigned identifiers to label, or identify, them. The identifier should be selected to suggest the use of the variable. For example, X could be used rather than HOURS but is more difficult to remember when writing the program.

A constant is a specific value, or number, that does not change during the execution of the program. In PL/I, there are several different kinds of constants; the only ones we will be using are decimal numbers. A constant can be written as an integer, or whole number, with or without a sign, such as:

1   +147   −31   0   3672

or as a real number (a number with a decimal point). It can be called a floating-point constant. Examples are:

1.372   +3.1416   −9.7   0.00

These represent a fixed format. Another format for real constants is the floating-point format. It is similar to the scientific notation which is frequently used in technical work. In scientific notation, the number is written as a decimal value, usually lower than 10, followed by 10 to the appropriate power. The power of 10 indicates the number of places the decimal point must be moved to the right ($-$) or left ($+$) in the original number to equal its scientific notation. For example:

70000 in scientific notation is 7.0×10^4,

.00312 in scientific notation is 3.12×10^{-3}.

Converting scientific notation to PL/I floating point notation is accomplished by using the letter E in place of the times sign and the number 10 in the scientific notation and writing the power as a regular number, since PL/I has no raised numbers.

For example:

7.0×10^4 is   `7.0E4`

3.12×10^{-3} is   `3.12E-3`

BASIC STRUCTURE OF A PL/I PROGRAM

The writing of a PL/I program has fewer restrictions and requirements in its structure than either COBOL or FORTRAN. The only requirement is that the statements be grouped; these groups of statements are called *blocks*. A short, relatively simple program might consist of only one block, whereas a longer, more complex program might consist of many blocks.

PROCEDURE STATEMENT

Each program begins with a Procedure statement in the following form.

identifier: `PROCEDURE OPTIONS (MAIN) ;`

The specific identifier is determined by the programmer. The keywords PROCEDURE, OPTIONS, and MAIN have special significance when compiling the object program. A sample procedure statement is:

`STEP1:   PROCEDURE OPTIONS (MAIN) ;`

COMMENTS

A comment is used to aid the programmer and others in understanding the operation of the program. It is not a statement and is not used by the computer when executing the program; therefore, it does not end with a semicolon. The general form of a comment is:

`/* comment */`

The comment may contain any message and be of any length, but it may not contain the pair of characters */ before its end. No blank space may separate the / and * at either end of the comment. A comment may be placed almost anywhere in a program. A sample comment is:

```
/* SAMPLE PROGRAM_COMPUTE AREA OF CIRCLES */
```

DECLARE STATEMENT

A Declare statement lists the names of all the variables used in the program and in many cases becomes quite complex. The form of the Declare statement we will use is:

```
DECLARE ( identifier, . . . , identifier) FLOAT ;
```

The words DECLARE and FLOAT are keywords. All the identifiers are placed inside the parentheses with a comma after each one except the last one. The keyword FLOAT indicates the manner in which the identifier will be used. It is not always necessary to list all the variables in a Declare statement, but at this time we will do so; it is easier to put them all in than to remember when they may be omitted. A sample Declare statement is:

```
DECLARE (RADIUS, AREA) FLOAT ;
```

GET STATEMENT

The Get statement provides the input data. It contains the names of the identifiers whose values are read into the computer from the input data. Its form is:

```
GET LIST (identifier, . . . , identifier) ;
```

As is in the Declare statement, the identifiers are separated by commas, but no comma is placed after the last one. It may contain one or more identifiers. A sample Get statement is:

```
GET LIST (RADIUS) ;
```

ASSIGNMENT STATEMENT

An Assignment statement gives the value that is indicated on the right side of the equals sign to the variable name on the left side of the equals sign. The general form of the Assignment statement is:

```
variable name = expression;
```

Although the equals sign is used, this statement does not mean that the two sides of the statement are equal; it means that the value of the expression on the right should be assigned to the variable name on the left. It therefore states an action to be performed, not a condition of equality. The equals sign is called the assignment operator for this reason. The computer interprets the expression, performs any calculations that are necessary, and assigns the resulting value to the variable name. The expression may be a single number or an arithmetic operation. The following are examples of Assignment statements:

```
PI = 3.1416 ;
AREA = PI*RADIUS**2 ;
```

A multiple assignment statement can assign the same value to more than one variable, as is frequently necessary. The general form of a multiple assignment statement is:

variable$_1$, variable$_2$, . . . , variable$_n$ = expression;

The variables are listed and separated by commas, such as:

```
A, B, C = 0 ;
```

The Assignment statement is the fundamental operation statement in PL/I, as it is with other programming languages. It is the only way to direct the computer to determine a value and save it for future use. All that may be to the left of the Assignment operator is the name of the variable, or the names of the variables in a multiple assignment statement. The arithmetic expressions that may be to the right of the assignment operator are explained next.

ARITHMETIC EXPRESSIONS

Arithmetic statements in the PL/I language differ somewhat from the way they are written in algebra. These differences are due primarily to limitations in the computer input/output media. For example, exponents cannot be raised, the square root sign cannot be used, and fractions have to be written with the numerator and denominator on the same line separated by the diagonal.

Arithmetic expressions consist of operators, operands, and parentheses. The operators indicate the operations to be performed and consist of + − * / ** in PL/I. The ** means exponentiation. The * for multiply cannot be omitted as it frequently is in algebra; for example, AB must be written A*B. The following table gives examples of algebraic notations and their equivalents in PL/I.

Algebraic	$m + n$	$a - b$	$2\pi r$	$a \times b$	$\dfrac{x + y}{z}$	x^2
PL/I	M + N	A − B	2*PI*R	A*B	(X + Y)/Z	X**2

The order in which the operations are performed is determined by their strength, which is:

1. Strongest   exponentiation
2. Next strongest   multiplication and division
3. Weakest   addition and subtraction

Multiplication and division have equal strength, and the order does not matter within these two operations. Therefore, the leftmost operation is done first. The same is true with addition and subtraction. This order may be changed with the use of parentheses. When changing algebraic expressions into PL/I we frequently find it necessary to use parentheses. For example:

$$\dfrac{a + b}{m - \dfrac{n}{x}} \qquad \text{becomes} \qquad \text{(A + B) / (M − N/X)}$$

$$x^{n+1} \qquad \text{becomes} \qquad \text{X**(N + 1)}$$

$$\dfrac{ABC}{2/3} \qquad \text{becomes} \qquad \text{A*B*C / (2/3)}$$

When in doubt as to whether or not you need parentheses, remember that having too many is better than not having enough.

ARITHMETIC FUNCTIONS

Arithmetic functions are built into PL/I. Standard operations that would be difficult and very time consuming for the programmer to write are perfomed. One such function is finding a square root, indicated by SQRT in this form:

```
SQRT (expression) ;
```

The expression may contain one or more variables and/or constants. The PL/I contains many functions, not needed in the programs of this chapter.

PUT STATEMENT

The Put statement is the output statement used for printing the results of the computations required in the program. It can also print the original input data if instructed to do so. The general form of the Put statement is:

    PUT LIST (identifier, . . . , identifier) ;

This statement provides a printout of all the values represented by identifiers inside the parentheses. They are separated by commas in this statement. This form of the Put statement prints as many decimal places in the result as were used in the computer for the computation, usually between 6 and 16 decimal places. A sample Put statement is:

    PUT LIST (RADIUS, AREA) ;

It is also helpful to print the initial input for the problem. Doing so enables you to associate the answer with the proper input values and to check any of the input values, if necessary. Checking is particularly useful in some complex problems when you must be sure that none are missing or out of order.

There are several special Put statements. One is for controlling the line of print, and its form is:

    PUT SKIP (n) (identifier, . . . , identifier) ;

The letter n in parentheses refers to a number. If n is 1 or is omitted, the printer skips to the next line, giving single-spaced printing. If the number is 0 or is negative, the printer returns to the beginning of the current line; this means that it might print over data previously printed on the line. If n is 2, the printer will go down 2 lines, giving double-spaced printing. Another form of the Put statement above is:

    PUT LIST (identifier, . . . , identifier) SKIP (n) ;

Another special Put statement is for controlling the page of print, and its form is:

    PUT LINE (n) (identifier, . . . , identifier) ;

The letter n refers to the specific line on the page, and the print begins at the left margin on that line. It does not indicate how many lines to go down as does the Put Skip form. Another form of this Put statement is:

    PUT LIST (identifier, . . . , identifier) LINE (n) ;

The Put statement that indicates to print on line 1 of the next page is:

    PUT PAGE (identifier, . . . , identifier) ;

or

    PUT (identifier, . . . , identifier) PAGE ;

These Put statements specify some action to be taken by the printer before any data are transmitted. A sample Put statement is:

```
PUT LIST (RADIUS, AREA) SKIP ;
```

Another special Put statement is required when it is necessary to specify the format of the output. The general form of this statement is:

```
PUT EDIT (list) (format) ;
```

The "list" refers to the identifiers, and the "format" indicates the desired form of the data on the printed page. Capital letters frequently placed in the "format" portion of this Put statement are:

A (n) Place the data in output with the length indicated by the number. If n is greater than the length of the data, they will be left-justified and followed by blanks. Data that are left-justified are usually alphabetic data.

E (n,d) Place the data in output as a floating-point number written in scientific notation. The number is right-justified if it requires fewer characters than indicated by n. The d indicates the number of decimal places.

F (n,d) Place the data in output as a fixed-point number with a total of n digits and d digits to the right of the decimal point. The number is right-justified with leading zeros omitted.

X (n) Leave n blanks.

The X (n) notation may be omitted if you allow more spaces than necessary in an E or F phrase. For example, F (12) is the same as X (4) F (8) if it is known that the largest number occupies 8 spaces.

Most of these special characteristics of the Put Edit statement also apply to the Get statement.

END STATEMENT

Each Procedure block is terminated by an End statement with the form:

```
END identifier ;
```

This identifier must be the same one that was used with the Procedure statement at the beginning of the Procedure block. A sample is:

```
END STEP1 ;
```

Now, we can combine the sample statements shown in this chapter to make up a Procedure block, as shown in Fig. 19.1.

```
STEP1:    PROCEDURE OPTIONS (MAIN) ;
          /* SAMPLE PROGRAM _ COMPUTE AREA OF CIRCLES */
          DECLARE (RADIUS, AREA) FLOAT ;
          GET LIST (RADIUS) ;
          PI = 3.1416 ;
          AREA = PI*RADIUS**2 ;
          PUT LIST (RADIUS, AREA) SKIP ;
          END STEP1 ;
```

**FIG. 19.1 One procedure
block of a
program**

Several additional items must be added to make the Procedure block in Fig. 19.1 become a complete program. As it is now, the statements would be executed once and the computer would stop. We want the computer to continue as long as there are new input data to be processed. The next sections add the details to this Procedure block to make it a functional program.

LABELS

We use labels to identify statements in PL/I so that we can transfer control to them later in the program if we wish. The form of a label is:
    name:
Although it is usually written on the same line as the statement to which it refers, the label may be on a line by itself, followed by the statement on the following line. The initial Get statement is labeled START, since it is the first statement needed when the computer is ready to process the next input data. The End statement is labeled FINISH, since it is to be referred to when there are no more input data. Any labels can be used, such as START1, START2, and START3 to indicate different sections that are referred to later in the program.

GO TO STATEMENT

The Go To statement can be used to alter the sequence of execution. The general form of a Go To statement is:
    GO TO (label) ;
The label must be the same word that was used to identify the state-

ment to which the computer is to transfer its processing. In our sample problem, we insert the following Go To statement after the Put List statement:

    GO TO START ;

In this case, the End statement is not executed; instead, the computer transfers its processing to the Get List statement.

IF STATEMENT

The If statement allows the computer to decide what path to follow by testing a condition. The general form of the If statement is:

    IF (condition) THEN (statement) ;

The condition is specified by two expressions separated by a comparison operator. The only comparison operator we have used so far is the *replaced-by,* or equals, sign (=), but we might use the *greater than* (>), *less than* (<), or any of several other operators. *The statement is what is to be done if the comparison is true.* If the comparison is not true, then the rest of this statement is ignored, and the next statement in sequence is executed. To determine whether or not the last card has been processed (whether or not there is another card in input to be read), compare an input item to zero. If its value is zero, the "compare" results in a "true," and the statement after the word is then executed. This statement is usually directing control to some final-step or steps in the program. If the value of the input is not zero, the compare results in a "false," and the next statement in sequence is executed to make the necessary calculations with the new input data.

The If statement in our sample problem is:

    IF RADIUS = 0 THEN GO TO FINISH ;

The If statement is considered a conditional transfer, since it is used only if the specified condition is met. The Go To statement is considered an unconditional transfer, since it is used every time it is encountered.

Now our sample program, in Fig. 19.2, is complete and can be executed. After each answer has been printed, control is transferred (unconditionally) to read new data as input. Whenever the Get statement is executed, the computer checks to determine whether it actually read new input data. If it did, it continues to perform the calculations. If it did not read new input data, it is instructed to stop.

```
STEP1:  PROCEDURE OPTIONS (MAIN) ;
        /* SAMPLE PROGRAM _ COMPUTE AREA OF CIRCLES */
        DECLARE (RADIUS, AREA) FLOAT ;
START:  GET LIST (RADIUS) ;
        IF RADIUS = 0 THEN GO TO FINISH ;
        PI = 3.1416 ;
        AREA = PI*RADIUS**2 ;
        PUT LIST (RADIUS, AREA) SKIP ;
FINISH: END STEP1 ;
```

**FIG. 19.2   A complete
short program**

Several additional statements needed in more complex problems
will be explained in the following sections.

MORE IF STATEMENTS

If statements are used for numerous conditions in addition to determining whether or not the last card has been processed. Most of these
statements use the same general form as the basic If statement. The
conditions are listed in Fig. 19.3.

Condition	In Words
A □< B	A is not less than B
A < B	A is less than B
A < = B	A is less than or equal to B
A = B	A is equal to B
A □= B	A is not equal to B
A > = B	A is greater than or equal to B
A > B	A is greater than B
A □> B	A is not greater than B

**FIG. 19.3   "If" statement
conditions**

Frequently, several conditions are possible, and the next sequence
to follow is different for each possible condition. Let us look at an
example in which several If statements follow each other. When an
employee has produced exactly his quota of items for the week, the

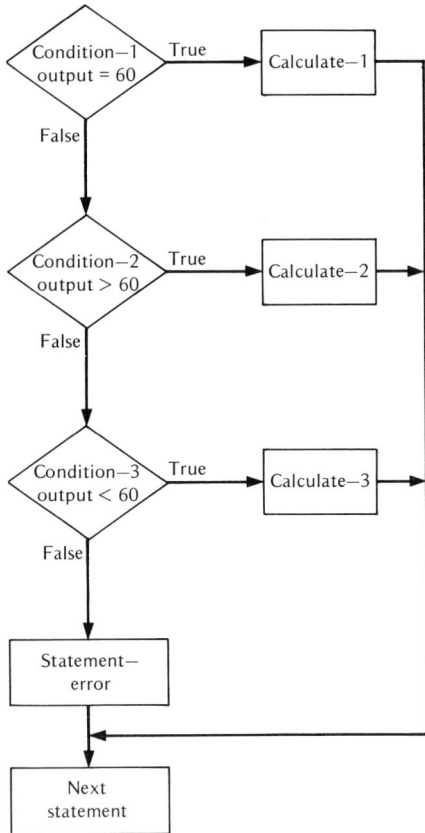

IF OUTPUT = 60 THEN GO TO CALCULATE −1;

IF OUTPUT > 60 THEN GO TO CALCULATE −2;

IF OUTPUT < 60 THEN GO TO CALCULATE −3:

FIG. 19.4 Sample partial flowchart and program— Different sequence for each possible condition

calculation of his pay is based on one set of figures; when he has produced less than his quota, it is based on another set of figures; and when he has produced more than his quota, it is based on still another set of figures. Follow the partial flowchart and program in Fig. 19.4.

It is best to state first the condition that exists or is expected to exist most frequently and to state last the condition that is expected to exist least frequently so that the computer does not have to go through an unnecessary number of statements.

Another form of the If statement can be used when choosing between two conditions and courses of action. It is the If . . . Then and Else statement and its form is:

IF condition THEN statement-1 ;
  ELSE statement-2 ;

It means that if the condition is met, the computer follows statement-1 which is immediately after the word THEN; and if the condition is not met, the computer follows statement-2 which is immediately after the word ELSE. This form is generally used when one specific step is followed for each of the two conditions, and then the computer goes back to the regular sequence; neither Statement-1 nor Statement-2 indicates a branch. For example, assume that value A is assigned to the identifier CLASS if the person scored 10 on a test, and the value X is assigned if the person did not score 10 on the test. After this step, the regular steps are followed for both conditions. Follow the partial flowchart and program in Fig. 19.5.

THE DO STATEMENT

The If statements we have used so far indicate whether or not a single statement is to be executed or which one of several alternative single statements should be executed. Even the Go To statement is a single statement, although it refers to other statements. Often it is convenient or necessary for an If statement to indicate the execution of a group of statements rather than just one statement. The Do statement serves this function and has the form:

DO ;

It has any number of statements after it and terminates with the End statement. The Do statement, End statement, and all statements between these make up a Do group. We use a Do group in a program

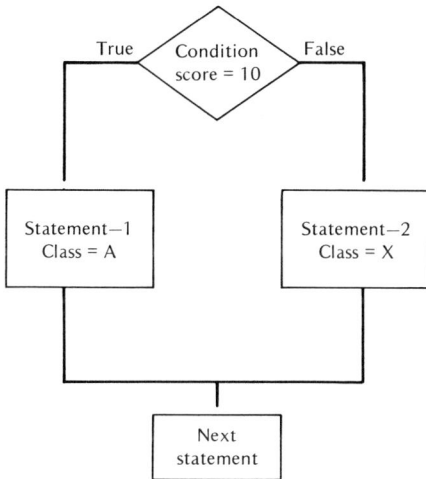

```
IF SCORE = 10 THEN CLASS = A;

ELSE CLASS = X:
```

**FIG. 19.5 Sample partial
flowchart and program—
Single statement
after each condition**

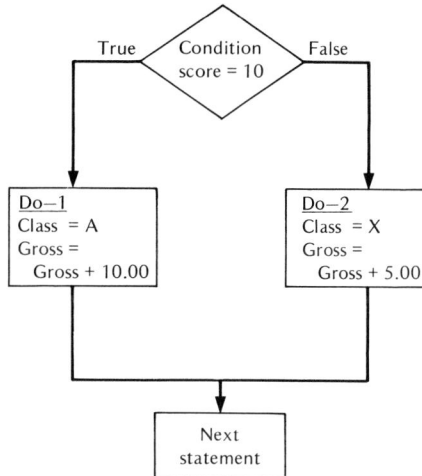

```
IF SCORE = 10 THEN DO;
      CLASS = A;
      GROSS = GROSS + 10.00;
      END;
ELSE DO;
      CLASS = X;
      GROSS = GROSS + 5.00;
      END:
```

**FIG. 19.6 Sample partial
flowchart and program—
Several statements
after each condition**

in a manner similar to the way we use a single statement. Consider
the situation in Fig. 19.5, and assume that several steps are to be followed rather than just one for each condition. If the person gets the
top score of 10, he is to be assigned to Class A and he is to receive a
bonus of $10. If his score was not 10, he is to be assigned to Class X
and is to receive a bonus of $5 for having participated. Compare the
partial flowchart and program in Fig. 19.6 with the one in Fig. 19.5.

ATTRIBUTES AND PICTURE SPECIFICATIONS

Attributes are the characteristics of data; for arithmetic data these
refer to the range of values they can assume and the form they maintain. Constants are specified by writing their values directly in the
program, so the form in which they are written determines their

attributes. Variables are referred to by writing their names or identifiers; their attributes are described in the Declare statement. Then their attributes remain the same throughout the program. The form of the Declare statement is:

    DECLARE (name attributes) ;

If several identifiers have the same attributes, they can all be listed in one Declare statement:

    DECLARE (name₁, name₂, . . .) attributes ;

For fixed numeric data, the statement is:

    DECLARE (name) (n, d) ;

The letter n refers to the number of digits in the entire item, and the d refers to the number of decimal places. For example, (8,3) means that the entire number can consist of eight digits, three of which are decimal places. Therefore the range of the number is 0 through 99999.999 in steps of .001.

For floating-point numeric data the statement is:

    DECLARE (name) FLOAT (n) ;

The letter n refers to the number of digits in the entire number.

It is not always necessary to specify the number of digits. In such cases, the computer uses its maximum, which varies for different computer models.

The Picture attribute defines the form of arithmetic items by a *symbolic representation* of their contents, *or a picture.* Fortunately, it is seldom necessary to do this; the rules concerning when it is necessary to do this are rather complex. In general, the picture is a part of a special Declare statement and its form is:

    DECLARE (name) PICTURE "specifications" ;

Its specifications are written in much the same way as a COBOL statement and they provide a similar function.

COMPILING THE SOURCE PROGRAM

After the source program has been written, it is punched on punched cards. A compiler program in the computer translates the source program into the object program, and then the computer uses this to execute the program. In a PL/I program, there are two basic kinds of statements: executable and nonexecutable. *Executable statements* tell the compiler what instructions to generate for the computer to use to execute the program. The Get, Assignment, and Put statements are executable statements, as are others. For example, the compiler generates an entire series of steps for the computer to follow when it encounters a square root or a divide instruction. *Nonexecutable statements* tell the compiler how to generate instructions for the executable statements. The Procedure, Declare, and End statements are nonexecutable. For example, when the compiler sees the End statement, it knows that the end of a procedure or the end of the entire program has been reached.

SUMMARY

The PL/I language has more capabilities than either COBOL or FORTRAN because it is more extensive and contains more options in programming statements. Its potential is great. As with the other programming languages, the programmer must understand all available details if he is to take full advantage of the options in the language.

QUESTIONS AND PROBLEMS

1. What types of problems are suited to PL/I?
2. What is the PL/I character set?
3. How does each PL/I statement end?
4. Does each statement have to be written on a separate line?
5. What are the restrictions of the PL/I word?
6. What are the two basic categories of PL/I words?
7. Which of the following can be PL/I words?

   a) SUM1   e) A-B-C
   b) 1SUM   f) X
   c) GROSS__SALES   g) 9
   d) SALES#1   h) TOT.SLS

8. How are PL/I keywords different from COBOL reserved words?
9. Can keywords also be used as identifiers?
10. What are variables and constants in a program?
11. Write the following numbers in floating-point notation:
    .910000   .61798.3

12. What is the purpose of a comment in a PL/I program?

13. What is the general form of the statement that provides the input data?

14. How does the computer manipulate an Assignment statement?

15. In an Assignment statement, what does the equals sign actually represent?

16. What does a multiple assignment statement do?

17. Which of the following are valid PL/I statements?
    a) A = M + N   d) D = PI * D
    b) X = YZ   e) A = (X + Y)/Z
    c) A*B = C   f) A = b + c

18. In what order are the arithmetic operations performed if there are no parentheses?

19. What are arithmetic functions?

20. Why is it frequently helpful to print the initial input for the problem along with the answer?

21. How can you control the line of print on a form?

22. Indicate the format section of the Put statement for each of the following:
    a) Use scientific notation for a number consisting of six digits, three of which are decimals.
    b) A fixed-point number with eight digits, four of which are to the right of the decimal place.
    c) Seven blank spaces.

23. How does each procedure block end?

24. What statements need labels?

25. Is the Go To statement a conditional or an unconditional branch?

26. What happens when the conditions in an If statement are not met?

27. When would several If statements follow each other?

28. When several If statements are placed together, which one should be first?

29. In what way does the Do statement help?

30. What are the attributes of numeric data?

31. What do executable statements tell the compiler?

32. What do nonexecutable statements tell the compiler?

33. Why is PL/I considered to have more potential than either COBOL or FORTRAN?

34. Write a program to convert each input, which is in yards on a punched card, to feet and to inches. The maximum input is 9999 yards. The required output is a line of print per input indicating the yards, feet, and inches.

PLANNING THE DATA PROCESSING FUNCTION:

OBJECTIVES, POLICIES, AND ORGANIZATION

CHAPTER 20

Every phase of the managerial process starts with planning. The data processing manager has been effective if what is happening now is the successful culmination of what he planned a long time ago. Effective operation demands skilled long-range strategic and manpower planning. The data processing manager must determine what he wants the future of the data processing function to be, and then lead or direct the efforts of his subordinates toward the achievement of these goals.

Planning is predetermining what action the firm or function should take. Plans take the form of objectives, goals, policies, procedures, methods, systems, standards, organizational arrangements, and so forth. To the data processing manager, planning means determining the objectives, policies, etc., toward a course of action for his function, based upon both the short-run and the long-run plans of the firm. The ability to initiate change is becoming just as important as the ability to adjust to change. A good plan defines the adjustment, addition, or change which may affect the survival and growth of any function within the firm.

Data processing activities, in themselves, range from simple to complex in many ways, and they are subject to change and development because they extend through long periods of time. In managing the data processing function one must think not only of conditions

341

as they presently exist, but also of what they will probably become. Accordingly, the data processing manager may have tangible people, materials, equipment, and systems before him to work with, or he may have only facts, ideas, and theories. In either case, he is constantly shifting his thoughts from present to future, from what is now to what ought to be or what he desires to bring about. Thus the data processing manager's task of planning involves:

1. Translating the plans of the firm into immediate plans for his function,
2. Establishing in detail the objectives and goals of his function,
3. Formulating the policies and procedures to be followed,
4. Establishing the organization structure and authority relationship for his function, and
5. Determining the systems analysis and design.

TRANSLATING PLANS OF THE FIRM

Today's organizations are becoming more complex every day. Rapidly changing technology and social patterns and the enormous capital investments required in business today have created a real need for data processing systems which are capable of providing timely and accurate information. They must be flexible enough to meet changing business conditions rapidly. The obvious need is to shorten the time between the discovery and application of data.

The data processing function is composed of tools and materials that provide the decision-makers of an organization with complete and up-to-date information with which to direct the operations of the company. The forms, records, communication lines, and electronic computers become interacting elements in an integrated system. It is a staggering task to integrate all company activities—from the receipt and entry of customer orders, through forecasting, engineering, manufacturing, inventory control, marketing, services, and accounting.

An integrated data processing system that enables the top executives to base decisions on today's facts, not yesterday's predictions, leads to more centralized and effective control over even highly decentralized operations. Modern communication and powerful on-line, real-time computing brings top management right back into the center of the business. Lines of communication are clean and direct, with no detours or delays. Urgently needed information is readily available because it can be automatically channeled directly to the man who requests it.

FORMULATING OBJECTIVES AND GOALS FOR THE DATA PROCESSING FUNCTION

Sensing a need for planning and exercising one's authority and knowledge are the first steps toward action. A need must be defined and clarified before one can decide what, if any, planning to do. It is one thing to have a vague idea that training within the data processing function is weak and quite a different thing to decide to do something about it. After a fire, the need for a new office building may be obvious, but the steps to take in developing plans for a new building would be less obvious.

Any list of objectives and goals for the data processing function may, of course, be improved, some parts deleted, or others added. The purpose of this section is to give you a starting point for your thinking concerning objectives and goals for the data processing function. You may find yourself wanting to change the objectives according to your own experience and environment. This reaction is good; it shows that you are beginning to challenge and to think. There is only one precaution: *Be sure that your thinking is realistic as well as logical.* Concentrate on logical, realistic premises to determine what the data processing function is to produce. Detailed objectives and goals for the data processing manager would begin with the following:

1. Participating in determining the types of information that managers on all levels need for their decision-making,

2. Improving the timeliness of information for all managers,

3. Increasing the speed of delivering information,

4. Improving the accuracy of the information,

5. Reducing data processing efforts and costs, and

6. Providing better service to customers.

Each member of the management team must be given the information he needs to perform his particular function. Let's review briefly what we said earlier on this subject. In designing the data processing system for any organization, the data processing manager will have to determine a number of levels of contribution.

At the very lowest level of contribution, data may have to be indexed according to pertinent documents necessary for operation planning, organizing, and directing. There is a first line of operation in all functions, whether it is production, finance, or corporate planning. The production function is usually charged with producing a quality product at as low a cost as possible consistent with the predetermined quality standards. The marketing function is usually charged with product sales, sales forecasting, advertising, and so forth. The finance function is usually charged with maintaining adequate working capital, managing wisely the investments of the firm, and providing funds for development or expansion. The corporate planning function is charged with planning for and coordinating the activities of the production, marketing, and finance functions. The vice-president in charge of these functions will have different information needs than the lowest executive in each function. Thus we see that the data processing manager must determine and establish levels of contribution for the users of information.

Furthermore, the data processing manager will have to use people, techniques, and equipment in such a way that redundant and duplicative sources of data are eliminated. These goals may very well be the objective of quality and quantity control, if the firm has such a division.

The managerial functions are not independent or separate activities. The manager has to think in terms of all the managerial functions as he makes a decision concerning any one function. The first step in control is to set standards. These standards may be objectives, policies, systems, and so forth, which are, in reality, plans.

Whether the reader uses his own list of objectives or the one listed above, he will want to examine his objectives and goals by asking himself the following questions:

1. Have plans and objectives of the total firm been considered in the proposed alternative(s)?

2. Are departmental or divisional plans and objectives in harmony with the overall plans and objectives?

3. Does management agree with stated plans and objectives?

4. Do the proposed alternatives accomplish stated plans and objectives?[1]

POLICIES AND PROCEDURES OF THE DATA PROCESSING FUNCTION

When the organization structure has been established, when major plans are outlined, and when competent people are obtained to do the necessary work, the need for guidelines for action and decision-making is the data processing manager's next concern in carrying out his function. Policies and procedures establish the tone of the data processing function and provide authorized guidance to all supervisors within the data processing function on the constraints within which work will be done. Criteria which will be applied to decision-making and the actions which may be taken to carry out the major plans have to be settled. If this guidance is not available, action to attain objectives will be varied, irregular, and inconsistent. A policy is the means to the objective and must be definite as to purpose.

Professor Ziegler of Merrimack College points out that "policy is a means by which company objectives are effectively reconciled with internal factors and organizational factors."[2] Internal factors are the firm's resources, both human and nonhuman. Why do we find the human resources the more difficult to manage? Because nonhuman resources are inanimate objects and, within the limits of their capacity, we can make them do precisely what we want them to do. On the other hand, people have basic drives that include biological, psychological, and social factors.

The data processing manager can formulate definite policies in order to integrate efficiently the physical facilities such as equipment, materials, building, space, office forms, and environment which includes lighting, color, music, and so forth. In large organizations, the modern data processing function is made up of synchronized pieces of equipment which use paper, tape, etc., all sheltered in appropriately designed buildings. The company's management outlines the scope of data processing activities by setting policies stipulating the data to be processed, the size of the unit, the degree of flexibility, and the anticipated future expansion. Thus management guides the selection and organization of the physical facilities. Intelligent selection of facilities depends upon an accurate appraisal of equipment with respect to its suitability for the work to be handled, rate of output, reliability and adaptability, and the purchase price and economy of operation.

The usefulness and economic advantages of the data processing function depend largely on how one tackles the critical job of analyzing and then selecting the physical facilities, including the computer. Poor judgment on this fundamental decision can be very costly. In addition to the tremendous cost of the physical facilities, use of a computer and the auxiliary facilities will probably cause gradual changes in policies, procedures, practices, and organizational relationships.

ORGANIZATIONAL PLANNING FOR THE DATA PROCESSING FUNCTION

As a company grows larger, it finds that it has many independent subsystems of data processing such as the payroll system, the customer billing system, the general ledger system, and others. It may still retain many manual systems such as filing systems, duplicating systems, and so forth. As the firm grows larger the need arises to integrate these automated and/or manual systems. Organizations have found themselves with private empires that have proliferated without any apparent pattern or without any significant coordination. The problems are how to organize to obtain effective integration of these many systems, and how best to provide operating management with a reasonable amount of control over the data and information it receives and transmits.

Organizations today rely heavily on receiving prompt and accurate information necessary for decision-making. The person or persons responsible for providing managers with this information are an important "key" in the effective operation of the organization. The data processing manager not only has the responsibility to get information to top management, but he must also see that managers of separate divisions of the firm have all information relating to the internal operation of their divisions.

The organization of the data processing function is probably the most difficult and critical problem with which any firm is faced today. The success of the entire effort may depend upon it, yet there are no hard rules to be used as guides. The principle problems are the place of the data processing function within the organization, the degree of specialization (centralization), and the type of authority for the data processing function.

DATA PROCESSING POSITION WITHIN THE ORGANIZATION

The organization chart shows every position in the organization and who is responsible to whom. A sample organization chart is shown in Fig. 20.1, but of course it is not typical of all companies. This or-

FIG. 20.1 Organization chart —centralized arrangement for data processing

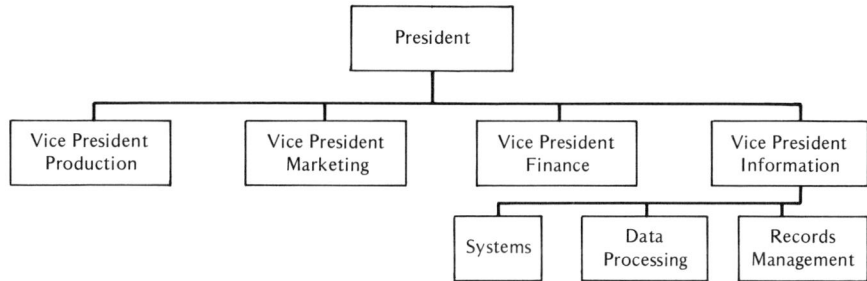

```
                              ┌───────────┐
                              │ President │
                              └───────────┘
        ┌──────────────┬──────────────┬──────────────┐
  ┌───────────┐ ┌───────────┐ ┌───────────┐ ┌───────────┐
  │Vice President│ │Vice President│ │Vice President│ │Vice President│
  │  Production  │ │  Marketing   │ │   Finance    │ │ Information  │
  └───────────┘ └───────────┘ └───────────┘ └───────────┘
                              ┌──────────┬──────────┬──────────┐
                          ┌────────┐ ┌────────┐ ┌──────────┐
                          │Systems │ │  Data  │ │ Records  │
                          │        │ │Processing│ │Management│
                          └────────┘ └────────┘ └──────────┘
```

FIG. 20.2 Organization chart —decentralized arrangement for data processing

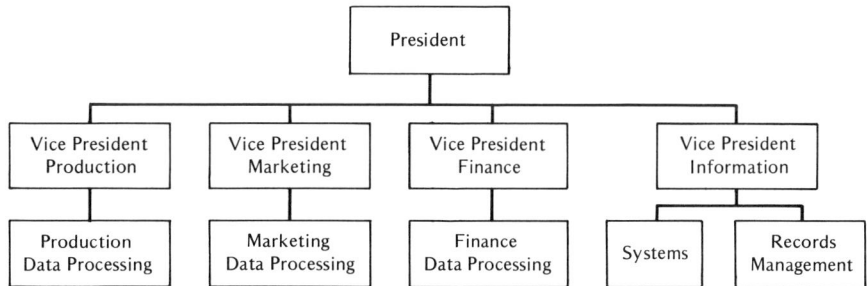

```
                              ┌───────────┐
                              │ President │
                              └───────────┘
        ┌──────────────┬──────────────┬──────────────┐
  ┌───────────┐ ┌───────────┐ ┌───────────┐ ┌───────────┐
  │Vice President│ │Vice President│ │Vice President│ │Vice President│
  │  Production  │ │  Marketing   │ │   Finance    │ │ Information  │
  └───────────┘ └───────────┘ └───────────┘ └───────────┘
  ┌───────────┐ ┌───────────┐ ┌───────────┐ ┌──────────┬──────────┐
  │ Production │ │ Marketing  │ │  Finance   │ ┌────────┐ ┌──────────┐
  │Data Processing│ │Data Processing│ │Data Processing│ │Systems │ │ Records  │
  └───────────┘ └───────────┘ └───────────┘ │        │ │Management│
                                            └────────┘ └──────────┘
```

FIG. 20.3 Organization charts —physical decentralization and centralized management of data processing

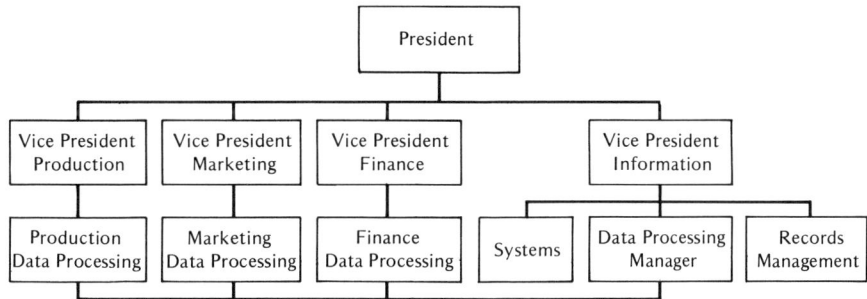

```
                              ┌───────────┐
                              │ President │
                              └───────────┘
        ┌──────────────┬──────────────┬──────────────┐
  ┌───────────┐ ┌───────────┐ ┌───────────┐ ┌───────────┐
  │Vice President│ │Vice President│ │Vice President│ │Vice President│
  │  Production  │ │  Marketing   │ │   Finance    │ │ Information  │
  └───────────┘ └───────────┘ └───────────┘ └───────────┘
  ┌───────────┐ ┌───────────┐ ┌───────────┐ ┌────────┬────────────┬──────────┐
  │ Production │ │ Marketing  │ │  Finance   │ ┌──────┐ ┌──────────┐ ┌──────────┐
  │Data Processing│ │Data Processing│ │Data Processing│ │Systems│ │Data Processing│ │ Records  │
  └───────────┘ └───────────┘ └───────────┘ │      │ │ Manager  │ │Management│
                                            └──────┘ └──────────┘ └──────────┘
```

ganization chart takes into consideration the place of data processing. This figure illustrates a data processing unit that is centralized and independent of nearly all its users. Reports are made directly to the vice president in charge of information. The systems and records management functions are also centralized physically and managerially. Figure 20.2 illustrates a decentralized data processing unit in which each important user has his own data processing facility. The production manager has his computer, the marketing manager has his, and so on. In Fig. 20.3 we have a data processing function that is decentralized physically, but centralized as to management. It appears, then, that even location becomes a problem of the degree of centralization and the type of authority for the data processing activity.

CENTRALIZATION VERSUS DECENTRALIZATION OF THE DATA PROCESSING FUNCTION

R. W. Fairbanks, President of Fairbanks Associates, Inc., and a pioneer writer in the field of office automation, very ably pointed out the problem indicated by the variety of organization charts when he said:

The tremendous increase in office paper work has made it impossible for the general office, as we knew it 50 years ago, to continue to carry all the clerical responsibilities for a modern company. This increase has led to decentralization of clerical functions, first within the operating divisions of the company, and then between widely separated units of the company.

Decentralization made the paperwork load manageable within each unit, but increased by a very great degree the overall paperwork burden of the company, and made it necessary to duplicate in a dozen different places the same information, the same reports, the same processes.

Our problem today is to take advantage of the new system concepts and new office machines available to reconcentrate the great mass of clerical functions in one central point—the counterpart of the old general office—at the same time preserving the principle of decentralized management.[3]

The problem of decentralization has been twofold: (1) when and how far to decentralize, and (2) how to maintain centralized control with decentralized function. It is sometimes difficult for a firm to recognize the point beyond which a centralized organization can no longer operate effectively. Too much decentralization makes it impossible to operate the whole firm as one company. At the same time, whenever decentralization is justified, the size and the complexities of the operations have made it virtually impossible for the central office to operate all divisions. Furthermore, too much centralization discourages the members of the divisions, and more specifically their managers.

Robert A. Shiff, President of Naremco Services, Inc., provided one perspective to the physical decentralization and managerial centralization of data processing activities when he said:

One of the most successfully profit-oriented concepts being applied in offices today is that of the satellite administrative service station.

Serving the logistic requirements of work stations, within close proximity to user needs, all satellite stations are linked with each other as well as central services. They thereby operate under centralized direction and control.

Typical satellite service stations operate as profit centers, with localized administrative services, including stationery and supplies; fast copies, secretarial and clerical assistance; mail and communications; sub-library and information retrieval. . . .[4]

One important point to remember is that under this concept, substations should be linked with other substations used by the organization as well as with centralized services. Substations thereby operate under centralized direction and control. One finds that actually this concept is not new but is being re-emphasized as one good way to increase work efficiency of the data processing function, as Mr. Shiff pointed out when he said further:

Each station is directed by an administrative supervisor who controls work distribution and monitors input to make sure that no girl is overloaded or underloaded. Private secretaries make the best candidates for this responsibility. . . They are also deputies to the company's administrative vice-president. He gives the orders, but the administrative services supervisor is the one on the firing line who comes in and sees that they are translated into working programs.[5]

In organizations that have adopted a positive approach to analysis and improvement of data processing activities, responsibility for the data processing function is placed on a single person and not delegated to a person who has other functional responsibilities. The question was raised: Will a computer-based data processing system function differently if the responsibility for it rests with the controller rather than with a vice-president of operations or vice president of information systems? A study made by Reichenbach and Tasso, both members of the research staff of Industrial Relations Counselors, Inc., reports:

. . . Based on the findings reported in this study, the answer is that it will. The location of the responsibility for EDP activities has a great deal to do with the nature of that responsibility and the effectiveness with which it is carried out.[6]

In this study, they also examined, "(1) why responsibility for the computer complex in a given company is assigned where it is, (2) what effect this assignment has on what the computer does and how well it does it, and (3) what developments cause changes in the location of the computer responsibility as management's need for information continues to expand, both in breadth and depth."[7] They go on with the following comments:

The organizational aspects of this study are:

Responsibility for computer activities is moving toward higher levels in the corporate structure . . . is independent of any specific function, with the individual heading up the computer activity reporting directly to top management—to the chairman, president, or executive vice-president.

The responsibility for computer-based information systems becomes increasingly centralized. . . .

Centralized computer activities do not necessarily lead to centralized operations and management within the company. . . .

Instead of the computer's centralizing the company, it is the underlying characteristic management style of the company that is the significant factor in the determination of how centralized EDP operations should be. . . .

Middle managers in companies with sophisticated information systems that use data from their functions find that they are relieved of some of the detailed routine and are able to spend the optimum time in managing. . . .

Responsibility for the computer complex, including information systems, should be apart from any existing traditional function. The function should report directly to top management.[8]

This example shows that the data processing function should not only be physically centralized but should also have its own centralized management. Let's explore the more common advantages of this kind of centralization.

One advantage is that of *consistency*. Obviously, all companies have organizational policies and practices, and all managerial people are interested in the morale of their subordinates. Having the data processing activities centralized makes possible more *consistency* in the administration of organization policies and practices.

Centralization also facilitates establishing standard operating and quality control procedures. It encourages workers to give specialized attention to developing and improving skills and acquiring a greater knowledge of the systems, methods, procedures, and machines that are available. A higher degree of overall efficiency is encouraged and maintained.

In a centralized data processing division, functional managers do not have to take time from other responsibilities to direct the data processing. This function is the responsibility of one man. In a sizable operation he would have supervisory personnel to carry out the operations. The head of data processing may direct others in hiring, training, scheduling, and supervising all activities pertaining to this specialized function. Under a decentralized plan, these activities would be handled by a manager whose primary responsibilities were not data processing.

Another advantage of centralization lies in the handling of work fluctuation. The broader base makes it possible to level off peak and valley workloads and to produce results during workers' vacations or temporary absences. Furthermore, the greater flexibility and more efficient utilization of manpower means that more work can be accomplished by fewer personnel.

THE DATA-PROCESSING FUNCTION AND FUNCTIONAL AUTHORITY

Since we cannot go into detail about all types of business organizations, let us discuss the three types most commonly recognized: (1) line organization, (2) staff organization (which may evolve into functional), and (3) a combination of line and staff or line and functional.

Line Organization

In this kind of setup, the authority originates at the top and flows directly to subordinate executives (see Fig. 20.4). One authority, Professor McFarland of Michigan State University, says that "Line authority is the basic and fundamental authority in an organization. It is the ultimate authority to command, act, or decide in matters affecting others."[9] This implies that line activities are directly concerned with attaining a firm's objectives. Professor McFarland goes on to say:

The primary purpose of line authority is to make the organization work. It does so in numerous ways. First of all, it provides the basic decisions involved in operating an enterprise . . . Secondly, it serves as a means of control by setting limits to the scope of authority of individuals. It helps to assure that employees conform to the plans and policies of the enterprise. A third purpose of line authority is to provide points of reference for the sanctioning and approval of proposals or actions. Without the existence of this ultimate

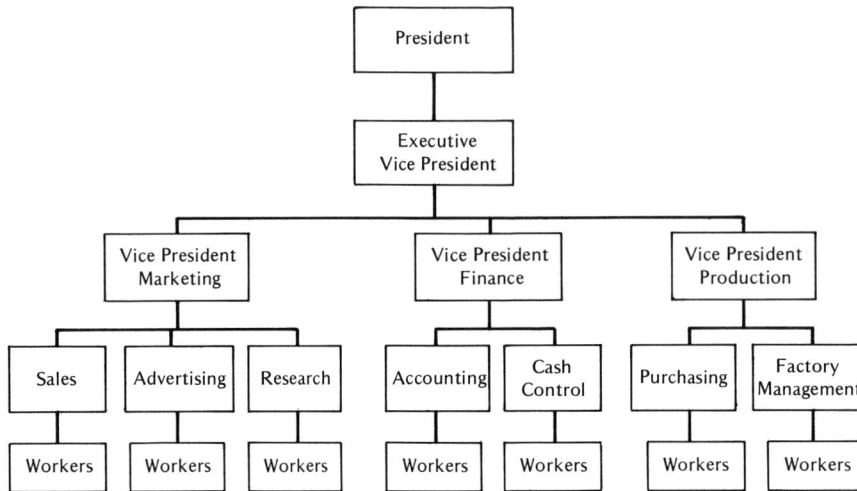

FIG. 20.4 Chart of line organization. Each manager has direct responsibility without aid of expert advice and counsel.

authority, persons in an organization could not be certain that their activities would be beneficial or effective. Securing the approval of line authority for actions outside the scope of their routine affairs frees the individual to think flexibly and plan more effectively.[10]

The main point appears to be that line authority is directly involved in attaining the organization's objectives and provides direct managerial control. Each executive handles the activities of his unit alone, without aid of expert advice and counsel except as it is developed by superiors and people within his own unit.

Staff Organization

An organization in which the authority originates at the top and flows functionally to subordinate executives is known as staff organization. McFarland writes, "Staff authority is best defined as authority whose scope is limited, by the absence of the right to command, to auxiliary and such facilitating activities as planning, recommending, advising, or assisting."[11] Thus, staff functions help attain the organizational objectives through expert advice and counsel. Staff members, therefore, do not have direct responsibility for accomplishing the organization's objectives. The "pure" staff organization does not exist in firms today.

According to McFarland's definition, the staff officer's major activ-

FIG. 20.5 Chart of line-and-staff organization. The staff officers give advice to the Executive Vice President who then makes the decisions for Marketing, Finance, and Production. Thus the line officers have the aid of expert advice and counsel.

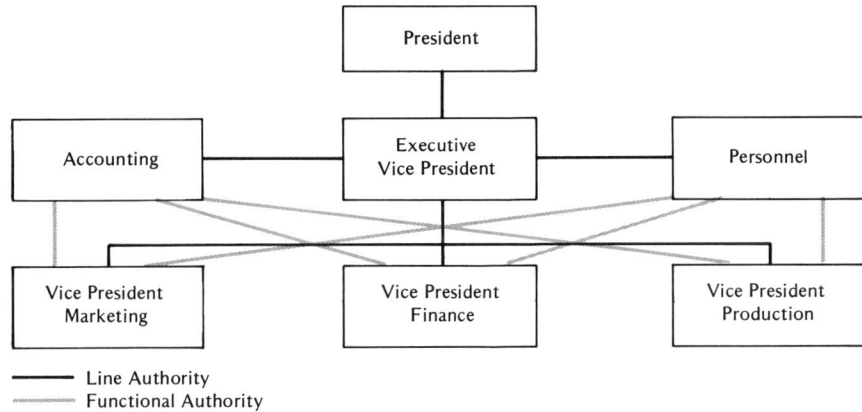

ity is dealing with information and advice. The particular responsibility of the staff officer is to supply information to those managers who are entitled to receive it. His job is to get this information, pertaining to any given specialized field, and pass it on. The staff officer also usually has the responsibility of interpreting this information, transforming it into useful form, and assisting and advising in its use.

Line-and-Staff Organization

An organization of this kind combines the two types mentioned above. The line organization determines the main departments of the organization and shows the definite line of authority. The staff organization provides expert staff officers who are available to give the line managers advice and assistance in the performance of tasks and activities outside their specialized line. The line-and-staff type of organization is the one in most general use (see Fig. 20.5).

Researchers agree, however, that the line-and-staff form of organization, as presently defined in most textbooks, does not adequately meet the demands of most firms with advanced technologies. These needs are summarized in Professor Uris's statement:

The line-staff type of organization is seldom flexible enough for the new functions and duties of the specialist. Where he is involved in line activity, functional relationship and flow of information often become fuzzy. Also, a split develops in the source of operating knowledge between supervisor and specialist.[12]

The traditional view of line-staff relationships is being challenged with the advent of more specialists, including the data processing specialists, in today's organization. With the advent of the computer, the changing role of data processing has been given a new dimension —the emergence of what management scholars call "functional authority." Functional authority utilizes both line and staff authority. Professor Ziegler describes "functional authority" very accurately when he says:

In functional organization the activities of the business are assigned to specialists; in addition, the flow of authority is greatly modified. Therefore, each of these specialists exercises authority not only over his own group, but also in any area where the activity in which he specializes takes place. This feature is referred to as functional authority. To illustrate, a company may have a specialist in charge of material handling. Regardless of where the material is moved—production department, shipping department, or storeroom— authority over this activity will be in the hands of the specialist. A policy, then, handed down from the top level, given to material handling, affects more than just the specific foreman and his workers. It now affects any foreman and worker involved in the section in which the material is moved.[13]

The specialist in material handling could be replaced by the specialist in data processing. Both would appear to have the same authority in order to be effective in performing their duties. Thus, functional authority differs from line authority in that the functional officer has specially delegated authority only over the proper performance of his particular specialty or function. His right to command is limited to his specialized area. The staff officer has the authority only to advise on activities pertaining to his specialized field; the functional officer has the right to command activities pertaining to his specialized field (see Fig. 20.6).

The line superior has the right to delegate authority to his subordinates as he sees fit. He delegates to the staff officer the right to collect information and pass it on to other line officers. He delegates to the functional officer the right to command only within his prescribed functional area. Thus subordinate line officers appear to have what could be called residual authority (that authority which is not specifically delegated to others). It is no wonder that one finds a line-staff-functional conflict in organizations. Line managers feel that they are not really free to utilize full authority over their activities.

The difference between functional and staff authority is often hard to distinguish, for in some cases it is more nearly a difference in degree

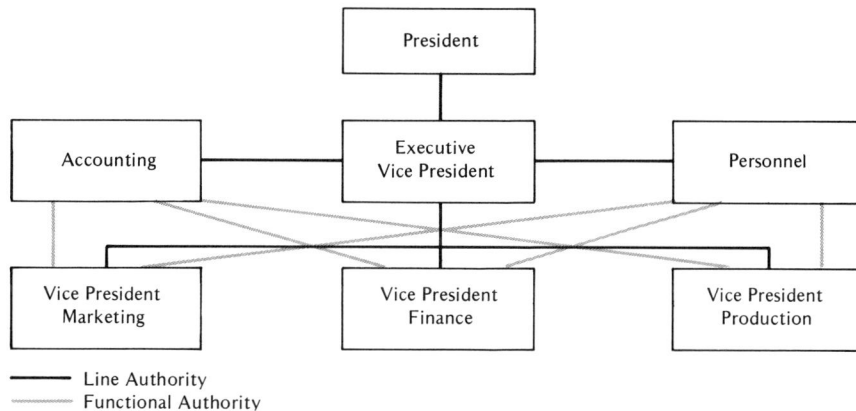

FIG. 20.6   Chart of line-functional organization. The function officer has direct authority over his specialty, wherever it occurs.

(right to advise, right to command) than a difference in kind (information). Functional authority is that degree of authority somewhere between the command authority of the line manager and the informational authority of the staff manager. In thinking about this difference in degree, one begins to wonder how the function of informational advice evolves into the right to command. According to Professors Koontz and O'Donnell of the University of California at Los Angeles, this development proceeds in three phases.

The successive steps by which a line manager gradually gives up his authority over particular activities make an interesting study. As has already been emphasized, the pure staff specialist offers advice or recommendations to his line superior, who has issued them as instructions to be filtered down the organization hierarchy. The first modification of this relationship ordinarily occurs when the superior delegates authority to the staff man to transmit information, proposals, and advice directly to the former's subordinates. . . .

A second modification might be to allow the staff specialist not only to transmit information and advice to the line managers but to consult with them and show them how the information should be used or how the recommendations should be put into effect. . . .

The transition to functional authority is accomplished when the assistant is delegated specific authority to *prescribe* processes, methods, or even policy to be followed in all subdivisions of either staff or operating departments. The personnel assistant, for example, who once could only advise, now may be given limited authority to supervise a special function or process of the line organization.[14]

The growing need for the information with functional authority is dictated, generally speaking, by the growing size and complexity of present-day organizations. It is emphasized by the growing recognition of the importance of the data processing function. As it becomes more important to and more centralized in the organization, the data processing function is acquiring the same status as the "hard core" functions of finance, marketing, or production. Converting from the concept of office services to that of data processing is a major undertaking in today's large, complex organizations.

The fact that the data processing manager has more opportunity to develop the necessary specialized knowledge of office machines, equipment, EDP machines, and methods is often used to support the delegation to him of firm-wide procedures and systems analysis, design, and improvement in data processing. However, it should be made clear that at no time should the data processing manager be responsible for firm-wide procedures any more than a functional specialist should "wear two hats." Departmental and interdepartmental procedures should be the responsibility of department heads and general management. The data processing manager's realm should rightfully be only that of machines, equipment, and methods pertaining to data-processing activities, not functional activities such as production. The data processing manager's position should be one of service in helping to increase the effectiveness of data processing throughout the entire organization.

The data processing manager should not be concerned with what work is to be done, who is to do it, and when each step in the task is to be carried out. He should rightfully be concerned with how individual data processing activities are to be performed. The authority of data processing extends into the organization wherever its services are needed; thus it exercises line authority over its function. Its authority is functional in that it exercises control, or command, over a given functional area across functional lines.

Two points must be remembered. The first is that functional authority is in the nature of a routine, or procedural routing, *how to do it* rather than *what to do*. The matter of what to do and when is still in the line officer's realm. Secondly, there should be a clear specification of the types of questions and the particular groups in which functional authority is recognized, such as the data processing function.

QUESTIONS AND PROBLEMS

1. Discuss translating the plans of the firm into immediate plans for the data processing function.

2. Discuss formulating objectives and goals for the data processing function.

3. What are the detailed objectives and goals for the data processing manager?

4. What questions should the data processing manager ask himself in examining his objectives and goals? Compare these questions with the steps of planning.

5. Discuss the policies and procedures of the data processing manager.

6. How does the success or failure of the data processing function depend upon organization planning for this function?

7. What are the advantages of centralized management of the data processing function?

8. What is planning?

9. In what ways is the data processing manager concerned with planning?

10. What are the characteristics of a good plan?

11. Why should objectives of a company be clearly understood before an organization is developed?

12. Distinguish as clearly as you can between "line function" and "staff function."

13. In what ways, or for what reasons, does the role of "staff" now appear to be changing?

14. Explain how functional authority evolves from staff work.

15. Discuss why there is a confusion between the concepts of line, staff, and functional authority.

16. Discuss how the computer is affecting management.

17. Discuss how the introduction of the computer has changed the type of employee that management is supervising and directing.

REFERENCES

1. LeRoy A. Pemberton and E. Dana Gibson, *Administrative Systems Management*, Belmont, California: Wadsworth Publishing, p. 76.

2. Raymond J. Zeigler, *Business Policies and Decision Making*, New York: Appleton-Century-Crofts, 1966, p. 2.

3. Ralph W. Fairbanks, *Successful Office Automation,* Englewood Cliffs, N. J.: Prentice-Hall, 1956, p. 32.

4. Robert A. Shiff, "Satellite Administration Service Centers," *Administrative Management,* Vol. XXX, No. 1, Jan. 1969, p. 26.

5. *Idem.*

6. Robert A. Reichenbach and Charles A. Tasso, *Organizing for Data Processing,* AMA Research Study 92, New York: American Management Association, 1968, p. 11.

7. *Idem.*

8. *Ibid.,* pp. 12, 13, and 22.

9. Dalton E. McFarland, *Management: Principles and Practices,* New York: Macmillan, 3rd ed., 1970, p. 410.

10. *Ibid.,* p. 411.

11. *Idem.*

12. Auren Uris, "Fitting Today's New Specialist into Your Plant Organization," *Factory,* **117:** No. 9, Sept. 1959, p. 226.

13. Raymond Ziegler, *op. cit.,* p. 6.

14. Harold Koontz and Cyril O'Donnell, *Principles of Management: An Analysis of Managerial Functions,* New York: McGraw-Hill, 4th ed., 1968, p. 302.

PLANNING
THE
DATA
PROCESSING
FUNCTION:

SYSTEMS
ANALYSIS
AND
DESIGN

CHAPTER 21

The "total systems" concept has been considered one of the most important developments in the past twenty years. The total systems approach views a business as an entity composed of interrelated systems designed to achieve the objectives of the business. The systems approach, whether applied to functional areas or to the total business, requires coordination of all subsystems. The subsystems designed to achieve a particular objective within a functional area are called *integrated systems. Total systems,* however, goes further; it means that all functions of an organization are systematized and integrated. Data processing plays a vital role in furnishing the means by which the total systems operation can be implemented.

Let's re-examine a data processing system. Figure 21.1 is a very simple diagram of the data processing system. Data are facts that we use as a basis for reckoning, and processing involves a series of related operations definitely leading toward an end. Thus facts are the raw material for the function of data processing. In the modern business firm the relevant facts for decision-making at various levels are so numerous that only the most pertinent ones can be reported in the normal course of operations. One of the prime purposes of a data processing system is to screen, collate, etc., the various facts that are collected in the day-to-day operations in order to develop meaningful information for managerial decision-making on all levels.

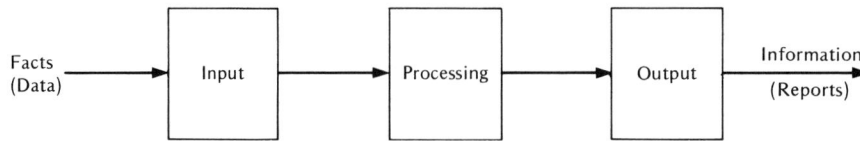

Facts (Data) → Input → Processing → Output → Information (Reports)

FIG. 21.1 A data processing system

The entire data processing system began to undergo gradual changes as the modern data processing equipment became more widely used. In many instances, these information-handling systems could not be completely planned in advance; they have grown through the years and are still growing as new developments are introduced. However, computers have now reached a rather mature stage, and the future developments will probably be in refinements that do not greatly affect the overall operation of the system. It is, therefore, imperative that firms conduct systematic studies before making any changes in their data processing operations. This job would be relatively easy if specific computer systems had been planned and set up for standardized business purposes. An automatic method of minimizing time, equipment, and cost for each business data processing function would be of immense value. Such a solution is nearly impossible, though, because each firm has its own unique needs. There are so many combinations of needs that it is difficult to have only a few standardized systems.

With the growing popularity of data processing, management has become more systems conscious. Robert Slater, of the John Hancock Mutual Life Insurance Company, emphasizes the need for efficient planning.

In the days ahead, simply having a computer will bestow no competitive advantage. Everyone will be using one. The determining factor will be the efficiency with which it is operated.

Those companies that insist on doing business in the same old way will soon fall behind because they are not going to be squeezing the maximum use out of their equipment at the minimum expense. In a tight competitive situation, this slight extra cost of office inefficiency could make the difference in maintaining a sales position.[1]

When the systems analyst studies a functional problem (sales, accounting, finance, etc.), he has to know the functional objectives, goals, procedures, and organizational relationships, as well as the plans of the firm. It is hard to say who should take the initiative in closing the communication gap between the computer group and the functional group. Both parties must be willing to communicate. The important point is that a decision has to be made on the information needs and how the computer can fill these needs.

SYSTEMS ANALYSIS AND DESIGN

The value of systems analysis and design are clearer than ever. As an introduction to systems analysis, Frank Greenwood says,

Although the term "systems analysis" is relatively new, and although it has come into vogue recently with respect to planning systems for automatic computers, its underlying idea is not new. Systems analysis may be broadly defined as the function of devising an appropriate procedure to achieve a particular purpose.

Good planners and efficient administrators have always done systems analysis in this sense. . . . Today usage of the term is normally confined to information systems for office and administrative purposes, but the approach and general techniques apply to engineering and other fields as well. For information systems, the analysis is not necessarily limited to procedures carried out by computers, but encompasses all that must be done to meet the needs of a situation whether the procedures are manual or mental and whether they involve the use of computers or other kinds of equipment.[2]

The purpose of systems analysis and design is to develop a data processing structure that will efficiently meet the information needs of a business. "Systems analysis" is an orderly study of the detailed procedures for collecting, organizing, and evaluating information within an organization, with the objective of improving control of the operations of the organization. "Systems design" is determining a system for definite functions or operations and establishing the specifications to be used for selecting the equipment best suited to meet the specific needs.

Systems analysis and design, applied to data processing, concentrates on how to gather, coordinate, and process data desired by general management and functional managers and how to select the best alternative (system) for processing data. We may be interested in revising existing systems as well as in designing new systems. Our general objective is to increase the effectiveness of data processing operations.

OBJECTIVES OF SYSTEMS ANALYSIS AND DESIGN

The general objective of a systems analysis and design program is to increase the effectiveness of the operations and bring about greater economy. Perhaps we can be more specific in looking at the ways to increase efficiency. We should have as goals

1. Better information to management, in quantity and quality,
2. Increased speed in processing data and preparing reports,
3. Elimination of overlapping tasks or duplication of service,
4. Increased efficiency of employees, both data processing personnel and management personnel,
5. Better service to customers, and
6. Improved public relations.

The specific steps involved in an orderly, planned systems study and design should consist of four phases:

Phase 1. Plan the systems study and get the approval of top management.

Phase 2. Gather, record, and analyze facts concerning the present system.

Phase 3. Determine the systems requirements.

Phase 4. Design the new system.

PHASE 1. Planning the Systems Study and Getting the Approval of Top Management

We should approach systems analysis and design by getting the approval of top management. George Berkwitt, senior editor of *Dun's Review,* says:

But if the human element in the management machine is hard to pin down, one thing is certain: Unless top management takes a personal and involved interest in it, the machine cannot possibly work. Middle-level executives are constantly heard to complain about their troubles in using new formulas or techniques because the company president gives the okay to go ahead with them and then shows no interest in how they are working.[3]

No system will be successful if each system or subsystem must be adapted for the people involved and their system alone so that each direction of a function performs independently. No system will produce efficient results if each manager of a subsystem is a "prima donna," executing his duties in whatever manner seems best to him.

Whether one thinks in terms of manual operations or computer-based data processing systems, data processing systems tie together all functions of a business—manufacturing, marketing, finance, etc. Thus the systems analyst must have top management's participation. Top management personnel must make an effort to understand the capabilities of systems analysis and design as applied to the data processing function. They often resist learning, of course. Today's sophisticated data processing equipment is formidable, and the proliferation of equipment makes understanding more and more difficult. However, the data processing function, data processing systems, and data processing equipment are no more complicated than most production functions, systems, and equipment, and they can be mastered with the proper effort.

The data processing manager has another problem that is not so obvious. Sometimes top managers feel that they are technically competent when they learn some of the technical jargon concerning the data processing function, systems, and equipment. The old saying that a little knowledge is a dangerous thing applies here. Systems analysis and design needs the approval of top management, but a false sense of competency by top management is a drawback, especially when they want to become involved in the detailed aspects of systems analysis and design. Thus, the data processing manager has a two-fold problem: (1) getting top management's approval, and (2) selling top management on the idea of delegating decisions concerning details of the systems analysis, design, development, and operation to skilled systems analysts and data processing specialists.

Let's assume now that top management understands the capabilities of systems analysis and design as applied to the data processing function. Now we take the following planning steps. We

1. Define the objective of the study and show how it relates to each function of the company,

2. Outline the scope of the study, and

3. Prepare a time schedule and plan of action.

In defining the objective of the study, we would specify adequate details to give direction and guidance to the plan. Specific objectives for a data processing system pertaining, for example, to the research and development function might very well be:

1. To provide current awareness advisories or to utilize selective dissemination techniques to minimize the time required for scanning the current literature,
2. To provide coverage of overlapping specializations as well as coverage of the primary area of interest,
3. To identify and remove from the system redundant and duplicating sources of information,
4. To minimize the need for searchers to be dependent on chance recall for retrieval of needed references,
5. To enable professional people to concentrate their current reading only to specific specialized sources pertinent to their interest.
6. To minimize time required for retrospective searches,
7. To minimize duplication of research effort resulting from unsuccessful literature searches,
8. To facilitate decision making by reducing delay time in delivery of needed information,
9. To provide retrieval techniques which will eliminate the traditional literature search which produces a product of use to only one specific question.[4]

Although the managers have loads of literature available from outside sources as well as from their company's own computer processing, they cannot search and retrieve the information within the response time permitted by superiors, subordinates, customers, or competitors. Managers should be able to retrieve relevant information quickly. Data can be extracted from any part of memory by *random access,* which is made possible through the use of magnetic cores.

The outline of the scope of the study is actually determined as a part of the objective of the study. We must determine what parts of the current data processing system are to be included in the study— for example, whether the study is to include the entire system or specified portions of it, what personnel are affected, and who must be satisfied.

A time schedule and a plan of action can be realistically estimated only after the objectives and the scope of the study are definite. The plan of action indicates the specific steps necessary for the successful completion of the entire study. The time required to complete each of these steps is estimated in order to make the overall time schedule of the study.

The thoroughness and skill with which these preliminary planning steps are undertaken are important to the success of the study. A system is no better than the planning that goes into it.

PHASE 2.   Gather, Record, and Analyze Facts Concerning the Present System

The objective of Phase 2 is a thorough understanding of the present business and its data processing needs. It is best to organize the information into a "Present Business Description" report. Making such a report helps to ensure completeness of the analysis and provides a point of reference during the steps that follow. It includes an analysis of the personnel, equipment, facilities, and finances and shows their relationships to the entire system. In assembling the information you make use of interviews with personnel, organization charts, procedure manuals, systems flowcharts, program flowcharts, and decision tables.

Your first step will be interviewing management and operating personnel. Next, you will observe actual performance of the work and analyze what you discover. Then, you will review formalized organization charts, definitions of authority and responsibility, job descriptions, skills and knowledge of personnel, standard operating instructions, and the ability of the supervisors of the respective units within the data processing function. You must keep in mind the fact that many items of input data may be useful for a number of different outputs. It is also obvious that data should not be independently gathered in many instances for special purposes, but rather that these data should be made available for multiple uses.

What management and operating personnel should be included? Perhaps one good approach is that recommended by Dearden: to recognize that we are dealing, in the typical organization, with three major information systems and many minor systems.[5] Dearden points out that the three major information systems normally found are financial, personnel, and logistics. This means, then, that we will be concerned with the employees of the finance, personnel and production functions. Other information systems identified by Dearden are those dealing with marketing information, strategic planning, and research and development. Thus we will also be concerned with the personnel of the marketing function, top management, and research functions.

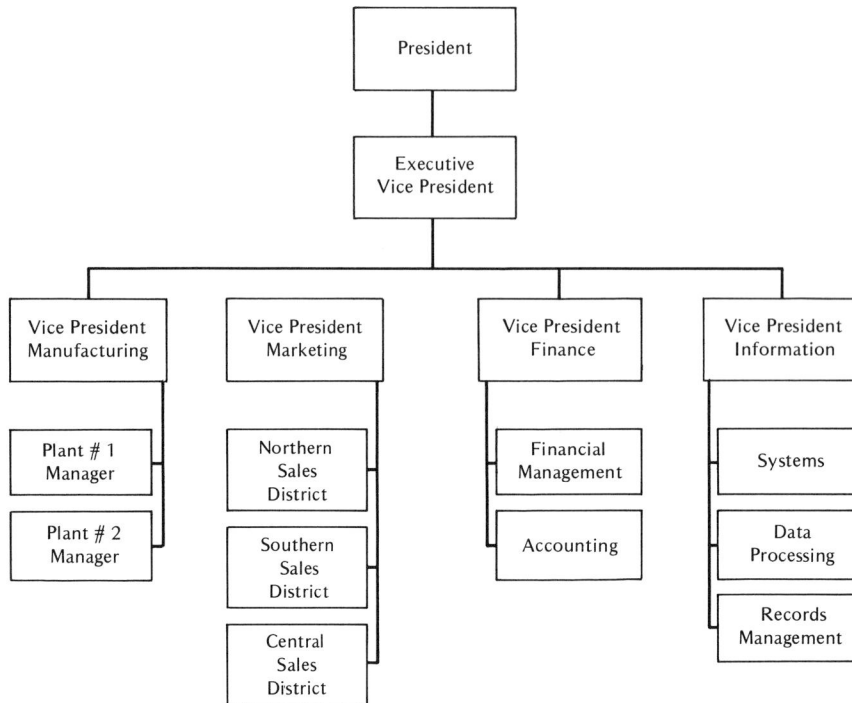

FIG. 21.2 Organization for a hypothetical manufacturing company

We have already discussed where the data processing function should be placed within the organization. Now let us turn to a chart showing a more complete view of the organization. We can make a chart showing every position in the company and who has formal authority and responsibility. The organization chart for a hypothetical company is shown in Fig. 21.2, but of course no chart is typical of all companies. Names of people holding the various positions can be inserted, but using names requires more frequent changes in the chart than are necessary if only titles are used. If no organization chart is available, the systems analyst should prepare one so that he has a clear picture of the formal lines of authority, lines of communication, and the decision points within the organization. The systems analyst must attempt to understand the organization structure as well as to identify the objectives of the different organization units within the company.

Frequently an informal organization has evolved that slightly alters the formal structure and must also be recognized. The formal structure at best gives only a limited picture. It does not show, for example, the many informal relationships that exist, the interactions that take place daily, or whether the manager involved uses democratic or autocratic leadership in discharging the responsibilities charted in the formal organization chart. Analyzing the informal organization basis is very complex. Research specialists in sociology, social psychology, and psychology are beginning to give us a better insight to informal organizations and the workings of employee groups. They are beginning to recognize that work groups can be studied from the clinical viewpoint just as individuals can be. Perhaps the most commonly used approach in understanding informal relationships is the *sociogram,* a device employed chiefly by psychologists and sociologists to indicate lines of preference. Each employee is asked such questions as "For which person or persons would you prefer to work?" "With which person or persons would you prefer to work?" and "With which person or persons would you prefer to socialize?" The manager can plot the responses to these questions in the form of a sociogram and can use the information in planning work assignments.

Despite its limitations, the conventional organization chart is used to depict the skeletal structure of the organization. The essential value of the organization chart appears to lie in the fact that it does strip the organization to the skeletal framework. In so doing, it serves a useful purpose as a tool of both organizational analysis and systems analysis and design.

The procedures manual is useful when reviewing the operating procedures. These manuals identify the equipment and facilities used in the system and explain their uses. The systems analyst must, however, check with the various functional managers to be sure that the procedure manuals are up to date. If not, he should have them changed. If there are no procedure manuals, the systems analyst must spend more time with the functional managers to determine what equipment and facilities are being used and exactly how they are being used.

When studying the systems flowchart, the systems analyst might find that this also is not up to date. This might be determined at the same time that the procedure manuals are being verified. A systems flowchart illustrates the flow of data and operations in a general manner. Although it indicates where manual, mechanical, and computer data processing methods are used, its primary purpose is to trace the flow of data through the system and the general sequence of opera-

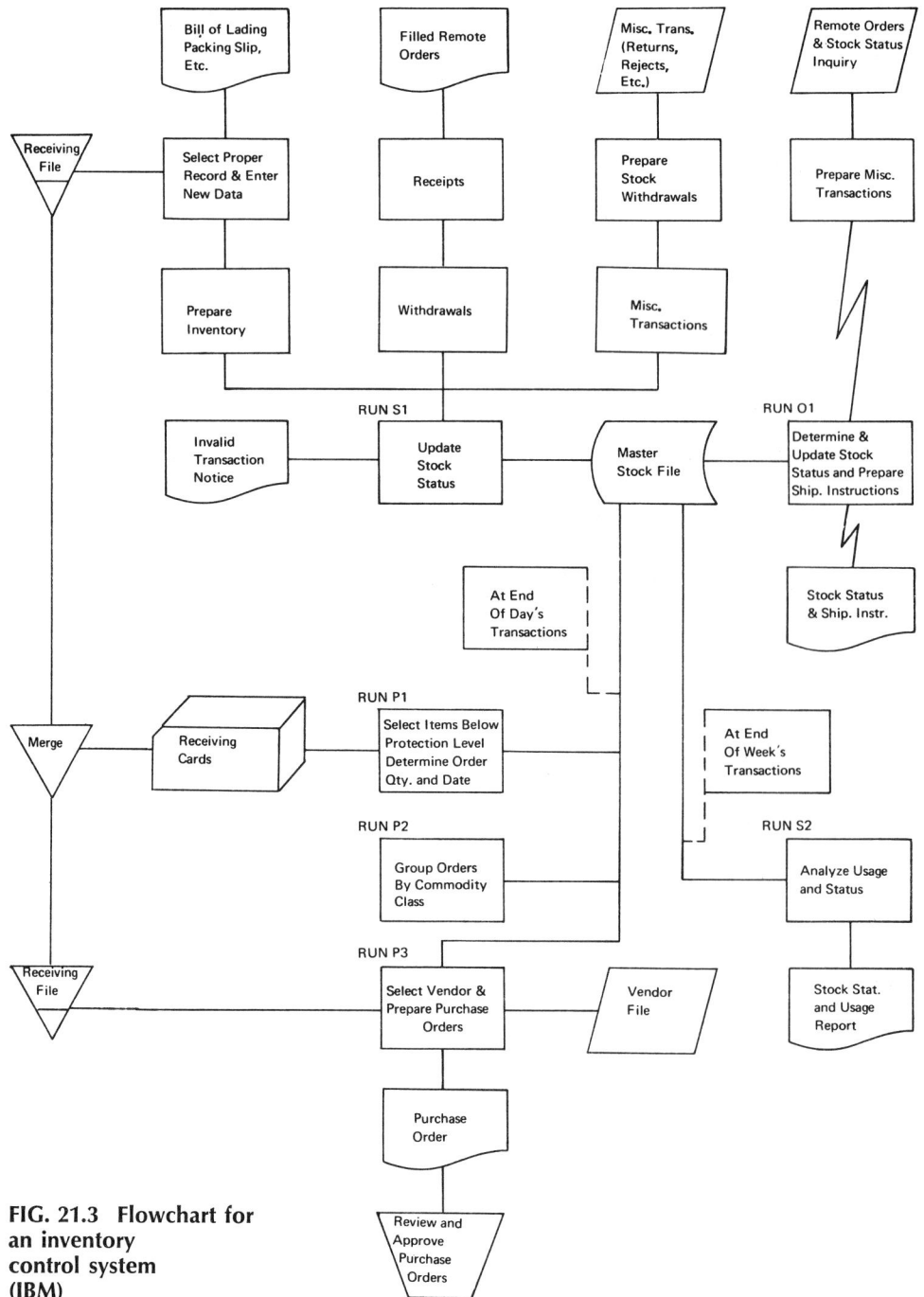

FIG. 21.3 Flowchart for an inventory control system (IBM)

tions rather than to show how specific operations are performed. A systems flowchart is shown in Fig. 21.3. If systems flowcharts are not available, they will have to be prepared after having meetings with the people operating the system.

In addition to getting operating details, the systems analyst can learn a great deal from his interviews with personnel. The people actually operating the system often see things differently from the managers and may give some very practical suggestions. Asking for their advice increases their self-respect and makes them feel a part of what is going on. A cooperative attitude when we are installing the new system will be a help to everyone's morale. The operating details should be checked against the program flowcharts that indicate the specific processing steps.

Flowcharting worksheets are helpful in making good flowcharts, as shown in the partially constructed flowchart in Fig. 21.4. When studying the operations details, close attention should be given to the input data, the output data, and the resources available. The important considerations concerning the input data include: its form, its source, when it is available, how often it is available, and where it comes from. The important considerations concerning the output data include: its form, when it is needed, why it is needed, who uses it, how often it is prepared, and its correlation with the input data. The resources available include the personnel, equipment, facilities, finances, and materials.

Decision tables are an aid to the systems analyst. A decision table usually corresponds to a decision block on a flowchart; it defines all the conditions and the various corresponding actions that can be taken. It provides information concerning the problems and their solutions in a concise form that is easy to read and understand. If decision tables are not available, the systems analyst must prepare them. An examination of the decision table in Fig. 21.5 helps to point out the advantages of using such a device. This decision table represents the handling of requests for $8, $5, and $3 tickets for a musical concert. First the possible conditions are listed, then the possible actions are listed. Then each possible combination of conditions and actions is indicated as a "rule."

Consider each rule (column) separately, reading first the conditions and then the actions. For example, Rule 1 states that if a check for $8.00 has been sent, the request is for an $8 seat, and if an $8 seat is available, then an $8 ticket is issued with no refund. Rule 6 states that

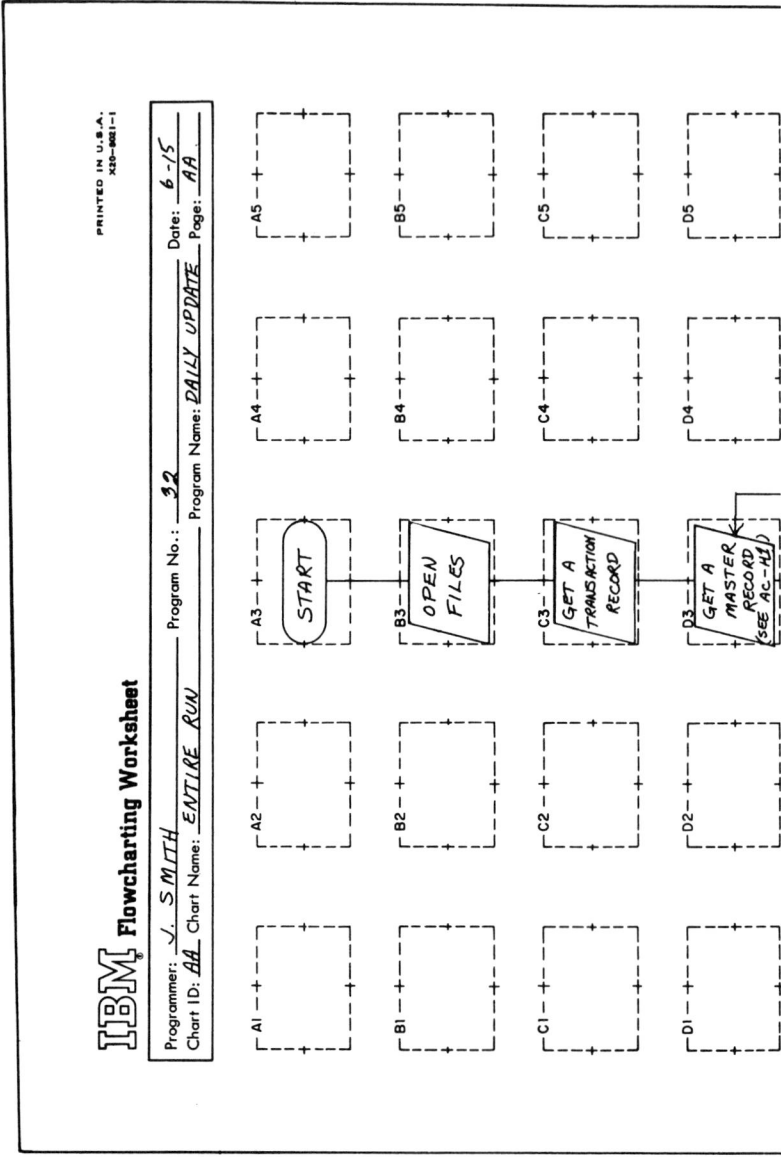

FIG. 21.4 First sheet of a sample program (IBM)

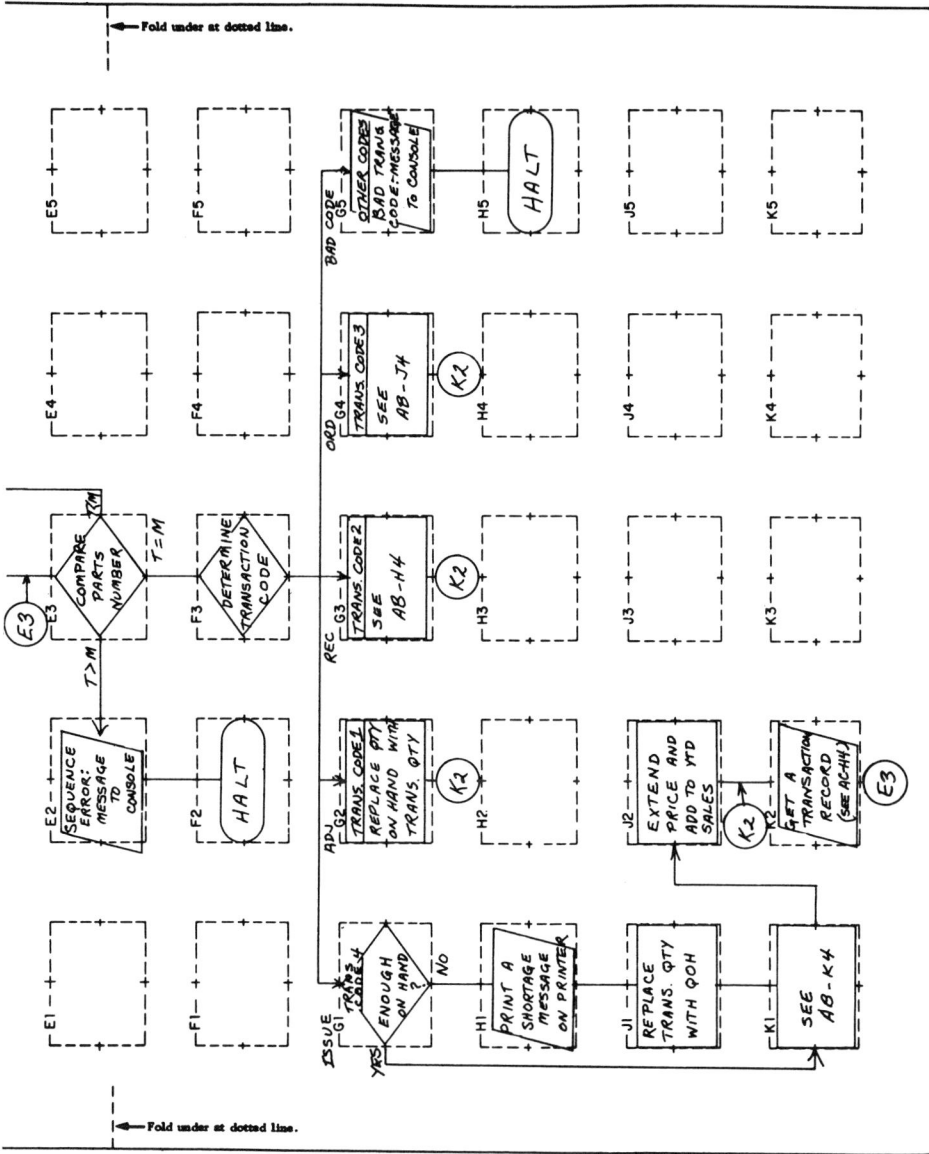

Rules

Condition	1	2	3	4	5	6	7	8	9
If request is for	$8	$8	$8	$8	$5	$5	$5	$3	$3
If $8 seats available	Y	N	N	N					
If $5 seats available		Y	N		Y	N	N		
If $3 seats available			Y			Y		Y	N
Will accept lower priced seats?		Y	Y	N		Y	N		
Send tickets costing $8	Y								
Send tickets costing $5		Y			Y				
Send tickets costing $3			Y			Y		Y	
Send refund of $8				Y					
Send refund of $5			Y				Y		
Send refund of $3		Y							Y
Send refund of $2						Y			

Y = Yes   N = No   Blank = Does not apply

FIG. 21.5 Decision table for processing ticket orders for a musical concert

if a check for $5.00 has been sent, the request is for a $5 seat. But if a $5 seat is not available and a $3 seat is, and if the person has stated that he will accept a lower-priced seat, then a $3 ticket will be issued and $2 will be refunded. From this example, the advantages of making decision tables can be seen. This form makes it easy to see whether all logical possibilities have been considered and to specify the relationship between the conditions and actions.

Now that you have followed the steps carefully and have made a complete and accurate analysis of the present system, you can go on to define the systems requirements.

PHASE 3. Determine the System Requirements

So far in the system analysis and design, all the attention has been concentrated on the past and the present. At this point, attention must be focused on the future. Our next decision has to be made on the information needs and how the computer can best fulfill them.

What is the nature and the scope of the information desired? What data will be included or excluded? Who will use this information and, perhaps more important, how will they use it? How large are the documents on which the information is recorded? Must the information be altered and, if so, with what frequency and regularity? Do the individual documents or units of information stand alone or do they relate to one another in some well-defined way?

Ways of identifying and retrieving information must be understood. Is the information classified so that it can be filed and located when needed? No system will be successful if there is a lack of proper classification. During this phase the systems analyst will describe the required inputs, outputs, operations, and resources to be used in order to get information to those who need it, and in the most reliable, fastest, and economical way. The current system must be re-evaluated and possibly modified. The activities required to ensure efficient performance must be determined. Even with the same information needs, alternative processing operations or modifications of the system may represent improvement.

When determining the requirements of the new system, the systems analyst must be careful to maintain adequate controls, good bookkeeping and accounting practices, simplicity, and effective scheduling. Adequate controls must be set up to check the accuracy of the system. Means for correcting errors must also be provided. Because of the time and cost involved in detecting errors, the analyst must decide what types and magnitude of errors will warrant correction.

The systems analyst must keep up to date with changes in accounting practices and their consequent effect on bookkeeping. He must maintain consistency in the records, nevertheless, adjusting if necessary. The systems analyst must also keep up with the laws and regulations of the government, seeing that all necessary records are kept and properly reported. A surprisingly large proportion of record requirements come from direct or indirect government requirements.

The systems analyst must keep the system as easy to follow as possible so that there will be few possibilities for making errors. Exceptions to routine should be kept to a minimum because they require alternative actions and quite often cause interruptions in the normal processing. It is true that some of these interruptions are unavoidable, but the fewer there are, the more efficient the system will be.

Effective scheduling of the data processing operations is necessary, especially when a timetable for accomplishing office work becomes important to management. Scheduling involves the establishment of time schedules for each operation required for the completion of a job. Scheduling systems may be as simple as a folder which contains a specified number of work units or as elaborate as Gantt or scheduling charts.

PHASE 4.   Design the New System

So far in the system analysis and design discussion, the concentration has been on the analysis phase; at this point the design phase begins. The overall objective of this phase is to create a data processing system that best satisfies the requirements of the organization as determined in Phase 3. The system must be designed, documented, and evaluated; then, a plan for its installation must be made.

Designing the new system requires reference to the report from Phase 3 and usually includes the following steps:

1. Determine input, output, file, and operational methods.
2. Select the equipment.
3. Determine the codes.
4. Design forms.
5. Describe the new system.

As we have already seen, there are numerous ways in which the input, output, file, and operational functions can be performed. The selection of equipment becomes more difficult and challenging each year as new machines and techniques are introduced. The systems analyst must have a thorough understanding of the uses of all the equipment available and the advantages and disadvantages of each. He must carefully consider not only the general requirements of the system, but also the volume of data to be processed, probable future needs, financial resources available, and the relative costs of the various data processing methods available. The systems analyst may use the following procedures in his analysis:

1. Manual and mechanical methods	when an application is not repetitive.
2. Punched card methods	when the application is repetitive but does not require random processing or real-time processing.
3. Computer	when the application is highly repetitive and/or requires a considerable amount of calculation in each repetitive cycle.

In deciding whether the required equipment should be rented or purchased, the analyst must consider some of these factors.

1. Purchased equipment may become obsolete before it is fully depreciated.
   a) Purchased equipment can be sold only at a depreciated current market price, which is quite low when newer models make it obsolete.
   b) Because purchased equipment is less likely to be replaced, improvements in data processing may lag behind methods used by competitors.
   c) Purchase contracts usually provide maintenance during only a relatively short warranty period.
   d) Capital must be made available for the initial outlay on purchased equipment. Interest on the capital over the period must be considered as a cost item.

2. Rented equipment can easily be replaced by newer equipment as it is developed.
   a) Equipment rental rates usually include maintenance.
   b) The number of hours per day of planned usage should be considered. Extra rentals are charged for overtime.
      1) Purchased equipment can be used overtime without additional capital, even though maintenance cost will increase.
      2) Rental for overtime is lower than for the regular shift.

The representatives of the equipment manufacturers can provide valuable assistance; they know the capabilities and limitations of the machines available and have had experience helping other companies handle similar problems. One important point to remember is that no commitment for equipment should be made until a very precise idea of what is needed has been formed.

The selection of codes for the transactions must be made very carefully; a merely adequate code or a wrong code can make an otherwise superior system become ineffective. The purposes of the codes must be fully understood and considered when making up the coding system. Data must be classified in numerous ways so that they may be used for as many different purposes as are required. In addition to assisting in identifying data, a good coding system can facilitate the machine processing that is required. The system must be sufficiently flexible so that additional entries can be made; it should have a large enough range so that new categories can be added; it should be able to handle all the segments within each category; and it should be easy to apply and capable of meeting all the needs with a minimum number of digits.

Forms must be designed for both input and output; many factors affect the design. Forms flow is usually thought of as involving only printed pieces of paper. EDP, however, has necessitated the development of forms not only for processing data by hand but also by means of automated equipment. Firms that have established integrated data processing systems (with or without electronic computers) no longer require as many forms as were formerly used to record and transmit information. Although the number of forms is fewer in the EDP systems, they are much more complex, and, as integrated parts of the overall data processing system, they should be designed only by someone who is familiar with the requirements, logic, possibilities, and limitations of the type of equipment being used in the data processing system.

A few years ago, a large percentage of the forms in the average large firm did were not for use in EDP systems. Today, however, this is not true. The forms specialist has a challenge to keep up with business forms—not only ones printed on paper, but special forms for EDP— punched cards, tapes, printed records, and other input/output forms.

After all possible alternatives have been considered, the systems analyst must combine them into one best plan or into a few alternative good plans, discussing the advantages and disadvantages of each plan. Once a decision has been made as to the system, it is time to outline it in greater detail. This is called documentation.

A detailed report must be prepared for top management in a form that is as easy to understand as possible. The systems analyst must keep in mind that they are not familiar with all the processing requirements and procedures. The report should include:

1. A system flowchart of the proposed system, along with a more detailed description of each step on the flowchart.

2. An organization chart pointing out the necessary changes in the company's organization structure. Job descriptions should be included to show the detailed duties.

3. Formats of the required forms with any necessary details explained. Forms flowcharts may be necessary to show the forms flow.

4. Facilities and equipment required by the system, including descriptions and costs. New layouts should be included.

5. Estimated volume of work and proposed schedules.

6. Schedule and estimate of costs for implementation.

7. Summary of advantages of proposed system over current procedures, and comparative cost figures.

Final Steps in Implementing the Plan

Top management must now approve or disapprove the proposed new system. If the plan is approved, the systems analyst will have programmers help him complete the documentation and installation. Some firms do not have the systems analyst assist in these final steps, since they may need him to immediately begin an analysis of another portion of the firm's data processing operations. It is best, however, for him to continue working with the documentation and installation at least on a limited basis; in this way, he can help interpret points that might not be quite clear to others. Seeing where problems arise and where modifications are necessary will help him avoid these problems in his future systems planning. These final steps include writing the procedures manuals, preparing punched card machine wiring panel charts and/or computer program flowcharts, wiring the panels and/or writing the computer programs, testing them, and installing the new system. Equipment must be ordered as well as forms and other supplies, and personnel must be hired and trained.

One point should be emphasized: Although new systems with or without the newer equipment on the market today may look very promising, one must take time to study and evaluate carefully every proposed change. Almost any system can be improved, but the advantages of improvement may not justify the cost of making the change. A system may be effective, however, but only at unnecessarily high costs; thus it may be inefficient. No organization has unlimited resources, so we have to think in terms of profit. This means one of our objectives is cost reduction. But when we are looking at the advantage of any system improvement, we have to consider the cost of time spent in analyzing the problem and thinking through the desired changing of new forms and acquiring additional equipment; of instruction and retraining; and of errors which will result until the new system is fully understood and accepted by subordinates. The final answer rests on a consideration of all the pros and cons, and on the good judgment of the systems analyst and top management.

QUESTIONS AND PROBLEMS

1. Define systems analysis and design.
2. What are the objectives of systems analysis and design?
3. List and discuss the steps necessary for systems analysis and design.
4. What should the systems report include?
5. What are the problems involved in making an analysis of data processing activities?
6. What is involved in defining the problem and the objectives of an EDP system?
7. How does the work of a data processing manager complement that of a systems analyst?

REFERENCES

1. Robert Slater, "How Near is the Automatic Office?" *Systems Magazine*, November–December 1958, p. 14.
2. Frank Greenwood, *Managing the Systems Analysis Function*, American Management Association, New York, 1968, p. 1.
3. George Berkwitt, "The Management Machine—Can it Work?" Vol. 94, No. 6 (December 1969), p. 27.
4. David Liston, Jr., "Information Systems," *Machine Design*, July 21, 1966, p. 190.
5. J. Dearden, "How to Organize Information Systems," *Harvard Business Review*, Vol. 43, No. 2 (March–April, 1965), pp. 65–73.

PART V

COMPUTERS
AND
ORGANIZATION

HOW
THE
COMPUTER
IS
AFFECTING
WORKERS
AND
ORGANIZATIONS

CHAPTER 22

INTRODUCTION

Through the decade of the sixties, two major phenomena occurred in parallel. One was the so-called information explosion. More information became available in every facet of human endeavor and, with the development of data processing techniques, became more accessible. The other major development was the computer revolution which has been having a profound effect on the lives of all of us.

In 1960, the computer was used primarily by scientists for the solution of intricate, isolated problems. By the end of the sixties, this machine had become the chief information processor in the American business, government, and academic communities. Clerical workers who now represent approximately one-sixth of the nation's labor force will be affected to a large extent, because much of the work they do is well suited for automatic electronic data processing.

CHANGING MANAGEMENT ROLE

The role of the manager has also been modified during the past decade, because the adoption of the computer has brought with it the use of systems analysts and designers. The increasing participation of the systems analyst and designer in the planning, design, and operation of computerized data processing systems has raised the question of how best to carry on with a minimum disturbance of existing relationships.

The evidence that the role of the manager has been modified in the light of the computer consists of noting the qualifications, train-

381

ing, activities, and responsibilities of managers as they existed before and after the installation of a computer. It is commonplace for firms to have systems which, starting from basic data concerning a worker's weekly activity, produce his check, payroll statistics, and basic documents for reporting and documenting taxes and benefits. In addition, most systems can produce cost information by product and work station, and finally, will coordinate material as the basis for reports to the management level for decision-making or corrective action.

The individual worker usually participates by reporting information which relates to his work activity by job or work station and by time period. Computerized aids assist in speedy and accurate recording. Then the computer proceeds almost automatically to carry out whatever processing and printing operations are necessary.

Not so long ago the steps outlined in the illustration above were performed by a large number of separate machine operations carried on and checked by various individuals. Managers directed the flow of the work from station to station. Today much of this work is accomplished by the computer.

When we remember that most businesses began using computers as recently as 1955, we realize the managers have adjusted to their new roles very rapidly. The business functions of computers are not new—they use the same methods and perform the same kinds of work humans have been doing for years. When the people are familiar with a procedure and know that it works, they are naturally reluctant to change to a new procedure. Most human beings resist change. Although the systems analyst and designer may have trained the workers, they look to their manager for direction and guidance once the changing process has actually begun. Unless the managers support the change and are enthusiastic about it, the subordinates will probably not try to help in making it a success. Change, then, is dependent upon the manager.

The initiative for accomplishing change must come from the top. Traditional management methods for leadership and control give way to new forms. Structures and systems for planning are increasing in importance. Management must decide whether to deal with revolutionary forces of change such as the advent of the computer, or whether to go along with the slower, evolutionary methods for development. There is a big difference between a managerial philosophy to simply react, and a managerial philosophy to initiate action based on well-planned premises about the future of the firm.

The strategy for accomplishing change must interrelate the systems, organizational structure, and organizational behavior. These three variables are interdependent and require parallel attention in any well-planned effort toward change.

Managers must be actively involved in the accomplishment of change at all levels. The alert manager realizes his own responsibility for continuous self-development and top leadership. He realizes that change must be continuous and based on long-term plans. Flexibility, however, and awareness of contemporary conditions must become a management way of life.

The computer has brought about a change in the role of the manager, one that we might call a behavior change in that he has adjusted to new styles of managing in terms of both equipment and people.

MANAGEMENT AND SPECIALISTS

It has been pointed out that management is affected by the participation of systems analysts and designers. In computer work, they include the systems analysts, programmers, machine designers, and designers of programming languages. Each is a specialist in his area of work and is primarily concerned with the machines or techniques—not with people and their behavior. These people do not have to manage the day-to-day problems with employees after their new systems and ways of doing things are put into use. This occasionally is a drawback. Some of their plans work out well, but others have serious flaws that have to be worked out by those who actually carry out the work.

Top and second level managers now realize that they are supervising subordinates whose knowledge and skills are different from theirs, both in amount and in kind. Conversely, the systems specialist is reporting to a manager whose training and experience undoubtedly has been in a field other than data processing. Since it is impossible to have a complete matching of training, experience, aptitude, and interests on the part of the systems specialist, top management, and work supervisors, there will always be some lack of understanding, inefficiency of communication, and frustration. Time will eventually remedy this situation, as it has similar ones at other times in the history of technology. Junior colleges, colleges, and universities are now attacking the problem of how to manage the new and rapidly growing field of specialization, and simultaneously, management training programs are in effect to assist data processing specialists.

EFFECTS OF THE COMPUTER ON INDIVIDUALS

Effects of the computer on individuals have been both good and bad; some individuals have benefited, some have suffered, and some have been affected by varying degrees of benefit and suffering. Individuals working for organizations that use computers are naturally affected, but individuals in private life are also affected by the computer, although they may never have access to a computer. We generally benefit from increases in scientific knowledge and medical knowledge. We receive our computerized bills with lower service charges than would be necessary if many clerks were needed to process them. Some of the benefits are so indirect that we do not realize them, and others affect only specific groups of people. For example, stockholders benefit from increased efficiencies in the company's operations brought about by the use of the computer. Airline reservations can be made and confirmed more quickly. Stock market reports are more current and accurate. Credit cards could not be used economically without computers to handle all the commissions and charges associated with them, because of the tremendous number of individuals and stores where they are used.

Some people are inconvenienced because the computer was improperly programmed. The programmers might not have provided for all possible exceptional situations that can arise. The person with the exceptional problem could receive incorrect results from the computer's processing.

Individuals and Their Jobs

The day-to-day use of the computer requires personnel for preparing the data, operating the equipment, scheduling the use of it, performing clerical tasks associated with it, and supervising and managing these functions. People who gain the necessary skill and obtain these jobs benefit from the introduction of the computer. As the data processing functions in the organization become more important, more centralized, and more directly related to the management activities, these people, even at the lower levels, feel more and more important to the company. Many of the jobs, however, such as data preparation and machine operation, involve repetitive mechanical work. There is no freedom to innovate or create. Some of these people take the initiative and gain more knowledge so that they can advance to higher positions; others are happy and have a feeling of prestige and self-importance by being associated with the modern and impressive "space-age" machines.

While the computer is a source of new opportunity to those who obtain the necessary knowledge and skills, it is also a source of fear and anxiety to many people. It symbolizes impersonality, conformity, the reduction of the individual to a number, and most important, the reduction of jobs for some people. Some groups of people have suffered in definite direct ways, others only indirectly.

The sales personnel in certain types of work—those involved in making airline reservations, for example, have benefited by being able to get complete information more quickly and thus please their customers.

Managers in organizations with computers have increased data available to help them make better decisions. More is expected of them, however; they are under greater pressure, and their jobs become more difficult. Many managers feel they are losing control with the increase of centralized information processing.

Most supervisors are hurt because their decisions are centered around scheduling of products and personnel, much of which can be handled now by the computer. They spent many years learning to make accurate and rapid decisions for the organization. It is difficult for them to adjust to the fact that computers have made these skills worthless.

Many professional people have been helped by the computer. Accountants, lawyers, and medical doctors can obtain certain required facts more quickly. Teachers have assistance in some test-scoring and record-keeping functions.

Clerical workers suffer in several ways. In organizations that are making frequent or gradual conversions to the computer, the clerical workers fear that they might not have a job or that they will have to learn a new job and be with different co-workers. The uncertainty about what is going to take place and when it might take place causes tension and anxiety. When a clerical worker knows that her work will be fed into a computer rather than going to another clerk, she feels uncomfortable. Other clerks are usually understanding when there are errors or deviations from the expected procedures whereas the computer is not, and more people in higher positions are likely to learn of the errors.

Students will be affected more and more by computer-assisted instruction (CAI) in the future for subjects adaptable to drill and practice in factual data. It is particularly appropriate in some industrial and armed forces training programs and in grade schools. Students who actually have access to a computer for computations in some subjects have a definite advantage over other students. If students are able to learn computer programming, their job opportunites in many areas of work immediately broaden.

Centralized Personal Data

Keeping personal data centralized in computer files will hurt some people. Only part of these data are needed by a specific inquirer. For example, a credit bureau needs only a man's employment record and credit rating; it does not need his arrest record. In some cases, the brief data kept in these files can be misinterpreted. Also, a seemingly unfavorable record could be explained, but space does not permit this. Some unfavorable conditions should be erased when they have been corrected, but these records remain permanently. At the present time, many of these records are computer centered, to great advantage. They are not centrally located, though. The Internal Revenue Service, Social Security, Federal Bureau of Investigation, Veterans Administration, large police departments, credit bureaus, and many other agencies have computer-centered files for personal data, but each has its own files. All the data about one individual cannot be obtained from one centralized file. Therefore, in general, this type of individual suffering has not yet resulted.

In this discussion, organizational effects on individuals have centered around office work, as the main concern in business data processing, with only a few comments concerning the computer in manufacturing operations. Many of the effects of the computer on office personnel, supervisors, and managers have their parallel in manufacturing.

Scientists and Engineers Change too!

Scientists and engineers in research have been able to advance some branches of study into degrees of complexity that would not have been possible without the use of the computer. Engineers can perform design calculations more rapidly and can feasibly try more alternative solutions. As with business modeling, not all the relationships can be represented numerically, as is the case with designing dams, dikes, and levees to control water; modeling can be used, though, to aid in making the best decisions. Now the engineer can devote more time to perfecting models while the computer takes care of the formulas for him. He must be careful to make some actual experiments to check the various modeling techniques for errors.

As each engineer or scientist needs to spend less time making calculations, fewer scientists or engineers are needed to perform any given job. In fact, the United States Navy Ship System Command is working on a computer system programmed to compute stresses, make the geometric calculations, and specify the decisions needed for the drawings in ship designing. With plotting boards, the computer could produce the engineering drawings. This changeover would reduce the need for both lower-level engineers and draftsmen, since an enormous amount of time is spent in producing the necessary drawings after the design is complete. Scientists and engineers suffer because they have to continually study the new developments which are occurring at a faster rate than they did in the past. The methods and techniques they learned in school become partially, if not wholly, obsolete very quickly. It takes real effort for top engineers just to keep pace before they can even consider advantageous developments.

EFFECTS OF THE COMPUTER ON ORGANIZATIONS

Organizations have undergone changes with each advance in technology, whether in the manufacturing or data processing operations. Some changes are directly caused by the computer. Such changes are seen in the operation of the routine function, in the planning function, and in the organization's basic structure.

Organizations Most Affected by the Computer

The organizations most affected by the computer are the ones to which it is most useful. Basically, these organizations are the ones that require large volumes of transactions each day, the ones that provide many small (in cost) items or services and have large numbers of customers. Number one examples of this kind are the utility companies, especially telephone companies that have to keep a record of so many calls and customer accounts. Many manufacturing companies, distributors, and retail stores also have a large number of customers and products in relation to their volume of business. Banks and savings and loan associations also fit into this category. Even organizations that have relatively few customers and products in relation to their dollar-sales volume have become computerized. Manufacturers of automobiles, for example, deal in products that sell for more than $1,000 each and have a limited number of authorized dealers. But they, too, have enormous data processing needs in other ways—in the number of employees and number of parts going into each finished product. Some government agencies fit into the category of organizations with enormous record-keeping problems—the Internal Revenue Service, the Social Security Administration, the Veterans Administration, among others.

Change in Routine Functions

A change in the operation of the routine functions of companies that use the computer is in the number and types of personnel employed. Many companies think they will need fewer employees when they make the change. The fact is that many find that they are not employing fewer people, but neither are they employing more. They usually find that they can increase the volume of work without needing additional personnel in the data processing function. Computers have not caused any large-scale immediate replacement of people, but they do reduce the future needs for people. This is true because during the changeover, the total volume of data to be processed increases so that the same number of employees are needed. However, without a computer, the new volume would require many additional employees—in effect, then, use of the computer means fewer office jobs will be available.

The Bell System points out this situation very well. The computer is used with direct dialing to establish the toll charge. The effect of this use of the computer in reducing the number of operating personnel is shown in these figures:

Category	1957	1965
Employees	640,868	611,931
Number of telephones	52,252,595	75,866,254
Number of local telephone calls (daily average)	180,084,000	266,165,000
Number of toll and long distance calls (daily average)	8,192,000	13,349,000

Source: "Annual Report," American Telephone and Telegraph Company, 1966.

Types of Jobs Available

Changes in the types of jobs available have become apparent. Fewer clerks are needed for the same volume of record keeping. Jobs on which one supervisor could manage 25 clerks without a computer, might now require one supervisor for 10 clerks. The supervisor is no longer in charge of people performing routine tasks; he now supervises a system which requires monitoring, control of errors, and improvements. The emphasis has changed from skill in guiding people to technical, computer-oriented knowledge. It is increasingly difficult for an employee to advance to a supervisory position based on knowledge required for a lower-echelon job. As more and more supervisory positions become available, more people with technical computer background are needed.

Miscellaneous Operating Effects

Another effect of the computer in the operations of organizations is the requirement of greater rigidity in the procedures of operating personnel. More forms have to be filled out, and they must be filled out completely and accurately, expressed in codes and symbols rather than descriptive terms. With the computers to keep records, it is no longer so important to manufacture only standard products. In the past, the cost and difficulty of record keeping prevented many companies from producing many variations, particularly in colors and styles. Companies also have found that they need smaller inventories of both finished products and materials for production. The records are accurate, and an order can be automatically produced when the balance on hand in inventory records gets down to a specific quantity.

If an organization had manufacturing operations or warehouses for shipping goods at more than one location, each location had to do its own scheduling and planning in the past. Now one centrally located computer can do it all with the use of data communication equipment. In some situations, the computer can also provide instructions to the workers. Foremen and supervisors no longer have to explain these instructions over and over again. Fewer foremen and supervisors are needed in some companies, since major portions of their duties are performed by the computer. Their remaining duties include personnel administration, training, and troubleshooting.

In summary, the computers' effects on the operating function of the organization are to facilitate its handling larger volumes of work, allow greater flexibility in products, and a smaller investment in inventories. They do bring about a greater rigidity in procedures, however, and changes in types of jobs.

The Computer Aids in Planning

If the computer is being used in the day-to-day data processing functions, it can also provide statistics from this day-to-day data. These statistics and summary reports keep management fully informed so that they make better plans for the future. The computer is also used to schedule operations. Then it begins to be used in "modeling," as explained earlier. It can be used to test the results of alternative investment decisions and management policies by simulating the probable future sequence of events. Although this procedure cannot predict with 100% accuracy because of events that are not foreseeable or not controllable, the computer can evaluate major alternatives. As these procedures are improved and better understood, they will become more widely used.

The computer can help to point out problems before they become major or serious. For humans to find small problems requires that many people constantly review the operating data and decide when a problem is serious enough to warrant action. With the aid of the computer, large quantities of operating data can be quickly reviewed, and every trend away from the manager's goals or standards can be revealed. For example, when the total cost of all the items going into a specific product reaches a specified point, this is reported immediately, rather than a week or month later.

As the use of the computer continues to grow, its effects on managers at all levels will continue to grow. The better understanding each manager in the entire company has of the uses of the computer, the better he will be able to make the necessary adjustments and the better he will be able to help his subordinates make the adjustments.

Changes in Organization Structure—To Come?

The overall structure of the organization may change, although most organizations using computers have not yet experienced any drastic changes. Traditionally, the organization has been divided into units that are small enough for one manager's span of control so that the detailed operations can be managed satisfactorily. Each group of unit managers has reported to successively higher levels, so that top management actually had frequent contact only with relatively few regional or upper-echelon managers. Since it becomes possible to bring all the transactions to a central computer operations center now, all the detailed day-to-day operations can be managed in this area. Theoretically, the computer operations center can become the center of the organization, with no need for regional or district managers.

Managers' duties, however, extend further than day-to-day data processing needs. They still need to make operating decisions that can be better made by a person or group of people at the actual location—they see the situation better and they are the ones who are most affected by the decision. However, the increases in efficiency brought about by the computer have resulted in managers' being able to oversee larger units of work, with the result that some centralization in managing the more routine operations has occurred. Some companies have been able to centralize clerical operations; some of the physical handling, storage, and manufacturing functions have also been consolidated. However, this change is limited because shipping costs make it more economical to conduct manufacturing operations involving products with heavy weight or large size in dispersed plants near their markets.

CONCLUSION

American business operates in an environment of change, the inevitable consequence of operating in a dynamic business climate. Rapidly advancing data processing systems have emphasized the need for planning. Firms that do not keep abreast of current technology are in trouble even over the short run, but firms unaware of the technical changes likely to occur over the next five to twenty years will be at a distinct disadvantage.

The impact of computers on integrated systems of information flow has revealed some reluctance on the part of the clerical workers and management personnel with vested interests to accept the required modifications in organization and status relationships. The data processing manager has one very important function to perform, then: He must sell both management personnel and clerical workers on the positive advantages of installing a computer. The present trend in our general political, economic, social, ethical, and moral philosophies is toward an atmosphere of freedom for change even for the business firm. Continued success for any firm demands adaptation and innovation.

QUESTIONS AND PROBLEMS

1. During the 1960's what two major phenomena occurred that were correlated with data processing?

2. What percent of the American labor force were clerical workers?

3. What caused the change in the role of the manager during the 1960's?

4. Have managers been able to adjust to the computer very rapidly?

5. Why are people reluctant to change?

6. Briefly describe the ways management can help make changes.

7. Why do some of the plans of the systems analysts and designers not always work out when in practice?

8. Why is there a lack of understanding between the systems specialists and their supervisors?

9. Can people who never actually have access to a computer be affected by one? Explain your answer.

10. How can individuals on their jobs benefit from the use of the computer?

11. In what ways does the computer cause suffering by people on their jobs?

12. Are managers under more pressure in a computerized system?

13. Overall, does the idea of centralized computer files for keeping personal data of individuals seem good or bad? Why?

14. In what ways do computers help engineers and scientists?

15. In what ways has the computer caused engineers and scientists to suffer?

16. What types of companies are most affected by the computer?

17. What do many companies find about the number of employees after they begin using the computer? Why?

18. Is the computer, in effect, causing fewer jobs to be available? Explain.

19. What changes take place in the role of the supervisor?

20. List five miscellaneous effects the computer has had on the operation of an organization.

21. How can statistics and summary reports be used?

22. How can the computer help with problems and exceptions?

23. How can the computer change the office structure?

24. State several reasons why this extreme change in the organizational structure has not taken place.

25. What very important function must the data processing manager perform?

26. What is the present trend in our general political, economic, social, ethical, and moral philosophies?

STRENGTHS AND WEAKNESSES OF THE COMPUTER

CHAPTER 23

As computers came into widespread use, the market for them increased enormously. Growth in the computer business has been fed by technological advances that have made computing equipment less expensive and better each year. However, one finds that the computer has become a friend to some and a foe to others. To some users, the computer has many benefits, and to others it has many drawbacks. Those who doubt the practicality of its implementation are quick to point out the weaknesses of the computer. The computer as an important technological development is still in its infancy stage; any one point of view will be proved only by future developments about which we can only speculate. With this in mind, let us consider strengths and the weaknesses of the computer.

STRENGTHS OF THE COMPUTER

The computer does save money by enabling firms to handle routine operations with fewer workers and by reducing the possibility of errors in figures. It can help in the solution of clerical labor shortages, and it can provide new information needed for decision-making in a very short time.

The fact that so many computers are being used today makes it obvious that the advantages have widespread appeal. Most of the publicity the computers receive point out their unusual and spectacular abilities and the experiments. While these aspects show great promise for the future, an objective evaluation of the actual strengths of computers must consider their current or more ordinary uses today.

Repetitive, Accurate, and Fast Work

The computer appeared on the scene at a time of increasing regulations and population growth, which certainly helped its growth and success. It was able to handle and process large numbers of individual transactions in a formal, predetermined sequence. By nature, humans are very poor at performing this type of repetitive mathematical work. They become bored, disinterested, slower, and very inaccurate. The fact that the computers do the job more accurately and much faster is the greatest strength of the computers today. The computer works constantly and consistently—it can work 24 hours a day, 7 days a week, with proper maintenance. So long as the programs are complete and accurate, it will function correctly, and each transaction will be accurately and precisely processed. Computers have been called "robot clerks" because of this repetitive ability with such a high degree of accuracy. A large majority of computers in current use perform only this type of work.

The computer's speed is also important. However, even if it could produce the same results no faster than people, and at the same cost, the computer would still be used because of its accuracy. The cost of computers is high, however, and they must be able to do the work of many humans in order to justify this cost. If the operating costs of a computer are equivalent to the costs for 30 human clerks and they can produce as much output as 60 or more human clerks, the cost of the computer is certainly justified.

Computers provide savings in more ways than in wages for human clerks. For example, the United States Internal Revenue Service (IRS) uses computers to process all the documents associated with both individual and corporation income tax returns. In 1966, the IRS used 27 computers worth approximately $12,000,000.* It is said that during 1966 these 27 computers

1. Did the work of 12,000 humans.

2. Produced additional revenues of $27,000,000.

3. Held back $61,000,000 in refunds to cover past tax debts.

4. Yielded $19,000,000 by discovering mathematical errors.

---

* *Inventory of Automatic Data Processing Equipment in the Federal Government,* U. S. Bureau of the Budget, July 1966.

5. Noted 700,000 missing returns with potential tax collections of $156,000,000.

6. Uncovered 416,000 duplicate refund claims.*

The capacity of the computer to perform routine data handling operations at high speeds is significant not only in the area of business. Science has benefited greatly—the space program, the design of jets, and many areas of theoretical physics involve experiments that produce such great volumes of data that human clerks could not be expected to perform these functions. Important, too, in these fields is the fact that the computer can predict the outcome of an event in time for the course of the event to be changed. For example, computers provide new predictions every few seconds of the impact point of each missile being tested at missile ranges. When a predicted impact point becomes unacceptable, the flight path is changed if possible; otherwise, the missile is destroyed. This is considered as "real time" use of a computer. The methods or formulas for making such calculations have been known for a long while, but the time required for human calculations made the knowledge useless for practical application. The "real time" concept also applies to business situations in which it would be possible for humans to perform the calculations before the results were actually required. However, the volume of such problems is so great that it would become enormously expensive to have an adequate number of human clerks available to do the work—and do it perfectly each time. Examples include the utility companies' billing procedures and individuals' bank account transactions.

Modeling

Although computers cannot actually make business decisions, they can provide useful data to help the managers make decisions. A problem that arises is the fact that there are uncontrollable variables such as government taxes, demands by customers, and subsidy policies. Usually, it is possible to develop a mathematical representation of the process or system, which is called a "model." Although it is not accurate in every detail, it is approximately correct—as nearly correct as possible. The manager can use the model to test various possibilities and make a much better decision than he would otherwise be able

---

* *Internal Revenue Service Automatic Data Processing,* Honeywell Corporation, 1967.

to make. For example, a manufacturing company has a limited amount of material, limited number of employees, and limited number of machines available for making its many products. Each product requires different input costs (material, labor, machinery) and has a different profit and demand for it. All these factors must be considered when deciding future production schedules. Using even imperfect models to test the many possibilities helps the manager select the best solution—seldom does one best solution result, but several that emerge are better than the many others. Once a manager begins to use the modeling technique, he can learn more about the process he is studying, can have the model improved as experience accumulates in using it, and can compare projections with the actual results.

A large amount of the current computer development work is being devoted to developing simulation models for both business systems and scientific systems. Models are used if definite relationships between causes and effects cannot be determined ahead of time. A company can be saved a great deal of time and expense by testing new hypotheses by new combinations of the input variables on a computer model, rather than by actually going through the manufacturing process or by actually carrying out some other "real world" situation. The ability of the computer to manipulate models is not yet used nearly as extensively as its ability to do clerical work, due primarily to current difficulties of developing models and programs to manipulate the models. This use for the computer is considered by many to be more fundamental and of greater potential importance and to have greater benefits to its users in the long run. It will certainly continue to develop, and as it does, the influence on individuals and organizations will be more greatly noticed.

Computer Controlled Machines

The computer controls other machines that are attached to it, particularly the numerous input and output devices. These "peripheral" devices to the computer have become so much faster and more reliable over the years that the computer does not have to stop and wait for them to operate. Some of these devices have such speed and capability that the computer is primarily a control device to them. For example, computers are used to control teletype switching centers and devices that compose type for printing operations.

The computer can also be connected to many other kinds of machinery through electrical devices. It can now be used to control industrial processes in addition to processing information. A major steel company reports that a computer applied to control the repetitive operation in a hot strip rolling mill provided these effects.*

1. Scrap was reduced by 25–50% compared to results obtained by earlier models.

2. Total production increased 2%.

3. The percentage of product having the acceptable thickness after only one rolling operation increased from between 72% and 85% to 95%. The need for a second rolling operation was thus reduced.

Summary of the Strengths of the Computer

The numerous abilities of the computer represent such a tremendous advance that we see its potentials are just beginning to be used—and its effects on humans and organizations are just beginning to be noticed. The primary emphasis in the past has been applied to clerical operations. In the future, more emphasis will be on its strengths and capacities to manipulate models, to control external devices, to improve control of rapidly occurring events while they are still taking place, and probably to extend to uses not yet discovered.

WEAKNESSES OF THE COMPUTER

Although the computer has such tremendous advantages, it is not perfect—there are also weaknesses, or disadvantages. Its limitations and drawbacks prevent its being used in some of the ways people have wanted and even tried to use it. In other attempted applications, great difficulties have evidently been encountered in getting it to do its intended work—some of which undoubtedly are unknown to us because people frequently do not like to admit failures.

Adaptation to the Human Language

The computer cannot communicate in a human language. An audio I/O device enables it to accept and emit audible sounds, but these are merely syllables of words selected by the program. It can work only with a very limited, predetermined group of responses or words. It cannot use an audible language in a real sense. The language limitation is not frequently considered a problem, because computers can

---

* *Datamation,* August 1967.

work with relatively large vocabularies of recorded words in human language. However, the computer must be specifically programmed to recognize certain words and symbols that have meaning to humans. This vocabulary provides the computer with a limited response—exactly the same each time the same word or symbol is used. A person who does not understand the way computers actually work sees large varieties of human language words being fed into it and coming out of it; he thinks the computer is using the language in the same way that we use it. He does not realize that these words are merely being used as symbols with no more meaning than mathematical formulas.

One area in which the language barrier between humans and computers has proved to be a problem is in information retrieval. Many people, especially scientists and engineers, must keep up to date in reading published material in their areas of work. Currently so much is being published that one person cannot keep up with it all. Furthermore, the data are being reported through so many media that one person or entity could not subscribe to or purchase them all. Because the computer can search through large files of data at such great speeds, humans have tried to program computers to store and retrieve such data ever since computers began to be used. Many efforts have been made and are continuing to be made to develop files and computer programs that will enable computers to identify and reproduce data about which a person inquires. In relation to the number of people and organizations that have been working on this problem, very few effective computer-based information retrieval systems exist at this time, and there is still a problem for the user due to their limited use of terminology. For example, there are many pairs of synonymous words, even in technical areas. When the inquirer uses one such word, the computer searches only for data with reference to that one word, but not to its synonym. Therefore, anyone making an inquiry has to check each word in a special dictionary made specifically for his area of work. Another problem is that many technical words have minute differences in meaning, so the inquirer has to be especially careful to use the correct one. The language barrier between humans and computers is especially significant in information retrieval attempts. The need for this use of the computer is so great that work will continue in an effort to improve such applications.

The use of the computer in education is especially desirable in areas affected by the enormous growth in both population and technology. Advances in technology are especially important; it is difficult for teachers to keep up with these changes. For this reason, computer-assisted instruction is desirable. However, its use encounters the same problem faced in information retrieval—limited language ability. In our broadening and ever-increasing educational process, the human language is used to its fullest extent. The communicating of ideas and understanding of concepts requires dialogue, either spoken or written, between student and teacher. The teacher must analyze each response in order to determine the student's level of comprehension. So the use of the computer is limited in education to subject areas in which a specific skill rather than abstract comprehension is being learned and tested. Most of these skills where the computer could be used do not actually need a computer. They involve the student's choosing among several answers which suggest the next page he should use. This type of instruction can be handled adequately with books designed as the computer program would be. Currently the computer is used only in instructional programs that encompass so many branches that it is impractical or inconvenient to print the alternatives in a book.

Programming Problems

Although programming the computer has always been a tedious job, it has been greatly improved over the years. Originally the programmer had to write each instruction, many of which were for the same sequence of instructions being used over and over again; but in the past they had to all be written each time they were needed. Then the programmer was provided with a set of symbols, each representing a specific group of machine instructions that perform a frequently used function. The computer could recognize each symbol and convert it to the group of required instructions. Thus began the use of compiler programs. Compiler programs have been developed for both business problems and mathematical problems.

Computer Costs

The cost of a computer is a major consideration. Even if there are reductions in the cost of building computers, the overall cost to a company will not be greatly affected, because the total "computer cost" includes numerous factors—some of which are the peripheral equipment, the software, and the number and caliber of the employees required in a computer installation.

The cost of the electronic circuits that are required to perform the computer's functions has gone down and is expected to go down even further. The costs of the peripheral devices have gone down only slightly and are not expected to go down much further. Many of these machines are basically mechanical, and the techniques in manufacturing them seem to be relatively complete and stable. Usually these peripheral media make up at least half the total manufacturing cost of the complete computer system. So reduced manufacturing costs of the installation will not be substantial. Also to be remembered is the fact that as increasingly more complex computers are made, production of them becomes more expensive. Newer and added requirements of the computer include electronic devices used in communication networks attached to computers for remote users and greater internal storage to keep each user's work separate from that of others. Computers needed for real-time applications such as airline reservations cannot be unavailable for very long. In fact, in some cases it is necessary to have duplicate facilities to accommodate the work load in such situations.

The cost of providing input data remains very high. Many keypunch operators are needed to provide input fast enough, with the result that both their wages and the total cost of the many keypunch machines needed is high. Attempts to surmount or alleviate this problem have resulted in numerous optical machines. But these machines are also very expensive and require that the source documents be very consistent. Consequently, the input remains a problem, and one so important that it is currently an area of major concern.

Costs for planning the entire system and making the specific programs cannot be avoided. At the present time, almost every company using a computer has to make up its own programs. For some users, this cost is beginning to be reduced. Sometimes it is possible to develop programs that can be used by several groups of users who have similar problems. For example, keeping records of bank accounts is similar for most banks, and keeping records of customer charge accounts might be similar for many department stores and even manufacturers. Some of the large computer manufacturers are preparing standard programs that need only slight modification for some users within a group.

In the past another problem in programming has been in hiring qualified personnel. If the company was able to hire a person with any programming experience, the person usually had to be retrained for the specific purposes and equipment the company had. The use of problem-oriented languages has reduced the programmer's need for detailed knowledge about the specific computer. Also, many students graduating from the post-secondary institutions have either gained an in-depth knowledge of programming or have at least been exposed to it.

Initially installing a computer is a definite expense. This investment is frequently referred to as "startup" cost and usually involves completely redesigning the way the work is done. New forms have to be designed, employees have to be reoriented (which is a later and separate topic), and even the customers have to get used to some of the changes. Much time and money is spent in planning all the necessary changes before any positive returns can be expected.

Many companies, however, have experienced gradually increased costs in their total computer installation each year. This situation is due primarily to the fact that they keep investing more money by increasing the number and size of computers and by increasing the use of peripheral equipment. At the same time, these companies obtain better results and more useful information. Thus the cost in terms of value received is not increased. It is apparent that the cost factor in using computers will continue to be a drawback. But this investment challenges each user to develop increased performance and increased satisfaction from his computer.

Lack of "Personality" and "Perception"

A computer lacks emotion, of course, and occasionally people say it "has no personality." Since humans are used to and adjusted to working with other humans, working with a computer requires a frequently difficult adjustment. An individual cannot use his own personality to influence the computer to help him or to do what he wants it to do. He can function with a computer only by presenting very definite and factual data in a logical manner for a specific purpose. There is little or no variation. Some people who work with computers begin to feel that they are becoming impersonal agents and losing their own personalities and that all people are the same.

A computer cannot perceive relationships as a human can, but it does not forget any item stored in it; humans forget and even have difficulty memorizing. For a computer, a relationship must be broken down into its many factors. For example, a human gains experience in evaluating visual relationships that help him decide whether or not he has time to walk across the street before a car gets to him. A computer would have to measure the car's speed, the distance between the person and the car, make the necessary calculations, and report the answer. Fortunately, a human does not have to solve this type of problem in this way; it would take quite some time for him to do. A computer could solve such a problem as fast as a person could decide what to do, but the two processes are entirely different.

If computers could handle relationships easily, they could be used advantageously in many desirable ways, such as in fingerprint detection and facial identifications. A computer would require an enormous quantity of its memory and computing time to record the mass of numerical measurements and relationships needed to describe any large number of human faces. No computer program has yet been developed to enable the computer to differentiate among them. This job certainly seems to be out of the reach of the computer. Some partial screening of fingerprints can be performed by the computer, however, and thus reduce the number of specimens a person must check.

Summary of Weaknesses of the Computer

Work is being done to solve each of the weaknesses of the computer. The probability is, however, that many of these weaknesses will remain: high cost, incapacity to perceive relationships and handle human languages, and a lack of personality. Having an understanding of these weaknesses, though, can help all who work with computers to overcome them. Only human efforts can solve these problems.

QUESTIONS AND PROBLEMS

1. What are the greatest strengths of computers today?
2. Most of the publicity that computers receive is geared toward what aspects?
3. Why are humans poor at performing repetitive mathematical work?
4. Why are computers called "robot clerks"?
5. How do computers help at missile sites?
6. What is a "model" in computer terminology?
7. How is a model used?
8. Toward what is a large amount of the current computer development work geared?
9. What other types of operations can a computer control in addition to processing information?

10. List four areas of computer usage that will probably receive more emphasis in the next few years.

11. Why is the human language limitation of the computer not considered an actual problem in some cases?

12. Does the computer use the English language in the same way that we use it?

13. Why is it advantageous to have computerized information retrieval?

14. What are the main problems in developing good information retrieval systems?

15. What is the major limitation in using computer-assisted instruction?

16. What developments have made computer programming easier?

17. List several of the computer costs that will probably not be reduced to any significant degree in the future.

18. How does the cost of a computer challenge the user?

19. Why is it frequently difficult for a person to adjust to working with a computer?

20. Why is it helpful for a person who works with computers to have a good understanding of the weaknesses of computers?

BUSINESS,
SCIENTIFIC,
AND
MANUFACTURING
USES
OF
COMPUTERS

CHAPTER 24

AN ANALOG COMPUTER USED FOR SOME MANUFACTURING AND SCIENTIFIC WORK

Computers are needed in business, science, and industry to solve different types of problems. The basic reason why each uses computers is the same, though: the need for rapid and accurate calculations. Business needs rapid calculations to handle the tremendous volume of data. Science needs rapid calculations because of the increasing complexity of the problems being explored. Industry needs rapid calculations to keep pace with the speed and preciseness with which items must be manufactured.

BUSINESS USES OF COMPUTERS

Many uses for computers have been developed by business since the middle 1950's when they began to be used. Business uses them primarily to handle sales data, employee payrolls, inventory control, customer accounts, and purchases.

A large company can use a computer very advantageously both for keeping records and producing information that helps managers to make decisions. The owners of a chain of retail stores or a manufacturer with numerous plants and sales office locations would find the computer particularly useful in bringing together data from widespread areas. The computer program that processes the sales records can produce, for example,

1. Accurate and up-to-date inventory figures,

2. Daily, weekly, or monthly sales figures,

405

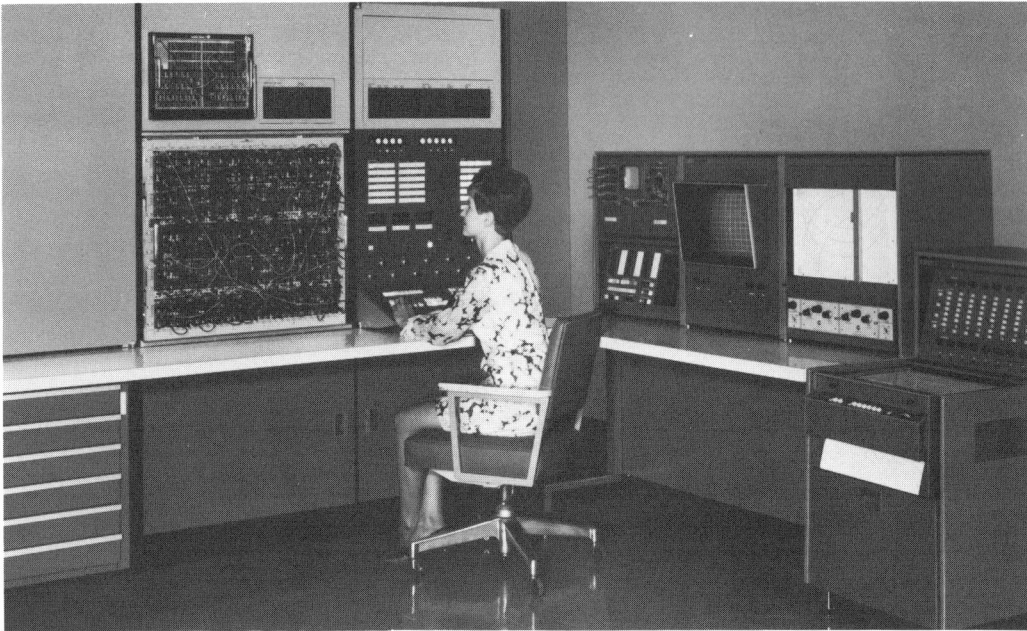

**FIG. 24.1 EAI 7800
Analog/Hybrid Computer**

3. Weekly or monthly purchases,
4. Style or model sales reports,
5. Sales by geographic areas,
6. Information received by salesmen.

The company needs an up-to-date inventory record in order to schedule its purchasing and manufacturing. The analysis of sales can be useful in many ways. For example, past records help management predict future sales and what items to purchase or manufacture; recent trends by geographic area help management determine future advertising plans for each area; comparisons of reports by different salesmen help determine each man's weak and strong areas. You can think of more ways these reports can be used.

Large banks have turned to the use of computers not only for handling employee payrolls, but more importantly for handling depositors' accounts and loans. Both checking accounts and savings accounts can be processed by computers. As we discussed earlier, the magnetic ink characters printed on checks are used directly as computer input; there is no need to transfer that information to punched cards or another input media. The account balances are kept on record by the computer's external storage hookup which may utilize disk packs, magnetic tape, or magnetic drums. Although all the data for each account could not possibly be held in the computer's internal storage, the external facilities make it possible for the computer to obtain the necessary data very quickly.

Smaller banks usually do not have a computer. They would not use one enough hours a week to justify its expense. Many companies other than banks are in the same situation—their data could be processed faster and more accurately by the use of a computer, but they would not use one enough to warrant its expense. For these companies, special services have been developed whereby several companies use the same computer, and each pays according to the amount of time he uses it. Companies with limited needs for a computer can install a computer terminal which provides communication with a computer in another location. The computer can be in another room of the same building, in a building in another part of town, or in a distant city. The computer might be one that belongs to the same company in another location, one that belongs to another company that does not need it all the time, or one that a service company has set up specifically for this purpose. When several different companies use the same computer, we frequently refer to it as *time sharing*.

The terminal might be a Teletype machine. A person punches the data into paper tape, or a machine has already prepared the paper tape. Then the specified number is called on the telephone and the punched tape is run through the transmitting section of the machine, which is at the left-hand side of the machine. These codes are converted into codes that can be transmitted over the telephone wires and received by a Teletype machine or another type of machine where the computer is located. Data are converted and used as input for the computer. If all the input lines at the computer location are being used when you call, you wait a few minutes and call again. Your data wait to be processed by the computer. If nothing else is being processed, your data are processed immediately. Your answer is transmitted to you in the same way in which you sent the information. Some Teletypes both send and receive data. The machine that does this can punch the data on tape and print them on paper at the same time (whether it is sending or receiving), or it can do just one of the two.

FIG. 24.2   Teletype only for receiving data

The Teletype machine in Fig. 24.2 can receive, but cannot send data. In actual practice you may receive your results within a few minutes or you may have to wait several hours, depending on how much other data is ahead of yours and how much material you need to have processed. Some schools use a terminal hooked up to a computer at a university or a service company so that the students can use the programs they write.

SCIENTIFIC AND ENGINEERING USES OF COMPUTERS

An application of computers that is particularly useful to scientists is called the *automated library*, or *data retrieval system.* Technical papers and magazine articles are punched on paper tape. A computer can detect the key technical words, make an index of topics and articles, and then make an abstract of each article. When a researcher needs data about a specific topic, his request is put into the computer; the output is a bibliography listing the articles that contain this type of data. Some computers can keep in memory a list of the interests of each researcher. When a new article is put into the machine, output is automatically produced to tell the person or persons who would be interested in the particular new article. Other types of data, such as legal reports for legal researchers, can be handled in similar fashion.

Most engineering and scientific work involves the use of formulas. This need resulted in the development of FORTRAN, which we discussed in Chapter 18.

As we have seen, most business uses of computers justify the cost of operation by reducing expenses, particularly for payroll. Some computers are used for jobs that would not be feasible to do at all without a computer. A method of weather forecasting is a good example. This method was initiated in 1962, and although the results are still not 100 percent accurate, the forecasts are much more accurate than those achieved by previous methods. This method could not be used without a computer because of the number of calculations needed, the accuracy required, and the number of decimal places to which computations must be carried out.

A one-day forecast requires nearly 100 million individual calculations from the measurements of the current conditions at weather stations around the world. It would take humans so long to make these calculations that the weather would be history before the forecast could be completed. Once the program has been written and perfected, a computer can produce the forecast in about an hour. Human beings making such calculations would inevitably make mistakes. One error in the final calculations would be so significant that it would result in a snow prediction in the middle of the summer, thus making all the calculations useless. The computer can make these calculations without error and without rounding off decimals to simplify the calculations. It can use numbers with many decimals without difficulty or much loss of speed.

The need for extreme accuracy and the use of many decimals is apparent in space flights. Very small changes in the course of flight must be detected in order to make the necessary corrections. Extreme accuracy is required to fly close enough to the moon to take pictures of it; to actually land there takes even greater accuracy. The moon is 239,000 miles from the planet earth!

The use of computers for space-age pursuits and weather forecasting is not determined by cost factors as it is in business. For these purposes computers are the tools that make such achievements possible.

USES OF COMPUTERS BY INDUSTRY

In industry, computers have numerous uses; in fact, some of the computers are special purpose ones designed specifically for a particular use. The general uses that can be employed by many types of manufacturing companies include controlling inventory, controlling processes, and numerical control of machine processes.

The inventory control use of computers in industry can actually be considered as a business use because it is an office function of updating numeric records. The special output, in addition to updated records of inventory items, includes summaries of items made and items sold; these figures help management plan the future manufacturing schedules.

Many types of industrial processes can be measured and controlled by computer, such as paper drying, oil refining, and steel making. Special devices measure what is going on, such as temperature ranges or humidity, and convert the findings into input data for the computer. With proper programming, the computer can interpret these input data and determine what should be done next. The computer then directs what is to be done next. The computer controls the actual process, its timing, and its operation. The computer can also produce output such as printed words reporting what has taken place, and flashing lights on the console informing the operator what he should do.

Numerical control of machine tools is used when extreme accuracy is required in the parts being made. For example, many parts in jets and missiles must be accurate to the ten-thousandth of an inch, a measurement so small we cannot detect it by eye. The machine is usually controlled by paper tape. The instructions tell the machine exactly where to drill the hole and how large the hole should be. The control unit causes the machine to move by power; it is not controlled by an operator.

These machines are used when many duplicates of the same part are to be made in order to avoid having people do such repetitive jobs. The machine can perform several operations at once or in auto-

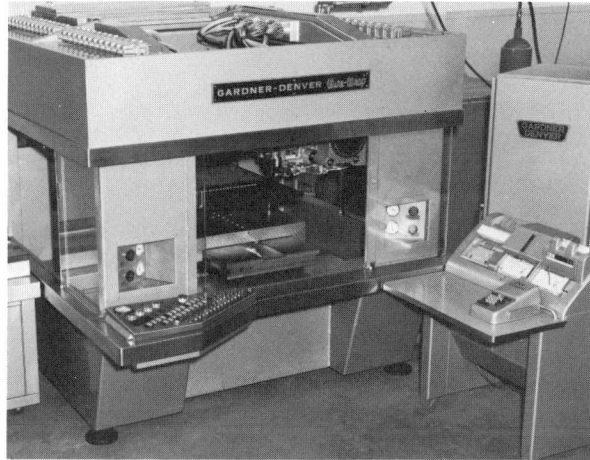

**FIG. 24.3 Gardner-
Denver Inc.
14F-22x22
Automatic Wire-
Wrap Machine**

**FIG. 24.4 Close-up
of back panel
as wired on
14F-22x22
Automatic Wire-
Wrap Machine**

matic succession. This advantage does away with the necessity of
taking the part manually to each individual machine for a specific
operation.

These numerical control machines, called N/C machines, are also
used when only a few experimental parts are needed if extreme accuracy is important. Figure 24.3 shows an automatic wire-wrap machine. Figure 24.4 shows a sample part made by this machine.

FIG. 24.5 John Hancock
Mutual Life
Insurance Company,
Chicago.

A SPECIAL USE OF A COMPUTER

The John Hancock Center in Chicago (shown in Fig. 24.5), is one of the first large office-apartment buildings designed to taper toward the top. This building, along with other extremely high buildings, was designed to compensate for a difference of as much as 10° between the temperatures at the ground level and at the top of the building; it is 1107 feet high. For this and other reasons, the John Hancock Center uses a computer as an electronic building superintendent to monitor more than 1000 checkpoints, keep a weather eye on the changing outside conditions, and turn out lights to save money on electricity.

FIG. 24.6 Honeywell
data center
in John Hancock
building

A Honeywell data center (Fig. 24.6) performs many duties that would otherwise require numerous employees and provide results much more slowly. It can perform duties that range from taking the temperature of the water in the swimming pool on the 44th floor to determining "waste" heat from people, machines, and high-intensity lights. The computer checks and controls hundreds of temperatures and pressures, opens and closes dampers, and adjusts temperatures throughout the entire building. A device on the roof constantly feeds information about wind direction and speed to the data center, which determines the effects of the wind chill on the building's air conditioning system. Every fifteen minutes, an electric device prints out information from dozens of other instruments scattered throughout the tower. If a report is not normal, the data center flashes an alarm to the operator while an electric log prints the details of what is wrong. One man who touches buttons and views 100 color-coded schematics of mechanical systems is able to check and control 10,000 remote points.

The Hancock Center uses more electricity than a town with a population of more than 30,000. Therefore, small savings in electricity on various operations become significant when they are added up. Whenever the overall power consumption gets too high, the computer automatically turns off nonessential equipment and lights. When the situation gets back to normal, this equipment can be started again.

QUESTIONS AND PROBLEMS

1. Why do business, science, and industry need computers?
2. Why do business, science, and industry have a need for rapid calculations?
3. What do banks find are the most important uses of computers?
4. Why is computer time-sharing advantageous for some companies?
5. Briefly describe an automated library, or information retrieval system.
6. Why could most currently used methods of producing weather forecasts not be used without computers?
7. Briefly describe how a computer can control manufacturing processes.
8. What are the advantages of N/C?
9. In what ways can large buildings use a computer as an "electronic building superintendent"?
10. How does the "electronic building superintendent" report abnormal conditions?

When students are taken on a tour through a company, the tour guide stops in front of a glass window and lets the students look at several large boxlike machines. He tells the students that this is the computer operation. At most, there are ten people in the room with the computer. We know, though, that many people "behind the scenes" are needed before the computer can be used.

A computer is expensive, so each company uses it for as many different types of jobs as possible. Careful planning is essential so that each job will be completed on time—the employees want their

FIG. 25.1 Typical configuration of Honeywell Information System's Model 3200

415

paychecks on Friday, not on Sunday. Efficient operation of the computer and other machines is necessary so that time is not wasted. Careful planning is also needed to determine what jobs should be performed by the computer and what jobs should be performed by the unit record data processing machines.

Every company that uses punched card machines and computers must hire employees to fill the positions or job classifications described in this chapter. People with these jobs work mainly for insurance companies, manufacturing companies, banks, wholesale and retail businesses, and the state and federal governments. A smaller but increasing number work for universities and independent service organizations which provide computer services on a fee basis. Table 25.1 shows the total number of personnel in the United States who worked directly with computers each year from 1951 through 1970. These figures include only the systems analysts, programmers, and computer operators. They do not include any managers, engineers, or punched card personnel. Remember that business uses of computers did not begin until the middle 1950's. The table also shows the total number of computers being used for each of these years. A comparison of the number of employees per computer shows that greater efficiency has taken place over these years. In 1951, approximately 27 people worked with each computer. In 1970, approximately 6 people worked with each computer. Table 25.2 shows the gradual change. Although the number of employees per computer has drastically declined, there have been so many more computers in use each year that the total number of employees involved has increased steadily.

Jobs are available for men and women ranging from keypunching and operating other machines to programming, operating, debugging, and managing computer systems. Each company has its own job classifications and job titles for the employees who work in the data processing section. The job titles given in this book are general titles that are used by many companies. The job duties are described, and the qualifications are stated. Our list begins with the jobs that require the smallest amount of training or special education, because many people begin at the lower level jobs and work their way upward. These jobs are classified as operations positions, because the people operate the various punched card machines and computers. The second classification consists of planning positions, those jobs that relate to planning the use of the punched card machines and the computer.

TABLE 25.1 Personnel and Number of Computers in United States, 1951–1970[a]

Year	Personnel[a]	Number of Computers
1951	324	12
1952	2,400	95
1953	3,200	135
1954	5,600	235
1955	9,200	400
1956	17,000	800
1957	29,000	1,400
1958	50,000	2,500
1959	54,000	3,000
1960	96,000	6,000
1961	112,000	8,000
1962	120,000	10,000
1963	132,000	12,000
1964	160,000	20,000
1965	180,000	30,000
1966	240,000	40,000
1967	312,000	52,000
1968	390,000	65,000
1969	480,000	70,000
1970	600,000[b]	100,000[b]

[a] Systems analysts, programmers, and operators.

[b] Estimated.

Source: *Computer Education Directory*, Data Processing Horizons, South Pasadena, Calif., 1968, p. 38.

TABLE 25.2 Number of Employees Working Directly with Computers (derived from Table 25.1)

Year	Employees per Computer
1951	27
1955	23
1959	18
1963	11
1967	6
1970	6

The third classification consists of management positions, which relate to the overall operation or organization and day-to-day operation of the punched card and computer systems. The basic job titles in each classification are explained.

OPERATIONS POSITIONS

Operations positions are ones in which the people operate one or more machines. They include classifications such as keypunch operator, punched card equipment operator, and computer operator. These positions do not usually require college training but do require some technical training.

Keypunch Operator

This person copies data from the original source document to punched cards, using the keypunch machine. If a large amount of alphabetic data is involved, the keypunch operator must be an accurate typist, but not necessarily a very fast typist. A rate of 30–40 words a minute would be sufficient. If the job requires mostly numeric data and very little alphabetic data, no typewriting skill is needed. Some companies hire people who have never operated a keypunch machine as keypunch operator trainees. Other companies hire only people who already have had some training in the operation of a keypunch machine. This training might be at a private business school in a short course ranging from one week to about fifteen weeks, depending how many hours a week are required. Most junior colleges or community colleges offer keypunch training as a regular college course and as a special evening class for people who are employed during the day. These classes take place over a period of ten to sixteen weeks. Some high schools are beginning to offer keypunch training to junior and senior students.

Most keypunch jobs are held by women. A keypunch operator spends most of the day sitting at the keypunch machine. She may be expected to deliver the punched cards to the person who needs them or to place them and the original source documents in the correct files. A keypunch operator seldom has the varied duties of a secretary —answering the telephone, greeting guests, and so on. Finger dexterity to operate switches and keys on the machine is essential. The person must enjoy organized and routine activities and be able to follow specific instructions.

Verifier operators are considered under the heading of keypunch operator because a verifier is like a keypunch machine, although it checks the punched holes rather than punches them. Little additional instruction is required to teach a keypunch operator how to operate a verifier.

All companies that use punched card data processing equipment and most companies that use computers need keypunch operators. Optical scanning machines are replacing keypunch machines for a few specific operations, but at the present time the need for keypunch operators continues and will continue in the foreseeable future.

Punched Card Equipment Operator

This person operates the punched card data processing machines. Since this equipment is sometimes called tabulating equipment, the name *tab operator* is sometimes used. The person must have a good understanding of the use of each machine so that he uses the correct one at the right time and so that he operates it properly. The machines include the sorter, interpreter, collator, reproducer, and accounting machines. He should also be able to operate the keypunch machine in an emergency. Some punched card machine operators are also able to wire the control panels of the machines. The person must have adequate coordination to be able to push buttons on the machines, insert cards, and remove cards. The operator is standing or walking most of the time, and he must enjoy working in a routine and organized manner.

Some companies conduct training programs to teach people this job; sometimes people begin by performing only the relatively simple duties and gradually learn all the job duties. Some people obtain training for this type of job at a private business school. Taking a full-time three- to six-month course, a person could learn to operate and to wire all these machines. Many junior colleges and community colleges offer a complete two-year program, preparing the student to obtain this type of position while acquiring two years of college credit. Very few high schools offer this training at the present time. These positions are held both by men and by women.

Computer Operator

This person controls the computer. He loads the program, inserts the input data, and watches for errors in the functioning of the computer.

He places the output data wherever specified on the program operation instruction sheet. Larger companies have classifications of computer operators such as A, B, and C grade operators. The C grade operators are the beginners; top computer operators are called senior operators. Senior operators do not write computer programs—they are operators, not programmers—but they do help the programmer test a new program and correct the errors.

The position of computer operator has changed in the last several years, just as the computers have changed. The operators with third-generation computers require a higher degree of mental alertness and knowledge than did the operators of second-generation computers. Operators in these larger multi-programmed operating system environments need more training and skill. The computer takes care of the more routine manual functions previously required of the operator; but the system is so complex that the operator needs more in-depth knowledge.

In the future, companies will have to do less training of people themselves. More and more schools are offering appropriate courses so that companies can hire trained people and conduct only brief training orientation for the specific operations of the computer system they have.

Schools that offer training for computer operators include private business schools and colleges, junior colleges, and universities. Most people holding this job have attended a private school or taken a two-year course at a junior college. Many of them are continuing their education on a part-time basis in order to become programmers. The training for a computer operator usually includes courses such as data processing mathematics, accounting, general business practices, elementary programming, computer operation, and punched card machine operation.

A computer operator must have a good technical vocabulary to be able to discuss the problems with the programmer and the systems analyst. He must be able to work in a very systematic and organized manner because he must operate the machines according to detailed and specific instructions. He is standing and walking much of the time, performing the variety of tasks which his job requires. Even while the computer is processing a job, a computer operator must watch the console, input media, and output media very closely. These jobs are held more often by men than by women.

PLANNING POSITIONS

Programmer

The programmer works closely with the systems analyst to prepare the detailed flowchart, or block diagram, of the best solution to the problem and convert it into the step-by-step instructions which describe the *computer program*. He must then test the program and make any necessary corrections. A programmer needs a knowledge of the operations of the computer and a knowledge of business or scientific problems.

A computer programmer must be able to think logically and work with details, and he must have patience. Some complex programs take several months to write and weeks to test and correct.

There are two basic types of computer programmers: those who program for business and those who program for engineering or science. The business programmer is sometimes referred to as a *digital-computer programmer*. He works with business problems such as payroll, inventory, and market analysis. The tendency is for business programmers not to have college degrees. However, many do have A.A. (Associate of Arts) degrees from community colleges or certificates from private schools. The person's first job is usually as programmer trainee for about one year; some details must still be learned about the specific computer system the company uses and the operations of the company. In installations concerned with the application of the computer to more complex areas such as market research or statistical forecasting, a college degree in mathematics is usually necessary. Some people are able to advance from computer operator to programmer trainee by showing extreme interest and by self-instruction.

The engineering and scientific programmer is sometimes referred to as a *technical programmer* (as shown in Fig. 25.2). He works with scientific, engineering, and other technical problems and uses his knowledge of advanced mathematics, including differential equations and numerical analysis. Because of the types of problems he must solve, the technical programmer usually has a college degree in computer science, mathematics, or engineering. From two to four years of on-the-job training with problems gradually increasing in complexity are necessary to make a person completely familiar with and competent at this work. The amount of training time is gradually decreasing,

FIG. 25.2 Computer programmers (IBM)

the programming languages are being simplified, and more computer courses are being offered by colleges. Programmers who must analyze extremely complex problems which involve research usually have either a master's degree or a doctorate in computer science, mathematics, or engineering.

Systems Analyst

This person is responsible for creating a logical system for collecting data, processing it, and producing useful output. He must make the best and most efficient use of the data processing equipment that is available. He must be very familiar with the uses of all the unit record data processing machines and have a good understanding of the capabilities of the computer. This position requires a logical and creative mind. A systems analyst plans punched card systems if the company does not have a computer. He plans systems that use both punched card machines and the computer if the company has a computer system.

The systems analyst must confer with managers and department heads to understand the output requirements for the managers' reports. He must confer with the programmers and even the operating personnel, who frequently provide suggestions for improving the system. He develops the general flowcharts or diagrams in order to give the programmer an understanding of what he is to do.

A person does not go to school to learn the specific job of systems analysis. He has gained an understanding of how all the machines work together to produce the required output, usually by having been a programmer. The systems analyst usually has a college degree in business administration, a two-year junior college certificate, or considerable work experience. These positions are generally held by men.

Programmers and systems analysts must continue their education while working in order to keep up with what is new in this ever-changing field. Special courses to explain the latest developments are frequently offered by computer manufacturers and by professional associations.

MANAGEMENT POSITIONS

Tab Supervisor

This person is responsible for the preparation and processing of punched cards. He must supervise the operations of the unit record data processing machines, schedule specific uses of the machines, and assign the operators to specific jobs. He frequently helps plan new applications for the equipment and modify existing uses of the equipment. Therefore he must be completely familiar with all the unit record data processing machines.

A person does not go to school to learn to be a tab supervisor. He starts as a tab operator (punched card machine operator). If he possesses the ability to supervise other people and the ability to plan and schedule both people and jobs, he is promoted to the position of tab supervisor.

Manager of Computer Operations

This person directs the computer installation, plans the scheduling of computer time, assigns personnel, maintains the file of programs (called a library), and controls the overall operations in the computer center. The person who advances to this position has managing abilities and the necessary technical background. He has probably been either an exceptional computer operator or a systems analyst.

Data Processing Manager

This person is responsible for planning, coordinating, and directing the data processing activities of the entire organization, involving both unit record data processing machines and computers. He must direct the work of others and have both managerial and technical skills. The person who obtains this position has usually had experience either as a manager of computer operations or as a systems analyst. He has acquired the necessary overall understanding of the complete system.

MISCELLANEOUS POSITIONS

The numerous other jobs necessary in most computer installations require fewer employees than we find in the positions already described. Because these positions are important and necessary, however, they deserve brief descriptions.

Computer Engineer

This person works with analog computers. He consults with the person who originates the problem and plans the complete program. He prepares the data flowchart, figures all the detailed settings of the computer, draws computer-circuit diagrams, wires computer patchboards, controls the computer during operation, and prepares the technical reports of the output or solution to the problem. Actually, he is performing functions comparable to those of the business computer programmer and the computer operator, but he works an analog computer. The person must have a college degree in engineering, physics, or some other field of science with a strong mathematical background. He must always keep informed of developments in mathematics and new equipment.

Field Service Technician (Computer Technician)

This person repairs analog or digital computers and peripheral equipment such as I/O media. He operates and observes the computer and peripheral equipment to determine the trouble, locate the defective circuits, and isolate faulty units. He uses specially prepared test programs and data to find the trouble; he uses an oscilloscope and other instruments to diagnose defects. His repairs include soldering faulty connections, replacing defective electronic and mechanical components, and making adjustments where necessary. He also provides preventive maintenance by cleaning the units periodically and testing circuitry and components.

The computer technician has completed a two-year course in electronics at a technical school or at least two years of a four-year electrical engineering program in a college. Additional courses in computer theory and repair are helpful. Military training and experience in complex electronic systems such as radar or computer systems for uses in fire control or flight simulation are desirable. Special training courses, provided by computer manufacturers, include classroom and on-the-job training for up to one year, with the time for each trainee depending on his background.

Tape Librarian

This person classifies, catalogs, and maintains the library, which consists of reels of magnetic tape, punched paper tape, or punched cards for the punched card system or the computer system. The materials must be stored and recorded according to systematic classifications and catalog numbers. Accurate records must be kept so that information can be located quickly. In small systems, the librarian may also operate the keypunch machine to replace damaged cards or work in the computer room to load and unload the I/O media. A high school graduate with a knowledge of business terminology would expect to spend a few months at on-the-job training. This experience handling the data is sufficient to enable a person to become proficient as a tape librarian.

AN AREA OF CONTINUOUS CHANGE

At the present time, there are many inconsistencies in these jobs because they have all come into being so recently. In 1940, there were just keypunch operators and tab operators, along with their supervisors. Since computers did not begin to be used in business until the middle 1950's, the need for most of these jobs did not exist until that time.

In the early 1970's many people who became systems analysts or took management positions did not have formal training for these specific jobs. Few colleges offered such courses. Most of the men had earned college degrees in business administration (either management, accounting, or mathematics) and had gained their computer knowledge through company training programs and actual experience. Most colleges and universities began offering unit record data processing and computer courses in the middle 1960's. Many high schools and most junior colleges or community colleges have begun to offer programs in data processing and computers, but very few offer more than an introductory course. Junior colleges and community colleges are rapidly gearing their curricula to fill this need; they are offering such courses in both full-time and evening programs. In fact, many have developed complete two-year data processing and computer programs.

If you are interested in pursuing a career in the area of data processing and computers, you have many opportunities available to you. If you are a girl who plans to work for only a few years, several of the jobs are immediately available to you. If you are a man planning your working career, which will extend for as many as 40–45 years, many jobs are available to you, and the better ones require special training. When making your career choice, be sure to consider the types of jobs available in the geographic area where you plan to live, the amount of education you want or can obtain, and the job duties that would be satisfying to you.

QUESTIONS AND PROBLEMS

1. What types of businesses most frequently use computers?
2. What does the chart showing the number of employees per computer point out?
3. What are the three general classifications of data processing personnel?
4. What are the more common operations positions?
5. Why is it not always necessary to be a skilled typist to become a keypunch operator?

6. What changes will probably take place in companies regarding computer operators?

7. How has the position of computer operator changed with the third generation of computers?

8. To be a good computer programmer, what abilities must the person have?

9. How does the systems analyst provide the programmer with instructions?

10. What details does a tab supervisor oversee?

11. Briefly describe the training required for each type of job listed.

Operations positions   Computer engineers
Programmers   Computer electronics mechanics
Systems analysts   Tape librarians
Management positions

12. When selecting a career in data processing, what basic considerations should a person keep in mind?

TODAY
AND
TOMORROW
WITH
COMPUTERS

CHAPTER 26

Today computers are used in many ways besides for payroll calculations, inventory control, manufacturing numerical control, and scientific problems—mostly in ways we do not even realize. They help us get our new car faster, guide our learning, or select the best college for our needs; they are used to analyze us medically or to match us with a compatible date! When we realize that the first computer was used in the middle 1940's and the first business computer in the middle 1950's, we really wonder what lies ahead! Let's see.

COMPUTER ELIMINATES LONG WAIT AFTER ORDERING THAT NEW CAR*

The computer has come to the rescue in eliminating that impatient post-order wait for a new car.

Com-Tel Corporation, based in suburban Lincolnwood, operates a Computer Locator Inventory Control (CLIC) system which enables about 20 Chicago-area Ford Motor Company dealers to determine for a customer in about two minutes whether the car he wants is among thousands stocked by the 92 Ford dealers in the Chicago district. Ronald L. Fenton, Com-Tel president and developer of CLIC, says his one-of-a-kind system has eliminated the "five-week wait" for Ford customers and has helped CLIC Ford dealers ring up additional sales.

Fenton says he got the idea for CLIC while working in May, 1967, as assistant general manager at Jim Aikey Ford, in suburban DesPlaines, one of the first dealers to use CLIC. At that time, Ford dealers trying to locate a particular car could call only one dealer at a time.

"The phone service went off at 6 p.m., and most people were coming to buy cars in the evening," Fenton recalls. So 34-year-old Fenton,

---

* Adapted from *Chicaco Sun-Times*, Business News, Monday, November 25, 1968, page 73.

who had computer training in the Marine Corps, quit and "invented" the system "with a great deal of encouragement from Ford." He formed the privately held company with a small group of investors, and the system became operational in August, 1957, with 10 dealers.

Fenton says most CLIC users are high-volume, low-markup dealers "who don't want to let a customer go" and suburban dealers, who have many requests for cars equipped with a wide variety of options.

Though the variety of options available can result in 500,000 differently equipped Fords, Fenton says that about 90 percent of the cars customers order can be found among the 14,000 cars usually in the district.

Asking the computer

Com-Tel rents time from Michigan-based Com-Share, Inc., on two Xerox Data Systems (XDS) 940 computers, which have on record Chicago-area Ford dealers' stocks. If a customer wants a black Mustang with a radio, the CLIC dealer who doesn't have the car simply dials the computer, hooked by telephone lines to the showroom, and asks via a small teletype machine whether one is in the district. If the computer through the teletype says it is, he can obtain it from the indicated dealer.

Seven basic questions (including a car's interior and exterior color) are answered first. Then the computer "asks" about options. For instance, the dealer will type "CS" if a console is desired. What makes the CLIC operation possible is computer time-sharing, by which a number of customers purchase time on a computer.

Although the 940 computers, which can handle 40 customers simultaneously, are valued at $1,200,000 each, CLIC Ford dealers pay Com-Tel only 26¼ cents a minute while on line and $88 monthly for the equipment and maintenance.

Reactions of dealers

"Customers sit there with their mouths open when we use the equipment," says Edward France, vice president of Burt Rose Ford Sales, a Chicago dealership. "If the car isn't available, he won't go to another dealer because he knows it's not in the area. Then we can switch him to a different color or equipment, or we can order the car."

"The important thing in our business is to make a delivery," France stressed. "The only time you make a profit is when the car goes out the door. People sometimes order a car and then call back and cancel. And often if we didn't have the car in stock, they'd just go to another dealer."

Owner James Aikey of Jim Aikey Ford says, "Before CLIC was installed, we'd spend an hour calling around looking for a particular car. People like to touch it before they buy it, and we order it as a last resort." Aikey explains that many buyers come in two weeks before their vacation and want their new car immediately. And he notes that when the Ford plant shuts down in July, you can't order any car.

COMPUTER "LIBRARY" HELPS COUNSELORS*

A computerized "library" of career information to help students explore vocational opportunities and to provide them with facts upon which to base mature vocational decisions is being used at Willowbrook High School.

The IBM system provides students with data on more than 400 vocations and with specifics on the training and academic preparation required for each. It also stores—for use by authorized personnel—information on grades and the results of interest and achievement tests for the 1700 sophomores, juniors, and seniors at the school. Some 1800 records of current eighth-graders and freshmen were added in the fall of 1969.

The innovative program, called Computerized Vocational Information System (CVIS), gives students access to the career data through two IBM 2260 visual display terminals. The terminals, which resemble small television sets and are equipped with typewriter-like keyboards, are linked by telephone lines to a System/360 Model 30 computer at the College of DuPage near Naperville. The college is cooperating with Willowbrook in implementing CVIS and has begun organization of a computer cooperative with other schools in DuPage County. (A terminal is shown in Fig. 26.1.)

Students in the upper three grades can use CVIS during free periods. To begin, a student sits at a terminal and identifies himself to the computer by entering his student number on the keyboard. The computer recalls the student's record, checks to see whether he has used CVIC previously and then explains the system's purpose.

---

* Adapted from *Press Publications*, TF-1/9-1/10, 1969, page 8.

FIG. 26.1
Computerized
vocational
information
system (CVIS)

Next the computer asks the student questions about his standing in class and his performance on special achievement tests. The system also asks him to state his post-high-school education or job-training plans, giving him choices ranging from none to the earning of an advanced degree.

If the student's answers are not consistent with the achievement records on file, the computer flashes a message on the screen to this effect and suggests that he talk to his counselor. The computer permits the student to continue with the program even if his answers are inconsistent, and it proceeds to list the jobs available at the training level the student has specified.

The occupations are divided into eight interest categories and six levels of training: service, business contact, organization, technology, outdoor, science, general culture, and arts and entertainment. The system describes each category and asks the student to select the one of greatest interest to him. Once the selection is made, a list of all jobs in that category is printed on an IBM 1053 communications terminal located next to the visual device.

The student can select from this list a job of special interest, and a 50-word description will appear on the visual terminal screen. If he wants more information, he can ask for a 300-word message to be printed on the 1053 terminal.

In subsequent uses of the CVIS, a student does not repeat the self-evaluation part of the program. Instead, he is reminded of the educational level and interest category of the job he was last exploring, and he is asked if he wishes to continue with that list or make a new decision. He may also get occupational briefs about any jobs stored in the system by typing in their code numbers.

SOMETHING AILING YOU? TELL IT TO THE FRIENDLY COMPUTER*

If no one else will listen to your medical problems, tell them to the computer. It will hear you out, lend a sympathetic ear, ask concerned questions, and give you a helping hand.

What for so long has been considered a cold, calculating, and inhuman jumble of wires and lights is becoming a useful aid to over-burdened doctors. The computer can be programmed to take medical histories of patients, ask them how they feel, both physically and mentally, and find out what ails them. And certainly in initial interviews, it is doing as well as the harried doctor and even sometimes a little better.

Advantages of the Computer in Diagnosis

A computer can listen with infinite patience while the patient relates his problems, a task that busy doctors often don't have time for. It usually asks more questions about a person's health than a physician

---

* Adapted from *Chicago Tribune*, Sunday, February 9, 1969.

with a crowded practice can. It can compare your symptoms with those of many others to help find out what is wrong; the computer can even quietly detect a person heading for a mental breakdown.

Doctors who use the medical electronic brain are finding that the machine is thorough, fast, and time-saving. Surprisingly, some patients tell the computer more about themselves than they tell their physicians. Although the potential value of computers is being studied in every medical area from diagnosis to mass screening, the two areas where they are reaching the application stage in doctors' offices are history-taking and psychological testing. For example, Dr. Irving F. Kanner, of the University of Kentucky College of Medicine, Lexington, has been able to double the number of new patients he can examine each day by using a programmed history-taker.

In a typical computer interview the patient faces a typewriter-like console with a screen. Questions about his health appear on the screen, and he can push buttons answering Yes or No, or he can ask for an explanation of the question. When the patient answers Yes to a question, the computer zeroes in and asks more detailed questions about that particular problem. For example, if he complains of headaches, the computer may ask how many times a week he has them, what part of his head hurts, and whether he has had any dizzy spells, vomiting, or slurred speech. In this way the patient may be asked as many as 90 questions if his medical condition calls for frequent Yes answers. One of these systems, developed by Medidata Scientists, Waltham, Massachusetts, a subsidiary of C. D. Searle and Company, Skokie, Illinois, takes 15 to 25 minutes to interview a patient. The results are printed out in the doctor's office in a matter of minutes. Doctors anywhere in the country will be able to have the small unit installed in their offices. It is hooked up to the computer in Waltham by telephone lines. The cost for the Medidata system ranges from $4 to $5 per history, but that expense is likely to go down as use of the computer goes up, a spokesman said.

Spanish-speaking patients can be asked questions in Spanish with the Medidata system, and the results are typed in English. Other languages are expected to become available.

Dr. Kanner said that the histories taken by the computer are as good as those available in a thorough questioning by a doctor. The time saved is 20 to 25 minutes per patient, he added. Printed reports have the additional advantage of being more valuable as records than reports in the doctor's traditionally illegible handwriting, which sometimes makes them useless to another doctor or to a nurse who has to follow instructions.

Using computers for psychiatric diagnosis may open the door for better treatment of more patients. In tests conducted by both computers and a battery of psychiatrists, diagnoses by the electronic brains compared favorably with those reached by the psychiatrists, according to Dr. Richard Stillman of Stanford University, Palo Alto, California. Since mental health experts are in short supply everywhere, computers can be valuable because persons with less professional training can use them to reach a reliable diagnosis, he said. Here is what one electronic wizard said about a 37-year-old male subject:

He appears to be a person who represses and denies emotional distress. In times of prolonged emotional stress, he is likely to develop physical symptoms. He is particularly vulnerable to psychophysiological symptoms such as headaches, tachyardia (rapid heart beat), and gastrointestinal disorders. This patient has test features which resemble those of psychiatric outpatients who later require in-patient care. Continued professional care and observation are suggested.

Computers used in psychiatric work are completely reliable in the sense that, given the basic information describing a subject, a computer will always arrive at the same diagnosis, said Dr. Robert L. Spitter of the department of mental hygiene of the state of New York.

Another advantage in using programmed interviews is that the patient is not so apt to say what he thinks the physician wants to hear, Dr. Kanner said. "Although a questionnaire cannot elicit such information as a physician obtains by noting the patient's tone of voice or facial expression, the patient is not biased by the physician's attitude," he said. What do patients think about being interviewed by a computer? "Apparently they like it," said Dr. Warner V. Slack of the University of Wisconsin. A survey of 275 patients who were interviewed about their health by an electronic brain showed that 96 percent liked it and more than 80 percent said they actually enjoyed it, Dr. Slack said.

INNOVATION IN TEACHING*

In California, around 1961, an electronics firm introduced a new teaching method and reduced its engineering training program from six

---

*Adapted from *Computers and Automation*, Newtonville, Mass.: Berkeley Enterprises, October, 1968.

months to three months. Veteran company engineers soon asked to be allowed to enter the program. They saw that they were missing something.

In Nigeria in 1964, a group of 50 Africans from six nations studied for 10 to 14 hours a day, month after month, using a new method.

In Belgium in 1966, one instructor conducted two classes, covering two slightly different technical subjects in two different languages simultaneously, using a new method.

In Canada in 1966, a young man started conducting a six-week technical class for twelve students who had a better formal education than he. He had never taught before, and he had less than a week to prepare. Most students thought the class was a great success. The teacher enjoyed every minute of it. He used a new method.

A host of new and different techniques has come into being in the past 15 years or so. Most famous for several years was *programmed instruction* (PI), developed by B. F. Skinner of Harvard. Today it is *computer aided instruction* (CAI) that makes the headlines. In between were many variations on the theme, each with some applicability in the field of education. Running through nearly all these innovations in instruction are some common threads:

1. The student can learn on his own, rather than in a group.
2. The student can set his own pace.
3. The material is carefully structured in order to minimize the time required for learning a given amount of information.
4. The student is actively involved in the learning process—he's not just sitting there listening.
5. The student is kept abreast of his progress or lack of progress.

As was true in the Industrial Revolution, the real effect of innovations in the Computer Revolution has been job displacement, not job replacement. Stagecoach drivers learned to drive buses. Wood carvers learned to operate wood lathes. Clerks learned to program computers. Now the Teaching Revolution is upon us. What will the teachers do?

DATE-MATCHING SERVICES

Numerous services have emerged throughout the country to attempt to match a person with a perfect date. You merely answer a list of from 30 to more than 100 questions and send in the required fee (from $4 to $20 and more). You will receive a list of several people whose likes and dislikes closely resemble yours. The only problem is that the only people this service can match you with are others who have sent questionnaires and fees to the same service you are using. Here are some sample questions from a typical questionnaire.

1. Your sex: _____male _____female

2. Years of high school completed: _____years

3. Years of college completed: _____years

4. How often do you read newspapers?
    _____every day   _____several times a week   _____seldom

5. What are your favorite kinds of movies? (Check all that apply.)

    _____westerns   _____musicals   _____war
    _____adventure   _____drama   _____cartoon
    _____comedies   _____foreign   _____document
    _____horror   _____travel   _____none

6. What do you most look for in a date?

    _____physique   _____loyalty   _____compliance
    _____intelligence   _____sensitivity   _____sense of humor
    _____honesty   _____daring   _____understanding
    _____looks   _____virtue   _____sophistication
    _____money   _____mystery   _____self-assurance
    _____popularity   _____decisiveness   _____excitement

7. How much is usually spent when you date?
    _____less than $5   _____$5–10   _____$10–20   _____over $20

8. What type of community were you brought up in?
    _____small town   _____small city   _____medium city   _____large city

9. Have you been engaged?
    _____yes, several times   _____yes, once   _____no

10. When would you like to get married?
    _____soon   _____in a few years   _____not for a long time

11. Do you enjoy wearing old clothes?
    _____often   _____sometimes   _____never

12. How much do you smoke?
    _____a lot   _____occasionally   _____not at all

TIME-SHARING

Another innovation is time-sharing, a system by which many people in different places can use the same computer at the same time. On a teletypewriter plugged into the computer by telephone lines, a user may need 30 seconds to think up and write out a question the computer can answer in one second. Instead of frittering away the extra time, the computer turns to the problems other users are posing. Like a glutton for work, it hops from problem to problem, pausing a split second on each, and going on so long as problems keep coming in.

Time-sharing is growing by leaps and bounds. It is being used to test computer programs, to let college students and teachers get full computer service from a single machine, and to reserve airline seats on a coast-to-coast basis, just to name a few applications.

The ability of computers goes beyond high-speed arithmetic and into analysis. Electrocardiograms can be taken of normal hearts, for example, and the pulses converted into binary language and stored in the machines as a pattern of how a healthy heart should beat. Using the model as a basis for comparison, doctors can rapidly screen ECG's for abnormalities.

More and more, computers are being successfully used to simulate real conditions, ranging from purchasing and maintaining the inventory for a prospective chain store to predicting the effects of a massive missile attack on a nation. Other computers play chess, write musical scores, analyze Shakespearean syntax, create a dubious kind of poetry. A limit to their versatility seems nowhere in sight.

Since man is in charge of the definition of thought, computers haven't yet been credited with "thinking." But as the calculating speed of the machines nears the speed of light and they proliferate in numbers and sophistication, the question might well be: "How long will man be in charge of the definition?"

COMING: A CASHLESS SOCIETY*

The day may be fast approaching when cash and checks will be obsolete—replaced by electronic "money". . . . The future may hold a computer to keep track of almost every cent the average American spends. He will use cash only for incidentals like tipping. In fact, the nature of his money will change from folding paper to electronic bleeps—or no bleeps—in the memory of a computer. Life in a "cashless society" will be easier in many ways. The individual will be relieved of details but not of responsibility. He will not have to scurry to his bank to withdraw cash for a weekend trip to the shore or to

---

* RCA Electronic Age, Winter 1968–1969, pages 30–34.

deposit money to cover a check his wife wrote. His salary will automatically be deposited in his account, and he will be notified that he can begin using it at, say, 9 a.m. on Friday. Upon his authorization, amounts to pay all his regular bills, such as mortgage payments, will be transferred to the accounts of his creditors.

He will use an all-purpose identification and credit card to purchase food, entertainment, gasoline, and many other items. In the earlier years he will utilize a change machine to obtain silver and small bills for vending machines and such. But even that need will be eliminated, because eventually, every financial transaction will be initiated by the identification card, and every vendor except the shoeshine boy will have a credit card terminal linked to a nationwide computer system that will instantly record all financial transactions. The system is most likely to include personal computers, neighborhood time-sharing electronic data processing centers, and gigantic processors operated by banks and leading retailers.

Such a network will help eliminate a variety of financial headaches, ranging from the familiar backlogs on Wall Street to the annoying delays in receiving receipts and canceled checks. And with terminals in the home, it will be possible for computers to report on the financial status of individuals as well as businesses. The computer will display on a screen the balance in an account, payments due in the near future, and the number of loans outstanding, including the various interest rates on each. There will be no need to wait until the end of the month to find out exactly how much money is in an account. Electronic safeguards against unauthorized persons' gaining access to the data will protect the individual's right to privacy. Many payments will be made immediately, by instructing the computer to subtract a charge from a customer's account, for example, and add it to the grocer's account. Any deferred payment will become a charge account sale; after a certain period of time this will automatically incur interest. The average man's life will be simpler because he will have access to a computer to keep track of these financial transactions. It will be more complicated because virtually an unlimited number of opportunities to make loans or to borrow money will be open to him.

Despite objections from some quarters, there are definite signs that the coming of the "cashless society" is simply a matter of time. One authority points out that most of the technology needed to operate an "electronic" monetary system is already available. He further states that if the needed technology is available but not economically feasible today, it soon will be. Yet even today there are holdouts against modern fiscal methods. Some people refuse to use banks, checks, or money orders. Instead, they hide huge sums in the mattress, send hundreds of dollars in cash through the mails, and consider it both sinful and foolish to borrow money or purchase goods with a credit card. Nevertheless, statistics are proving the popularity of credit cards and the coming of the "cashless society."

In the first half of 1968, the use of credit cards by national banks expanded by 15 percent over use in the first six months of 1967. The amount of credit outstanding under credit card and revolving charge plans reached $1.13 billion at the end of June, 1968, compared with $985 million a year earlier. Credit cards alone accounted for $724 million of the mid-year total, and the number of national banks using credit card plans increased from 187 to 217 in that six-month period. And that's just national banks. In the autumn of 1968, the Federal Reserve Board (FRB) reported that 416 commercial banks were operating credit card programs, many with tie-ins with other banks.

Under most plans, cardholders can obtain merchandise or services on credit from local retail outlets, and they are billed through their banks. Interest on unpaid balances ranges from 1 to 1.5 percent a month, or up to 18 percent a year, depending on local usury laws. The average credit limit, according to the FRB, is $350.

Many of the nation's large retailers also have charge card and credit card plans. People also carry travel, entertainment, and airline cards, and at least two banks, located in Miami and New York, even issue a card that triggers a money-dispensing machine. In addition, one of the nation's largest supermarket chains recently began an experimental credit card program. The A & P, traditionally a cash-and-carry firm, introduced the program in six stores in Ohio and West Virginia.

Credit card plans are considered the first step toward the "cashless society," and their rapid proliferation is an indication that some day checks and paper money will not be able to compete with efficient "electronic" money. Other fiscal innovations in many industries are leading to the establishment of a national network for checking the credit and verifying the identity of the cardholder.

In an effort to reduce frequent holdups of bus drivers, the Philadelphia Transportation Company recently inaugurated an "exact fare" plan. Passengers who do not have the exact fare deposit a larger amount in a locked box and receive a certificate entitling them to a refund for the difference, obtainable at centrally located refund centers. It is expected that, within a few years, buses in many metropolitan areas will carry devices that can read credit cards. Fares charged against these cards will be recorded on magnetic tape or miniaturized magnetic disks. These records will be processed by computers, and each passenger will receive a monthly bill for all his bus and subway rides. Adapting to the exact fare plan will help Philadelphians adjust to any computerized billing that may be introduced. A credit card system would practically eliminate the handling of money by the driver and do away with trips to collect the refund.

In another case, the Ripley Company will soon run tests to prove the feasibility of automatic utility meter reading via public telephone lines. A spokesman claims that when such a system is operable, a computer will be programmed to interrogate the meters periodically and prepare the bills from the readings. With the customer's permission, the system could be tied to bank computers for automatic payment of utility bills.

The military forces are already using "cashless" money and computers to help curb black market activities in Vietnam. The United States military command has issued plastic currency control cards that must be used when a serviceman converts his military scrip into cash or when he spends it on certain high-priced goods at a post exchange. Data from the cards give officials a constant watch on the volume of converted scrip as well as on PX purchases. For example, if a man converts more than the authorized amount of scrip, the computer "kicks" out a card identifying him and showing all his recent transactions.

A major factor in speeding the establishment of the "cashless society" is the continuing decline in data processing costs and in the cost of transmitting information over telephone lines. In the late 1950's, it cost $1.35 to perform 100,000 mutiplications on the most efficient computer available, according to a data processing consultant. Today, the same function costs less than three cents.

Dr. James Hillier, RCA Executive Vice President, Research and Engineering, has frequently stated that the "cashless society" is inevitable. In fact, he points out that, on the basis of past economic and technological development, society may even be able to determine when it will be a reality.

A certain concept of this development, which he calls "the tyranny of numbers versus the constancy of humans," may hold the answer.

To illustrate, a department store clerk is essentially a constant in regard to her ability to write out sales slips, manually verify credit authorization, or handle the transactions of the people who line up at her counter. On the other hand, the number of credit cards, volume of financial transactions, and degree to which individuals depend on others to produce food, clothing, and personal protection are expanding at a rate faster than that of the population. If this continues, there will not be enough people in the world to handle the financial transactions generated by the people of the United States.

In the past, when the constancy of humans was violently coupled with the tyranny of numbers, the resulting explosions gave birth to technological breakthroughs and important innovations. An example can be found in the history of the telephone industry. The rapid increases in the use of telephones, combined with the geometric expansion in the number of possible connections that could be made by the operators, eventually produced direct dialing and computerized switching. If switchboards were still operated manually, there would not be enough girls in the world to handle all the calls made today. Thus, according to Dr. Hillier, it is only a matter of time before the number and complexity of financial transactions make it economically necessary to convert to "electronic" money. The reduced cost of communications and data processing, the public's growing familiarity with credit cards, computerized billing, and automatic meter reading, and the more efficient manufacture of computer terminals will combine to force the conversion.

Despite these forces, there are still a few technological hang-ups that the nation's scientists and engineers have not completely solved. One is the need for a foolproof, inexpensive method of verifying the identity of the cardholder. No one looks forward to an "electronic" money system if it means that a thief will have unlimited access to the financial accounts of others. A lost wallet containing a code number could lead to total financial ruin. This is such a problem today that at least one company has sprung up to help protect consumers against lost or stolen credit cards. The company claims that, within 30 seconds of notification, it can put a computer to work identifying the cards owned by a subscriber. Then the issuing companies are notified by telegram that the cards are missing and credit privileges should be canceled. Although this is a partial solution to the problem, it still puts the burden on the owners of cards to notify the firms. Any purchases charged on those cards are still their liabilities. What is really needed is a system that would deny credit privileges to the cardholder unless he could positively identify himself as the rightful owner.

Dr. Donald S. McCoy of the RCA Laboratories has suggested a speech-recognition system that employs both code words and voice-signature prints to positively identify cardholders. A person would voice an assigned code phrase of easily identified sounds—"This is six one one tango"—and then speak his name. By means of the code phrase, the computer would be directed immediately to the place in its memory where that person's voice-signature file is stored. These voice-signature prints have been demonstrated to be as efficient and forgery-proof as are fingerprints. This speaker-identification system is already possible with the speech technology of today. Its cost is still high, but it is rapidly approaching economic feasibility.

One of the first developments that must take place is the establishment of a large, computerized credit card system. At the present time, one of the primary obstacles to such a pilot project is the high cost of terminals capable of reading credit cards. To attract widespread use, the terminals for the remote interrogation of credit files and the collection of credit transactions must be small and inexpensive. A credit card system will not function properly unless a remote credit card terminal is located wherever a charge can be made. Every hardware store, jewelry shop, grocery store, gasoline station, and restaurant must have at least one. These terminals must be small and easy to operate because they will be handled by proprietors and clerks who currently operate machines no more sophisticated than a cash register. The main function of these devices is to read and transmit the credit account number and to accept variable data, like the dollar amount of the transaction. Also, these devices must have the capability of signaling the terminal operator that the sale has been approved and recorded or that it has been rejected and not recorded.

One of the chief factors that will contribute to the practicality of on-line credit card networks is the development of internal computer systems. The Marine Midland Grand Trust Company of New York typifies the banks that are developing computerized information networks linking all their branches to a centralized computer. If banks develop central information files containing information on all their customers, it will become a relatively simple matter to add an automatic credit card system. Actually, credit card validation and purchase authorization require a very small fraction of computer time. Banks can continue to do batch processing and handle the credit card system through the use of multi-programming and time-sharing techniques. It is then possible for credit card terminals to interrupt the processor, request information, and receive it in only a fraction of a second. These techniques permit the handling of bulk processing and on-line communications at the same time.

However, many other problems must be worked out before the "cashless society" becomes a reality. For example, the competitive struggles between the banking industry, large retailers, the telephone companies, and the federal government must be resolved. The lines separating the proper fields of activities for these industries begin to blur when their operations project into the age of "electronic" money. Many state and federal laws will have to be modified to permit banks to engage in merchandising and also to allow retailers to perform some typical banking functions.

This would be only one of a variety of changes in the economic life of the nation. With the advent of the "cashless society," many new jobs will be created, and some pedestrian ones will be eliminated. It may even be a built-in answer to the problem of crime in the streets. Armed robbery would be obsolete if nobody carried money and a voice check was needed to use a credit card. A new breed of criminal would probably be developed, electronic embezzlers who could tamper with computer systems to inflate their accounts, but computer experts are already working on methods to foil such a move. In addition, federal investigators would merely have to check employers' computers to discover the honest income of a suspect.

One thing is certain. A nationwide "cashless society" would provide everyone with his own electronic accountant: a computer that could handle almost all financial details but would make none of the critical decisions.

CONCLUSION

Although the idea of a cashless society and its implications seem impractical to us today, think back a few years. When the telephone was invented, people probably thought "This is ridiculous. Ordinary people will never have one of these things in their homes. Special wires would have to go to each house. How could you speedily be connected with the person you want to talk to? How can voices be magnified so you can hear a person even in another town? Who could afford it anyway?" It took years of development, but all these problems were solved. Will we see the problems arising from the cashless society concept solved during our lifetime?

QUESTIONS AND PROBLEMS

1. Describe how a computer can help a person ordering a new car.
2. How can a computerized library or career information center help counselors and students?
3. In what ways can the computer help the medical doctor in treating his patients?
4. The numerous developments in teaching, ranging from PI to CAI, are all based on some common advantages. List them.
5. Name one limitation of a computer date-matching service. Are there other limitations?
6. What are the advantages of the suggested cashless society?
7. What are the disadvantages of the suggested cashless society?
8. Would you like to see the cashless society concept become reality? Why or why not?
9. Are there other advantages and/or disadvantages to this system that were not mentioned in the book?

INDEX